REORIENTING ECONOMICS

In this wide ranging, thought provoking, book Tony Lawson further advances the basic thesis of his much acclaimed *Economics and Reality* that social theorising, in particular economics, needs to give more explicit and systematic attention than hitherto to considering the nature of its subject matter. Formally put, the author continues his call for an ontological turn in social theorising.

Tony Lawson finds the discipline of economics to be in a non too-healthy condition, and demonstrates that the problems arise largely because of a widespread tendency of economists to make stipulations on method independently of considerations of context or conditions of analysis. In addressing this situation the author argues for a radical reorientation of the discipline allowing a more pluralistic forum, one that is accommodating of ontology and critical thinking amongst much else.

The emphasis on pluralism is basic to Lawson's argument. Far from being a polemic against the currently dominant set of economic practices, Lawson sustains the thesis that if economics is to be saved from itself it is highly desirable to seek, where feasible, a continual dialogue between all interested parties.

The coverage of *Reorienting Economics* includes commentaries on the current state of economics, the nature of ontological theorising (including the nature of its consequences), possibilities for social explanation, the scope of economics, evolutionary thinking, the contribution of heterodox traditions including feminist economics, post Keynesianism and old institutionalism, the historical process whereby economics came to take its current orientation, and much else.

As with Lawson's previous writings, *Reorienting Economics* will be of interest not only to economists but also to philosophers, the variety of social theorists, and indeed anyone interested in understanding the current state of social theorising and contemplating how it might be improved.

Tony Lawson is a member of the Faculty of Economics and Politics at the University of Cambridge, UK.

ECONOMICS AS SOCIAL THEORY
Series edited by Tony Lawson
University of Cambridge

Social theory is experiencing something of a revival within economics. Critical analyses of the particular nature of the subject matter of social studies and of the types of method, categories and modes of explanation that can legitimately be endorsed for the scientific study of social objects, are reemerging. Economists are again addressing such issues as the relationship between agency and structure, between economy and the rest of society, and between the enquirer and the object of enquiry. There is a renewed interest in elaborating basic categories such as causation, competition, culture, discrimination, evolution, money, need, order, organisation, power probability, process, rationality, technology, time, truth, uncertainty, value, etc.

The objective for this series is to facilitate this revival further. In contemporary economics the label 'theory' has been appropriated by a group that confines itself to largely asocial, ahistorical, mathematical 'modelling'. Economics as Social Theory thus reclaims the 'theory' label, offering a platform for alternative rigorous, but broader and more critical conceptions of theorising.

Other titles in this series include:

ECONOMICS AND LANGUAGE
Edited by Willie Henderson

RATIONALITY, INSTITUTIONS AND ECONOMIC METHODOLOGY
Edited by Uskali Mäki, Bo Gustafsson and Christian Knudsen

NEW DIRECTIONS IN ECONOMIC METHODOLOGY
Edited by Roger Backhouse

WHO PAYS FOR THE KIDS?
Nancy Folbre

RULES AND CHOICE IN ECONOMICS
Viktor Vanberg

BEYOND RHETORIC AND REALISM IN ECONOMICS
Thomas A. Boylan and Paschal F. O'Gorman

REORIENTING
ECONOMICS

Books are to be returned on or before
the last date below.

Withdrawn

First published 2003
by Routledge
11 New Fetter Lane, London EC4P 4EE

Simultaneously published in the USA and Canada
by Routledge
29 West 35th Street, New York, NY 10001

Routledge is an imprint of the Taylor & Francis Group

© 2003 Tony Lawson

Typeset in Palatino by Taylor & Francis Books Ltd
Printed and bound in Great Britain by TJ International Ltd, Padstow,
Cornwall

British Library Cataloguing in Publication Data
A catalogue record for this book is available from the British Library

Library of Congress Cataloging in Publication Data
A catalog record for this book has been requested

ISBN 0–415–25335–7 (hbk)
ISBN 0–415–25336–5 (pbk)

FOR J.P.

CONTENTS

CONTENTS

PREFACE AND ACKNOWLEDGEMENTS

The central contention of this book is that the discipline of modern economics stands in need of a significant change of orientation. Specifically, the thesis is advanced that modern economics can profit from a more explicit, systematic and sustained concern with *ontology* than has been its custom.

Ontology may be an unfamiliar term. But if so I hope that this will not deter the reader from proceeding further. The matters addressed here are rather important to the future of the discipline. Indeed, I want to make clear from the outset that this book is addressed not just, or even mainly, to those who pursue methodology for its own sake, but to anyone at all concerned about the state of modern economics and of social theorising more generally.

By ontology I mean enquiry into (or a theory of) the nature of being or existence. It is an endeavour concerned with determining the broad nature, including the structure, of reality. In this book, I am especially concerned with the nature of *social* reality, with the question of social being.

By canvassing a reorientation of the economics discipline I am obviously wanting to suggest that there is something amiss with the way things currently stand. I am also intimating that the problems which I have in mind are of a sort that the proposed transformation can help rectify. Let me briefly sketch an outline of my argument.

I start from a recognition that, as an intellectual pursuit, much of modern economics is not in a healthy condition at all. This much is frequently affirmed even by many of the discipline's mainstream spokespersons, as we shall see in Chapter 1 below. It is also significant that over the last two or three decades many university (as well as secondary school) departments of economics have experienced steadily declining enrolments (Abelson 1996; Chote 1995; Parker 1993; du Pisanie 1997; Kirman 2001), whilst existing students, most notably in France, openly criticise the lack of relevance of both their lectures and the accounts of social reality found in modern economics textbooks (for overview and references see e.g. Kirman 2001; Fullbrook 2003). As I write these lines, indeed, petitions criticising the state of the modern discipline appear to be receiving widespread support from disaffected economists and others throughout the world (see, Fullbrook, 2003).

Given the nature of this situation, it may be thought that advocating a turn to philosophy in the guise of ontology is not an adequate response at all. A seemingly more obvious reaction, perhaps, especially for those of a practical disposition, would be to counsel a greater emphasis on a theorising which seeks to incorporate accepted insights and to address issues of immediate economic import.

The problem with the latter response is that such a course of action has long been recommended and even pursued, but without any perceivable improvement in the relevance of the discipline (see Lawson 1997a). Something is standing in the way of theoretical and practical progress. It is my assessment that ontological analysis is required in order fully to identify and understand the nature of the blockage. Indeed, we shall see that a central reason for the hold-up in achieving greater relevance is precisely the subject's continuing ontological neglect. Ontology can never be a substitute for a more relevant and empowering economics. But it can certainly under labour for this goal, and at this point in time is probably essential for this goal to be realised.

To see how ontology can be especially helpful at this point in time it is important to consider two of the roles that can be accepted for it. Now, it is a thesis central to this whole book that specific methods and criteria of analysis are appropriate to the illumination of *some* kinds of objects or materials *but not others*. Marx once observed that 'In the analysis of economic forms…neither microscopes nor chemical reagents are of use' (*Capital*, vol. I, 19). His point, of course, was that the nature of the subject-matter in question is such that the noted tools are not appropriate to its investigation. But the point being made is a general one. The properties of material studied will always make a difference to how we can and cannot know it.

One role for ontological enquiry, then, is to determine the (usually implicit) conceptions of the nature and structure of reality presupposed by the use of any specific set of research practices and procedures. Equivalently, it can identify conditions under which specific procedures are relevant and likely to bear fruit.

A second, and at least as fundamental a role for ontology, indeed one I take to be primary, is the elaboration of as complete and encompassing as possible a conception of the broad nature and structure of (a relevant domain of) reality as appears feasible. The aim is to derive a general conception that seems to include all actual developments as special configurations. Put differently, a central objective is to provide a categorial grammar for expressing all the particular types of realisation in specific contexts.

The results achieved by ontology in each of these roles can be used in numerous ways, as we shall see. But of particular interest at this juncture is a recognition that the results obtained in these two roles can be used to especially good effect in combination. For if, by employing ontology in its second role, we can achieve a general framework, this in turn can reveal the particularity of many scientific and practical ontologies (i.e. the conceptions of reality presupposed by specific methods of science, or policy claims) uncovered by employing ontology in its former role. In other words, applying ontology in both of the roles discussed allows us to compare the ontological presuppositions of specific methods with our best account of the nature of social reality. The application of ontological insight in this fashion can reveal in particular both the error, and the non-necessity, of universalising any highly specific approach or stance *a priori*. Ontology, so fashioned, can identify the error of treating special cases as though they are universal or ubiquitous. Relatedly, it can also highlight the error of treating abstractions as isolations, i.e. as if they are more concrete than they are (see Chapter 2).

I run through all this because it is my assessment that the noted problems of modern economics stem from a widespread failure of the modern discipline to match its methods to the nature of its subject-matter. Indeed, modern economics provides a very clear example of a rather narrow way of doing research being unthinkingly and erroneously universalised *a priori*, with unfortunate consequences.

The significant feature here is the emphasis of the modern discipline on method. Modern economics situates itself within, or as a, social science. It thus orientates itself to the social realm. But unlike any other academic discipline of which I am aware, modern economics, or more accurately its hugely dominant mainstream tradition, is best identified or distinguished by its concern with method, and specifically by its insistence that economics necessarily relies on techniques of mathematical modelling. This insistence on mathematical formalism is the one feature common to all developments within the modern mainstream tradition. But formalistic methods are not insisted upon because they are found to be appropriate to the analysis of social material. In fact, the possibility of a lack of fit between such methods and the nature of the subject-matter of economics is rarely even contemplated.

Here, then, as I say, we have an example of a particular stance being universalised *a priori*, a practice that is risky at best. And it is fairly easy to establish that the sorts of formalistic methods everywhere advocated by modern mainstream economists are in fact only rarely appropriate to the analysis of social material, given its nature. In other words, it is easy to show that these methods which are universalised *a priori* are so erroneously. This, I argue, is why the modern discipline of economics is in such disarray. The theories formulated by economists are necessarily restricted so as to conform to the worldview presupposed by their formalistic methods. Because there is reason to suppose that this latter worldview characterises very little of human society, it is not surprising that mainstream theories are found hardly to advance understanding in most of the contexts for which they are constructed.

So a basic thesis motivating this book is that modern economics is largely characterised by a mismatch between its methods of analysis and the nature of the material it seeks to illuminate. There is a mismatch between the ontological presuppositions of the methods of formalistic modelling and the nature of the social world in which we actually live. This mismatch, indeed, explains not only the widespread and continuing failures of the discipline, but also the limitations of those previous responses to the discipline's various problems which have sought to make the subject more insightful and policy-relevant. For they have mostly left unchallenged the formalistic modelling methodology of the mainstream tradition and, in doing so, inevitably fashioned or adapted their insights and policy questions to an implicit worldview (such as is presupposed by use of these methods) that continues to be at odds with the nature of (seemingly most of) social reality.

The persistence of this mismatch of method and subject material is really only comprehensible in the context of a continuing failure to address ontological issues in any very explicit and sustained fashion. Hence my urging of an ontological turn as being especially of value at this point.

However, my use of ontological argument to demonstrate the questionable *a priori* universalisation of rather specific claims is not restricted, in the following chapters, to the modern emphasis on methods of mathematical modelling. Other theorists, also critical of tendencies to universalise *a priori*, have rejected the common assumption that human beings are everywhere the same (an assumption itself ultimately encouraged by the emphasis on mathematical formalism, as I note in Chapters 1 and 9). But by focusing on the uniqueness of individual experiences and personal identities, these theorists have tended, instead, to converge on a conception that acknowledges *only* differences. From the ontological perspective defended in the following chapters, however, it is found that the universalisation of difference is itself illegitimate, that it neglects such commonalities in the human and social world as there are (see especially Chapter 9).

Ontology, then, can be useful in identifying examples of what might be termed the fallacy of misplaced universality. It helps us identify cases where specific methods or theoretical claims are treated as being more widely useful or relevant than is the case.

This, however, is not its only useful function. Ontology, especially under its primary role of uncovering the nature of a domain of reality, can also be of assistance in more positive ways, particularly in providing insights as to the sorts of conditions or contingencies for which it is prudent that researchers be methodologically prepared, as well as indicating potentially fruitful directions in which to proceed. It can aid in a number of further ways still, depending on context, as we shall see in many of the chapters which follow.

I might emphasise at this point that, by urging an ontological turn, I do not propose that all economists necessarily become involved in contributing to (i.e. doing) social ontology. Rather, I suggest only that the discipline everywhere stands to benefit if more of its practitioners are at least aware of the ontological presuppositions of their broader visions, and (at a minimum) concerned with ensuring that these worldviews or ontological assessments are not at odds with the ontological preconditions of their adopted methods and substantive orientations.

Let me systematise all approaches to theorising which are in this way ontologically explicit and concerned (whether or not constituting a contribution to ontology) under the heading of *realist social theorising*. Ontological elaboration, then, is part of the latter but not exhaustive of it. In counselling a greater concern with ontological issues, while not insisting that we all need to develop our own ontological theories (especially where sustainable developed conceptions are usefully appropriated) I am, more precisely, urging a wider take-up of realist social theorising.

I might also stress that I am not here proposing that ontology be prioritised in any context-independent sense. I do, though, think explicit and sustained ontological analysis, or its results, can be invaluable, and at this juncture, given the state of the modern discipline, probably essential. But ontology, like all other forms of theorising, is itself a situated, partial, fallible process, producing results that to some degree at least are likely to be transient. I thus urge a rounded approach to theorising in economics. I advocate only that developments in ontology and those in method and substantive theorising evolve in tandem, with each informing or otherwise enriching the other, where possible.

Let me elaborate a little on my orientation to formalistic modelling. Although parts of this book, and most specifically Chapter 1, are critical of the way formal modelling methods are taken up in modern economics, I hope by now the highly conditional nature of my criticism is apparent. It is not, and has never been, my intention to oppose the use of formalistic methods in themselves. My primary opposition, rather, is to the manner in which they are everywhere imposed, to the insistence on their being almost universally wielded, irrespective of, and prior to, considerations of explanatory relevance, and in the face of repeated failures. My aim with this collection of essays thus truly is a reorientation of the discipline: towards a way of proceeding that more obviously prioritises the goal of illuminating social reality. Once, or if, this realist priority is re-established formalism can be fitted in where it is found to be appropriate, or retained as part of the variety on offer. The last thing I wish to do is support any efforts to prohibit forms of activity, or limit the range of methodological options.

I do not deny that I am rather pessimistic about the prospects of significant success with mathematical methods in economics. In the light of the conception of social ontology defended in the chapters below, along with the assessment made of the ontological presuppositions of formalistic modelling methods, I find it not at all surprising that these latter methods have fared somewhat poorly. But in acknowledging my pessimism, I do not oppose a share of resources being used in endeavours to study social material mathematically. Amongst other things, all knowledge is fallible, as I have already stressed, so that, in particular, the grounds of my pessimism may yet prove erroneous. Rather, the primary object of my criticism is as stated. In its most general formulation, my opposition is directed at any kind of *a priori* dogma. The realist approach I defend is contrasted with any kind of ungrounded insistence that certain methods only, or almost only, should be followed. Such an insistence seems especially unfortunate when, as currently, the methods laid down persistently perform rather badly, whilst that unhappy performance can be explained.

I also want to emphasise that, in portraying the modern mainstream project as overly narrow (in its insistence on universalising an approach likely to have limited relevance) I do not join with those who impute necessary disreputable or questionable intent to its practitioners. Some critics of the modern mainstream project in economics do appear convinced that the emphasis on formalism somehow flows from the political ambitions or orientations of mainstream contributors, or from other unstated goals unrelated to the science process. This is not my position (as I make clear in Chapter 10). Rather, my experience is just that, for most mainstream economists, the thought that economics might very often be better done without using mathematical methods either does not occur or, if it does, appears to be too unlikely a possibility or too subversive an idea to accept.

For many modern economists, in fact, mathematical deductive reasoning is regarded as essential to science. It follows, for this group, that to relax the existing emphasis on mathematical methods is effectively to give up on the possibility of economics as science.

One response to this line of reasoning is to question why economics has to be a science. Many critics indeed have rejected the possibility of economics as science. But this is not my position. To the contrary, my concern is more with the recovery of economics as science. Ontology helps us better understand the nature of science, and, as we shall see, to appreciate that mathematics is not essential to it. To suppose that scientific practice even in the natural realm reduces to, or even necessitates, mathematical formalism is once more erroneously to universalise *a priori* a special case (in this case a particular form of scientific practice) as we shall see in due course.

If I am here criticising the *emphasis* that mainstream economists place on methods of formalistic modelling, I recognise (of course) that these same economists occasionally write non-mathematical presidential addresses or guest editorials and the like. Further, even highly formalistic papers often carry insightful discursive introductions or asides. But it is the orientation to formalistic modelling that, in the context of the modern economics academy, determines whether any given individual qualifies as a card-carrying member of the mainstream. And it is formalistic modelling methods that, again in modern economics faculties (as opposed to business schools, institutes of management studies, human geography departments, and the like), now almost exclusively constitute the 'core' material of modern economics courses.

I do not deny that a good deal of relevant and insightful economics is pursued outside the modern economics academy. Much of this is discursive, concerned to address pressing questions of significant import, and highly sensitive to context-specific issues and considerations. When earlier I referred to a stumbling block in the path of progress to a more relevant economics, I was referring to economics as prosecuted within the economics academy. It is on this latter site that the emphasis on formalistic modelling methods is so uncritically universalised.

I might also observe that various different (non-ontological) reasons are sometimes offered for opposing the use of mathematics in economics, but these I mostly do *not* accept (see Lawson 1997c; 2002; Chapter 1 below). Some individuals appear to oppose formalistic analysis merely because they are unfamiliar with it. Others play it down because of its apparent inaccessibility. Marshall, for example, albeit as but one step of his strategy, suggests that after results have been achieved using mathematics, the mathematical derivations should be burnt even if the results achieved have relevance (Marshall 1906). I do not subscribe to this view. If it were widely found that mathematics of the form utilised by economists is helpful to furthering our understanding of social reality, I believe more people would choose to acquire the relevant skills. And as a general stance I certainly favour the provision of opportunities for as many as possible to acquire the relevant skills to benefit from, and enjoy, mathematics at first hand.

Further, I well understand those who emphasise pragmatic grounds for the pursuit of mathematics in any domain. Mathematical proofs can be elegant, and the use of mathematics does tend to impose a high degree of clarity and rigour. However, while mathematical procedures are not unique in this respect, where the goal is to increase social understanding, the meeting of these pragmatic criteria clearly ought not to be regarded as sufficient.

If an increased understanding of social reality is an approved goal, and I am maintaining that it ought to be primary, there is some onus on those who insist that almost all (or even a significant share of) resources be allocated to the development, application and teaching of methods of mathematical modelling, to reassure the rest of us that there are grounds for supposing that these methods have at least the potential to be explanatorily successful and (so) practically useful. But so far there is little evidence or argument that such formalistic procedures have much relevance to social analysis at all.

If it is by now clear that the central contention of this book *is* that a reorientation of the modern economics discipline is warranted, I must now emphasise that I do not attempt to make my case merely in the abstract. Rather, I consider how best to begin moving in the preferred direction. Specifically, in the following chapters an ontologically oriented contribution is everywhere attempted. The various results achieved are systematised as part of, or are informed by, a specific project in realist social theory, one often referred to as *critical realism*. In other words, I not only defend the irreducibility of ontology, but seek, for the social domain especially, to establish something of its substance or contours as well. I not only argue for a reorientation of economics, I also endeavour to contribute to a specific ontologically oriented position.

It is the case, then, that the basic thesis of this book has both a highly abstract as well as a more concrete or specific formulation. At its most abstract and basic, my argument is just for a turn to ontology in social theorising including economics. My central claim here is that the discipline warrants a reorientation away from merely (or mainly) *a priori* stances towards realist social theorising. The more concrete or specific formulation of my thesis is that the modern discipline of economics requires a turn away from the currently dominant methods of mathematical-deductivist modelling, and a take-up of the (more general and inclusive) framework of critical realism. For if the mainstream formalistic modelling emphasis is the chief modern manifestation of *a priori* thinking and itself the main contributor to the modern discipline's failings, the project of critical realism, I believe, is currently the most sustainable (if, of course, always fallible) project of a mostly *a posteriori* or realist social theorising sort, capable of (at least pointing the way to) transcending the discipline's numerous ills.

Although the essays which follow interrelate and overlap, I have thought it useful to give the book a four-part structure. Part I, 'The current orientation of the discipline and the proposed alternative', contains three essays. The first sets out my assessment of the current state of modern economics, focusing on the role of the mathematising tradition. I abandoned an original intention to include further chapters criticising the mainstream orientation. This, in some significant part at least, is because I want, with this book, to emphasise the more constructive side of the project with which I am involved. Although roughly half of *Economics and Reality* (Lawson 1997a) concerns itself with advancing an alternative approach to that of the current mainstream, it is my criticisms of the mainstream project, found mainly in the first half of that book, which have received most of the attention from reviewers. A hope I retain for the current book is that more of the constructive aspects of the project will be noticed. Chapter 2 is concerned with clarifying the basic orientation to ontology I seek to promote. This includes a discussion of the manner in which the position I defend is derived. For it seems a reasonable demand of any contribution of the sort I am proposing that it is able to situate, describe and explain itself. Chapter 3, containing a brief overview of my basic position, is included in the hope that it serves further to clarify the argument.

Part II is entitled 'Possibilities for economics'. My objective here is to explore the manner in which the ontological conception I defend can be brought to bear on other issues. In this part of the book I focus specifically (though by no means exclusively) on three 'e's: explanation, evolutionary theorising and economics. I deal especially with issues that reviewers of *Economics and Reality* have felt received insufficient coverage, elaboration or at least prominence.

Part III is entitled 'Heterodox traditions of modern economics'. By heterodox I mean those traditions critical of doctrines currently held to be correct and most fundamental by a majority of modern economists, specifically by those who collectively comprise the current mainstream. Contributors to the heterodox traditions tend to view mainstream economics as rather unsuccessful in its attempts at explaining social phenomena. In this part of the book I examine the nature of the projects whereby the various alternative or heterodox traditions endeavour to do better.

It is my contention that these heterodox traditions have been working to achieve a more relevant economics by advancing forms of criticism, or defending perspectives on theory and method, all consistent with a wider and richer ontology than the revealed presuppositions of the modern mainstream. And it is my further view that these projects (or at least prominent strands within them) can benefit at this juncture from making their ontological theorising or commitments more explicit, systematic and sustained, from reformulating themselves explicitly as contributions to what I am calling realist social theorising.

The fourth and final part of the book, 'A historical perspective on economic practice', consists in just one chapter. Here I examine how the current orientation of economics in the academy has arisen and is sustained. For if it is widely perceived that the modern mathematising tendency fares rather poorly in explanatory terms, and that potentially fruitful alternative approaches are feasible, it seems warranted that light be thrown on how this mathematising project has achieved, and maintains, its position of dominance. A provisional explanation of this clearly relevant and even urgent issue, one that *prima facie* requires a historical investigation, is sketched in the final chapter of the book.

It will be apparent to anyone who has read *Economics and Reality* that the current book comprises an extension of the same basic project. I have already indicated my intention of giving greater consideration to aspects treated rather cursorily in the previous book. As a consequence some topics that previously figured in a central way inevitably receive somewhat less emphasis here and in a few cases are temporarily put aside. The resulting field of vision of *Reorienting Economics* is thus both broader and narrower than that of *Economics and Reality*. Where the coverage is the same I take the opportunity to clarify aspects of earlier arguments, particularly where misunderstandings have arisen. In this latter endeavour I recognise a recurring need, and frequently seek, to convey the basic structure and background presuppositions of my arguments. This is so, for example, where I run through the nature of, and motivation for, my project, explain why it is appropriately identified as realist, sketch how ontological reasoning can be initiated, and elaborate the manner in which its results are achieved (see especially chapters 2 to 6). Hence on such matters in particular, but on others as well, this book is especially concerned to reveal the basic framework and perspective that supports or conditions, that lies behind, the seemingly more finished, or more fully coloured-in, picture of *Economics and Reality*.

Finally, I should perhaps warn the reader that although this book is a response to the situation of the modern economics academy (so that the latter provides the context for my various arguments), its analysis leads me away from the view that economics is legitimately a subject of isolated study. Indeed, the position I develop is very much an interdisciplinary one in social theory and science. My conclusion is that economics, appropriately reoriented and (so) more reasonably prosecuted, is at most a division of a wider social science, not a separate or autonomous science in its own right (see Chapter 6). Thus, although this book is nominally addressed to actual and potential economists, and its motivating context is the situation within the modern academic institution of economics, many and perhaps most of its conclusions bear upon social theorising in general.

Most of the essays included below are previously unpublished, and of these not all have been wholly conceived with this book in mind. In fact, early drafts of some of the previously unpublished essays were originally intended for *Economics and Reality*.

In truth, not only is it the case that the essays included below were not all initiated with this book in mind, but, to the contrary, this book started life as a response to an invitation by Alan Jarvis of Routledge to put together a collection of already published papers. In so selecting various papers for this purpose, however, I also felt the need to fill some gaps. As the 'gap fillers' became more numerous, individually longer and integrated with each other, as I reworked them (by that stage with this current book clearly in mind), I found I had less and less space for those essays already published. Thus many of the previously published essays that I originally intended for inclusion (in fact the majority) have since been dropped.

It is in such a manner, then, that this book has come about. It is as much the product of an evolutionary process as one of prior design. Nevertheless, I am not unhappy with the result. In particular, I think the structure of the book, including the partitioning of perspectives described above, does work to a sufficient degree. And the structure has allowed me to cover many of the things I have thought important at this juncture.

A consequence of producing a book of essays in this fashion is some repetition across chapters, especially in those comprising the three previously published essays (Chapters 3, 6 and 9). However, the resulting relative autonomy of each chapter means the reader can more easily embark from or concentrate her or his focus more or less anywhere, whilst the combined collection constitutes, or so I believe and hope, a reasonably coherent whole picture.

Acknowledgements

Finally, I reach the point where I get to thank particular individuals. In truth, though, it is impossible to acknowledge all those who, directly or indirectly, have influenced me in writing this book. Because I have discussed and debated the topics covered so regularly and with so many others, I doubt I am even capable of recognising most of my debts. But I know I owe a good deal to the people who have attended the Cambridge Realist Workshop over the last twelve years or so, as well to all those who have attended seminars throughout the world where I have been fortunate enough to present my ideas. To all these people I express my deepest gratitude.

The one set of helpers I can (hopefully mostly) name are those who have read and commented on one or more chapters (including chapters in the end excluded). For this I especially thank Margaret Archer, Richard Arena, Leonard Bauer, Roy Bhaskar, Antonio Califati, Andrew Collier, Kurt Dopfer, Philip Faulkner, Steven Fleetwood, John Foster, Elisabetta Galeotti, Mário da Graça Moura, Geoffrey Harcourt, Nick Hostettler, Geoffrey Hodgson, Clive Lawson, John Latsis, Paul Lewis, Leonidas Montes, Ann Newton, Alan Norrie, Jenneth Parker, Eugenia Perona, Stephen Pratten, Carlos Rodrigues, Jochen Runde, Roy Rotheim, Marco Schejtman, Diana Strassmann, Ulrich Witt and Gregor Zwirn (who also helped with the checking of the quotes and references).

From the foregoing list I must single out two groups in particular. First, Philip Faulkner, Clive Lawson, Leonides Montes and Stephen Pratten each read an early draft of the book in its entirety and collectively joined me in a whole-day seminar criticising its form and contents. Second, Paul Lewis, Stephen Pratten and Jochen Runde read the whole of a penultimate draft and provided further helpful criticism. For such an input from those concerned I am grateful indeed.

I must also thank Alan Jarvis of Routledge for instigating the project that turned into this book, and Rob Langham for help and encouragement on taking over from Alan as well as Terry Clague for help on various matters when he later joined the Routledge team.

And I also thank my family. I must mention Heather, in particular, who not only, as with my earlier book, allowed me some access to the family computer (albeit this time rather more begrudgingly) but also, especially when I was preparing material for seminars on early versions of the manuscript, taught me how better to use some of the computer packages I drew upon. Last but not least, I thank my partner Joëlle Patient, for continuing encouragement, support and advice. It is to Joëlle that this book is dedicated.

Finally, I thank the editors and publishers of the relevant journals for permission to reproduce the following papers:

'What Has Realism Got to Do with It?', *Economics and Philosophy*, 1999, vol. 15, 269–82.

'Economics as a Distinct Social Science? On the Nature, Scope and Method of Economics', *Economie Appliqué*, 1997, tome L, no. 2, 5–35.

'Feminism, Realism and Universalism', *Journal of Feminist Economics*, 1999, vol. 5, no. 2, 25–59.

In addition I have used revised versions of material also found in the following:

'The Varying Fortunes of the Project of Mathematising Economics: An Evolutionary Explanation', *European Journal of Economic and Social Systems*, 2001, vol. 15, no. 4, 241–68.

'*Should* Economics be an Evolutionary Science? Veblen's Concern and Philosophical Legacy', *Journal of Economic Issues*, 2002, vol. XXXVI, no. 2, 279–92.

Part I

THE CURRENT ORIENTATION OF THE DISCIPLINE AND THE PROPOSED ALTERNATIVE

This first part of the book is concerned with setting out my basic position and providing a framework that is drawn upon in Parts II–IV. It contains three chapters which to a significant extent systematise arguments that I have made elsewhere. A central aim here is clarification and consolidation. But there is also some development of my previous argument.

The first of the three chapters is the most critical. Here I note the less than satisfactory state of modern economics. I concentrate on those features of the discipline which I regard as its most problematic, and which can be shown to contribute significantly to its current unfortunate situation.

In the second chapter I urge a particular reorientation of the discipline as a way forward. Here the focus is on ontology. In particular I outline an approach to ontological theorising, discuss the sorts of results that are achieved, and also indicate very briefly something of the consequences of these results (a more detailed account of the latter is provided in the rest of the book).

The third chapter, a relatively brief note previously published in Economics and Philosophy, *addresses the specific question as to why it is appropriate to identify my project as realist.*

1

FOUR THESES ON THE STATE OF MODERN ECONOMICS

How might we characterise the state of modern economics? In this opening chapter I advance four basic 'theses' which bear quite fundamentally on this question. Because I have defended each one to some degree before I will not go into very great detail here. My purpose in reconsidering them side-by-side at this point is to systematise and clarify relevant background preconceptions. For the picture they collectively convey is taken as given (if further developed) in most of the chapters which follow. These four theses are quickly stated:

1   Academic economics is currently dominated to a very significant degree by a mainstream tradition or orthodoxy, the essence of which is an insistence on methods of mathematical-deductivist modelling.
2   This mainstream project is not in too healthy a condition.
3   A major reason why the mainstream project performs so poorly is that mathematical-deductivist methods are being applied in conditions for which they are not appropriate.
4   Despite ambitions to the contrary, the modern mainstream project mostly serves to constrain economics from realising its (nevertheless real) potential to be not only explanatorily powerful, but scientific in the sense of natural science.

Let me consider each of these assessments in turn.

Thesis 1: Academic economics is currently dominated to a very significant degree by a mainstream tradition or orthodoxy, the essence of which is an insistence on methods of mathematical-deductivist modelling

There can be little doubt that modern economics is dominated by a project that attempts to apply mathematical methods to all areas of study. Currently, graduate programmes in university faculties of economics concentrate on the use of mathematical methods[1] and often consist in little more than micro (mathematical) modelling, macro (mathematical) modelling and econometric modelling.[2] And most journals regarded as core or prestigious publish almost only articles formulated in mathematical terms.[3]

So dominant is this mathematising project in economics, in fact, that many of its modern perpetrators (unlike their predecessors[4]) hardly (or are not willing to) recognise that there are alternative ways of proceeding. For most members of the project, indeed, categories like 'economic theory' or even just plain 'theory' have become synonymous with mathematical modelling.[5] For a contribution even to be counted as economics (or to gain an audience) in mainstream circles, it is requisite that the author takes a mathematical approach and ultimately produces a formal model. Consider Richard Lipsey's observation:

> to get an article published in most of today's top rank economic journals, you must provide a mathematical model, even if it adds nothing to your verbal analysis. I have been at seminars where the presenter was asked after a few minutes, 'Where is your model?'. When he answered 'I have not got one as I do not need one, or cannot yet develop one, to consider my problem' the response was to turn off and figuratively, if not literally, to walk out.
>
> (Lipsey 2001: 184)

To recognise this situation is not to deny that the project in question is always, in some way, also concerned with social phenomena, or at least with social categories. Economists do not usually deal abstractly just with the properties of (mathematical) operators and elements of sets, but concern themselves with variables labelled 'consumption', 'income' and so forth.[6] Although some, like Debreu (1959), profess attachment to the Bourbaki ideal of a framework free of any interpretation (see Chapter 10), this ideal seems never to be realised in its entirety. It does serve the function of loosening up the project from achieving immediate contact with reality (as again we shall see in Chapter 10). But practitioners of modern economics appear never to abandon all concern with social categories, or the hope of illuminating social reality sooner or later. Ultimately the aim, it seems, is to render aspects of the social world intelligible. There is a sense, then, in which the project always remains in essence an explanatory endeavour.

The point to emphasise here, though, is that this project's conception, or mode, of explanation is necessarily one that facilitates the widespread usage of mathematical formalism including formalistic modelling.[7] That mode of explanation called into play is *deductivism*.

4

Deductivism

By deductivism I mean a type of explanation in which regularities of the form 'whenever event x then event y' (or stochastic near equivalents) are a necessary condition. Such regularities are held to persist, and are often treated, in effect, as laws, allowing the deductive generation of consequences, or predictions, when accompanied with the specification of initial conditions. Systems in which such regularities occur are said to be *closed*.[8] Of course, a closure is not restricted to the case of a correlation between just two events or 'variables'; there can be as many of the latter as you like. Nor is a closed system avoided by assuming a non-linear functional relationship or by pointing out, as in chaos theory or some such, that what happens may be extremely sensitive to initial conditions. If, given the exact same conditions, the same outcome does (or would) follow (or follows on average, etc., in a probabilistic formulation) the system is closed in the sense I am using the term.

Notice that it is the *structure* of explanation that is at issue here. The possibility that either many of the entities which economists interpret as outcomes, including events or states of affairs, are fictitious, or claimed correlations do not actually hold, does not undermine the thesis that deductivism is the explanatory mode of this project. In other words, by deductivism I refer only to forms of explanation for which closed systems are an essential component; no commitment to the realisticness of any closures or regularities posited is presupposed.

Observe, too, that it does not make any difference whether an inductive or *a priori* deductive emphasis is taken. If mathematical methods of the sort economists mostly fall back on are to be employed, closures are required (or presupposed), whether they are sought-after in observation reports or 'data' or are purely invented. Deductivism is an explanatory form that posits or requires such closures whether or not any are actually found. And deductivism, so understood, clearly encompasses the greater part of modern economics, including most of modern microeconomics, macroeconomics and econometrics.[9]

So characterised, the modern mainstream project might be labelled in various ways. In the sections which follow I refer to its activities interchangeably as mathematical-deductivist modelling, formalistic closed-system modelling, or just as formal (or mathematical) modelling, amongst other things. Such descriptions amount to the same thing and can be loosely systematised under the head of (modern) mathematical economics.[10] It is this approach, however we label it, that now pervades the discipline. And it is an insistence on this approach, I am suggesting, that characterises the highly dominant modern mainstream component within it (see also Dow 1997; Setterfield 1997).

If the mainstream mathematising endeavour is so dominant that its contributors often take it to be the whole of the discipline, this nevertheless is a mistake. Though marginalised, there are not only dissenting individuals but also various highly productive heterodox traditions that pursue understanding in economics whilst rejecting the mainstream insistence on mathematical modelling methods. Amongst the more prominent of the latter traditions we find, for example, Austrianism, feminist economics, (old) institutionalism, post Keynesianism, Marxian economics and social economics. Although sub-groupings or individuals within these projects do sometimes turn to formalistic modelling, there is not a reduction of economic method to techniques of formalistic modelling. Let me quote Diana Strassmann, the editor of *Feminist Economics*, who very well captures the orientation of the modern mainstream project as viewed from a heterodox perspective:

> To a mainstream economist, theory means model, and model means ideas expressed in mathematical form. In learning how to 'think like an economist,' students learn certain critical concepts and models, ideas which typically are taught initially through simple mathematical analyses. These models, students learn, are theory. In more advanced courses, economic theories are presented in more mathematically elaborate models. Mainstream economists believe proper models – good models – take a recognizable form: presentation in equations, with mathematically expressed definitions, assumptions, and theoretical developments clearly laid out. Students also learn how economists argue. They learn that the legitimate way to argue is with models and econometrically constructed forms of evidence. While students are also presented with verbal and geometric masterpieces produced in bygone eras, they quickly learn that novices who want jobs should emulate their current teachers rather than deceased luminaries.
>
> Because all models are incomplete, students also learn that no model is perfect. Indeed, students learn that it is bad manners to engage in excessive questioning of simplifying assumptions. Claiming that a model is deficient is a minor feat – presumably anyone can do that. What is really valued is coming up with a better model, a better theory. And so, goes the accumulated wisdom of properly taught economists, those who criticize without coming up with better models are only pedestrian snipers. Major scientific triumphs call for a better theory with a better model in recognizable form. In this way economists learn their trade; it is how I learned mine.
>
> Therefore, imagine my reaction when I heard feminists from other disciplines apply the term *theory* to ideas presented in

verbal form, ideas not containing even the remotest potential for mathematical expression. 'This is theory?' I asked. 'Where's the math?'

(1994: 153–4)

Although Strassmann here recognises the close association of mathematical modelling with the current mainstream project, there are some economists who have sought instead to characterise the modern mainstream in terms of features of its substantive theorising. Such endeavour, though, has not proven successful. Most typically, it has associated mainstream economics with theories of human rationality or conceptions of equilibrium, or some such. The problem here is that such features as are identified are found not to survive across the numerous (and consequential) flits in fads and fashion that the project in question repeatedly experiences at the level of its substantive interests.[11]

On recognising this situation, critical observers conclude that the current mainstream is just too slippery a project to pin down. Some even wonder if there is any continuity to, or commonality to the various strands of, the mainstream project at all. In Mirowski's view,

> the historian is forced to concede that, in fact, it is best described as a sequence of distinct orthodoxies, surrounded by a penumbra of quasi-rivals; and that it is this, more than any deductive or inductive 'successes', which accounts for its longevity.

(1994: 68)

Overlooking the mainstream project's continuous reliance on methods of mathematical-deductivist reasoning, Mirowski feels we must question whether this project can be said to 'consist of anything more than a bold assertion of continuity in the face of repeated ruptures every two or three generations?' (*ibid.*: 69).

Those who reason in this sort of manner take the mathematisation of modern economics (if not necessarily any specific form of mathematics[12]) for granted. No doubt the common tendency to do so is reinforced by the widespread failure of most within the mainstream itself to defend or even comment on the mathematical emphasis. In consequence, I think it is worth recalling Whitehead's warning when considering philosophy more generally:

> When you are criticising the philosophy of an epoch, do not chiefly direct your attention to those intellectual positions which its exponents feel it necessary explicitly to defend. There will be some fundamental assumptions which adherents of all the variant systems within the epoch unconsciously presuppose.

7

Such assumptions appear so obvious that people do not know what they are assuming because no other way of putting things has ever occurred to them. With these assumptions a certain limited number of types of philosophic systems are possible, and this group of systems constitutes the philosophy of the epoch.

(1926: 61)

In any case, in the face of the seemingly unquestioned acceptance of the reliance of modern economics on methods of mathematical deductivist reasoning, it is worth emphasising over and again that mathematical modelling is certainly not essential to social theorising and understanding. This is a point I establish under the heading of thesis 4 below, where I argue, in fact, that the current formalistic emphasis is likely often debilitating of explanatorily insightful social analysis. My concern at this stage, though, is to emphasise that with mathematical methods being insisted upon by the mainstream but regarded as *in*essential by heterodox traditions and others, we can see that the various strands of orthodoxy have not only a common, but also a distinguishing, feature after all. This, as I say, just is the *insistence* that mathematical-deductivist methods be used in just about all endeavour to advance knowledge of phenomena regarded as economic (for further discussion see Lawson 1997c; 2002).

Thesis 2: This mainstream project is not in too healthy a condition

A second assessment of the current situation I want to advance is that this mainstream project, when viewed as an endeavour concerned with social explanation (as opposed to being considered under its aspect of seeking to maintain its dominant position within the academy), is actually not too successful.

In fact the problems of the modern mainstream project are sufficiently widely recognised (and recorded) by those who reflect on the issue that I need say very little indeed here. Heterodox economists have for a long time pointed to the failings of the project (see, for example, Ferber and Nelson 1993; Fine 2001; Hodgson 1988; 1993; Kanth 1997; Srassmann 1993a) as have close observers of the discipline (see e.g. Parker[13] 1993; *The Economist*[14] 1997; Howell 2000[15]). But even some proponents of the mainstream project themselves are showing signs of increased concern. Certainly some contributors to this project acknowledge that it performs rather poorly according to its own (explanatory/predictive) criteria of success (Kay 1995; Rubinstein 1991; 1995) and is plagued by tension and inconsistency between how it claims to proceed and actually does so (Leamer 1978; Hendry *et al.* 1990). Basically, the project is recognised as being in a state of some disarray and unclear even as to its own rationale (see e.g. Bell and Kristol 1981; Blaug 1997; Kirman 1989; Leamer 1978; 1983; Leontief 1982; Parker 1993; Rubinstein 1991; 1995; Wiles and Routh 1984). Consider for example Rubinstein's reflections:

> The issue of interpreting economic theory is … the most serious problem now facing economic theorists. The feeling among many of us can be summarized as follows. Economic theory should deal with the real world. It is not a branch of abstract mathematics even though it utilizes mathematical tools. Since it is about the real world, people expect the theory to prove useful in achieving practical goals. But economic theory has not delivered the goods. Predictions from economic theory are not nearly as accurate as those offered by the natural sciences, and the link between economic theory and practical problems … is tenuous at best.
>
> (Rubinstein 1995: 12)

This mainstream 'theorist' continues:

> Economic theory lacks a consensus as to its purpose and interpretation. Again and again, we find ourselves asking the question 'where does it lead?'.
>
> (Rubinstein 1995: 12)

More than ten years earlier, Leontief, a Nobel Memorial Prize winner in economic science, was already bemoaning the project's continuing failure to advance understanding:

> Page after page of professional economic journals are filled with mathematical formulas leading the reader from sets of more or less plausible but entirely arbitrary assumptions to precisely stated but irrelevant theoretical conclusions. … Year after year economic theorists continue to produce scores of mathematical models and to explore in great detail their formal properties; and the econometricians fit algebraic functions of all possible shapes to essentially the same sets of data without being able to advance, in any perceptible way, a systematic understanding of the structure and the operations of a real economic system.
>
> (Leontief 1982: 104)

Recently, Blaug, perhaps the foremost methodologist of the mainstream, formulates matters at least as starkly:

Modern economics is sick. Economics has increasingly become an intellectual game played for its own sake and not for its practical consequences for understanding the economic world. Economists have converted the subject into a sort of social mathematics in which analytical rigour is everything and practical relevance is nothing.

(Blaug 1997: 3)

Friedman, also a Nobel Prize winner, adds:

economics has become increasingly an arcane branch of mathematics rather than dealing with real economic problems.

(Friedman 1999: 137)

And Coase, yet another Nobel Prize winner, further remarks that

Existing economics is a theoretical system which floats in the air and which bears little relation to what happens in the real world.

(Coase 1999: 2)

Of course, of those who acknowledge the less than satisfactory state of the modern (mainstream) project, not all actually associate its problems with its mathematical nature. To the contrary, this will tend to be the last consideration of most mainstream economists, just because to question the widespread reliance on mathematical methods is to query the very essence of their programme. Consider the response of the (mainstream) 'economic theorist' Alan Kirman (1989). In an admirable piece entitled *The Intrinsic Limits of Modern Economic Theory: The Emperor Has No Clothes*, a title which clearly indicates the critical and reflective predispositions of the author, Kirman is concerned about aspects of 'economic theory' as currently practised. However, despite an openness to change, Kirman seemingly cannot bring himself to sanction the possibility that something other than a form of mathematics is required. In attempting to 'identify the source of the problem' of modern 'economic theory', Kirman writes:

The argument that the root of the problem ... [is] that we are confined by a mathematical strait jacket which allows us no escape, does not seem very persuasive. That the mathematical frameworks that we have used made the task of changing or at least modifying our paradigm hard, is undeniable but it is difficult to believe that had a clear well-formulated new approach been suggested then we would not have adopted the appropriate mathematical tools.

(Kirman 1989: 137)

10

The failings of econometrics has met with the same sort of response. For example, Edward Leamer, who, like Kirman, is clearly a critical and reflective contributor to his subject (with published papers carrying titles like *Let's take the con out of econometrics*), acknowledges both that the 'opinion that econometric theory is largely irrelevant is held by an embarrassingly large share of the economics profession', and also the existence of a 'wide gap between econometric theory and econometric practice' (Leamer 1978: vi). However, after failing to resolve the noted inconsistencies Leamer writes:

> Nor do I foresee developments on the horizon that will make any mathematical theory of inference fully applicable. For better or for worse, real inference will remain a highly complicated, poorly understood phenomenon.
>
> (Leamer 1978: vi)

The idea of a non-mathematical theory of inference, though, goes unconsidered.

The central point here, however, is that all responses of the sort noted rest upon recognitions of the less-than-buoyant state of the discipline. Whatever the types of diagnoses sought or offered, there is quite widespread agreement that the modern discipline is not in too healthy a condition, and that whatever explains the fact that the formalistic mainstream project has risen to such dominance (see Chapter 10 on this), it has little to do with this project's record so far at explaining the social world in which we live.

Thesis 3: A major reason the mainstream project performs so poorly is that mathematical-deductivist methods are being applied in conditions for which they are not appropriate

I now want to suggest that the continuing poor performance of the project in question is explained precisely by the persistent application of methods of formalistic modelling just in (social) conditions for which they are mostly not appropriate.

I am aware that such a possibility is almost unthinkable to many economists. Frank Hahn probably captures widespread sentiment when he declares of any such suggestion that it is 'a view surely not worth discussing' (Hahn 1985: 18). In fact, Hahn later counsels us 'to avoid discussions of "mathematics in economics" like the plague and to give no thought at all to "methodology"' (Hahn 1992a; see also Hahn 1992b). However, given the record of the modern mathematising project in economics, I think the need for a detailed discussion and analysis of its nature and relevance grows more urgent by the day.

Behind much of the incredulity many experience in any thesis of the sort I am advancing (i.e. in the idea that the mathematising tendency may itself be at least part of the problem) is a view, sometimes stated explicitly but I suspect more widely held, that mathematics, as used in economics, is just (another) language (see e.g. Samuelson 1952). I believe this perception is, at best, misleading. We are mostly dealing here with the ways economists apply to their discipline already worked-out mathematical procedures. And the problems that arise are more easily brought into relief by drawing parallels not so much with language as with tools more generally.[16] Few people, I suspect, would attempt to use a comb to write a letter, a knife to ride to work, or a drill to clean a window. Yet all these tools have their uses in appropriate conditions. And so it is with modelling methods of the sort that economists wield. Of course, with these examples I am being somewhat less than subtle. But if bringing them to mind helps challenge the complacency involved in the idea that any tool, including formalistic mathematical reasoning, can be universally applicable, they will have served a purpose.

Ontology

These considerations lead into the topic of ontology. By ontology I mean the study (or a theory) of being or existence, a concern with the nature and structure of the 'stuff' of reality. Now, all methods have ontological presuppositions or preconditions, that is conditions under which their usage is appropriate. To use any research method is immediately to presuppose a worldview of sorts.

It seems to be the case, however, that the ontological presuppositions of the methods of mathematical modelling used by economists are rarely questioned or even acknowledged, at least not in any systematic or sustained way. As a result, the possibility of a lack of ontological fit (a mis-matching of the presuppositions of these modelling methods with [the nature of] those features of social reality being investigated) is not considered. Yet, as I say, methods of mathematical-deductivist modelling, like all methods, do have ontological presuppositions. And my assessment, simply stated (and defended below), is that these preconditions of mathematical-deductivist methods appear not to arise very often in the social realm.

Closed systems

To move towards justifying this assessment, let me first note that the sorts of formalistic methods which economists wield mostly require, for their application, the existence (or positing) of event regularities; they presuppose the occurrence of closed systems. Mainstream economics, as I say, is a

12

form of deductivism. By deductivism, I repeat, I simply mean any form of explanatory endeavour which assumes or posits or constructs regularities (deterministic or stochastic) connecting actualities such as events or states of affairs.

Of course, the fact that formalistic modelling methods require the identification or construction of event regularities is well recognised by mainstream economists. Allais (1992), taking the association of deductivist modelling and science for granted, expresses the conventional situation well:

> The essential condition of any science is the existence of regularities which can be analyzed and forecast. This is the case in celestial mechanics. But it is also true of many economic phenomena. Indeed their thorough analysis displays the existence of regularities which are just as striking as those found in the physical sciences. This is why economics is a science, and why this science rests on the same general principles and methods as physics.
>
> (Allais 1992: 25)

But if Allais correctly points to the modern mainstream emphasis on identifying or formulating social event regularities, his description of the situation of modern economics is actually quite wrong in two of its aspects. Econometricians repeatedly find that correlations of the sort formulated are no sooner reported than found to break down. Social event regularities of the requisite kind are hard to come by (see Lawson 1997a: ch. 7). And it is just not the case that 'striking' event regularities of the sort Allais appears to reference, and which modern mainstream economists pursue, are essential to science. Their prevalence is a precondition for the mathematical-deductivist methods that economists emphasise having relevance, but the application of these methods cannot be equated to science. This latter claim I will defend below. For the time being I merely note that any presumption of the universal relevance of mathematical-modelling methods in economics ultimately presupposes a ubiquity of (strict) event regularities.

Atomism and isolationism

But this is not the end to the ontological preconditions of methods of mathematical-deductivist modelling as employed in modern economics. A further important feature, which is less often recognised (or at least rarely explicitly acknowledged), is that the dependency of mathematical-deductivist methods on closed systems in turn more or less necessitates, and certainly encourages, formulations couched in terms of (i) isolated (ii) atoms. The metaphorical reference to atoms here is not intended to convey anything about size. Rather the reference is to items which exercise their own separate, independent and invariable (and so predictable) effects (relative to, or as a function of, initial conditions).

Deductivist theorising of the sort pursued in modern economics ultimately has to be couched in terms of such 'atoms' just to ensure that under given conditions x the same (predictable or deducible) outcome y always follows. If any agent in the theory could do other than some given y in specific conditions x – either because the agent is intrinsically structured and can just act differently each time x occurs, or because the agent's action possibilities are affected by whatever else is going on – the individuals of the analysis could not be said to be atomic, and deductive inference could never be guaranteed.

Why do I qualify the inferences drawn, insisting the modern emphasis only *encourages* (and does not fully necessitate) atomism? And why do I refer only to deductivism 'of the sort pursued in modern economics'?

When I refer to deductivism as pursued in modern economics, I have in mind those closures in which the connected events might be said to stand in a relation of causal sequence. This qualification is required to the extent it might be suggested that the latter closures are not exhaustive of deductivism. Let me briefly elaborate.

By describing two events as standing in causal sequence I mean that one event, y say, happens in some sense because, or as an eventual result, of the other event, x say, which is prior. To describe two such events as standing in causal sequence carries no necessary implication that y happens (or is thought to happen) as a *direct* result of x. In the social realm events regarded as economic, and standing in causal sequence, are usually mediated at least by human agency. Thus for an increase in a person's income to result, say, in an increased expenditure on certain commodities the individual usually has to act, to exercise essential causal agency. But still the increased income is an event in the causal process or sequence resulting in additional expenditure. To say of two events that they stand in causal sequence is to assert that one is in the causal history of the other.

Why might it be retorted that deductivism does not require that events stand in a relation of causal sequence to each other? Situations may arise in which variations in two events x and y are merely concomitant, being caused, perhaps, by movements in a third (set of) factor(s). Examples of this sort abound in the economic realm as in any other. When the sterling price of US dollars (or of petrol or any imported items) rises in the east of England the price often rises in the west as well. When the striking refuse collectors fail to turn up to remove my neighbour's rubbish they also fail to turn up to remove mine. Clearly in such examples, the correlated events do not, or need not, stand in a relation of causal sequence. Neither event need be (even indirectly) a cause of the other.

Because I have defined a closed system as any in which an event regularity occurs, we might want to refer to a system where the events are correlated, but where neither causally conditions the other, as a *closure of concomitance* to differentiate it from a *closure of causal sequence*, where some event (the consequent event or dependent variable) is causally conditioned by the other(s) (the antecedent event(s) or independent variable(s)). The former type of closure can be extremely useful in social life, including (non-deductivist) explanatory work, as we shall see in Chapter 4. I focus upon this form of closure here, just to acknowledge that it does not presuppose an ontology of atomism. If x and y move together because they are both related to a third (set of) factor(s), there is no necessary presumption about how movements in the latter are related to movements in either (or both) of the former.

Having noted these qualificatory considerations, they need not detain us here. Although they will prove useful to my own project in due course, they have little bearing on the practices of modern mainstream economics. For, as a rule, mainstream economists, though committed to positing or detecting closures, are simultaneously concerned with theoretical formulations or explanations of a causal sequence sort. When, in constructing their models, modern economists relate consumption to disposable income, wages to consumer prices, imports to total final expenditure, investment to interest rates, and so forth, they are hypothesising that the posited relations arise because, in each event pair, movements in the former are somehow ultimately brought about because of, or in response to, changes in the latter.

Actually, I have to acknowledge that even faith in closures of the causal sequence sort ultimately, or formally, does not necessitate atomism. That is why, above, I acknowledge that the latter is only (albeit strongly) *encouraged*. I make the qualification just because an event regularity even of this (causal sequence) kind could come about by chance, with a different causal complex connecting the *a posteriori* associated events on each occasion. Such a possibility, however improbable, cannot be ruled out in principle. Of course, economists need more than this; they need to construct their theories in a way that event regularities are guaranteed, allowing deductive reasoning, etc. Thus although there is strictly no formal necessity for it, if economists are to theorise general connections between given events, if they are to persist in their micro- and macro- and econometric modelling endeavour, an atomistic ontology will be involved.

Atomism, then, is essential, if closures of the sort economists usually require are to be assured. However, even in the noted scenarios the assumption of atomism is not yet sufficient to ensure closure and facilitate deductivist explanation including prediction. For even with an atomistic ontology, the total effect on an outcome of interest may be changed to almost any extent if all the other accompanying causes are different. That is why, in concrete economic analyses, the (atomistic) individuals tend to be treated as part of an assumed-to-be isolated and self-contained set or system.

The ontological presuppositions of (or encouraged by) the insistence on mathematical modelling, then, are of subsets of the social domain constituted by isolated sets of atoms. Most typically, such deductivist modelling endeavour encourages a view of atomistic human agents (social atomism) where these are the sole explanatory units of social analysis (methodological individualism).[17]

I have not yet indicated precisely why I am suggesting the modern mainstream tradition fares so poorly as an explanatory endeavour. I have merely indicated that if the methods of mathematical deductivist modelling (as employed in modern economics) are insisted upon as universally valid for the social realm, a tacit presupposition is that the social realm everywhere comprises (closed) systems of isolated atoms.

Now it is immediately clear, I think, that these latter conditions need not characterise the social realm.[18] I want to suggest, in fact, that the noted conditions for closure may actually be rather rare in the social realm. I draw this conclusion on the basis of the (*a posteriori* derived) theory of social ontology, a conception of the nature of the material of social reality, defended in the chapters below (especially Chapter 2) and elsewhere (especially Lawson 1997a), and often systematised as critical realism. To avoid excessive repetition, let me postpone a defence of this ontology until the following chapter, and at this point turn and give a brief overview of aspects of the ontological conception in question.

A theory of social ontology

By *social reality* or the social realm I mean that domain of all phenomena whose existence depends at least in part on us. Thus it includes items like social relations, which depend on us entirely, but also others like technological objects, where I take technology to be that domain of phenomena with a material content but social form.

Now if social reality depends on transformative human agency, its state of being must be intrinsically dynamic or *processual*. Think of a language system. Its existence is a condition of our communicating via speech acts, etc. And through the sum total of these speech acts the language system is continuously being reproduced and, under some of its aspects at least, transformed. A language system, then, is intrinsically dynamic, its mode of being is a process of transformation. It exists in a continual process of becoming. But this is ultimately true of all aspects of social reality, including many aspects of ourselves including our personal and social identities. The social world turns on human practice.

The social realm is also highly *internally related*. Aspects or items are said to be internally related when they are what they are, or can do what they do, by virtue of the relation to others in which they stand. Obvious examples are employer and employee, teacher and student, landlord/lady and tenant or parent and offspring. In each case you cannot have the one without the other.

In fact, in the social realm it is found that it is social *positions* that are significantly internally related. It is the position I hold as a university lecturer that is internally related to the positions of students. Each year different individuals slot into the positions of students and accept the obligations, privileges and tasks determined by the relation. Ultimately we all slot into a very large number of different and changing positions, each making a difference to what we can do. The social realm, then, is highly internally related or 'organic'.

The social realm is also found to be *structured* (it does not reduce to human practices and other actualities but includes underlying structures and processes of the sort just noted and [their] powers and tendencies). And the stuff of the social realm is found, in addition, to include *value* and *meaning* and to be *polyvalent* (for example absences are real), and so forth.

This broad perspective, as I say, is elaborated and defended in the chapters below (especially Chapter 2). But I doubt that, once reflected upon, the conception is especially contentious. Nor in its basic emphasis on organicism or internal-relationality is it especially novel (see Part III below). However, it should be clear that if the perspective defended is at all correct, it is *prima facie* quite conceivable that the atomistic and closure preconceptions of mainstream economics may hold not very often at all.

That said, I repeat that the possibility of closures of the causal sequence kind, i.e. of the sort pursued by modern mainstream econ-omists, cannot be ruled out *a priori*. Certainly, there is nothing in the ontological conception sketched above and defended in the following chapters which rules out entirely the possibility of regularities of events standing in causal sequence in the social realm. But the conception sustained does render the practice of universalising *a priori* the sorts of mathematical-deductivist methods economists wield somewhat risky if not foolhardy, requiring or presupposing, as it does, that social event regularities of the relevant sort are ubiquitous. And to the point, if the social ontology systematised in the following chapters (and sketched above) does not altogether rule out the possibility of social event regular-ities of the sort in question occurring here and there, it does provide a rather compelling explanation of the *a posteriori* rather generalised lack of (or at best limited) successes with mathematical-deductivist or closed-systems explanatory methods to date.

Actually the ontological conception I defend is more explanatorily powerful still. For not only does it ground a likely explanation of the widespread continued explanatory failures of much of modern economics over the last fifty years or so, but also it can account for both

(i) the *prima facie* puzzling phenomenon that mainstream economists everywhere, in a manner quite unlike researchers in other disciplines, suppose that (acknowledged) fictionalising is always necessary, and
(ii) the types of conditions that prevail when mathematical methods in economics achieve such (limited) successes as are experienced.

Let me briefly consider the latter two claims in turn.

Fictions

It is not only the case that modern economics mostly fails as a predictive and explanatory endeavour. It is also evident, and equally remarkable, that the mainstream project's theories are everywhere couched in terms of constructs that are absurd fictions, and acknowledged as such. Assumptions abound even to the effect that individuals possess perfect foresight (or, only slightly weaker, have rational expectations), or are selfish without limit, or are omniscient, or live for ever. Moreover, these sorts of assumptions are not a recent innovation but have always been thrown up by those who would mathematise the discipline. They are found, for example, in the contributions of Walras and his predecessors (see Chapter 10 below) just as they are found today.

Rather than invidiously pick on examples to illustrate the point that fictions abound (for any mainstream contribution would suffice), let me instead consider a commentary on the ways of the mainstream project by a prominent and reflective contributor. Admitting that modern mainstream economics rests on fictitious claims, the mainstream theorist Hahn (1994) writes:

> there is ... a lesson which has only gradually been borne in on me which perhaps inclines me a little more favourably to the 'anti-mathematics' group.
>
> The great virtue of mathematical reasoning in economics is that by its precise account of assumptions it becomes crystal clear that applications to the 'real' world could at best be provisional. When a mathematical economist assumes that there is a three good economy lasting two periods, or that agents are infinitely lived (perhaps because they value the utility of their descendants which they know!), everyone can see that we are not dealing with any

actual economy. The assumptions are there to enable certain results to emerge and not because they are to be taken descriptively.

(Hahn 1994: 246)

This passage captures well the sorts of assumptions that abound in modern economics, and various aspects are worth emphasising.

Notice, first, that the sort of fictitious assumptions thrown up within modern mainstream economics do not involve claims that could be true in some really possible counterfactual state of our world. I interpret the latter as part of the domain of the real. Real possibilities are as real as actualities. Both can have a causal impact. Mainstream economics continually falls back on states of affairs, etc., that could not possibly come about (see also Lawson 1997a: ch. 9).

Observe, second, that the set of fictitious assumptions does not reduce to those (if any) that are *in*essential to the results of the analysis. Rather fictitious constructions are usually vital in generating the results obtained. As Hahn expressly acknowledges, these sorts of assumptions are there precisely 'to enable certain results to emerge and not because they are to be taken descriptively'.

But how, though, is this emphasis on fictions to be explained? Notice, at this point, a third feature of the mainstream formulations illustrated by Hahn's assessments. Just as a class of assumptions, such as rationality, omniscience or total greed, always appears in order to render the human agent atomistic, a further set of assumptions, like a given number of agents or (as in the above passage) three goods and two periods, are always in place serving to fix the boundaries of the analysis, to isolate the set of atoms on which the analysis focuses. In other words, in some form or other the assumptions of atomism and isolationism are ever present, resulting from the (typically unquestioned) reliance on methods of mathematical-deductive reasoning.[19]

The reason for the fictitious nature of modern economics, then, is clear. To the extent that human beings as well as society are, in reality, complex, evolving and open, a methodology which necessitates that the subject-matter addressed is everywhere atomistic and isolated is likely very often to throw up accounts of human individual and collective behaviour that are fictitious and rather superficial, to say the least.

It follows, though, that for the mainstream practitioner wishing to retain mathematical-deductivist methods for all situations, there may be no other option than putting on a brave face and insisting that accounts that, in terms of substantive claims made, are somewhat superficial may yet perform well according to some pragmatic criterion (such as elegance, simplicity, revealing of where assumptions lead, generating deductions/predictions, and so forth). Lucas provides an example of a self-conscious response of this sort:

> To observe that economics is based on a superficial view of individual and social behavior does not seem to me to be much of an insight. I think it is exactly this superficiality that gives economics much of the power that it has: its ability to predict human behavior without knowing very much about the make up and lives of the people whose behavior we are trying to understand.
>
> (Lucas 1986: 425)

A major problem for this particular 'justification', of course, (and for the quasi-instrumentalist stance of Friedman 1953 from which it derives[20] – see Lawson 1997a: 309–10) is that economists are actually not very good at predicting human behaviour (i.e. at making relatively accurate predictions as opposed to producing countless rather inaccurate ones – see Kay 1995: 19).

Modelling successes

How about my second claim that the ontological analysis provided above throws light on the sorts of conditions under which mathematical methods in economics are likely to prove most useful, and perhaps can be said to have achieved most success? If my arguments are correct, these conditions are precisely those in which, first, the agents of analysis are found to have little scope in what they (can) do (as with atoms, their activities are highly determined by context), and, second, only a few factors are found to bear any influence on the outcome of interest, or, equivalently, wherein one set of influences is so dominant that the effects of others are rendered marginal.

Possible examples that spring to mind are the behaviour of motorists in rush hours in busy cities, or perhaps decisions of those with extremely low incomes in western societies about whether to spend or save out of income received. Most generally, as in such examples, closures will occur when very basic biological needs are being satisfied. Clive Granger has argued convincingly[21] that it is possible to use econometrics to provide relatively successful short-run forecasts of phenomena such as electricity loads and peaks in regions wherein one factor, temperature, or more specifically the extreme cold, dominates behaviour. Even here it is found that the effect of the dominant factor depends on the time of day, and whether or not it is the weekend. But notably forecasters such as Engle *et al.* (1992) who, in focusing upon a particular period of the year, have attempted to forecast each hour of the day separately (twenty-four models) treating weekdays and weekends separately (making forty-eight models altogether) appear to have achieved a degree of all-round success that seems high by standards of modern econometric research.[22]

The point remains, however, that the sorts of conditions in question appear *a posteriori* not to be typical of the social realm. Rather, as I say, social reality is found to be a quintessentially open, structured, dynamic and highly internally-related system, amongst other things, whilst the conditions for achieving a local closure are seemingly rare. Thus our best explanation of the widespread failures of economics (as well as the fictions that abound) is just that mathematical-deductivist or closed-systems modelling methods are often applied to materials for which they are unsuited. It is conceivable, indeed, that the set of social situations for which they are appropriate is not very large at all.

The nature of the argument

My argument is ontological. I do emphasise this. For my impression is that the few explicit responses to criticism of the emphasis on formalistic modelling miss this and address instead to other forms of criticism which are often less significant. Perhaps to back up this observation I should mention explicitly some apparent criticisms to which responses have been forthcoming, but which I think are largely mistaken. Certainly they do not reflect my own worries.

Krugman (1998) for example, conjectures that criticisms of the mainstream emphasis on methods of formalistic modelling arise because exercises of the latter formalistic sort are often found to refute the preferred theories of the critics (1998: 1829)[23]. It should be clear, then, that my own concern is almost the opposite. It is that these formalistic methods seem rarely able to help refute (or support) anything.

Nor do I regard the emphasis on mathematical methods as especially elitist (see Krugman 1998: 1831).[24] Even less do I wish to minimise the value of clarity, rigour and consistency.[25] I do though insist that these attributes are not enough, that ability to illuminate the social realm counts as well.

Nor, further, do I deny that modellers often use data and pronounce on issues of policy.[26] I do, though, reject the presumption that such practices *per se* are sufficient to put a project like the mainstream in touch with reality.

Let me elaborate on the latter remark. Krugman (1998) sometimes gives the impression that dealing with data or mentioning policy issues is sufficient for relevance. And I am even aware of an endeavour to establish the relevance of modern mainstream economics which proceeds by determining the proportion of all articles in core or 'flagship' journals which make reference to 'empirical facts' or 'draw' policy implications, and reporting that this proportion is reasonably high.

Let me be clear. If economic data record phenomena generated within an open and highly internally-related social system, and mainstream economists uncritically insist on analysing them using methods which presuppose they record phenomena generated in systems that are closed and atomistic, any claims by these economists to be in touch with reality just because data are involved are not well founded. Indeed they merely reveal the level of misunderstanding involved. Similarly, if the whole framework of theoretical modelling is inevitably largely false, and known to be so, it is not obvious there need be any relevance or insight in policy conclusions drawn.[27]

To return to the central theme, however, I hope it is clear that the orientation I am taking is indeed ontological. Mathematical-deductive methods have many desirable features. But 'fit' with reality matters too.[28] The problem with the mainstream stance is that the ontological preconditions of its formalistic methods appear to be not only *not* ubiquitous in the social realm, but actually rather special occurrences. If we knew both that social life was everywhere atomistic, and also that for any type of outcome a fixed isolated set of causes was always responsible so that all other causal processes serve only as a kind of stable, non-intervening or homogeneous backdrop, we would have grounds for feeling confident in the emphasis that mainstream economists place on the sorts of deductivist methods they use. However, our best ontological analysis suggests that closures are but a special configuration of social reality, whilst our *a posteriori* experience is that this special case seems not to come about very often at all.[29]

Thesis 4: Despite ambitions to the contrary, the modern mainstream project mostly serves to constrain economics from realising its (nevertheless real) potential to be not only explanatorily powerful, but scientific in the sense of natural science

It does appear that a central reason so many economists persevere with methods of mathematical-deductivist modelling, despite a dearth of successes so far, is an ingrained belief that these methods are an essential component of all science (see e.g. Lantner 1997: 58). Not all hold to such a belief (e.g. Clower 1999; Kirman 1997); but very many seem to.[30] As Mayer (1997: 21) expresses matters, 'formal analysis provides a comforting feeling of doing work that is "scientific … "'.

Even so I think it can be demonstrated that mathematics is not essential to science after all. Further, there is every reason to anticipate that the study of social phenomena can be not only explanatorily powerful but scientific in the sense of natural science, even if mathematical-deductive methods are not used. In fact, the mainstream insistence on employing mathematical modelling methods in conditions for which they are not appropriate, actually serves as a barrier to economics proceeding in the manner of natural science. Let me briefly defend this fourth and final thesis by re-examining what we might mean when talking of natural science.

Now I think we can agree that natural science is carried on in numerous contexts. My claim defended in Lawson (1997a) and elsewhere is that if there is something fundamental to scientific explanation in the natural realm it is the move from phenomena at one level to their underlying causal conditions. And this move is often possible even where stable event regularities are not uncovered and mathematical formalism not applicable.

Against this claim the best (and a common) response of the deductivist modeller is to observe that whatever the extent of natural science the one sure component of it is the successful well controlled laboratory experiment. And experimental activity of this sort supports the image of science accepted by the formalistic modellers of modern economics. For in the well controlled laboratory experiment, event regularities (or closures) of the causal sequence type are regularly sought and often achieved, and where they are achieved forms of formalistic-deductivist modelling are indeed facilitated.

I acknowledge the import of this observation. But it is useful for my purposes to consider more closely what goes on in such conditions. In fact, problems for the deductivist arise as soon as we also recognise that

(i) most event regularities of the causal sequence sort regarded as of interest to natural scientists are actually restricted to conditions of experimental control, whilst
(ii) the results of these experiments are frequently successfully applied outside the experiments *where event regularities are not in evidence.*

The key to understanding this situation is already in place in the preceding discussion of the implicit ontology of economists' methods of mathematical-deductivist modelling. For the latter methods presuppose occurrences of event regularities of the causal sequence sort. And we have seen that in order to generate relevant results taking this form, economists need to specify their theories in terms of entities which both are isolated and produce constant and invariable responses to given conditions.

This analysis bears on how we must interpret experimentally produced event regularities. For we can make sense of the confinement of these regularities to experimental conditions just by viewing experimental practitioners as intervening in a sphere of reality and experimentally manipulating it in order that

(i) the workings of a specific intrinsically stable causal mechanism are
(ii) insulated from the effects of countervailing factors.

It is just because an intrinsically stable mechanism is isolated, where it is, that an event regularity is produced between the triggering conditions of the mechanism and the effects that ensue. If a mechanism being investigated were not stable, or countervailing factors are allowed to intervene, the regularity would not be produced.[31]

Notice, then, that to make sense of the experimental process, it is essential to recognise that the event regularity produced corresponds to the empirical identification of an underlying causal mechanism. In other words, even in experimental work, i.e. even in that branch of scientific work which is most bound up with the production of event regularities of the causal sequence sort, the primary concern is not with the production of an event regularity *per se*, but with the empirical identification of an underlying mechanism (co-responsible for any regularity so produced).

Notice, too, that it is only by way of this understanding of the experimental process that we can make sense of the observation, noted above but not yet addressed, that experimental knowledge is somehow successfully applied outside the laboratory, even in conditions where event regularities do not occur. For the knowledge or insights obtained relate primarily not to the (contingent and experiment-bound) regularity that is produced, but to a (experimentally empirically identified) mechanism that, when triggered, operates independently of scientists and their experimental work. For causal mechanisms normally act not actualistically (resulting in the same actual events or outcomes in all conditions), but transfactually (having effects all the time whatever the outcome). Thus gravitational mechanisms or tendencies will be acting on the autumn leaves not just as they fall to the ground but even as they fly over rooftops and chimneys.[32]

Science

There are many implications of this discussion that could be developed (see Lawson 1997a). But the central point I want to convey here is that even in those experimental situations where event regularities are successfully brought about, the real contribution of (successful) science is not the production of the event regularity *per se*, but the identification of an underlying causal factor. The aim of experimental practice is to increase our understanding (or to 'test' theories about) underlying powers, mechanisms and/or tendencies, etc., responsible for the events we produce or otherwise observe.

We find, then, that even the achievements of laboratory experimentation ultimately constitute evidence supporting the view that *if* anything is essential to the scientific process it is this movement from a surface phenomenon to its underlying cause. This is causal explanation (rather than event prediction – see Chapter 4 below). Now, the identification of causes is not restricted to situations where stable event regularities are produced. As we shall see in Chapter 4 especially, causes can be successfully uncovered in situations where mathematical-deductivist reasoning is not applicable at all. The point of relevance here, though, is that even the experimental work of science is found to concern itself with the understanding of causal factors.

In short, *if* science can be characterised by any one aspect of its activities, the analysis sustained here and elsewhere (Lawson 1997a) suggests that the prime candidate is the (explanatory) move from a conception of a phenomenon of interest at one level to a conception of its cause(s) lying at a different one. Science is characterised by causal explanation if by any one aspect or process. And, if the social ontology sketched above and defended in Chapter 2 below is at all correct, and specifically if social reality is indeed structured, this is a move available as much to those who study social phenomena as to those who study natural phenomena. Economists can seek to uncover, for example, the social processes governing unemployment, poverty or whatever.[33]

It follows, that even if the practice of applying methods of mathematical -deductivist modelling in economics continues to be rather unsuccessful, there remains every reason to suppose that economists can yet, and successfully, practice science in the sense of (successful) natural science.[34]

The mainstream project and science

The form of reasoning that takes us from observations on phenomena at one level to hypotheses about their causes lying at a different one is retroduction. Causal explanation depends on it (see Chapter 4 below). Can mainstream economists also adopt this causal explanatory move? If mainstream economists construct (novel) social theories in an endeavour to ground presumed event correlations of a causal-sequence sort, a form of retroductive move must be involved, even if this remains unrecognised.

The problem for modern mainstream economists adopting explanatory goals is not so much whether, as how, retroduction can be employed. Causal explanation is concerned with identifying the powers, mechanisms, tendencies and structures responsible for phenomena at a higher level. The purpose is to uncover how the surface phenomena were produced. Although mainstream economists do not eschew all talk of powers and mechanisms (as Hoover [1997] for example reminds us),[35] it is clear that in the retroductive process the range of feasible options is severely constrained by the prior and dominating goal of achieving conceptions that are (mathematically) tractable.

Thus, in mainstream models, agents are often endowed with powers such as rationality which (unlike those, say, of perfect foresight or omniscience) seem realistic up to a point. However, in order to facilitate deductivist or closed-systems formalistic modelling, any powers attributed to agents (whether realistic or not) must be assumed always to be exercised, and exercised in given ways. In order to generate event regularities it is not enough to assume that agents merely could (i.e. merely have the power to) do this or that. Powers have to be exercised, and exercised in predictable ways. Thus agents, if endowed with the power of rationality, must always be rational in their actual behaviour. The starting point in mainstream undertakings is the desire to engage in deductivist modelling, and so the end result is a theoretical system, or set of conceptions, that facilitates this.

In an open social world, the *representations* of structures, including powers, elaborated on the requirement that they facilitate a closed system of the causal sequence sort are, then, in most cases going to be to a significant degree fictitious, as I have already discussed. Indeed, they will be of a sort that guarantees a system of isolated atoms. And ultimately all such powers as are conceptualised will, *qua* powers, be in any case largely superfluous to the outcome. For the deductivist, analysis requires that underlying powers, etc. are always reflected fully in predictable behaviour, i.e. are actualised, and in ways where events could not have turned out otherwise.

Mainly of course, the mainstream economist starts out intending to show that any outcome is a result of individuals optimising their situation. This is the easiest, or anyway (widely considered to be) most compelling, way of constructing a set-up with a predictable or deducible outcome. An isolated situation constructed so as to contain a unique optimum, coupled with the assumption that agents always optimise, meets, with relative ease, the requirements for formalistic deductivist modelling to proceed (thus explaining, of course, why so many commentators have interpreted the mainstream project as defined by its attention to the optimising individual atom).

However, this strategy, though explicable, is not essential. Assumptions, say, to the effect that (isolated) agents follow fixed rules irrespective of context, will do the job equally well. And indeed the presumption of rationality does not figure in all contributions accepted as mainstream (for actual examples see Lawson 1997a: ch. 8).[36]

The point here, though, is that in a non-atomistic world the constraint of providing theories that presuppose an atomistic ontology diverts us from uncovering (realistic accounts of) the real causes of phenomena of interest. And such a constraint is an unavoidable consequence of the insistence that the primary goal be always a conception or 'model' that is mathematically tractable. In orienting itself in this way the modern mainstream project, despite its pretensions, actually serves to undermine its clear ambition of achieving an economics which proceeds in a manner that is scientific in the sense of natural science. At the same time it serves to constrain the discipline from realising more of its explanatory potential.

Implications for the discipline of economics

So what, in brief, are the implications of all this? Most clearly a rather significant reorienting of the modern discipline of economics is warranted. Specifically, there is good reason for economists to turn to ontology, to engage more explicitly than hitherto in practices of realist social theorising. And, if the particular realist analysis outlined here is at all correct, there are also good reasons for economists to accept a more pluralistic orientation to the discipline, and in particular for economists to give up their insistence on methods of formalistic closed-system modelling for all occasions.

In so concluding I am not at all suggesting that formalistic modelling methods should not exist in the battery of options available. My aim with the discussion of this chapter is not to narrow down the range of method-ological options by attempting to prohibit a particular method. Rather it is to widen the range of possibilities through criticising the fact that, and manner in which, in many quarters at least, the particular method in ques-tion is currently and often unthinkingly universalized.[37] The goal, as I say is a pluralistic forum[38] where explicitly prosecuted ontology and critical reflection can take their place amongst all the conceivable components of economics as social theorising. Only with this acheived, I believe, can we again, with reason, be optimistic about the possibility of economics proceeding in an explanatorily fruitful fashion.

2

AN ONTOLOGICAL TURN IN ECONOMICS

My primary purpose with this book is to argue that there is much to be gained from an ontological turn in social theorising, that there are significant advantages to making a concern with ontology more explicit and systematic than is the custom. A secondary goal, closely bound up with the first, and one with which I shall be expressly occupied in the current chapter, is to argue for a particular ontological conception. It is through demonstrating the sustainability as well as usefulness of this particular conception, one sometimes systematised as critical realism,[1] that I seek simultaneously to achieve my primary goal.

As with many broad conceptions in social theory and philosophy, the ontological one I defend here is usefully viewed under the following three of its aspects: the manner in which it is achieved, its central features or results, and the sorts of implications that follow from accepting it. The current chapter is structured by considering each of these aspects in turn. The framework and results of *Economics and Reality* (Lawson 1997a) do receive some development. However, my primary concern in the current chapter is with consolidation and clarification.[2]

Context and philosophical method

I start with method of derivation, with the manner in which the ontological conception I defend is achieved. The task of conveying the significant features of any approach to theorising, no less to theorising about methods of argumentation, is often aided by contrasting the approach in question with alternatives, especially if the latter are familiar. I adopt such a contrastive strategy here.

A study of the relevant literature reveals that many, and perhaps most, recent contributions to methodology in economics conform broadly to one or other of two basic approaches. On the one side are those who accept the scientificity of economics as practised and seek (for the time being at least) mostly to justify and/or clarify the way in which economics is already done, to demonstrate the nature and rationality of what goes on. On the other side are contributors who seek to impose onto economics conceptions of proper science or method determined outside of the discipline (by philosophers of physics, or some such).[3]

Now it may be because certain commentators on economic methodology suppose these particular versions of 'bottom up' and 'top down' approaches are the only options that are feasible, that they have inferred that the realist project to which I and many others have been contributing must itself adopt one or other of them. More specifically, because the realist project in question is somewhat critical of modern economic practice, it has been interpreted by some as thereby inevitably conforming to the externally imposing or 'top down' form of contribution.

The approach I take, however, is not of this sort at all. It is certainly self-consciously prescriptive in certain ways. But it proceeds in a fashion that is not well captured by either of the two noted models of methodological approach. Let me briefly elaborate, indicating something more of the two noted traditional approaches first.

Contending approaches to economic methodology

Prior to recent debate, perhaps the dominant view amongst economic methodologists was that philosophy's role, at least in economics, is to justify scientific practices already regarded as rational, to legitimise what already takes place. Friedman's (1953) early methodological essay is a well known example of this kind.

Easy criticism of philosophical activity so conceived can be offered. Most obviously, in the face of the recent dismal record of modern economics, any strategy which involves accepting unquestioningly the assumption that whatever economists are doing it must be broadly rational (or 'scientific' or sustainable) seems complacent at best. In particular, it forgoes the possibility of a significant *critical* philosophical input from the outset.[4] Methodologists taking such a stance tend to be restricted either to transforming the criteria by which to gauge the mainstream project, or to clarifying if not defending its procedures or types of formulation (see e.g. Friedman 1953, or more recently Mäki 1998). In such cases,[5] insight as to why economics is currently in such an unhappy state is largely absent,[6] and indeed appears hardly feasible.[7]

Further, where philosophers or methodologists are concerned to demonstrate merely that practices followed are rational (their rationality being already considered a fact), it is not obvious that economists who are already engaged in such practices need take a great deal of notice anyway (even if some clarification of how they are proceeding is achieved). On this conception philosophy/methodology appears to be running idle. This perception of the contribution of methodology seems to be held by a significant number of mainstream economists, presumably explaining in some part their often noted (albeit rarely skilfully articulated) impatience with it. Others have made this point before. Blaug, for example, writes:

> Too many writers on economic methodology have seen their role as simply rationalizing the traditional modes of argument of economists, and perhaps this is why the average modern economist has little use for methodological inquiries. To be perfectly frank, economic methodology has little place in the training of modern economists.
>
> (Blaug 1980: xiii)

It is perhaps not surprising, then, that in recent years certain methodologists and meta-methodologists in economics have tended to conclude that putting methodology to work merely to justify methods already regarded as rational is somewhat unrewarding, if not of questionable worth.

For some in this latter group, and in particular for those who remain reluctant to challenge the rationality of dominant practices but who abandon even the goal of clarifying, for the mainstream, the nature of their practices and presuppositions, the result has been an effective rejection of normative/prescriptive methodology. The conclusion drawn has indeed been that 'methodology has no consequences for practice' (Weintraub 1989: 487). If methodology is to retain any input at all, the argument from this quarter often runs, it should be reserved for the task merely of describing the practices of the discipline, along with its sociology.

There are also others, though, who are prepared to accept that the rationale of actual practices is indeed open to question and perhaps criticism. For members of this group, the main response has been to call upon the philosophy of (natural) science to furnish injunctions for economics.

This has been Blaug's (1980) approach. Blaug has taken note of both the continuing poor performance of the modern economics discipline, as well as the widespread disparity between actual practices of economists and their professed (typically Popperian) theory of practice or 'standard economic methodology' as set out in basic textbooks. In setting out his remedy for these ills, Blaug sides strongly with reorienting practice in line with the latter text book theorisations:

> economists have long been aware of the need to defend 'correct' principles of reasoning in their subject, and although the actual practice may bear little relationship to what is preached, the preaching is worth considering on its own ground.
>
> (Blaug 1980: xii)

And a few paragraphs later he explains:

> After many years of complacency about the scientific status of their subject, more and more economists are beginning to ask themselves deeper questions about what they are doing. At any rate, there are growing numbers who suspect that all is not well in the house that economics has built. … Like many other modern economists, I too have a view of *What's Wrong With Economics?* to cite the title of a book by Benjamin Ward, but my quarrel is less with the actual content of modern economics than with the way economists go about validating their theories. I hold that there is nothing much wrong with standard economic methodology as laid down in the first chapter of almost every textbook in economic theory; what is wrong is that economists do not practice what they preach.
>
> (1980: xiii)

The problem with Blaug's response, as with others like it, is that, typically, the theoretical or methodological principles called upon have been formulated externally to the discipline and even to the social realm, and merely asserted as relevant for economics. They have no obvious evidential grounding as generalised procedures for *social*-scientific practice. Rather they are mostly justified, if at all, by reference to the authority of their formulators, or their apparent or claimed successes in other domains.

Moreover, practitioners of economics aware of the disparity between what Blaug terms 'standard textbook methodology' and actual practices, have tended to conclude that, of the two, it is the former methodology that is most clearly wanting.[8] Standard textbook methodology has been found to be impractical in the context of economics. Leamer agues this case in the context of econometrics, for example, concluding, in the face of the supposed widespread 'sin' of not following standard methodology, that 'unavoidable sins cannot be sins at all' (1978: vi).[9] And McCloskey, reflecting on such matters, raises the question as to why methodological theorising unrelated to actual economic practices should be worthy of any consideration:

> The custom of methodological papers in economics is to scold economists for not allowing it to interfere more. Mark Blaug's useful book summarizing the state of play of economic methodology in 1980, *The Methodology of Economics*, is a recent case. Its subtitle promises to tell 'How Economists Explain'. It might better have been 'How the Young Karl Popper Explained', for it repeatedly attacks extant arguments in economics for failing to comply with the rules Popper laid down in *Logik der Forschung* in 1934.

Blaug's exordium is typical of the best of the methodologists in economics: 'Economists have long been aware of the need to defend "correct" principles of reasoning in their subject: although actual practice may bear little relationship to what is preached, the preaching is worth considering on its own ground' (Blaug 1980: xii). Such words flow easily from the modernist's pen. Yet it is unclear why preaching unrelated to actual practice should be worth considering at all. Why do economists have to defend in the abstract their principles of reasoning, and before what tribunal? The methodologists – whether logical positivist or Popperian or Austrian or Marxist – should have an answer, but do not. Ancient common sense and recently philosophy of science suggest they cannot.

(McCloskey 1986: 21)

And yet Blaug has a point: economics as a discipline is not very successful, even on its own terms. Indeed, it is recognised by many of its most prominent contributors as being in some disarray. Moreover its lack of direction as well as sense of purpose, its inability to tie its practice to its own methodological theory, along with its continued lack of explanatory successes (see Chapter 1), suggest *prima facie* that methodology ought to have a lot to contribute somehow.

Critical realism in economics

It is in this context, and against such varying assessments and strategies, that the project of critical realism has been developed within economics. Its entry points and motivations have been numerous.[10] A most obvious stimulus has been the just noted disarray of the discipline of economics, and especially its lack of empirical/explanatory successes combined with the widespread experience of theory/practice inconsistencies. For myself at least, a further relevant factor has been the regular assertions of colleagues and others that contributions that do not involve formalistic-deductivist models do not count as proper economics. The fact that such assertions are based not on analyses of social material but mostly on conceptions of naturalistic social science alerted me early on to the problem (as I see it) of ontological neglect in the modern discipline.[11]

Against this background, it has seemed evident that explicit philosophical/methodological analysis is called for. Here I side with Blaug. But there are varying ideas of how to proceed, and it is not good enough merely to assert the rationality or superiority of any methodological position or set of practices (whether deriving from within or from outside a discipline). Here I side with McCloskey and Weintraub. Rather it is necessary to provide an argument which does not beg the relevant

32

questions at the outset, and against which, indeed, there always remains a possibility that any, and even all, approaches might be shown to be wanting in some respect.

A question that, from the beginning, warranted being addressed by myself and others contributing to the project of critical realism, then, is whether it is possible to relax the assumption that the practices of researchers (whether of economists or of others) are necessarily rational, without imposing formulations concerning proper economic practice (especially those determined in other contexts). Or to frame the question slightly differently, how is philosophy or methodology to provide a non-arbitrary input to scientific practice? How can it legitimately make a difference?

Seen from this perspective, the realist project has in effect been concerned with determining the sorts of premises, if any, which can legitimately get a normative philosophical/methodological analysis going. If we reject the presumption that the practices of science are necessarily rational or justified, what alternative is there?

The alternative point of departure adopted is to suppose of scientific practices not that they are inevitably rational, but that they (and indeed all human practices) are *intelligible*. That is, it is accepted that all actual practices, whether or not scientific, and whether or not successful on their own terms, have explanations. There are conditions which render practices actually carried out (and their results) possible. Let me refer to this supposition as the *intelligibility principle* (to heighten the contrast with Popper's *rationality principle*, that individuals always act appropriately to their situations (see Popper 1967: 359). Thus, accepting the intelligibility principle, one strand of my strategy has just been to seek to explain (aspects of) certain human actions, to identify their conditions of possibility. Or, more precisely, my strategy has been to explain various generalised features of experience, including human actions, and so to uncover generalised insights regarding the structure or nature of reality. This of course, is precisely an exercise in ontology.

How does this move help? Basically, it gives a good deal of insight into the possibilities and limits to social analysis. I will discuss all this below in the third part of this chapter.[12] Let me at this point give a very brief overview of a mode of argumentation that is found to be particularly useful.

Transcendental analysis and social theory

The initiating presumption that human social activity is intelligible , i.e. the intelligibility principle, should not be especially contentious. We all act upon it. It is difficult, for example, to imagine anyone bothering to attempt to read and understand these lines who supposes or claims otherwise.

I have already noted that the premises of the sorts of (ontological) analyses to which I refer usually express certain fairly generalised features of experience. The form of reasoning that takes us from widespread features of experience (including here conceptions of generalised human practices, or of aspects of them) to their grounds or conditions of possibility, is the *transcendental argument*.[13] The transcendental argument (or transcendental 'deduction') is thus clearly a special case of the *retroductive argument*, where the latter moves from conceptions of specific phenomena at any one level to hypotheses about their underlying conditions or causes (see Lawson 1997a: ch. 2; Chapter 4 below).

Any results achieved by way of transcendental reasoning are clearly conditional. They are contingent upon the human practices selected as premises and our conceptions of them, as well as upon the adequacy of the transcendental arguments employed.

Moreover it is clear that philosophy so conceived, i.e. as method turning centrally upon the transcendental argument, considers the same world as do the sciences, and indeed serves, in its insights, to complement the latter's results. However, it proceeds on the basis of pure reason (albeit exercising it always on the basis of prior conceptions of historically rooted practices) and produces (fallible) knowledge of the necessary conditions of the production of knowledge.

Specific strategies

Contributors to the project of critical realism have made use of transcendental arguments in many different ways. It is true, for example, that, when initiating explanatory endeavour, some have adopted premises concerning the practices of natural science. I do not deny that I myself have made use of insights achieved in such exercises. Specifically, I have sought to uncover essential features of successful natural-scientific practice, and I have questioned the extent to which it is feasible to undertake similar practices in researching the social realm (see, for example, chapter 6 below). Alternatively put, I have examined the extent to which naturalism is possible, where naturalism is the thesis that the study of social phenomena can be scientific in the sense of natural science. But it is important to understand how and why.

The 'how', or manner in which the issue of naturalism has been pursued, has in no way involved imposing a conception of natural scientific practice onto the social realm. Rather, as I say, I have merely questioned the extent, if any, to which naturalism is possible. Thus the position on naturalism taken is an answer to this question. And determining an answer presupposes an independent analysis of social ontology; it is something determined only *after* a theory of social ontology, or other insights into the social realm, have been independently uncovered (see for example Lawson 1997e).

The 'why', or reason for my having pursued the question of naturalism, is, in part at least, strategic (see Lawson 1997e; Lewis 2002b). Currently, the discipline of economics is in a state of some disarray and, at the institutional level, dominated by a mainstream tradition distinguished by its insistence that economics mostly reduces to the application of methods of formalistic-deductivist modelling (see Chapter 1). Now this emphasis is often considered justified simply because the methods in question are regarded as essential components of all science. In other words, naturalism is, first, already on the agenda; second, asserted to be true by mainstream economists; and third, interpreted in terms of the application of methods of mathematico-deductivist modelling. As I say, I reject the idea that naturalism, however interpreted, can be merely asserted as correct. But the mainstream assessment of natural science is, in any case, erroneous (see Chapter 1). It has thus seemed to me important to reveal this.[14] For it removes one further barrier to a more informed and open discussion. This anyway has been a central aspect of my motivation and strategy.[15]

If all of this helps explain my orientation and strategy, there may yet remain some who suppose that the ontological conception I defend is somehow necessarily imposed from the outside. In case this is so, I now want briefly to run through, and in places also extend, my development of a theory of social ontology as found in *Economics and Reality* (especially chapters 12 and 13) without making any reference to the practices (or any philosophy) of natural science. By my doing so, it will hopefully be clear that natural scientific considerations are in no way necessary to, or part of, the basic argument and orientation achieved (even if they are, as I say, strategically useful to my overall project nevertheless). An elaboration of the ontological conception I defend provides the second theme of this chapter.

A theory of social ontology

By social reality, I understand that domain of phenomena whose existence depends, at least in part, on us. One useful starting point in determining aspects of its nature has been the observation that human action does generally seem to be rather successful. If *prima facie* the social world is somewhat complex, we do, most of us, appear to be fairly successful at negotiating it. At least we mostly do so after a certain (albeit often quite mature) age. Of course, the fact that we are able to do so only after a certain age (an observation which appears to hold for all societies) and only after a good deal of instruction and experience, lends credence to the idea that society is indeed complex. Its understanding and navigation are non-trivial affairs. This assessment is also borne out by the relative difficulties we all sometimes appear to encounter in getting by, or fitting in, when travelling away from our own familiar localities and culture.

35

However, in any specific setting we usually find that 'local' people not only get by, but also interact in seemingly competent ways, including with strangers. For this to be possible it must be the case that a good proportion of individual activities or practices are, under some of their aspects at least, comprehensible to others, and even to a degree predictable within limits; it seems inconceivable that capable human interaction such as we observe could arise otherwise.

In the twenty-first century UK, for example, I expect other road users to drive on the left side of the road, to stop at red traffic lights, and so forth. Indeed, I expect individuals in all walks of life to follow various other sets of practices known to me. Mostly they do. They do not always, however. And the latter is an important observation too, one to which I shall return in Chapter 4. But there are indeed situations in which, much of the time at least, certain practices have a routine or otherwise predictable aspect to them. There are occasions where it is at least feasible to anticipate limits within which the (highly routinised) actions of many (though rarely all) others do fall, at least much of the time.

Social rules

A necessary condition of possibility of this highly generalised state of affairs, and, in particular, of the experience that routinised behaviour is pervasive, is a social world structured by social rules or codes, which condition the practices people follow (Lawson 1997a: ch. 12). This could be (indeed is) a transcendental inference. But in truth we already know the inferred conditions to be so. We already know that social life is rule-conditioned.

Parenthetically, there are many aspects of capable human behaviour that do not reduce to routinised practices or rule following. I will have something to say about some of these below, and also in Chapter 4. But for the time being I focus on that aspect of social life that is highly structured by social rules.

Social rules can be conceptualised as generalised procedures of action, procedures that, under suitable transformations at least, can be expressed as injunctions of the form: 'if x do y under conditions z'. For example, 'if wishing to speak at a crowded seminar, hold your hand up, when in twentieth century Britain'. The stipulation 'under conditions z' will often be dropped or unacknowledged in any explicit formulation but will always be implicated. All action takes place over limited regions of time and space and in specific socio-cultural contexts.

This formulation is quite general and intended to apply equally to semantic, moral, constitutive, regulative, etc., forms, or aspects, of rules alike. The 'do y' in other words is to be interpreted widely and to include such injunctions as 'interpret … as', 'count … as' 'take … to mean', and so on. Of course, any rule only carries normative or legitimating or facilitating (constitutive/regulative/moral/semantic) force. A social rule, in other words, is a formulation of action that, under specified conditions, must, should, or can usefully, legitimately, meaningfully, or advisedly, etc., be carried out, rather than a prediction or observation of an action. It is a (possibly contested) directive, code, convention, or understanding about *how* an act could or should be performed; it is not *per se* a prediction or claim that the performance so indicated in fact always proceeds. As I have already noted, human behaviour is rarely if ever entirely predictable. Nevertheless, in a system in which social rules are widely respected, the result can be a degree of predictability of aspects, including the limits, of certain forms of behaviour, sufficient, it seems, for capable action to be possible. Thus just as a shared knowledge of, and adherence to, rules of the game allow us to play team sports (albeit not typically to predict the exact moves made, only the *sorts* of moves and their limits) – so shared knowledge and acceptance of, say, rules of language, or conventions of speech interactions, facilitate conversations.

If we already know that social reality is in part constituted by social rules, there are various aspects of these rules and their conditions that warrant elaboration. In particular, social rules are ontologically distinct from social practices.[16] A recognition of this follows once we observe, and enquire into (transcendentally deduce) the conditions of possibility of the already noted widespread feature of experience that practices governed by rules are not always, or on average, in conformity with our formulations of these rules. The (intentional) act of rebelling requires as much knowledge of the rules as does that of conforming. Currently, motorway drivers in the UK *mostly* drive at a speed above that laid down in law, albeit in each case usually not significantly faster than other motorists for fear of getting caught out by traffic police. And workers taking industrial action frequently *threaten* to work to rule. Making sense of the fact that rules are often (or even sometimes) so much, and possibly systematically, out of phase with the practices they condition, requires that we recognise the two aspects, rules and practices, as connected, but ontologically distinct.

The social realm, then, is structured; it does not consist only in actualities such as behaviour. The ontological distinction between social rules and practices is a (transcendentally inferred) necessary condition of the possibility of the former influencing, whilst simultaneously being often out of phase with, the latter.

Parenthetically, I might emphasise that I have made no claims about how a knowledge of rules, or of action that is legitimate because coherent with local rules, is acquired, or the manner in which social rules make a difference. It is likely the case, for example, that actions consistent with many rules (especially those to which there is wide and enduring conformity) can be learnt via trial and error or by way of imitating others, and that, for many individuals at least, many forms of rule-consistent action may never be given an explicit formulation. So a knowledge of rules may not always, or even usually, take a codified form.

But that recognised, it would be wrong to infer that in all such situations social rules had not had a causal impact in some manner. Where social rules are in place, forms of behaviour significantly inconsistent with them will tend to induce conflict. As a result, either the practices or the rules they contravene (or both) must be adjusted. Typically of course, the individual's mistakes do not lead to the prevailing rules being transformed. Thus a condition of survival of specific behaviour patterns, typically, just is that they are not radically inconsistent with operative rules. In other words, existing rules play a 'selecting' role. Irrespective of how each practice from the range of those tried is originally motivated, the prevalence of accepted rules will bear on the question of which come to be reproduced. The process or mechanism directly stimulating certain forms of behaviours may be quite different from any direct reading and following of systems of rules, but the sustainability of certain practices as habitually performed or routinised forms of behaviour will be in part explained by (the consistency of those practices with) prevailing systems of rules.[17]

Social positions

A further highly generalised feature of experience is that the practices people follow, including routines (which may or may not become habitual), are highly, and *systematically*, segmented or differentiated. It seems we are not in all cases all empowered to do the same sorts of things. Teachers follow routines and other recognisable practices which are different to those followed by students. Similarly there are differences between the regular practices of employers and those of employees, between those of landladies/landlords and those of tenants, and so forth. It is the case, then, that either we do not all follow the same rules, or that given social rules lay down contrasting obligations, etc., for different (sorts of) people.

How can this be? Notice, too, as a yet further generalised feature of experience, that practices which can be followed in any context, and so the rules governing the obligations and prerogatives in play, are often independent of the particular individuals carrying them out at any point in time. Each year, for example, I am, as a university lecturer, faced by an array of students who are expected to attend lectures, write essays and sit exams (just as I am expected to give the lectures, etc.). But equally, each year the set of individuals facing me as students is found to be different from that of the previous year. The practices are continued but the individuals enacting them frequently change.

We can make sense of all this by recognising that the constituents of social reality include *positions* into which people essentially slot, positions that have rules associated with them governing the obligations and perks, etc., that fall on, or are on offer to, their occupants. This real category of positions into which people slot is required to make sense of (is a necessary condition of the possibility of) the continuity of social life in the face of changing individuals; and it is the association of rules with these (different) positions that explains the systematic segmentation of routines followed. So, by way of a further transcendental argument, we find that the ontology of the social world includes not only social practices and social rules but equally social positions.

Internal relationality

The social world also includes other aspects of social structure. For example we can take note of (and seek to explain) the further generalised feature of experience that our practices are not only differentiated but typically systematically and constitutively other-oriented. The defining practices of any one group are usually oriented to the practices of others which, if often to a degree similar to the first set of practices, are typically quite distinct. Thus the practices of students are oriented towards (though mostly different from) those of teachers, and vice-versa. In similar fashion, this feature of being other-oriented characterises the practices of employers and employees, landladies/landlords and tenants, parents and children, preachers and congregations, performers and audiences, etc.

A condition of the possibility of this other-orientation of social practices is the existence of *internal relations* in the social domain. These are relations whereby the aspects related, the relata, just are what they are, and/or are able to do what they do, in virtue of the relation in which they stand. Internal relations hold for the natural world too, e.g. between a magnet and its field. Notice, though, that it is relations between positions (as opposed to people *per se*) that are likely to be of primary importance in the social domain (for an elaboration of the argument see Lawson 1997a: ch. 12).

Transformation and reproduction

More yet can be inferred regarding the socio-ontological picture. Because social structure is everywhere found to make a difference (we could not speak as we do without the prior existence of language, drive safely on motorways without knowing the already existing highway code, etc.), we can infer that social structure is both relatively autonomous (it pre-exists our current acts) and also real (it makes a difference to what is possible). Hence voluntarism must be rejected. Further, because social structure (in virtue of being social) depends on us (i.e. on transformative human agency), structural deterministic accounts must also be rejected.

In short, social structure is both condition of, as well as dependent upon, human action. So it is neither created by, nor creative of, human action. This means we must replace both voluntarist and determinist accounts of social life by a conception according to which social reality is recognised as being continuously reproduced or transformed. This is the *transformational model of social activity*. Only on such a conception does it follow that social structure is the (often unacknowledged) condition of our actions, and its reproduction/transformation the (often unintended) outcome.

Reproduction over space and time

Clearly the transformational model is consistent with the possibility of certain structures being found to be relatively enduring over space and/or time. Whether this possibility is actualised will depend on context, of course. However, there are various generalised features of experience which bear on this, i.e. features which, if we inquire into their conditions of possibility, afford an insight to processes of social reproduction.

One significant observation here is that there is an *a posteriori* degree of continuity in our everyday affairs. Although event patterns of the kind sought after by deductivist modellers appear to be relatively rare in the social realm, there are many regularities of the form 'whatever happens here (today) happens there (tomorrow)'. In the UK where I live, shops are usually in the same place each day, open on the same days of each week and at similar times. Similarly schools, banks and churches keep to reasonably regular times. And the hospitals are almost always open. Going further afield, we find that whatever the (current) local prices of postage stamps, national newspapers, television licences, etc., the same prices tend to hold in other UK towns. Mostly, too, we (currently) find that prices of these items and of numerous others remain the same from day to day, at least over significant periods of time. At a more abstract level, it is the case that throughout the UK and over time, people are buying and selling, driving cars, talking to each other, watching television, listening to the radio, and so forth.

Clearly, it is a condition of possibility of these particular generalised features of experience that social structures, at least in some of their aspects, are in fact relatively enduring, that some are reproduced over (perhaps considerable) stretches of space and/or time. That is, we can make sense of such patterns of continuity as we experience in everyday states of affairs by recognising that, although the social world turns on inherently transformative human agency, it happens that various aspects of social structure are continually reproduced over significant spans of time and/or space none-theless. The sorts of practices just noted, for

40

example, presuppose the continuity (of course through change) of certain structures of market capitalism, the English (or another) language, a broadcasting network, and so on.

I might note, parenthetically, that the sorts of event patterns which emerge (i.e. those that can be explained only through acknowledging a continuity of structures) often approximate (or in the limit can be viewed as restricted forms of) constant conjunctions of the sorts that are defining of closed systems. It is true that these closures are not (or do not reduce to) the sort pursued by mainstream deductivist modellers, where the correlated events stand in causal sequence (i.e. where the independent variable or antecedent [set of] event[s] x stands in the causal history of the dependent variable or consequent event y – see Chapter 1). Rather, in the sorts of examples mentioned above, such correlations as occur mostly arise because the events in question (x and y say) are influenced by a third set of factors (z say) or share a similar causal history. There need not be a fixed relation between z and both x and y. All that is required is that whatever the effect of z on x at a given point, it has the same effect on y at that point. Thus when the UK government has needed to raise revenue in the past it has sometimes sought to obtain it by increasing the level of car tax (or national insurance contributions, etc.). The outcome, however, is that whenever 'the price of car tax (or whatever) has increased in Cambridge' (event x), 'the price of car tax has increased by the same amount elsewhere in the UK' (event y).

I admit to not giving such patterns much explicit consideration in previous writing (as is illustrated by the discussion of closures in Chapters 3, 6 and 9 below, each published before this book was put together). I shall be making significant use of them in Chapter 4 below. For the time being I note that an upshot of rectifying their previous neglect here, is that we now have cause to distinguish two sorts of closed system. Remember a closure just is a system in which a constant conjunction of events occurs, i.e. which supports a regularity of the sort 'whenever event x then event y'. Where the correlated events are held to stand in causal sequence, a guaranteeing of an event regularity requires the insulating of a (stable) mechanism from all others, as we saw in Chapter 1. In this case, the term closure is appropriate in that it captures the idea of a specific mechanism being 'closed off' from the influence of others. However, where x and y are correlated because they share similar causal histories, the term closure better captures the idea of 'closing over'. The reference is to a similar set of causal forces covering a particular region. If the former captures the idea of isolation, the latter captures the idea of continuity or connection.

Thus, if considered under the aspect of causal forces in play, a closed system of the former type might be distinguished as a closure of isolation (or insulation) whilst one of the latter sort might appropriately be designated a closure of continuity. Alternatively, if considered under the aspect of events (being connected), a closed system of the former sort might be termed a closure of causal sequence, whilst an example of the latter type might be labelled a closure of concomitance.[18]

However, to return to the main point of the current set of considerations, the fact of continuity in social life can be rendered intelligible through recognising that social structures do often possess a high degree of space-time endurability. Social reproduction gives rise not just to continuity of patterns, but to endurability of underlying causal structures too.

Of course, even event patterns of the continuity sort being here considered are rarely other than partial (for example, even the price of UK national newspapers varies – students can get certain papers at reduced prices, and my local cinema is sponsored by a particular national newspaper with the result that in its adjoining cafe copies of that newspaper are provided for 'free'; the price of UK television licences was recently reduced for citizens over a certain age; postage stamps franked on the first day of their release and attached to a 'first day cover' often fetch a higher price). And many patterns appear and disappear only later to reappear; there is often a patchiness in actual patterns without their disappearing entirely (for example stability in the prices of financial assets – see Keynes 1973a: ch. 12; Lawson 1994c). We can make best sense of such variability by recognising that there is not a cessation of the underlying causal structures and mechanisms where a pattern does not strictly hold, but that countervailing mechanisms are also typically in play affecting the actual outcomes. This is consistent with underlying causal structures being often relatively enduring, but with the social world in general being *open* (events are determined by a multitude of shifting causes). All in all, then, such patterns as there are, and some appear quite strict, can be made sense of by recognising that some structures can, and often do, endure.

Now, if it is a generalised feature of our experience that patterns of the sort 'what happens here happens there' are common, it appears to be a further and related generalised feature of experience that where these (strict or partial) empirical patterns are the more abstract, the greater, very often, is their space-time reach or stretch. And a necessary condition of (the possibility of) this is that the more abstract patterns pick out (are manifestations of) those more sedimented, deeper and fundamental features of a society. Let me briefly elaborate.

Consider the retail prices of everyday items in a country like the UK in the early twenty-first century. As already noted, such prices are often found to be fairly constant, at least over days if not weeks. However, over longer periods all such prices tend to change. But the fact that each day over these longer periods there are nevertheless prices in place is itself a relatively enduring empirical phenomenon. So is the state of affairs that production is mostly oriented to supplying goods for exchange rather than for immediate use (whilst the range and types of commodities being produced is changing all the time). Or consider my own university. It has been around in some form for more than 700 years. In that period the practices of teaching and writing/research have been continually central to it. It is because these same practices have been repeatedly enacted, and at the same broad location (the sites of particular colleges and departments have changed, of course), that we can conceive Cambridge University as the same causal structure throughout. But at a lower level of abstraction aspects of this university are changing all the time. Since I have been in Cambridge new departments have emerged while others have all but disappeared. At the same time, any given department is usually more enduring than the specific practices that constitute it. In particular some lecture courses grow in popularity and are developed, others wither and die. Within a given course technologies change and with them teaching practices and so forth. In short, it appears to be the case that the more concrete and detailed the patterns found the more restricted their space-time location. The more abstract the patterns, the more sedimented or enduring the structures responsible. At least, this is very often so.

Perhaps we have here a handle for research into institutions. I have previously conceptualised the latter as particular social systems, or structured processes of interaction, that are relatively enduring and identified as such (Lawson 1997a: 317–18). If the above considerations are correct, it follows that there can be institutions within institutions within institutions (traditional courses within departments within faculties within a university as a whole); the institution becomes a nested concept. Certainly the category appears ripe for analysis using the framework to hand. The point here, though, is that transcendental analyses of (rough and ready) patterns of everyday life do reveal something of the way certain social structures can be, and have been, reproduced (through change) over wide swathes of space and (perhaps most interestingly) time. A degree of continuity in social life is evident at all levels, albeit that some features are more enduring than others.

Emergence and process

To move on from the issue of reproduction and transformation *per se*, we can note that the basic fact of social structure making a difference to human action, and so its ability to act, its possession of irreducible causal powers, presuppose an account of *emergence* (see Lawson 1997a: 63–5, 175–7). At the same time the dependence of social structure on inherently transformative human agency in the form expressed by the 'transformational model' (even acknowledging that some abstract features are often reproduced over wide stretches of time and space) establishes its dynamic mode of being: social reality is a *process*. Let me briefly indicate what I mean here by emergence and process.

A stratum of reality can be said to be emergent, or as possessing emergent powers, if there is a sense in which it

(i)   has arisen out of a lower stratum, being formed by principles operative at the lower level;
(ii) remains dependent on the lower stratum for its existence; but
(iii) contains causal powers of its own which are irreducible to those operating at the lower level and (perhaps) capable of acting back on the lower level.

Thus organic material emerged from inorganic material. And, according to the conception I am defending, the social realm is emergent from human (inter)action, though with properties irreducible to, yet capable of causally affecting, the latter. For example, a language system has powers irreducible to the human speech, and other communicative, acts on which it nevertheless depends.

What about the idea that society is a process? According to the conception sustained, social structures such as households, markets, universities, schools, hospitals and systems of industrial relations do not independently exist (and often endure over significant periods of time-space) and undergo change. Rather, change is essential to what they are, to their mode of being. They exist as processes of becoming (and decline). Although, for example, the University of Cambridge has always supported teaching and research, the form and content of this has (like that of any other aspect of university life) been changing all the time.

It is clear, then, that we are able to make sense of various generalised features of certain human practices, by transcendentally deducing their conditions of possibility. In so doing we are led to a definite conception of social reality. According to it, social reality is structured vertically (it includes underlying powers and tendencies as well as actualities such as social practices and other events), and horizontally (practices are differentiated), and consists in social rules, relations, positions and institutions, amongst other things. Social reality is an emergent realm, dependent upon, though irreducible to, inherently transformative human agency, and consisting of stuff that is intrinsically dynamic, i.e. everywhere a process, highly internally related and often relatively enduring, amongst much else.

Human being and subjectivity

Let me briefly turn to the topic of human being, including subjectivity. For by way of seeking to identify the conditions of possibility of noteworthy aspects of human practices, it is possible to infer numerous insights in this realm too. The topic is a complex one, and here I can only be relatively brief. But I cannot ignore it altogether without appearing to leave the rational atom of mainstream theorising unchallenged.[19] The transformational model derived above reveals the social world to turn on human practice. Here I concentrate on features of the human individual that relate fairly directly, or in a significant way, to that practice.

It is clearly the case that the human individual is structured. Think of all the things we do. We walk, talk, read, write, sing, interact, imitate, etc. In order to do these things we must possess the capacities to do these things. We could not, say, learn a language without the capacity to do so (not possessed by other species), and we could not engage in speech acts, without having already developed a capacity for one or more languages. So human beings are not reducible to what they do but also comprise the various capacities, dispositions, instincts, etc., presupposed by their activities.

Now, a capacity that is clearly significant to human practice is that which permits forms of action to be performed habitually. I refer to that generalised feature of experience that once we have followed a course of action long enough it can become (what I shall term) a habit, a form of behaviour carried out in appropriate conditions both repeatedly and seemingly unreflectively, i.e. tacitly. Thus we may, repeatedly and without reflecting on our behaviour, stop at red traffic lights, take certain routes home, eat at roughly the same given time each evening, etc. Ways of thinking are but forms of activity, of course, and these too can become habitual. Even the modelling practices of the modern mainstream economists appear, for the most part, to be carried through habitually.

Clearly it is the case that we could not act in such ways, i.e. follow habits, without possessing the capacity so to do. In other words, a transcendentally necessary condition of possibility of any habit is a disposition to act in the said manner, where a disposition just is a capacity so structured or weighted, essentially constrained, that it is perpetually oriented or directed to generating some form of behaviour (habit) in the appropriate conditions.

Habitus

We can note the further generalised feature of experience that we regularly act in many habitual ways simultaneously. It thus seems to follow (once more as a transcendentally necessary condition of possibility of this feature of experience) that an individual, in part, comprises a complex structure of (durable if also transposable) dispositions. This structure is one which, following Bourdieu (e.g. 1990: ch. 3), we might refer to as the habitus.[20] And because many dispositions to act in habitual fashion endure, the habitus (where each disposition is always marked by its conditions of acquisition) ensures the heavy weight of the past in the present, and helps account for the noted fact that we can achieve many things almost at once. It enables us to negotiate a number of obstacles in a manner that would be impossible if we had to reflect upon them all. Thus the habitus seems to be a further essential ingredient in an understanding of practical action.[21]

Of course, an awareness of the considerable role that features like habits and dispositions play in everyday life must not detract from our recognising that human beings are reflexive subjects. Especially important here is that further widespread feature of experience that human beings are forward-looking. Human beings are not just passive reactors but fundamentally initiators of action. Human beings are possessed of intentionality. We can make plans, instigate some of them and (often successfully) carry them out. These and other features presuppose that very significant capacity human beings possess, namely consciousness.

Consciousness

We all, it seems, have subjective, first person, or inner, experiences we call (or attribute to) consciousness. These clearly have their conditions of possibility, presumably including processes in the brain. But the subjective aspects appear irreducible to any neurobiological activity, suggesting that we are talking here of emergent powers, i.e. powers which emerge out of certain lower-level principles and depend upon, but are nevertheless irreducible to, them.[22]

Our consciousness allows some forms of doing to be influenced by that which we desire and understand. To acknowledge consciousness is not to suggest that an individual is always clear, or even able easily to be clear, about their conscious states. But consciousness is bound up with the idea that we are able to reflect on, and bring direction to, what we do.

Now it is a further generalised fact of experience that there are both things we do which we do not desire and were no part of our objectives (e.g. we trip over, or break the light cord) as well as things we do desire or plan (to walk safely from A to B, turn on the light). The distinction here refers not to separated human doings, but seemingly to all human behaviour viewed under its separate aspects. Thus the behaviour involved in pulling the light cord, when viewed under the aspect of its being oriented to illuminating the room, can be recognised as directed. When this same behaviour or doing is viewed under its aspect of breaking the light cord – or, if succeeding to illuminate the room, alerting the prowler, or disturbing the animal, outside the window – the behaviour is not seen as directed. These latter outcomes typically will not have been objects of the mental states which directed the behaviour.

Now, however we may categorise the various components and conditions of human behaviour, it seems that the distinction being made here is rather significant. Consciousness is required for human behaviour viewed under the former aspect of being subjectively directed. Such behaviour is directed by beliefs grounded in the practical interests of life. In *Economics and Reality* (see Lawson 1997a: ch. 13) and elsewhere I have referred to the directing of behaviour under the heading of intentionality. And I refer to behaviour that is intentional, i.e. behaviour viewed under its aspect of being directed, as action. In other words actions are intentional human doings. The beliefs grounded in the practical interests of life which appear able to motivate actions and make a difference to what occurs (and so must be assessed as functioning causally – see Lawson 1997a: 175)[23] I have collected under the heading of reasons.

So, in short, in the framework I defend, human actions are simply intentional human doings, meaning doings in the performance of which reasons have functioned causally, where reasons are beliefs grounded in the practical interests of life.

I acknowledge that other contributors may not only argue things differently but also define or use the above-noted (or similar) categories in contrasting ways.[24] But it remains the case that some, but not all, aspects of our doings occur because we desire them, given our knowledge, and seek to bring them about. And it appears that a (transcendentally necessary) condition of possibility of this is the causal efficacy of beliefs, desires, psychological or mental dispositions and other capacities, however we decide to name the various aspects and conditions of human doings.[25]

It appears to be a further generalised feature of experience that many, indeed most, of our intentional doings or actions are carried out without our reflecting upon them in a direct or explicit manner at all. After all, human activity is a continuous flow whilst each act of reflection or discursive commentary takes time. In order to render this continuous flow of action intelligible it seems we must distinguish within consciousness not only a level at which a discursive reflection and/or premeditation can occur, but also a level at which action can be facilitated without it. I have referred (and continue to refer) to the former as the level of discursive consciousness and the latter as the level of sub-, practical or tacit consciousness.

By distinguishing these different levels I do not suggest that consciousness is other than (or produces experiences that are other than) unified. But the different things we do can be motivated in different ways. Some aspects of our activities rest directly on discursive reflection. Others do not. Things we do at the level of practical consciousness, i.e. tacitly (get up and walk around the room while thinking about something else, apply some social conventions, drive cars while structuring a talk we are about to give, drink coffee while reading or watching television, apply the grammar of a language while debating an issue, etc.) can usually be brought into discursive consciousness if need be, albeit sometimes with a bit of effort. But it is because practical consciousness can function without conscious deliberation having to occur that it is so important to human activity. Indeed, as I say, it is at the latter practical level of consciousness that most human doings seem to happen.

To recognise that many human doings are carried out without being premeditated or reflected upon does not mean that they are undirected. A human being may get up and walk around while thinking or talking on the telephone, or whatever, without being fully aware that the journey has been undertaken. But this walking around may be directed all the same: to stretch legs or release frustration or to move to a quieter spot; and in its course, the walk will be directed in its navigation of furniture, and so forth. In other words, actions, i.e. intentional doings, can and do occur at different levels of consciousness. Of course, to suggest that reasons, or intentionality in action, apply at different levels of consciousness is not to diminish the importance of distinguishing levels of consciousness, but to raise the question as to how intentionality works at the different levels.[26]

I have acknowledged that the things we do at the level of practical consciousness can usually be brought into discursive consciousness, if need be. But some motivations etc., appear not to be recoverable through reflection. The likely explanation here is that they have been repressed, or were acquired prior to the formation of linguistic capabilities, or that the individual possessing them has suffered a degree of brain damage, etc. They remain aspects of consciousness, though. And if the level of consciousness at which they exist is typically termed unconsciousness, this must be distinguished from a state of non-consciousness, like that of a wooden stool.[27]

Now it should be clear that the various features discussed here presuppose each other. Discursive reflection, for example, is not carried out instead of (i.e. alternately with, or as a substitute for) a reliance on practical consciousness, other capacities, dispositions, tendencies, habits and the like, but presupposes them. If I am reflecting on the subject at hand while engaged in discussion, these other capacities and habits are in play simultaneously, thus allowing me to speak grammatically, stay upright, walk around without bumping into things, etc., all in one go.

And we can note too that, with the aid of reflection, we can, and in numerous situations must, come to transform many of our background capacities and dispositions and habits. For example, although I habitually keep to the left side of the road when driving in the UK, on crossing to the continent of Europe I must, and do actively work to, overcome this habit. I consciously (sometimes literally) tell myself to 'keep to the right'. At this point, certainly, the rule takes a codified form. After about twenty minutes or so, however, I usually find that I have become disposed to driving automatically on the right side of the road. I keep to the right side of the road habitually so that when I eventually return to the UK, I have actively to reorient myself once more, to restructure certain of my driving capacities.[28] Discursive reflection, other forms of human capacities, habits and so forth require, and causally condition, each other. Although everything in the social world turns on human practice, no feature of social life warrants explanatory/analytical priority.

There is always more that can be said and/or determined.[29] But hopefully enough has been covered both to clarify (and explain) my use of terminology, as well as to indicate that transcendental argument enables access not just to social ontology but to aspects of human subjectivity as well. I acknowledge that I merely touch on questions of psychology. Mostly, as I say, I focus on (some of) those of most direct relevance for understanding human action in society. However, if the conception defended has received limited elaboration here, the discussion provided ought to be more than sufficient to convince that this conception hardly reduces to the 'representative agent' of modern mainstream economics.

Agency/structure interaction

Let me briefly consider something of how human agency and social structure come together, and in particular how the latter bears on the former. The location of their coming together is society's positions. But the process of how each bears on the other, and specifically of how structure bears on agency, warrants further elaboration.

I have already derived the transformational model of social activity. In focusing on social structure I noted how the latter is not typically created in human activity, but is both a condition of such activity and something that is reproduced and transformed through it. But the same holds for the human agent, especially her or his embodied personality. That is, the transformational model applies as much to the human individual as it does to society. Let me briefly elaborate.

I have argued that the human individual is highly structured, that each individual possesses numerous capacities, dispositions and tendencies, etc. Clearly, the specific capacities developed, or the manner in which they are, is dependent on the particular individual's (positions within a) specific social-cultural and natural context. Consider language once more. Most individuals develop their capacity for language. But the specific language(s) acquired will depend on the individual's social situation. Indeed, just as the historical-geographical context will often bear on which languages are acquired, the socio-economic conditions and status of the individual will often bear on the number of languages learnt and the level of competence achieved.

Furthermore, if a given individual moves for significant durations in different language communities, their language capacities are likely to be repeatedly significantly transformed. And the sorts of things that can be said of the development and moulding of language capabilities apply in the development of most other human capabilities as well. The human being arrives in the world with a generalised capability for social being. But which of the individual's potentials are developed, and the manner in which capacities and dispositions are shaped and, in some cases at least, continuously reshaped, depends on the individual's particular practices, which are always situated in, and conditioned by, a socio-cultural context. Society acts on, and shapes the individual, just as individuals collectively (if mostly unintentionally) shape the social structures that make up society. The two, the individual and society, though irreducible to each other, are interdependent features of a socio-transformational process of linked or co-development.

It may be useful if I distinguish here the synchronic and diachronic aspects of agency/structure interaction. If I visit a country with a culture and traditions very different to my own, then this set of social structures, mediated by my understanding of it, will mainly constrain and enable, at least at first. This is the synchronic aspect. If I decide to turn my visit into a permanent stay, the new structures, the traditions and culture and relations, etc., will likely very soon begin to affect my personal and social identity, habits and dispositions, and so forth. That is, they will effect a transformation in my embodied personality. This is the diachronic aspect. It is important to recognise that the transformational model captures both aspects of agency/structure interdependency. It is a error of comprehension to reduce it to one or the other.

Of course, to say, as in the previous illustration, that the structures of the relevant society will come to reshape the social identity, etc., of an individual moving into it, is not to imply that in this context, or in any other, social structures are somehow able to bear down on the individual in some external unmediated fashion. It is human beings that do things. And everything that happens in the social world does so through human activity. Certainly it is through human activities that social structures have a causal influence, whether synchronically or diachronically. If the individual in moving to a different socio-cultural context or system wants to function capably within it, he or she must become knowledgeable and skilled in its rules and conventions, etc. Thus, although the latter do not force themselves on the individual, to the extent the individual seeks to become locally competent, her or his capacities and dispositions will likely become significantly reshaped in conformity with the traditions of the new society nonetheless.

Forward-looking behaviour

There is one last issue I want to consider here, one that in many ways serves to bring together various aspects of the conception so far outlined. I have suggested that it is an important aspect of human beings that they are forward-looking, that human beings are not just passive reactors, but fundamentally initiators of action. However, this realisation has also to be balanced with the recognition that (*pace* many formulations of mainstream economists) human beings have somewhat limited cognitive and computational capacities. In addition, social reality is found to be fundamentally open. Social event regularities of the causal sequence sort (such as pursued by modern economic modellers) are neither universal nor ubiquitous. Indeed, they are rather rare in the social realm and those that are found (especially where they do not comprise forms of routinised [rule-governed] behaviour) are very often not only severely restricted but highly partial. There are thus ontological and practical limits to anticipating future outcomes. Yet despite this, I think it can be accepted as a further generalised feature of experience that human beings not only make plans but are in many ways often rather successful in their forward-looking undertakings. And this can be so even with regard to objectives that individuals set themselves knowing that their realisation may take a matter of days, months or even years. Let me consider what must be the case for this to be possible in the light of everything else that has been argued.

Now it appears to be a condition of possibility of such achievements that some (knowable) features of social life do possess a significant degree of endurability. And from the discussion so far it would seem that the more enduring features of social life are mostly the more abstract, and in some sense deeper, more sedimented, or fundamental, features of society.

It seems to follow then, given that successful forward-oriented behaviour is in evidence, that individuals must form their longer-term goals mostly in terms of those highly abstract features of society which are found to be the more enduring. However, these aspects, being highly abstract, do not facilitate a knowledge of concrete details. So it must be the case that individuals

(i) form broad, somewhat abstract, *plans* (Lachmann 1971; 1991),[30] *projects* or *schemes* on the basis of a knowledge of such structures,
(ii) with the intention of filling in details, or adapting these plans to specific conditions and contexts, as the individuals move through life.

Individuals likely form plans in terms of broad goals or purposes which (from the individual's [always situated] perspective) are currently viewed as possible and desirable, leaving the details open to determination at a later date.

I do not consider in the current chapter *how* individuals come to learn about the more enduring (or indeed any) aspects of society. This is a matter I address in Chapter 4 which focuses on processes of social explanation. Here I merely accept that it is a generalised fact of experience that human beings are often successful in societal practices oriented to the longer term, and suggest (transcendentally infer) that it is a condition of the possibility of this that there are enduring aspects to social life (which I established above) and that people are knowledgable to a degree of these aspects, and base their practices, and specifically plans, projects or goals, upon them.

At a very high level of abstraction individuals may, for example, decide to seek positions of power whatever the form of society in which they find themselves may take. Or, somewhat less abstractly, they may suppose (with reason) that the society in which they are situated will continue, and seek goals that mesh with its most fundamental or otherwise enduring aspects. Thus, for example, an individual situated in early twenty-first century western society may form plans to pursue a certain type of career, to become a political or religious activist, to get married and/or have a family, to travel, to go to university, to teach, to care for others, to help preserve the environment, and so forth.

It seems entirely possible that our only feasible option, if we are to succeed in future-oriented behaviour in an open world, is to formulate abstract plans such as these. The task is then, as I say, to fill in the concrete details as we go along, depending on the nature of the contexts of action; to adapt plans formed to other plans (of one's own and/or of others) or to changed understandings or situations, etc.

Personal identities and meaning

Such considerations can throw light not just on the nature of agency/structure interaction at any point in time, but also on specific ways in which certain structures can bear considerably on the human subject and her or his identity over time. For at various points in a lifetime, each individual must use her or his own reflexive powers to deliberate about which sorts of (potentially achievable) broad plans or projects most facilitate her or his own concerns within the relevant environment. Where conflicting plans cannot be rendered coherent with each other, a process of prioritising may have to be undertaken (a particularly situated individual may feel the need to decide whether family plans dominate career goals or vice-versa, etc.).

Such processes of prioritising, where carried through, will result in, or underpin, the emergent personal identities of individuals (Archer 2000). And plans adopted impart an orientation on the part of their holders, giving meaning to their actions, and allowing, in turn, the possibility of the recovery of meaning through interpretive social science.

Further, emotionality, the disposition to express feeling about our concerns, is likely to become intimately bound up with (can become manifest as commentaries on) our plans and their progress. Of course, all of this, and the empirical fact of continuity in social life, presupposes too, as a necessary condition of their possibility, a continuous sense of (if always developing) self at the level of the (embodied personality of the) individual.

Transcendental reasoning, then, can help us to understand something of how human beings, as well as social structures, develop in an open system, and of how agency and structure interact in different ways.

It is always possible to determine more. And clearly there are many questions or issues raised by this discussion that warrant further elaboration. This is not something I propose to undertake here, however. My concern is merely to indicate that, and how, transcendental argument can be (and has been) used to facilitate insights relating not only to social ontology but also to the human condition or nature, and equally to the manner of human agency and structure coming together.

Limitations of perspective

Before finally turning to consider some of the implications of all this for social theorising in economics, let me once more acknowledge that an ontological conception, just like any other, is inevitably fallible and partial and, in some aspects at least, doubtless transient. I believe this is well recognised by those contributing to the project of critical realism, with the consequence that such individuals are continually endeavouring to extend the project's insights and rectify inadequacies.[31] Indeed, the overview sketched above must be seen as unavoidably partial, even within this realist project (and in some respects even with respect to the outline and arguments of Lawson 1997a). Hopefully, though, it succeeds in giving a sufficient feel for the sorts of results maintained and the manner of their attainment.

What use is a conception of social ontology once achieved? In particular, what follows from a conception of the sort just elaborated? A concern with discussing the implications of the conception sustained constitutes the third and final theme of the current chapter, and is the matter to which I now turn.

Implications of the ontological enquiry

There are actually very many uses to which the conception in question might be put. But before I discuss some of them, let me first be clear about the limits of ontological argument. Philosophy in the form of social ontology is very much an underlabouring practice for social theorising such as economics. It is never a substitute. This applies as much to the results of the project systematised as critical realism as to those of any other. Any derivation of substantive theoretical results, reliance on specific methods and/or support for concrete policy proposals, requires that the ontological conception sustained be augmented by specific empirical claims, as I have often stressed (see e.g. Lawson 1996).

It is quite legitimate (and not uncommon) for those accepting the broad framework of critical realism to disagree over additional empirical claims, with different individual contributors thus arriving at contrasting substantive, methodological or political orientations for specific contexts (see C. Lawson *et al.* 1996). The point is that although critical realism makes a difference to the sorts of approaches or frameworks adopted and so paths taken, it is never by itself determining of substantive positions reached. There is not a position on substantive theory, policy or practice, even in a particular context, that warrants being distinguished as *the* critical realist position (see Lawson 1996: 417–19).

All the same, if philosophy in the form of ontology cannot replace substantive theorising, research practice or policy analysis, it can, as I say, underlabour for these activities. In this it can reveal methodological errors and dangers, as well as help clarify and give directionality to research practice. Let me briefly elaborate.

Errors and dangers

How can ontology reveal errors of, or dangers for, research practice? It does so by (amongst other things) disclosing various outcomes or configurations as but special cases of the range of outcomes or configurations possible, and thereby revealing the risks involved in universalising them *a priori*.

For example, the ontological conception sustained above reveals social reality to be characterised by depth (or structure), openness and internal relationality, amongst other things. These insights respectively help guard against treating

(i)   actualities, such as the course of events (or features lying at any one level of reality), as though they are the sole constituents of the world,
(ii) particular conjunctions of events as though necessarily recurrent, or
(iii) features of reality that are rather abstract as though they are concrete.[32]

As I say, in these ways, amongst others, ontological analysis as defended above can help us avoid mistaking the particular for the general. Of course, we cannot rule out the possibility that, even in the social realm, a feature shown to be but one of many possible realisations will in fact turn up every time, any more than it is possible to stipulate *a priori* that a fair coin tossed over and again (even say a million times) will not always come up heads. But a conception of ontology such as sustained here does reveal the risky nature of any venture of universalising cases that can be identified as very particular, and *a posteriori* it does help explain numerous examples of failure, or of puzzlement when things turn out not as expected. Perhaps some specific examples of misplaced universalising would be useful here.

In Chapter 1 above I concentrated on the misplaced universalising of formalistic-deductivist methods in modern mainstream economics. I adopted this emphasis just because it is an error that so shapes the modern economics discipline. But there are other examples of universalising of this sort also prominent in modern economics, many of which follow in turn from this methodological one, and all of which are easily recognised once the ontological conception set out above is accepted. Such cases are obviously too numerous for a complete coverage to be attempted. But let me briefly give a few illustrations.

Consider the case of the human individual first. It is a practice of some modern mainstream economists to assume that everyone is everywhere the same. More specifically, it is not uncommonly supposed that because some individuals have developed a heightened ability for individualistic or selfish thought and behaviour (i.e. to act as much as possible in accordance with the optimising agent of modern economics), we all have. Notions of 'representative agents' of this sort are even invoked.

Others, though, have universalised in a somewhat contrary fashion. That is, they have focused on specific differences between human beings and their experiences or practices, and universalised the feature of difference instead. In other words, some recent social theorists have tended to treat the uniqueness of personal identities and individual experiences as a feature of all aspects of human nature or being (see Chapter 9 below). According to this latter perspective there are only differences.

Ontological analysis as sustained above, however, reveals both forms of universalising to be suspect. By uncovering the ontological depth of all human beings, such analysis identifies how commonality remains feasible *in the midst of difference*. For example, although we possibly all develop a unique mix of language capabilities, and everywhere engage in, and experience, unique forms of speech acts, all such developments presuppose a common capacity for language. More generally, although we daily experience possibly unique social encounters, we share a common capacity to enter social being, whatever the form or manner in which it is realised.

The same sorts of opposing, but equally suspect universalising tendencies are sometimes found in analyses of socio-economic systems. A first questionable move, here, lies in supposing that because specific relations, rules, positions, institutions or mechanisms of production, are features of one socio-economic system (say of capitalism), these same examples of rules and relations (say specific market or class relations), etc., must be present in all socio-economic systems (including, say, of feudalism).

This latter is an error recently addressed in Hodgson's aptly titled *How Economics Forgot History: The Problem of Historical Specificity in Social Science* (2001b). Although Hodgson does consider more general issues of generality and particularity, his primary focus is indeed the particular error of treating historically relatively specific features of certain socio-economic systems as though they are common to all such systems.[33]

An opposing move, equally suspect in that it relies on questionable forms of universalising, is to suppose that because everyday, including working, practices vary across social-economic systems, societies or communities, there cannot also be commonality in these systems. Ontological reasoning, however, reveals all such social systems to be composed of social relations, rules, positions, institutions and the like (see below). It is, indeed, just in virtue of some such features that we can distinguish the objects of reference as (examples of) social-economic systems (or whatever), i.e. as different examples of the same kind of thing.[34]

A further common example of misplaced universalising is the often-found presumption that where an agent acts in a certain way on a given occasion he or she (or we all) will act in that way on all occasions. Thus the observation that some individuals endeavour to calculate advantages and disadvantages in some situations is universalised as the claim that they do so (or we all do so) in all situations. Perhaps this might be termed the theory of 'representative action'.

In any case, ontological analysis such as sustained above, reveals human beings to be structured and possessed of capacities that may or may not be exercised. As such, it can sustain the possibility that even if capacities of calculation are possessed they may remain unexercised in certain contexts (or, if exercised, countervailed against, perhaps even by the individual's own competing tendencies). Of course, mainstream economists tend to insist that behaviour is everywhere rational in the calculative sense, i.e. that the relevant capacities are always exercised (and realised), just in order to render their (deductivist) models tractable.

A related example is the presumption that whatever the outcome associated with an action in one situation, the same outcome will follow from this particular action in all cases. Thus it is supposed that because on a previous occasion a specific amount (or form) of government expenditure led to a given increase in, say, the numbers employed, the same outcome will arise from a similar policy action on a different occasion. Ontological analysis, though, reveals social reality to be open, with the likelihood that, in each different context of policy action, a quite different array of accompanying causal forces and conditions will be in play, affecting the outcome that emerges.

As a final example, let me note the inference often made that because some features of social reality appear to be successfully explained in a certain sort of way (e.g. in terms of certain units of analysis), so all features can be. Most typically, it is reasoned that because some social phenomena appear to be explicable largely, or solely, in terms of individuals and their preference (e.g. the item selected from a short menu by an individual sitting alone in a restaurant), therefore all social events can be explained in merely individualistic terms. In this way a methodological individualist stance is considered justified.

56

Ontological analysis such as sustained above, however, quickly reveals any such reductionist orientation to be significantly misguided. Specifically, because of the fact of emergence (i.e. because social structure, though dependent on human agency, has powers that are irreducible to it), methodological individualism is seen to be false. For forms of social structure are as explanatory of (condition or facilitate) the things individuals do, as the actions of individuals in total are explanatory of the reproductions and transformations of social structure.

More generally, because of the complicated ways in which social structure (in all its forms) and human agency depend upon, but remain irreducible to, each other, all methodological reductionist positions must be rejected. This applies not only to methodological individualism but also to methodological holism (social wholes are always the main unit of analysis), methodological institutionalism (institutions are always the main unit of analysis), methodological evolutionism (evolutionary processes are always the main unit of analysis), and much else (see Chapter 5 below).[35]

As I say, I here provide merely a selection of examples where particularities not only may be, but frequently are, erroneously universalised in modern economics. I do emphasise this. Although the types of misplaced universalisation just discussed are easily recognised as such, at least in the light of the ontological perspective set out, the examples provided are actually very prominent. The ontological project to which this current book contributes aims to help avoid such errors. More generally, it seeks to underlabour for all social theorising where questions or issues of commonality and difference, generality and particularity, continuity and change, connection and distinction, etc., are found. It aims to provide insights to analytical possibilities and limitations for social theorising at large. In this way it helps avoid very many problems of specificity (or generality) as currently abound.[36]

I have already noted (see Chapter 1) that I doubt very much that the sort of ontological conception defended here will appear especially contentious. Indeed, it is a conception often presupposed by economists' wider visions. The problem, very frequently, is a failure to acknowledge the ontological presuppositions of methods, explanatory approaches, or specific substantive theories which economists adopt, and so to recognise any mismatch with the sort of ontological conception here sustained. Indeed, it is a mismatching of the (typically unrecognised) ontological preconditions of specific methods wielded and the (implicit) ontological presuppositions of expressed broader economic visions, that explains a range of often noted tensions and inconsistencies throughout the history of economics, including those detected in the rather influential accounts of Marshall (Pratten 1994; 1998), Menger (C. Lawson 1995; 1996), and Schumpeter (Garça Moura 1997; 2002), amongst others.

Clarification

So ontology can help identify errors including inconsistencies and fallacies (including that of misplaced universalisation). Can it, though, contribute in more positive ways, including being given a clarifying role? I believe it can. Amongst other things it provides a categorical grammar against which more substantive social theoretical conceptions and distinctions can sometimes be better understood. However, the manner and extent to which a conception of ontology will prove helpful in this way depends on numerous issues, including the conception itself, the context, the questions being pursued, and so forth.

For illustrative purposes, consider recent discussion and debate about whether the increased degree, scale and speed of global interaction is best conceptualised as one of *globalisation* or merely increased *inter-nationalisation* (Held and McGrew 2000). These social-substantive categories are rarely well defined, but the contrast in question seems usually to rest on the idea of increased integration versus increased interaction.[37] Once we are possessed of the categories of internal and external relations, and recognise that those talking of globalisation mostly refer to the spread of the former and those emphasising internationalisation mainly the latter, it is easier to see the nature of the issues involved and how they can be resolved. Once, too, we recognise that it is quite possible for two aspects of reality to be simultaneously both internally and externally related, we begin to understand the reasons for the continuing miscomprehension involved in such debates as this (we can see, for example, that when some participants to the debate maintain that aspect X is an example of increased internationalisation and others attribute it to globalisation, both may be right).

Various further social theoretic conceptions, many of which currently are either conflated with others or poorly articulated, can be systematically developed from the basic categories identified above. For example, all social systems and collectivities can be recognised as ensembles of networked, internally related positions (in process) with associated rules and practices. This applies to the state, schools, hospitals, trade unions, the household, and so forth. Sub-distinctions can be made. A social system can be recognised as a structured process of interaction; an institution, as already noted, as a social system/structure that is relatively enduring and perceived as such; a collectivity as an internally related set of social positions along with their occupants, and so forth (see Lawson 1997a: 165–6).

The basic categories elaborated also provide the framework for a theory of *situated rationality* (Lawson 1997a: ch. 13; 1997b). Various real interests, as well as possibilities for action, depend upon the internally related positions in which individuals are situated. Of course, we all stand in a large number of (evolving and relationally defined) positions (as parents, children, immigrants, indigenous, old, young, teachers, etc.). Hence there exist possibilities of conflicting, as well as unrecognised, individual, in addition to collective or shared, (evolving) interests (and intentions).[38]

This conception, then, also provides the basis for a meaningful theory of distribution. In particular it allows an analysis of the determinants of resources to positions, as well as of positions to people.

More generally, a conception such as that sustained encourages and informs a reconsideration of the many categories of social theorising taken for granted in modern economics. The list includes not only the already noted categories of institutions, systems and rationality, but also others equally central to economics, such as money, markets, uncertainty, technology, order and numerous others.[39]

Also, by examining a contributor's ontological preconceptions it is often possible to throw further light on the nature and/or meanings of their substantive claims and contributions, especially where the latter are found to be otherwise open to a large number of seemingly ill grounded interpretations.[40]

And ontology may assist in pursuing a range of further issues that gain their interest from context. It can bear, for example, on questions relating to the nature of the discipline of economics itself. What, for example, is the legitimate scope or subject-matter of economics? Is it possible and/or meaningful to demarcate a separate science or even domain of economics? Ontology, given its focus on the nature of being, including of the 'objects' of study, holds out some promise for providing a handle on these sorts of issues. The question of whether the specific conception of critical realism (suitably supplemented with other insights) is of any help in this is explored explicitly in Chapter 6.

Furthermore, there are issues to pursue concerning the heterodox traditions in modern economics. If the mainstream tradition is marked by a neglect of explicit ontology and an adherence to methods which presuppose a largely untenable ontology, presumably the persistent heterodox opposition to the mainstream must reflect a quite different orientation to ontology? This and related questions are pursued in Part III of this book, in the context of examining aspects of post Keynesianism, (old) institutionalism and feminist economics respectively.

Directionality

Let me turn to consider some of the numerous ways a conception of ontology, and in particular the conception defended here, may impart directionality to social research. Most clearly, because the social world is found to be structured (it is irreducible to such actualities as events and practices), it follows that actualism is a mistake, that social research will need to concern itself not only with correlating, or otherwise describing, surface actualities, but also, and seemingly primarily, with identifying the latter's underlying causal conditions. Indeed social research has, as a proper and compelling object, the explaining of surface phenomena in terms of its underlying causes. If patterns in surface social phenomena have scientific value, it is in some part through their providing access to the structural conditions in virtue of which the former are possible.[41] Of course, structural conditions in turn have their own conditions, so that the process of seeking to explain phenomena at one level in terms of causes at a deeper one may be without limit.

Further, to the extent that social phenomena not only depend upon transformative human agency and so are processual but also are highly internally related, it is *prima facie* rather unlikely that they are manipulable in any useful or meaningful way by experimental researchers and others. Social research, in consequence, will typically need to be backward-looking, being concerned to render intelligible what has already occurred, rather than interventionist/experimentalist and so predictionist. Certainly it would be rather risky to insist only on (learning and teaching) methods which presuppose that parts of social reality can be treated as isolatable and stable chunks.

It follows that the current excessive concentration (of skills, university research methods, courses, etc.) on methods of deductivist (macro-, micro- and econometric) modelling is likely shortsighted; and indeed, that methods relevant to open systems in process will prove fruitful at least as often. Now I am aware in this regard that some researchers worry that in social explanatory endeavour there is no alternative to using methods which presuppose that the social world is, and will continue to be, everywhere closed. To meet this concern, I outline a general approach appropriate to open systems analysis in Chapter 4 below. This, though, does not (and could not) derive from the critical realist conception directly. It is merely a conception for which there is reason to expect more than a degree of social theoretical success, given the perspective on the nature of the subject-matter of the discipline uncovered.

Further, it is easy to see that an ontological conception such as critical realism can carry implications for matters of ethics, and so for projects of a practical or policy sort. For example, because all human beings are both shaped by the evolving relations (to others) in which they stand, as well as being differently (or uniquely) positioned, it follows that all actions, because they are potentially other-affecting, bear a moral aspect, and also that any policy programmes formulated without attention to differences, that presume homogeneity of human populations, are likely to be question-begging from the outset. Certainly, programmes of action that ignore their likely impact on the wider community are immediately seen as potentially deficient. Eventually, of course, such considerations point to questions of power, democracy and legitimacy. They raise questions of who should be taking decisions in a world of different identities where most of us are probably in some way (differentially) affected by actions taken by others. And indeed they invite a questioning of whether anything less than the whole of humanity (and possibly much more) can constitute a relevant unit of focus in the shaping of emancipatory projects and actions.[42]

The context of ontology

One final observation warrants emphasis. I have stressed over and again (both above and elsewhere) that an ontological conception such as I defend, though practically conditioned, historical and fallible, always requires supplementing with rather more context-specific empirical claims before it can bear on substantive or concrete issues, whether concerning theory, method, politics or policy. However, it should be equally clear that although critical realism stops short of licensing any specific empirical claims, it does not follow that those who contribute to and/or defend this realist conception do, *or are even able to*, avoid invoking fairly context-specific empirical claims continuously. Ontological theorising everywhere goes hand-in-hand with such empirical assessments.[43]

It is easy to see how this is the case with the current book. Although my aim with it, particularly in the current chapter, is to make a case for an ontological turn in economics, the case made is in large part empirical in nature. It rests on the assessment that the state of modern economics is none too healthy, that a central feature of modern economics is a tendency to universalise certain (mathematical-deductivist) methods *a priori*, and that explicit ontological reasoning has, until very recently at least, been overly neglected in modern economics, and so on. All such assessments are, in some part at least, empirical in nature.

Irrespective of their validity, I might have avoided making them; but only at the cost of leaving my discussion and advocacy of ontology at this time without motivation, point or context. Thus I indicated above how the ontological conception sustained gives reason to be very cautious about universalising certain insights, or practices *a priori*. But to demonstrate just how relevant are the insights sustained for modern economics it was useful to remind the reader (i.e. to advance empirical assessments) of how widespread are existing practices of universalising highly particular conceptions of individuals, socio-economic systems, human practices and explanatory orientations.

The general point I am working towards here is that we each contribute always from within a context, being situated in particular ways, with very definite socio-cultural-political interests. In contributing we act on our situated interests, value assessments and perspectives.

There is no escaping from any of this, nor from the implication that there is always an empirical grounding of our particular pursuits, orientations, justifications and so on. Like everything else, critical realism is a product of its place and time, as in particular are the motivations of those who contribute to it and the uses to which it is put.

The reason I emphasise all this is to add support to the claim already made that there are very many ways an ontological conception such as sustained here can be utilised. And as I have also already emphasised, although any results derived from supplementing the ontological insights of the project with highly context specific empirical assessments ought not to be identified as critical realist, this is not to say that important results cannot be achieved in this fashion. In the conditions of modern economics, specifically, there is rather a lot that can be done and an increasing amount that is being initiated, at least in some quarters. In fact, a good deal is beginning to spring up in social theorising more widely.[44] How it all works out in practice will doubtless depend not only on the specific ontology defended but also the resources, including socio-cultural situation and perspective of the investigator.[45]

This all must be borne in mind in interpreting much of the discussion that follows. In the remaining parts of the book, and most particularly in Part II, I develop further examples of how the social ontology outlined above can make a difference. My primary aim is to depart as little as possible from the level of ontology. I intend not to descend too far into substantive reasoning. But I can utilise ontological insights only through also utilising some quite context-specific empirical claims here and there. The issues I raise and the supplementary empirical claims adopted, are, I believe, both important and reasonably well grounded. But because there are many ways of going forward even with this particular ontological conception, the ensuing chapters, particularly those of Part II, may, if the reader prefers, be viewed primarily as illustrations of the *sorts* of ways in which the conception of social ontology I defend is able to make a difference. Alternatively, because I do accept all the empirical and other supplementation which are incorporated (and regard the additional claims as significant), the chapters in question can equally be understood as my own (ontologically informed and explicit) contributions to (realist) social theorising.

Before turning to such issues, though, I complete Part I with a short chapter (reproduced from *Economics and Philosophy*) which serves to summarise the realist orientation I am here defending .

3

WHAT HAS REALISM GOT TO DO WITH IT?[1]

For several years now I and a number of others (see e.g. the contributions in Fleetwood 1999) have been developing a project in economics that is often described as realist. In a recent article in *Economics and Philosophy*, Dan Hausman questions whether realism is actually a feature of this project worth emphasising (Hausman 1998). In fact, Hausman goes as far as to suggest that making reference to this aspect of the project may actually be misleading or otherwise unhelpful. His basic worry is summarised in the concluding section of his paper where he writes:

> To label one's program for economic methodology as 'realist' inevitably suggests that the competing programs are not realist or fail to be realist enough. In the case of economic methodology, this suggestion is misleading, because there is no anti-realist school of economic methodology, and there are few methodologists (as opposed to economists) who are instrumentalists either. What is distinctive about Lawson's and Mäki's programs is not realism – which they share with the rest of economic methodology – but something else. That something else can, of course, be a particular formulation of realism, such as Lawson's critical realism. But it would be less misleading if what was distinctive was characterized in terms of what distinguishes it from alternatives, rather than in terms of what it shares with them.
>
> (Hausman 1998: 208–9)

Now I infer from this passage that Hausman's concern lies not with the project in question being *interpreted* as realist (for Hausman acknowledges that it is); nor necessarily (or primarily) with its being *distinguished* or *identified* as a *specific formulation* of realism (after all Hausman accepts that the 'something else' that can make a programme 'distinctive' 'can, of course, be a particular formulation of realism, such as Lawson's critical realism'); but with it sometimes being *distinguished* or *identified* simply as *realist*. For it is this practice before any other that '*inevitably* suggests that

63

the competing programs are not realist or fail to be realist enough' (emphasis added). In truth, however, I believe that even this latter practice is more than justified in the circumstances. My primary object here then is briefly to indicate why. In the course of pursuing it I take the opportunity to identify what I believe to be some significant differences between Hausman's programme and my own.

Realist as a contrast to non-realist

Notice first that Hausman identifies two possible inferences to be drawn where a project is identified explicitly as 'realist': that competing programmes either 'are not realist', or 'fail to be realist enough'. Let me consider each in turn.

Now I am (of course) ready to acknowledge that we are indeed all realists of sorts, and that this is so with regard to many interpretations of the term. Indeed I have usually taken pains to emphasise as much. In *Economics and Reality*, for example, I acknowledge that 'any position might be designated a *realism* (in the philosophical sense of the term) that asserts the existence of some disputed kind of entity' (Lawson 1997a: 15). And I add that 'Clearly on this definition we are all realists of a kind, and there are very many conceivable realisms' (15). I believe too that most scientists are scientific realists regarding (are committed to the independent or prior existence of) at least some of their posited objects of investigation.

To be sure, I usually use the term realism in a specific way, primarily to indicate an ontological orientation. However, I am equally ready to acknowledge that we are all realists, even in the particular sense of holding (or at least presupposing) ontological positions. In my writings, I have continually acknowledged that all methods and criteria, etc., presuppose an implicit ontology, an unstated account of reality (see for example Lawson 1997a: 49). Even explicit attempts to suppress ontology result only in the generation of an implicit one, as I have frequently pointed out in discussing Hume's empiricism or forms of postmodernism (see for example Lawson 1997a: ch. 6).

So we are all realists of some sorts, and perhaps of many. Does it follow thereby that a social-theory project oriented to economics should not identify itself as realist? Not at all. Specific projects, programmes and activities in all walks of life are regularly identified according to certain fundamental aspects or features which also figure in other projects, etc., but less centrally so.

For example, Hausman distinguishes his own project as one in methodology. I, Mäki, and others whom Hausman identifies explicitly, are all (and are interpreted by Hausman as being) involved with methodology in our projects. And so indeed are all economists. All approaches, methods, techniques, goals, criteria, etc., adopted by economists (and everyone else) presuppose conceptions of scientific or proper method. Thus all economists, and indeed all scientists or researchers, are inherently methodological. Does this mean that Hausman should desist from designating his particular project as explicitly methodological, in case he is erroneously interpreted as implying thereby that all other projects are not methodological? Are cooks not to be distinguished as cooks because we all cook? Or singers as singers, runners as runners, economists as economists, teachers as teachers, students as students, and so on?

Realist: more rather than less

The reason most of us do not distinguish ourselves as cooks, singers, runners, carers or cleaners, etc., is not because we do not engage in these activities, but because we do not pursue any of them sufficiently ardently or seriously, on a regular or consistent enough basis. This, I think, is the relevant point. And it brings me to Hausman's second worry about explicitly labelling a project realist: that so doing 'inevitably suggests that the competing programs ... fail to be realist enough'. There is a sense in which this is exactly what I *am* suggesting.

In identifying my project as realist I am first and foremost wanting to indicate a *conscious* and *sustained* orientation towards examining, and formulating *explicit* positions concerning, the nature and structure of social reality, as well as investigating the nature and grounds of ontological (and other) presuppositions of prominent or otherwise significant or interesting contributions. And I am wanting to suggest that it is precisely this sort of *explicit concern* with questions of ontology that is (or has been) lacking in modern economics. This is an absence, indeed, that I believe contributes significantly to the discipline's current malaise. In this sense of the term, in my view, most of the projects contributing to the development of modern economics are not nearly realist enough.

But there is (at least) a second, albeit related, sense in which projects in economics are not realist enough, and in which I want to distinguish my own. I refer here to the tendency of most projects in economics implicitly to conflate the real with what is or could be apparent (or is 'observable'), and fail in any meaningful, systematic or sustained fashion to go beyond appearances to the (equally real – but not necessarily wholly apparent) underlying structures, powers, mechanisms and tendencies that generate or condition the surface phenomena of reality.

Competing programmes

Before giving more detail on all this, however, I must refer once more to Hausman's specific formulation of his worry: that others may infer that I am suggesting 'that the competing programs are not realist or fail to be realist enough'. The feature of it I want focus upon here is Hausman's reference to 'competing programs'. It seems from the longer passage in which this inference is embedded (noted at the outset of the current chapter), that Hausman has in mind here only programmes of methodologists, where methodologists are explicitly contrasted (by Hausman) to economists. I should immediately emphasise, then, that Hausman is in error if he is presuming (as he seems to be) that, in adopting such a realist orientation, the 'competing programs' I am addressing are only, or even primarily, those of others who explicitly distinguish themselves as methodologists. I do address these. But they are by no means my main intended audiences, opponents or 'competitors'.

Economics and Reality, for example, is explicitly aimed at an audience of general economists, both mainstream and non-mainstream. I view it as a contribution to economics as social theory. The identified 'opponents' are contributors, or potential contributors, to the contemporary mainstream programme (Lawson 1997a: xvii). I optimistically saw (and continue to see) myself as attempting to contribute to a fruitful transformation of the discipline. And I saw, and see, the taking of an *explicitly* realist orientation as a significant step to this end (1997a: 15).

That said, it happens that I do believe that most contributions explicitly designated programmes in economic methodology are (or have been) also not realist enough. I return to this below. For the time being, however, I want to concentrate on the mainstream programme in economics. For, as I say, I believe that this is indeed not realist enough in the senses indicated, and that the contrast between this project and my own is alone sufficient justification (although not the only reason) for distinguishing the latter explicitly as realist.

The problem with modern mainstream economics

Let me be more specific. First, for anyone with an interest in metaphysics, it does not take too much familiarity with our discipline to recognise a continuing failure of modern economists to examine the nature and consistency, etc., of the ontological (and other) presuppositions of their various pronouncements on, and decisions concerning, matters of substantive theory and method. It follows immediately, I think, that any project concerned systematically so to examine these ontological questions can fairly be identified explicitly as a realist one. My own project can certainly be *identified* as realist in this sense.

But I do go much further in a direction that can (also) be reasonably described as realist. Specifically, I (along with others) have been engaged with a range of investigations aimed at attempting to provide a sustainable social metaphysics, a theory of social reality, to inform the fashioning of methods of social, including economic, analysis. Fundamental to this project has been the questioning of the nature of social material, investigating its mode of being, structure and peculiarities, conditions, and so forth.

The orientation of this project thus contrasts quite significantly with the mainstream approach of (unthinkingly) adopting methods assumed to be successfully utilised in the natural sciences or somehow thought, on an *a priori* basis, to characterise proper science. Fundamental to the mainstream position is an insistence on working with formalistic models. Indeed, the primary objective of this mainstream tradition is the production of theories that facilitate mathematical tractability. In contrast, my goal, naive though it may sound, is to pursue true theories, or at least to achieve those that are explanatorily powerful.

I have found that the two sets of objectives, explanatorily powerful theories and mathematically tractable models, are usually incompatible, just because of the nature of the social world. For whereas the latter has been found to be quintessentially open and seemingly insusceptible to scientifically interesting local closures, the generalised use of formalistic economic methods presupposes that the social world is everywhere closed. By a closure, here I mean merely a system in which event regularities (deterministic or probabilistic) occur.

Two sets of observations (at least) can be explained by this incompatibility: that formalistic models are rarely if ever found be to be empirically successful, and that the entities posited in mainstream theorising (determined on the basis of being facilitative of mathematical tractability and other mainly pragmatic criteria) are usually seen to be unrealistic in many essential ways.

Mainstream economists seem to suppose there is no other way of proceeding. For those econometricians (most if not all of them) who care about 'fit' with reality (the latter assumed to be captured by data on measurable events and states of affairs) the hope appears to be that empirically successful models will be uncovered in due course. But although some equally hope the positing of theoretical entities recognised as severely unrealistic is also a temporary situation, many act as if it does not matter. Here there are indeed *elements* of anti-realism in the mainstream position. Some are quite *explicitly* anti-realist when commenting on the perceived status of the 'theoretical entities' that are used to ground their models (if not in their conceptions of the events and states of affairs thought to be measured by the 'data'). That is, they explicitly pronounce a philosophical theory (about economic theories or models) to the effect that either it is not meaningful to talk of true models, or true models are not possible (for examples see the discussion in Lawson 1997a, especially page 325).

Now the primary problem or error of the mainstream project here, as I see it, is not the anti-realist orientation of many of its participants towards formalistic economic models *per se* (a stance which would appear to carry some justification), but the decision to persevere with (and to insist that all economists concern themselves with almost nothing but) the modelling project despite its long-term and continuing lack of clear empirical successes. The central mistake is one of not recognising that the near-exclusive focus upon closed systems modelling (a procedure mainly suited to certain natural [experimental] contexts) is itself questionable, and in need of justification. This, I believe, is the key to the mainstream discipline's shortfalls, turning on the more general avoidance of an explicit concern with ontology, of omitting to investigate the nature of social reality with a view to determining the basis of potentially more fruitful alternatives. In brief, the primary failing of modern economists is ontological neglect. It is in this specific sense especially, in my view, that most economists are not being realist enough.

A realist alternative

Of course the sorts of responses by modellers just noted mainly serve the purpose of allowing the modelling project in economics to continue unabated. In some quarters numerous pragmatic or coherentist criteria of model selection (elegance, parsimony, complexity, consistency with the equilibrium framework) are even invoked as if to obviate any need for the empirical assessment of models.

Such responses are certainly questionable. My alternative strategy, as I say, has been to investigate in a sustained and explicit way the nature of social reality, and to tailor methods of social investigation accordingly. This has certainly led me to doubt whether methods of formalistic analysis have much relevance to the social domain. And in the process I have come to defend a conception of the social realm as emergent from, but irreducible to, human interaction. I have argued for a theory of social ontology that includes forms of social structure, including social relationships, rules, positions, processes and totalities, etc., that collectively constitute a relatively autonomous realm, being dependent upon and resulting from human interaction, but with properties that are irreducible to human interaction, though acting back upon it. In *Economics and Reality* I argue, in effect, that this social ontology covers both a 'vertical realism', entailing a commitment to underlying social structures, powers and entities, etc., and also a 'horizontal realism' covering the transfactual operation of causal mechanisms in open and (any conceivable) closed systems alike, i.e. whatever the outcomes. In this I find that causally efficacious (and often largely unobservable) social structures and mechanisms, etc., indeed exist independently of our investigations of them and, individually and collectively, constitute proper objects of social scientific study.

The situation in 'economic methodology'

To this point I have been referring mainly to the ontological neglect (in the sense of failing to sustain explicit ontological reasoning as well as ontological depth) and the consequences of this in the methodological practices of mainstream economists. In comparison to the largely *a priori* unthinkingly reductionist and scientistic programme perpetrated by mainstream economists, then, the project in social theory to which I have contributed can, I believe, with good reason be *identified* as realist.

Hausman, though, appears to be more concerned with any implied contrasts with other projects explicitly designated methodological. Now if it is the case that such methodological projects in economics are concerned to engage in a significant way in social metaphysics explicitly, these projects, in my view, warrant being identified explicitly as realist as well. Certainly, I take this to be appropriate where any such project is concerned *in this manner* to confront and ultimately help transform (and so inevitably be contrasted with) the largely *a priori* scientistic set of practices that is the contemporary mainstream. Moreover, if in the course of such critical endeavour a definite perspective on the nature of nature, science and society were derived and defended, any such project would equally warrant being identified as a *specific formulation* of realism.

As it happens, however, I do believe that those projects in modern economics explicitly designated methodological have mostly (with a few exceptions) also failed to give sufficient attention to questions of ontology or metaphysics. In the main it is questions of epistemic appraisal (i.e. epistemological questions concerning the rational basis for accepting or rejecting theories) that have occupied the economic methodology discussion (for discussions see Lawson 1997a: xiii–xvi; Fleetwood 1999: 127–35).

I shall not survey the contributions of these projects here. However, in order to address some further rather important issues raised by Hausman, and to take the discussion further in the hope of bringing clarity to our differences, I might add at this point that I harbour doubts that even Hausman's own programme (highly productive and insightful though it is) pays sufficient attention to questions of metaphysics. It is more oriented to issues of metaphysics than most, and seems to be becoming increasingly so. Yet it seems to me that it, too, ultimately fails (so far) both to challenge sufficiently the relevance (including ontological presuppositions) of the contemporary mainstream (or any other) programme, or to elaborate an ontology that takes us very far beyond the course of actual events and states of affairs. I believe these claims can be shown to be true of Hausman's output broadly conceived. But for present purposes, let me concentrate on the *Economics and Philosophy* paper in question where Hausman, by explicit intent, is actually wanting to address issues of concern to realists.

Hausman and economics

At various stages in his *Economics and Philosophy* paper, in the course of establishing some point or other (e.g. that 'the debate between realists and epistemological anti-realists is largely irrelevant to economics' (1998: 185), Hausman makes assertions to the effect that 'economics does not postulate unobservables in the way physics does' (1998: 185). Indeed, a central thesis is formulated as follows:

> the ontological, semantic, and epistemological issues separating realists from anti-realists and from some instrumentalists, are largely irrelevant to economics. The reason is simple: economic theories for the most part do not postulate new unobservable entities.
>
> (Hausman 1998: 196)

The question I want to pursue, of course, is which economic theories are we talking about? All possible? Those formulated in heterodox approaches? Economists who have contributed to, or who have been informed by, the project of critical realism in economics have, in their more substantive contributions, generated economic theories that posit a variety of novel entities which in large part at least are unobservable. These include particular social relations (gender, race, employer/employee, student/teacher, money), other structures of power, social processes, social positions, social rules, evolving totalities, specific institutions, etc. (see e.g. Lawson 1997a: ch. 18). This research, like that of others on industrial districts, regions, collective learning and so on, is constantly positing new categories, relations, processes and totalities, etc., many (albeit not all) of which are (or possess essential aspects that are) inevitably unobservable. Indeed, human society itself can only be known, and not seen, to exist. Hausman is thus quite wrong when he supposes that I 'would not … dispute the claim that economic theories rarely posit the existence of new unobservable entities' (1998: 202). (For my conception of the nature of economics specifically, see especially Lawson 1997a; and Chapter 6 below.)

Why should Hausman conclude, despite everything, that 'economic theories for the most part do not posit new unobservable entities'? It may be because, at least at the relevant stage of his discussion, he is implicitly and unquestioningly reducing economic theory to the output of the current mainstream project in economics (or even to a specific strand of it, to something like mainstream 'theoretical' microeconomics). This, of course, is Hausman's explicit strategy in his recent (1992) book *The Inexact and Separate Science of Economics*. And it is in this light that we can most easily interpret his almost exclusive focus in the *Economics and Philosophy* paper on the question of whether 'the preferences and expectations that explain and predict choices are unobservable' (1998: 196). For only to the contemporary mainstream do such matters assume such a central role.

Of course, even if we focus only on this limited domain we are entitled to ask why, or in what sense, it matters that unobservables are or are not *new* (apparently meaning unfamiliar or non-commonsensical). For at one point Hausman accepts that beliefs and preferences, etc., are indeed *unob*servable and even contested, but seems to suggest that any realist/ anti-realist debate this might facilitate in economics is somehow less significant than the debates of physics just because the noted unobservable items are known to us:

> The point I want to insist on is a different one. Anti-realists seek to draw a line between the relatively unproblematic claims of everyday life and the problematic theoretical posits of science. Physics postulates new unobservables, to whose existence commonsense realism does not commit us. Although economics refers to unobservables, it does not, in contrast to physics, postulate new ones. Its unobservables – beliefs, preferences and the like – are venerable. They have been part of a commonsense understanding of the world for millennia.
>
> (Hausman 1998: 197–8)

And he adds below:

> There is no issue concerning realism versus anti-realism in economics that is not simultaneously an issue concerning the everyday understanding of the world.
>
> (198)

Now I concur with the latter remark. But I draw from it more or less the opposite inference to Hausman. Certainly, I do not take it to entail (as Hausman mostly does) that we should refrain from questioning the reality and nature of certain aspects of the social realm, just because there exists a commonsense understanding of them (that the unobservables are not in this sense 'new ones'); I do not suppose that 'the everyday understanding of the world' is incorrigible. Rather, I believe we should be continually reassessing even the most familiar of our everyday categories. For example, I take money (a feature of everyday modern life with presumably a commonsense understanding) to be a system of social relations (explaining why this piece of metal/paper/plastic functions differently from others). Is this interpretation part of commonsense understanding? Is it to be discounted if (and just because) it is not?

What, too, of the everyday gender-differentiated or class-differentiated, etc., practices, rights, obligations, etc., in any given location and their

structural conditions? I even take Hausman's tables and chairs to be constituted in part by social relations. When I go camping, for example,
numerous items have the potential to serve as tables (flat-topped tree
stumps, smooth-sided lumps of rock) or serve as chairs (rocks, upturned
buckets, etc.). Which items become so constituted depends in part on us
and our relations to them. Ultimately, of course, this is no less true of the
artefacts that we call tables and chairs in the home.

In other words, I am suggesting that just as Hausman allows that
'Physics postulates new unobservables, to whose existence commonsense does not commit us', so too can (and often does) social science,
including economics. Now, this perspective cannot be ruled out just
because it allows that we can and often ought to transcend/transform
commonsense. And in that it interprets or recognises daily life as internally related to underlying structures (including wider totalities), I think
the perspective sustained does warrant being interpreted as rather more
realist than Hausman's rather commonsensical and quasi-actualistic
(reducing reality to the actual course of events) account.

Still these sorts of considerations are not my only or even my primary
concern here. I return to my main point, that by mostly focusing on items
such as preferences and expectations, Hausman appears implicitly to be
interpreting economics as little more than the current, and hardly illuminating, mainstream set of contributions. It is true that Hausman includes
in his paper a sub-section with the more promising heading: 'Other
unobservables in economics'. But in essence only two sets of items –
'socially necessary labour time' on the one hand, and 'human capital'
and 'attributes' on the other – are identified as real possibilities. And
each is quickly dismissed merely on the supposed grounds of being
either not 'economically significant' (200) or 'relatively unimportant in
economics' (202). But we are once more entitled to ask what is this
economics in which these (and other unobservables) are unimportant? It
can only be the contemporary mainstream. This is precisely the project I
have criticised for its ontological neglect, and I worry that Hausman may
be unwittingly colluding in this by taking the output of that project as
sacrosanct.

Now it may seem that against this latter criticism at least, Hausman
can reply that he is justified in considering only this mainstream project
just because the latter accounts for most of the current output of the
economics academy. But this is not good enough for his argument.
Hausman is explicitly questioning the reasons for designating the project
with which I and others are involved, as realist. His chosen strategy turns
on showing that debates and discussions, etc., to which I am party in
economics do not involve the postulation of new unobservable entities,
and so forth. But for this to work his analysis must cover all debates, etc.,
to which I am a party, mainstream or otherwise. And for this, the focus

must be a far wider and richer conception than that which mainly turns on preferences and expectations.

Certainly Hausman could not simultaneously maintain both that the realist aspect of the project to which I have contributed is not distinctive in the context of modern economics, and also that because it is so distinctive it should not be considered a part of modern economics.

Hausman and critical realism

It must be admitted that Hausman does appear to go further in addressing my own project in the latter part of a later section of his paper, headed 'Transcendental realism'. Here he recognises the questioning of whether or not unobservables exist in the social realm cannot reasonably be restricted on an *a priori* basis, even to discussions of entities and properties; Hausman finally allows the possibility that I may be positing underlying structures and mechanisms, etc., as amongst the proper objects of economic study. Ultimately, though, this section mainly comprises various somewhat erroneous, if often tangential, remarks or assertions, mostly still reflecting Hausman's apparently unquestioning support for the mainstream tradition.

For example it is suggested that I offer 'economists a false dichotomy. Either they can accept a view of science as exclusively the search for exceptionless regularities among observable events … or they can accept critical realism' (Hausman 1998: 204). Now what is false about this dichotomy (if a dichotomy it is)? After all, critical realism argues that the world is open and structured in complex ways. It is because it is so that event regularities whether strict or partial (i.e. 'demi-regularities') can indeed be brought about under certain conditions. Critical realism thus entertains *a priori* the possibility of event regularities of varying degrees of strictness; it all depends. Mainstream (deductivist) economic modelling, in contrast, requires that strict event regularities (including those covered by well defined probabilistic laws) are ubiquitous. So the choice, the dichotomy, is indeed between science being or not being 'exclusively the search for exceptionless regularities among observable events', between the reductionist claims of deductivism and non-reductionist claims of critical realism.

Hausman supposes that the thesis in question, that economists should abandon deductivism (as a universalising claim), somehow follows from a 'controversial metaphysics' which, first, precisely maps distinctions in metaphysical categories onto those between observable and unobservables; and second, supposes that experiences and aspects of mechanisms cannot themselves be events. I am not sure why Hausman supposes that either set of claims is or would be defended. I personally have never entertained either and would not wish to (although I do not deny, of course, that *a posteriori* social structures, powers, mechanisms, processes and tendencies, etc., are found to be in large part unobservable).

Hausman further asks: 'What is gained by assimilating questions concerning the status of, for example, social norms [presumably amongst other social structures] to questions concerning the existence of electrons?' (1998: 205). But as I have already indicated, there is no assimilating going on; these simply are the same sorts of questions. Both reflect the postulating of the existence of some disputed kind(s) of entity; and both sets of postulations require investigating. Hausman's purpose in all this seems to be a misguided attempt to reduce all aspects of all structures and mechanisms to the level of 'everyday commonsense understanding' as if thereby all aspects can somehow be treated as free of realist/anti-realist controversy.

Hausman also includes a brief discussion of firms and the supposed 'law of diminishing returns' intended to demonstrate that 'Lawson's emphasis on realism distracts attention from the real issues' (1998: 205). But in this Hausman appears to suppose that my critique of economics if applied to discussions of the firm and 'returns to inputs' would amount to little more than a suggestion that more variables or factors should be included in the analysis ('the law of diminishing returns … captures only one factor that generates the complicated phenomena observed. One does not have to be a critical realist to recognize this crucial point' [Hausman 1998, 205]). The fact that I am arguing that the social world, including firms, is in part constituted by intrinsically dynamic (and mostly unobservable) highly internally related structures of powers or capacities, etc., irreducible to any actual realisation, appears to be less than fully appreciated.

Hausman also makes reference to other 'fundamental 'principles' of economics' (1998: 211) that I do not have space here to discuss. But my general observation is that in all such examples, like that of the supposed law of diminishing returns just noted, the constituents of economics are being too uncritically presumed. Indeed, from my own perspective a most striking feature of the contribution of Hausman (and of various other 'methodologists') is a failure to recognise the limited relevance to the social realm of 'principles' of the sort identified. And this failure can be explained, it seems to me, only by a continuing refusal to question the relevance of the entire mainstream (deductivist) tradition; to ignore, in particular, its continuing practice of ontological neglect.

Concluding remarks

Hausman's recent (1998) *Economics and Philosophy* article contains a number of claims to the effect that certain questions or issues are (or are not) relevant to economics. It seems that behind each such claim is a presumption that, in order to qualify as relevant or 'pressing', a question or issue must currently be a focus of attention or a topic of debate amongst (mainstream) economists. This line of reasoning appears itself to be underpinned by a more general presumption that economics reduces to what most economists (including economic methodologists) currently do.

My own rather different starting point has been the (widely recognised) phenomenon that modern economics mostly fails to illuminate the world in which we live and, indeed, is in a state of disarray, coupled with a conviction that we ought to do something about it, and specifically to seek to replace (or at least supplement) dominant strategies with others that are rather more capable of being explanatorily successful and useful. Addressing such matters seems to me to be as relevant or pressing as any issue facing modern economics.

Central to my project, then, has been the need to identify the cause of the discipline's failings. And I have certainly found that the problems turn not just on matters of current concern to modern economists, including methodologists, but at least as much on matters for which far too little concern is shown. Specifically, I have argued that the problems of the modern discipline relate fundamentally to ontological neglect. In consequence, my own endeavour to help improve things has involved explicit and sustained ontological elaboration, focusing on implications for explanatory conduct in the social realm. Others have contributed in similar fashion.

The result is a project that has been not only more explicitly and systematically oriented to ontological investigation in economics than most other projects, being concerned indeed to elaborate a social metaphysics for social science, but also found to sustain a conception of social life that is far richer, containing significantly more 'depth', than most competing conceptions in economics.

The conception defended is likely to be contentious, of course. And, whatever the worth of this project and its results, it is the case that its contribution will always be practically conditioned, fallible, partial and likely transient. But whatever else might or might not be claimed of the project I have been discussing, I think it clearly is the case that if we question what is distinctive about it in the context of modern economics, a realist orientation (in the senses indicated throughout) has got more than a little to do with it.

Part II

POSSIBILITIES FOR ECONOMICS

There are various ways in which the sort of ontological conception outlined in Part I can impact on social theorising. It is indicative, for example, of the range of conditions for which the social researcher might with reason be prepared. One question revealed to be of immediate interest and significance is how it is possible for explanatory endeavour to proceed in the face of a social system that is found to be fundamentally open. How in particular might an explanatory project get under way without the possibility of experimental intervention to fall back on? Is it in fact necessary to oversimplify in the sense of knowingly to fictionalise in order to get anywhere? Many economists appear to believe so. Perhaps most do. My concern in Chapter 4 is with establishing that any such belief is ill founded. I demonstrate that despite the fundamental openness of the social domain, successful social-explanatory endeavour which does not knowingly fictionalise is entirely feasible.

Economists need not always fashion their methods from the 'ground up'. Amongst other things they are at liberty to borrow from other disciplines. Indeed, economists have always done so. As I write these lines more and more economists appear to be interested in borrowing from evolutionary biology, and in applying the Darwinian 'natural selection' model in particular. In Chapter 5 I look at the implications of the understanding of social reality achieved in Part I for the way, if at all, the natural selection model might carry over to the social realm. I argue that ontological considerations are fundamental to processes of abducting from other realms.

To the extent that ontology is used to identify the nature of specific spheres of reality, its results also provide a non-arbitrary basis for distinguishing and identifying the different sciences. That is, ontological results can provide a basis for delineating the various sciences according to the different types of material and principles that are studied. It is in such terms, indeed, that sciences like physics, chemistry and biology have always been distinguished. It is only modern mainstream economists who have attempted to define a discipline according to its (supposed) methods. Once we abandon this orientation in favour of a realist one based on the properties of materials to be studied, it is possible to raise anew questions bearing on the nature and scope of the discipline. Specifically, how might we distinguish economics from other branches of social theorising? Further, is there a sense in which economics is or could be a science? If so, is it, or could it be, legitimately distinguished as a separate science, i.e. one with its own material of study? These are the sorts of issues addressed in Chapter 6, an essay reprinted from Economie Appliquée.

4

EXPLANATORY METHOD FOR SOCIAL SCIENCE

How does an ontological conception such as I defend in this book bear upon the project of social explanation? One thing it does not do is determine how we *must* proceed, certainly not in any very specific way.[1] It does, though, serve numerous purposes. One such, upon which I focus in the current chapter, is to indicate something of the sorts of conditions or scenarios for which it is prudent to prepare ourselves. In this it imparts directionality to social scientific endeavour.

Conditions of social explanatory endeavour

According to the conception I defend, social reality is open in a significant way. Patterns in events do occur. But where the phenomena being related are highly concrete (such as movements in actual prices, quantities of materials or outputs, and most of the other typical concerns of modern economic modellers), such patterns as are found tend to take the form of *demi-regularities* or *demi-regs*, that is, of regularities that are not only highly restricted but also somewhat partial and unstable (Lawson 1997a: 204–21). Moreover, patterns relating events standing in causal sequence (i.e. patterns where some of the associated events causally condition the others) seem to be rare indeed in the social realm. At least this is so once we look beyond situations involving rule-governed, reasonably routinised forms of behaviour (cars stopping at red traffic lights, and the like).

However, social reality is found to be not only open in the manner described but also structured. That is, it comprises not only actual events and states of affairs, some of which we may directly experience, but also deeper structures, powers, mechanisms and tendencies, etc., which produce, facilitate or otherwise condition these events and states of affairs (see Chapter 2). This assessment immediately guides us in the direction of causal explanatory research or *causal explanation*. For whether or not given phenomena are correlated with others at any one level of social reality, they can be explained in terms of (meaning shown to have been produced or facilitated by) their underlying causal structures and conditions.[2]

Causal explanation and retroduction

So the ontological conception defended in Chapter 2 directs us towards considering how, in economics, we might conduct causal explanatory projects. This emphasis, in turn, points to a need to develop modes of inference over and above (the usual forms of) deductive and inductive logic. A reliance on these latter forms of reasoning, as usually interpreted, restricts the researcher to considering only the level of reality at which the phenomenon to be explained is found. However, for causal explanation it is usually necessary to go deeper. Deduction, of course, moves from the general statement to the particular. For example, if we accept that 'all metals expand when heated' we can deduce that 'this metal before us will expand when heated'. Induction takes us from the particular statement to the general. If our research practices reveal that 'each examined (bit of) metal expands when heated' we might be tempted to speculate inductively that 'all metals expand when heated'. In each case we move from a statement about the behaviour of metals to a second statement at the level of the behaviour of metals.

To pursue causal explanation as interpreted here, we require a mode of inference that takes us behind the surface phenomenon to its causes, or more generally from phenomena lying at one level to causes often lying at a different deeper one. This is *retroduction*. It takes us from a recognition that 'this metal before us expands when heated' to a conception of the metal's intrinsic structure (or whatever) in virtue of which the metal has the power to expand when heated.

Little can be said outside a specific explanatory context about how in practice the retroductive process might proceed, other than it will often follow a logic of analogy and/or metaphor, and rest usually upon ingenuity as well as luck (see *Economics and Reality*, especially chapter 15). For example, following the discovery, in the late 1980s, that cows in the UK showed symptoms of the illness we now call 'mad cow disease', it was retroduced, by way of analogy with other illnesses, that a virus was causing the problem. This retroduced hypothesis, however, proved not to be correct. Only with a lot of skill and luck was the prion located as the most likely (explanatorily powerful) causal hypothesis (see for example Lawson 1997a: 293–4).

It is clearly significant, here, that causal explanation under the guidance of retroductive inference does not necessitate that only atomistic explanatory accounts be contemplated. Retroductive inference *per se* places no restriction on the sort of explanatory conception that may be uncovered. This is important here because the ontological conception I defend suggests that social reality, as well as being open and structured, is also highly internally related, intrinsically dynamic, and so forth. It may be that the conception which best explains some identified phenomenon of interest is a holistic entity, or an atomistic one, an evolutionary process, or of a momentary impulse. Each and all types of phenomena can be accommodated through retroductive reasoning. Thus in focusing on causal explanation and retroduction, we are staying well within the framework of the ontological conception I defend.

The central problem of social explanation

If the openness of social reality is a spur to pursuing causal explanation, is it not simultaneously a fundamental obstacle to success in doing so? Although the frequent productions of experimental event regularities in certain natural scientific contexts can themselves be adduced as evidence that these natural realms too are open (it is only if a domain of reality is open that an experimental closure [of part of it] can be humanly engineered), there is no doubting that the well controlled experiment aids causal analysis precisely because it allows a causal mechanism to be insulated from other factors and thereby empirically identified. A central challenge to much social explanatory endeavour, then, and in my view the most fundamental one, is to determine how explanatory work might proceed in an open system context that lacks the possibility of experimental intervention.[3] At least this is a fundamental challenge where social processes do not reduce to the rule-governed routinised sort.

There are three interlinked aspects or parts to the problem that arise here, three relative disadvantages facing non-experimental research. In the experimental context, causal explanatory endeavour is usefully viewed under the aspects of

(i)   identifying an event regularity
(ii) forming causal hypotheses that can account for the regularity
(iii) discriminating between competing hypotheses consistent with the regularity.

It is in relation to these three activities that the problem of social (or, more generally, non-experimentally aided) explanation can be viewed.

To elaborate, there is first of all the difficulty of determining how an explanatory project is to be initiated if, or where, event regularities of the sort engineered in controlled experimental conditions are not in evidence. How do we know where to start?

Second, if somehow it proves possible to initiate an explanatory project in a meaningful fashion, there arises the question of how to direct any causal explanatory research. The analysis of Chapter 1 suggests that experimentally produced event regularities correspond to situations where a single (set of) intrinsically stable mechanism(s) is effectively insulated from countervailing mechanisms. Causal hypotheses are, in this very particular case, directed at the underlying mechanism experimentally insulated. In an open system such as human society, the relative paucity of regularities of the causal sequence sort reflects the fact that events or outcomes are mostly each determined by a multiplicity of causes, with the possibility that at least some of the latter will be highly transient as well as unstable. From the perspective of this understanding, a *prima facie* problem of causal research in the social realm, is with determining how it is possible to pick out one particular cause from the conceivably very many acting on any phenomenon in which we might be interested.

Third, to the extent that an understanding of a single (set of) causal mechanism(s) can be pursued at all, there arises the likely task of discriminating between competing accounts of it, where such arise. In the experimental laboratory background factors can be varied in a controlled and systematic manner. What options are available in the non-experimental situation? Clearly because we are concerned with causal explanation rather than with correlation analysis *per se*, the criterion for selecting amongst any competing hypotheses will not be predictive accuracy but explanatory power. We can accept the hypothesis which makes sense of the widest range of phenomena within its scope. But in the absence of event regularities, what sort of empirical phenomena might we now expect to call upon in assessing the relative explanatory power of competing hypotheses where held?

It is this three-part problem of openness (of knowing how even to begin the explanatory process in the absence of event regularities of the sort produced in controlled experiments, of determining how to direct causal reasoning, and of being able to select amongst such competing alternative hypotheses as may be formulated) that remains to be addressed, and on which I propose to focus in much of the remainder of this chapter.

The usual recourse of mainstream economists faced with the noted situation, is to maintain, in effect, that universal and strict (or well behaved probabilistic) event regularities of the sort engineered in experimental laboratories are ubiquitous in the social realm, after all, if as yet remaining undiscovered. Mostly this course of action is driven not by any reflection on the ontological conditions of social reality, but by the (largely unexamined) triplet of a desire to be scientific in the sense of natural science, an unquestioning confidence that the latter is possible, along with an (erroneous) belief that science necessitates a reliance on mathematical methods. Certainly, the overriding goal, typically, is a tractable mathematical model. And if each modelling endeavour presupposes a closure of a certain sort, the insistence on formalistic methodology for all occasions requires precisely that social closures of the relevant sort are ubiquitous. The openness of social reality is assumed away.

As I say, this mainstream response is mostly driven by an unthinking *a priori* presumption that formalistic modelling must have relevance, and it is only a question of time before we get it right. There are others, though, who ultimately take the same deductivist path whilst adopting a different attitude (or 'justification'). Specifically, there are those who, though enamoured of neither the deductivist approach to explanation *per se*, nor by its desire-to-be-mathematical motivation, adopt the mainstream deductivist approach anyway. This group appears resigned to the idea that, because social reality is rather complex, there is little alternative but to proceed *merely as if* universal and strict (or well behaved probabilistic) closures of the causal sequence sort are ubiquitous in the social realm after all, even though they see good reason to reject any presumption that they are. Fundamental, here, is a common, if erroneous, apprehension that because, or where, social reality is complicated we must knowingly fictionalise so as to simplify enough to say anything. This is where isolationist procedures are often brought in (if occasionally misdescribed as methods of abstraction). For those accepting this outlook (which is easily shown to be misguided – see Lawson 1997a: ch. 9),[4] it is mostly an act of faith that deductivism through fictionalising can help (in so far ill defined ways). This act of faith follows on from a supposition that there is no alternative but to persevere with deductivism in the face of repeated failure so far. My aim here is to show that the latter supposition is as unfounded as the former resort to unreasoned hope is unnecessary.

I might note, parenthetically, that members of both these groups, in seeking formulations resting on correlations of the causal sequence sort, display a (seemingly increasing) tendency to refer to the results of stretching such rough and ready patterns as are found as stylised facts. The project undertaken, then, is a sort of stylised-facts-based deductivism. Now, Kaldor and others who earlier advanced the terminology of stylised facts in economics used it to indicate the rough and ready nature of such patterns as are found (Kaldor 1985: 9). Of course this is precisely the opposite of what stylised means in common parlance. And this has led some contributors to employ the category to cover formulations that are recognisably extreme idealisations, even plain fictions, whilst simultaneously apparently seeking to claim for their constructions the more realistic pedigree of the likes of Kaldor. At best the terminology serves to confuse. I thus continue the practice of referring to partial patterns in actual events and state of affairs not as stylised facts but as demi-regularities or demiregs. This label better conveys the insight that the patterns implied are usually indeed partial and unstable at best, not something to be stretched into the sorts of strict conjunctions that are the provenance of closed systems.

So my task, to state it now more fully, is to demonstrate that, and how, in social research that is concerned with wider issues than routinised behaviour, it is possible both to initiate and also to direct causal-explanatory endeavour, as well as to discriminate amongst any contending causal hypotheses, in an open-system context in which well controlled experimentation appears infeasible, making use only of such event patterns, and in particular demi-regularities, as are found to be available, i.e. without pretending the situation is entirely different to the way we continually find it.

It will be appreciated that, so conceived, my overall goal remains highly limited. This, as I noted at the outset, is necessarily the case. The most I can hope to achieve is a demonstration that successful explanatory work in such conditions is indeed possible. I can at most seek to identify a method or approach that carries the potential (and regularly proves) to be fruitful in such situations. The actual relevance of any specific method or approach elaborated will always depend on context. However, even this minimal objective seems to be regarded as unattainable by many, as I have just noted. Instead there is a widespread conviction that social explanatory research ultimately has to rely on methods whose usage require that we treat the relevant domain of reality as closed, even if, and where, we believe that it is not. So my aim here, though limited, appears not to be insignificant.

I might emphasise too that the limited approach I defend here cannot be formulated in any very great detail. My goal with this chapter is certainly to be as definite as possible in terms of how we might undertake the task of explaining social phenomena generated in an open system. Indeed, I want to set out and defend a way of proceeding that can be interpreted as a definite explanatory approach. But the aim is not, and in my assessment could not be, to provide a list of highly specific or concrete methodological rules that need only be registered and followed. Indeed, if the reader understands methodology as a narrow concern with specifying specific watertight rules for conducting research, then the project to which I have been contributing is not one in methodology (in this sense) at all.[5] It is, though, methodological in the broader sense of underlabouring for social science.

A point of departure

So where might we start? It is a matter of some significance here that most of us are quite successful every day in negotiating the open, dynamic and complex social world in which we find ourselves. And such successes do not reduce just to our following (rule-governed) routinised practices. Certainly the latter are essential for everyday interactions with others. But these interactions typically figure as but a component of broader (short-term and longer-term) projects. We may aim to get from A to B successfully; draw money from the bank, perhaps of an amount sufficient to cover activities for a fixed period of time (say a week); organise a meal for friends, neighbours or in-laws; deal with minor accidents or emergencies; choose a school (or holiday play scheme) for a child; organise a sabbatical period abroad; join a public demonstration (critical, say, of the way certain groups are oppressed by others or of how the world's resources are being used); prepare for, or attend, a wedding, an anniversary event, or a funeral; raise some finance for a project; show a continuous sensitivity to the projects and expectations of others, whether strangers, family or friends; and so on. Each such activity involves our (simultaneous) participation in a large number of complex social processes. And it is difficult to believe that our regular successes in these activities do not require that we are highly knowledgable of the social structures and processes, including systems, in which we so regularly partake. Clearly, we all make mistakes. But even the recognition of these mistakes reflects the degree of success most of us achieve in our everyday projects and actions. The question, then, is not if, but how, a knowledge of the range of causal structures of an open social reality is obtained. And one promising place to start in investigating this matter is with the sorts of successful explanatory strategies we all, on a day-to-day basis, undertake.

My specific orienting claim, here, is that we all very often advance our knowledge of aspects of the world in which we live, including of the social system, by way of first questioning why something is not quite as we expected it to be. And this observation, which I think is rather clearly a generalised fact of experience, proves to carry quite fundamental import for social scientific research.

Certainly, examples of the sort of questioning described come easily to mind. Why are my keys not in my pocket as usual? Why does my bicycle not work as well today as it did yesterday? Why did the students do so much worse/better in the exams this year compared with other years? Why, in so many parts of the world, are enrolments in economics currently declining when those in seemingly comparable subjects are increasing? Why has productivity growth in the UK over the last hundred years or so often fallen below that of other industrialised countries? Why have house prices in the UK recently been rising faster in the south-east than in the north? Why, in the 1990's, was the NATO reaction to the situation in Kosovo different to its earlier reaction to the events in Bosnia? Why do I feel so ill/tired today compared with normal? Why was the milk not delivered this morning? Why, in the UK, did less people than usual go away for the start of the New Year coinciding with the new millennium?

I think it will be recognised that surprised expectations or quizzical reflections of this sort are everyday occurrences. But, significantly, so too are their resolutions. We normally can and do figure out why our keys are not as usual in our pockets (perhaps there is a new hole); why our bicycle is not running smoothly (a stick caught in the mudguard); why the recent group of students fared relatively poorly/well in their exams (an exam setter who misunderstood the coverage of the course); etc.

Other questions may require more effort, but still seem open to explanation (I think, for example, the central thesis of this book, appropriately interpreted, effectively identifies significant reasons for the continuing decline in enrolments to study economics).

If it is accepted that the posing and answering of questions of the sort identified is rather widespread, it may yet seem that such practices are of only marginal significance at best to the task of determining explanatory procedures for social-scientific research. My contention, as I say, is that, to the contrary, they are fundamental to this issue. Indeed, through understanding certain central features of what is going on in these examples, it is possible to determine a somewhat (as it turns out) general basis for developing research methods appropriate to causal explanation in open and complexly structured systems lacking the experimental option.

So what do examples such as those briefly listed reveal? What accounts for successes, when achieved, in answering the sorts of questions formulated? We can address such matters, first by examining the structure or nature of the sorts of questions and answers noted in order to understand precisely what is going on, and second by determining their (ontological) preconditions, i.e. the conditions which must hold given that such successful practices occur. From an understanding of the latter conditions we can infer wider consequences for social explanatory work.

Contrasts and interest

I consider first, then, the structure or nature of questions of the sort posed and responses obtained. Here it is significant to note that in each case the question posed is not of the form 'why x?', but of the form 'why x rather than y?'. In each case there is a contrast made, and surprise, concern or interest revealed that the outcome is x rather than y as expected.

Correspondingly, in each case the answer is a causal factor that does not account for x *per se* but explains the contrast 'x rather than y'. It explains the observer's surprise or topic of concern. Here in a nutshell, I am going to suggest, we have one significant solution to the three-part problem of openness. This contrastive orientation allows the initiation of an explanatory endeavour and facilitates the process of identifying a particular mechanism. And competing hypotheses can be selected amongst simply by bringing a range of contrastive phenomena to bear.

Once this solution to our three-part problem of openness is accepted, we need only determine the conditions of possibility of proceeding in this way to appreciate the relevance of this approach. Before turning to this matter, however, the brief account of the structure of the relevant form of question and explanation just set out will likely benefit from some elaboration by way of an illustration. For I doubt that, from the discussion so far provided, it will be at all obvious that the contrastive structure singled out is either essential to such successes as are regularly achieved in social life, or adequate to facilitate explanatory scientific research in the context of open systems where opportunities for experimental closures are lacking. Moreover, there is rather more to the explanatory practices in question than is immediately apparent.

An illustrative example

To demonstrate the relevance of the contrastive form of the question posed, as well as to uncover the relevant conditions of such explanatory successes as are achieved, it is useful to look more closely at a particular example of a successful explanatory project. I need to focus on an explanatory exercise where it is clear both that, and how, success has been achieved. Here, though, I encounter a first significant problem. For although it is possible to turn to published social theoretical studies to see *how* results and conclusions have been derived, there is always going to be a difficulty in convincing the critical reader or opponent that such analyses are indeed successful. That is, before using any examples to illustrate an argument about how successful research may proceed, there has to be some agreement that the examples chosen do constitute, or in some way typify, explanatory successes. But of course, a major problem in the charged atmosphere of modern social science is that few if any sets of systematically laid-out practices or results are so regarded in an unambiguous fashion.

For strategic reasons only, then, I turn to the practices of certain natural sciences, or anyway to those of other 'accepted' forms of science (as I have previously and for related considerations – see Chapter 2). I do so, as I say, merely to identify examples of practices which illustrate the approach I wish to convey but are already widely regarded as successful. It will eventually be seen that the insights of the examples considered do indeed bear on the social realm too. I return to an explicit consideration of explanatory endeavour in the social domain in due course.

Scientific experiments once more

In fact, I turn to an example of controlled experiments, which most commentators seem to agree are (frequently) successful. But I do not want to focus on those most controlled of 'controlled experiments' in the natural sciences, those laboratory experiments wherein all factors, bar the one whose properties are being investigated, are held either constant or at bay. Such a scenario is hardly feasible in the social realm, and would not easily suit my purposes here. However, this precise scenario is largely infeasible in various other domains as well, including some where successful controlled experiments do nevertheless occur. Not all controlled experiments proceed on the same basis, and some occur in conditions where it is not feasible to hold off, or hold constant, all background factors. It is experiments of the latter sort I want to consider here, experiments which, it will be seen in due course, do bear implications that have a relevance for social science (even though such experiments may not actually be executable there). Experiments in plant breeding can serve as an illustrative example.

Plant breeding

In plant breeding experiments, researchers are often concerned with determining whether a substance, say a chemical compound, has the potential to act as a fertiliser, to increase the yield of certain crops. The context of such experiments, however, is that they are frequently carried out in open fields in which the sorts of factors that can affect crop yield are often large in number, variable, transient and/or immeasurable, frequently unknown, and seemingly capable of combining in organic (non-mechanistic) ways. Certainly, it is typically not possible to isolate the crops from the effects of all but one factor, or to hold the effects of other causal factors constant.

In this context, agricultural researchers have nevertheless been successful in their work. The successful strategy has usually been to divide the land into a set of plots, some of which receive (varying amounts of) the compound and some which receive none. To the extent that there is a systematically higher average yield where the compound is applied, researchers have with reason attributed this to the compound whose fertilizing capacity is being investigated.[6]

How does this discussion have any bearing on our social explanatory concerns, and, in particular, relate to the sorts of questions listed above? It has an immediate bearing in that the focus is not on a specific outcome *per se*, i.e. the level of yield of the crop, but on a comparison or contrast: whether or not the yield is significantly higher where the compound has been added.

Of course, the plant breeding example motivating the discussion is not directly analogous to the scenarios we expect to find in the social realm simply because there is an element of experimental design involved. I will consider what follows from this disanalogy for social explanatory research in due course. For the time being I think we can agree that agricultural experiments of the sort examined are often successful, and I want to examine their conditions of possibility. For we shall see that these conditions, only slightly modified, along with the possibilities for explanatory success they facilitate, carry over to social situations as well.

Conditions of possibility of successes

What then are the necessary conditions for successful plant breeding experiments of the sort discussed? First there must be an observation domain of some sort, one I shall refer to as the *contrast space*, over which the experiments are performed. A contrast space is merely a domain over which it is meaningful, given our current understandings (possibly reflecting experimental design, although not necessarily), to draw comparisons. It is a space over which any observed systematic contrasts can be regarded as *prima facie* significant or of interest. In plant breeding the contrast space stretches over geographical space (in time). It comprises the plots of land utilised throughout the period of the experiment.

A second essential condition for the experiment to be successful, or at least to be successful on its own terms (the relevance of this qualification will become clear in due course) is that all relevant parts or aspects of the contrast space are correctly assessed to be subject to roughly the same set of causal influences bar one, i.e. except for the compound which is deliberately applied to some plots only.

In this particular example of plant breeding, I repeat, there is no requirement that the causal factors operating throughout the contrast space remain constant over time. All may change and in unknowable ways. It may even be that some of the relevant factors in play change from day to day (or even second to second), either in having an effect, or in the nature of their effects. The relevant requirement, or condition of possibility of experimental success, is only that at any point in time, the relevant causal factors (excepting the compound being experimentally investigated) are roughly the same throughout the contrast space, i.e over the plots of land utilised in the experiment.[7] I further repeat that there is no presumption that any causal factor, including the compound under investigation, interacts with other causal factors mechanistically/atomistically. The success of such experiments is rendered intelligible simply if, over the plots utilised in the experiment at any point in time, the set of causal factors in play are sufficiently similar, excepting for the compound whose causal properties are the concern of the investigation.

Moving towards the social domain

Now consider a situation which is very similar to the one of plant breeding described above, excepting that there is no agricultural experimenter allocating the compound systematically to plots, but instead a farmer who discovers *a posteriori* to her or his surprise that the crop yield is twice as high on average at one end of the field. It is not too fanciful to suppose that on examining the field the farmer is successful in identifying a factor (the compound in question or shade from trees or a local river or whatever) located only at the end of the field where the yield is high, which is the cause of the observed contrast. The scenario of this example does seem analogous in relevant ways to the examples with which we started concerning the social realm, and (as we shall see) in essential respects it is equivalent to the plant breeding experimental situation as well.

Of course, a clear difference between this scenario of the surprised farmer and that of the plant breeding experimenter is that of orientation. The experimenter is forward-looking, concerned with designing the experiment, triggering a mechanism, and observing the result. The surprised farmer is backward-looking. He or she starts from a situation where the *a posteriori* result occasions a sense of interest or surprise. The experimenter engineers a scientifically significant situation (albeit only where conditions allow). For non-experimentalists such as the surprised farmer, it is necessary to 'wait' for scientifically significant situations to emerge. But these are differences not in the conditions in which an increase in knowledge is possible, only in how they come about. As long as surprising, or otherwise significant, contrasts of the sort in question abound in the social world, and I indicate below that they do, there is no reason to suppose that, in itself, backward-orientated research (like the farmer seeking the explanation of the *a posteriori* situation of high yields at one end of the field) cannot be as successful as research that is experimentally designed.

However, there remains a second and rather significant difference between the two scenarios, or at least between the experimental situation and a conception along the lines of the example of the surprised farmer (the example that most corresponds to the situation in the social realm). This relates to the accuracy of the judgement formed over the contrast space. If an experiment is to be successful on its own terms, it is essential that the conditions of the experiment are more or less as the experimenter supposes. If, for example, a second factor influencing yield just happens to be located in the field in places where the compound is added (perhaps something has infected all, or a sample, of the compound before it was applied) then the experiment may fail in that erroneous conclusions are drawn.

Now equally, of course, if the surprised farmer is to track down a previously unknown cause (of higher yield) at the end of the field, it is essential that his or her prior assessment about conditions in the field is broadly correct, excepting for the unknown causal factor at one end. At least this is so if progress in knowledge is to take the form of an awareness of a causal factor that has somehow newly entered the contrast space.

However, it is immediately apparent for the non-experimental situation at least, that we can relax this latter requirement or condition (actually we shall see below that the same holds for experimental situations as well). And this possibility turns out to be rather important. A surprising contrast may ultimately reveal not that a previously unknown causal factor has somehow emerged in the contrast space, but that the judgement made concerning the degree of continuity, homogeneity or sameness occurring over the contrast space, though based on the observer's best evidence to hand, was incorrect. In such situations there is (or can be) progress in knowledge all the same. It merely takes the form of a transformation in understandings previously taken for granted, rather than an insight into something newly in play.

In the case of our farmer, for example, it may be that the supplier of seed for the crop always mixed a variety of types. There never was homogeneity. Some types of seed produce more yield, some less. It just so happened that on this occasion seeds of the high-yield-producing variety became somehow grouped together in a container that was applied at one particular end of the field.

I am probably overdoing the plant breeding illustration by this point. However, a case along the sorts of line just illustrated remains a logical possibility, and its nature, as we shall see, is one that has some substantial relevance for learning in the social domain. The significance of the example is that there is more than one way to learn in a situation of surprised contrasts. The basis of our surprise may indeed be a new causal factor coming into play, but equally it may merely be that our prior assessment of the nature of the contrast space was significantly in error all along. From such considerations we can see that the possibility of a progressive transformation in our knowledge does not require that we have judged the contrast space correctly, merely that we had rational grounds for the judgement formed.

In the end, of course, even the controlled experiment can go wrong. A (fallible) judgement about the adequacy of the experimental conditions is always involved. If anomalies are produced, this may lead the experimenter to discover factors not sufficiently controlled for. But when this occurs, and it does seem to be a common occurrence, then the experimenter is simply in the situation of our surprised farmer, in both making a discovery of a factor hitherto unknown or previously unrecognised as an influence, and doing so after the event.

I emphasise, though, that in the non-experimental scenario (just as much as the experimental one) a situation of *informed* prior judgement concerning the contrast space remains essential if progress in explanatory understanding is to be at all feasible, including getting an explanatory endeavour off the ground. Although the observer may get things wrong somewhere, he or she must get things wrong in a nevertheless knowledgeable and informed way. An explanatory endeavour is not going to be triggered by any old contrast. It has to occasion surprise, concern, feelings of doubt, or interest.

To construct an (extremely simple) example specifically for the social realm, if X notices that her or his residence and that of person Y are painted in different colours on the outside, such a contrast normally (i.e. for most examples of X and Y, and in most contexts) is unlikely to occasion surprise, and thereby trigger an explanatory exercise into the cause of the contrast. If, however, the two residences are two halves of the same house, X owns them both, and a hired painter had been instructed to paint them in identical fashion, any observed *a posteriori* contrast in their colour may indeed occasion surprise and the seeking of an explanation.

Further, if an explanatory exercise is initiated, any new insight gained may, as I say, come in a variety of ways. The cause of the contrast may well be a new factor in play. Perhaps X's spouse and joint owner of the house contravened X's original instructions without telling X. However, it may also be that there is no new factor in play. Perhaps X is a (normally) absentee landlady/lord, and is in fact viewing the wrong property mistakenly. Even here there is something to be learned, albeit only for our landlady/lord to discover he or she is in the wrong street.

The general insight these sorts of considerations bring out is the transformative nature of the process by which progress in knowledge occurs. The complex structures of the world are not revealed just by our sensing them directly. Nor is knowledge created out of nothing. Rather we start out, at any point in time, with a stock of knowledge, hunches, data, anomalies, suspicions, guesses, interests, etc., and though interacting with the world we come to transform our understandings. Knowledge, then, is found to be a produced means of production of further knowledge.

The specific insight achieved concerns the nature of the explanatory process in an open system. Through illustrating how human knowledge and expectations are a vital input to the explanatory process, the above considerations lead to a model of explanatory discovery. It is a model of which the social examples originally listed, like those of plant breeding, are special cases.

Contrast explanation

The various illustrations and considerations reflected upon above in fact lead us to a model of scientific endeavour that can be referred to as *contrastive explanation* or, as I now prefer to call it, *contrast explanation*.[8] According to it, successful explanatory endeavour requires just the two basic conditions or ingredients identified.

The first essential ingredient is an informed (if often tacitly formed or implicit) judgement about conditions operating over some contrast space (which may stretch over geographical regions, time, cultures and so forth, where the range of the contrast space will be larger or smaller depending on context). All that is required of any judgement is that it be suitably informed. It is not necessary that the judgement be wholly correct. As we have seen, a correct judgement (about past conditions at least) is specifically a condition of learning by way of identifying a new mechanism coming into play. This scenario, then, is but a special case of contrast explanation.

The second essential ingredient of contrast explanation is that a relation between outcomes within the contrast space is eventually recorded that is regarded by the researcher (or whoever) as surprising or in some way of concern or interest.

The satisfaction of such conditions, I now want to suggest, gives us all we need to embark systematically, and with some reasonable expectation of success, on explanatory endeavour, and in particular on such endeavour as can proceed in the face of the three-part problem of openness identified earlier in this chapter. Let me recall what the three noted aspects to the problem are.

Causal explanation, in an experimentally closed system, is able to move from the detection of regularities, to the formulation of causal hypotheses, to a weighing of any competing hypotheses in terms of predictive power with respect to such regularities. The three-part problem that arises in situations lacking the possibility of producing the sorts of regularity often achieved in controlled experimental contexts, lies in determining how even to *start* the analysis, how to *direct* it to get at a specific (aspect of a) causal mechanism, and how to *discriminate* between competing hypotheses without event regularities to facilitate event prediction. Let me indicate how we are now in a position to deal with each aspect of this problem.

Initiating the explanatory process and interest relativity

An entry point can be occasioned by feelings of surprise, doubt, concern or interest, that accompany some contrastive observations. Because we always possess knowledge of sorts, and form expectations, we can be surprised by what occurs. Here, then, we have an obvious basis for initiating an analysis. Surprising contrasts serve to draw attention to the possibility that, and to indicate a 'location' where, a hitherto unknown or unidentified causal factor is (or may well be) in play. In an open and highly internally related system this is rather important. Without such surprising or otherwise *interesting* contrastive observations it is difficult to imagine how investigatory research can proceed in any meaningful or systematic fashion at all.

The notion of *interest* here denotes a relative assessment of course. Further it tends to presuppose a prior (equally relative) assessment of a scenario as *uninteresting*. For a contrast tends to be interesting precisely in situations where its absence would have been regarded as somewhat uninteresting in the sense of expected or taken for granted.[9] Many taken-for-granted things are going on all the time. We often only notice that they have been doing so when something different occurs.

Prior to the 1980s, the sight of cows standing and walking around the field was mostly not of great interest to a UK country person. Indeed, it was an unexceptional commonplace. It is because of this, however, that the later observation of many cows appearing to lose the ability to stand and walk (with the onset of 'mad cow disease') was of 'interest' to the point of disturbing.

As I walk down the street in which I live, people walk past, and birds fly in the air. I usually take it all for granted. But I would be quite interested if a passing fellow human being suddenly propelled herself or himself into the stratosphere (and even if certain birds of a particularly nervous disposition stayed on the ground and chose to pass me by).

So, when certain phenomena are described as uninteresting this must often be recognised as an achieved view, a relative and knowledgable perspective marking a site where potentially very interesting things may yet arise. The interesting is a realisation of that potential.

I might note, at this point, that in previous writings (e.g. Lawson 1997e: 79) I have often referred to some sorts of relatively strict event regularities as somewhat scientifically uninteresting. By this I have indeed meant something like 'unremarkable', 'well understood' or 'taken for granted'. Usually these event regularities have been of a merely concomitant kind, where the events are correlated not because one subset causally conditions the other but because they share a similar causal history. We can now see, indeed, that regularities of this 'uninteresting' sort are polar or limiting conceptions (i.e. strict versions) of the sorts of patterns that are projected for contrast spaces. When correlations of this sort are expected to be strict their failure or breakdown can be interesting in the sense relevant here. These event regularities of the merely concomitant sort, then, are limiting forms of the patterns that lay the basis for contrast explanation to be initiated.

In sum, if it is usually a mistake to take anything completely, or even largely, for granted, we can now see that it is often just because we do so that contrast explanation can go to work. Contrasts tend to be considered interesting precisely because, and where, their prior absence was, at that time, regarded as uninteresting in the sense of 'taken for the ordinary'.

So the first component of the three-part problem of openness is met in contrast explanation. The fundamental feature is the element of surprise, doubt, or more generally interest in 'surprising contrasts', a feature presupposing a concerned and knowledgeable orientation. It is the human interest that gets the explanatory project going.

Directing the explanatory process

The second problem, the issue of directionality, is resolved as much by the contrastive side of interesting or surprising contrastive observations as by the interest or surprise. For just as an event regularity produced in the experimental laboratory *prima facie* marks the site of a single (set of) causal mechanism(s) in play, so a surprising contrast *prima facie* directs us to a single (set of) causal mechanism(s). It directs us to the mechanism(s) explaining the discrepancy between outcomes (or between outcomes and expectations), that accounts for the contrast 'x rather than y'.

Consider again the farmer concerned with the yield of her or his crops. The total yield will depend on numerous, possibly complexly interacting factors, and typically be too difficult to explain. However, the yield differential, the contrast between the average yield at one end of the field and the average yield elsewhere, may, when we have reason to expect a high degree of uniformity throughout, give *prima facie* reason to suppose a single explanation.

Or consider once more the situation of cows and the case of 'mad cow disease'. Consider first someone concerned with explaining any and all aspects of a cow's state or behaviour. Conceivably, any aspect of the cow, its mouth, teeth, legs, tail, parents, all factors that entered into the evolution of cows, and ultimately many factors going back to any big bang, have had a causal impact and so are explanatory of some aspects of the behaviour or general state of cows. Explaining the behaviour or state of cows, in truth, is not a meaningful proposition.

However, consider the situation of someone familiar with cows, who is surprised and concerned to discover that, say, in local herds (this, and perhaps all previous herds, is the contrast space) some, but only some, are showing symptoms of the disease. By attempting to explain not the state of cows *per se* but the observed contrast, i.e. why these cows are ill and those are not, factors common to all cows can be standardised for, or factored out, allowing the possibility of identifying the (specific or most direct) cause of the (symptoms of the) disease.

Now, is this enough for our needs? It certainly helps us get at a causal mechanism. But what if we want to learn more about the event that emerges? More specifically, if contrast explanation is directed by an interesting contrast to a specific mechanism which, along with others, co-produces a phenomenon, is there any way of identifying other causal conditions of the phenomenon in question?

If we do indeed want to further our understanding of an open-system (multiply determined) event, i.e. to identify several of the causes bearing on it, one possible strategy is to seek out different interesting contrasts or 'foils' involving it.

Consider an example I explore in depth in Lawson 1997a. The primary outcome (or the 'fact' or actuality of interest) upon which I chose to focus was the UK's productivity record in the early post-World War II period.

The point is that various aspects of this phenomenon can be determined by setting it against a variety of contrasts or foils, and seeking then to explain the various contrasts.

If the selected foil is the UK's productivity record before that war, the more recent productivity performance (our primary concern) is found to be superior. Thus we can ask why the recent record is superior to, rather than the same as, that before the war. And the likely answer to this contrastive question is the postwar expansion of world demand in the period of reconstruction.

However, if the selected foil or contrast is instead the early postwar productivity record of certain countries of the continent of Europe, say of the old West Germany, the postwar UK productivity performance, our topic of interest, is found to be mostly inferior. In this example, our contrastive phenomenon turns on the discrepancy in cross-country performances. We are concerned to determine why the UK fared so much *worse* than counties like West Germany (rather than as well). The likely answer to this contrastive question is the UK's relatively unique system of localised (as opposed to centralised) collective bargaining, with its in-built slow responsiveness to change (see Lawson 1997a: ch. 18).

It is not necessary, here, that the reader accepts the explanations offered of the noted contrastive questions. It is enough that the example demonstrates that where different foils are involved, where different contrastive observations are used to initiate explanatory research, different causal mechanisms bearing on the object of our focus (here the UK's postwar measured productivity performance) are likely to be uncovered. The more contrastive questions we can pose which involve a given phenomenon x, the more, potentially, we learn about its different causes. The feasible result is a range of causal knowledge that might eventually be synthesised to give a more rounded and deeper understanding of the concrete phenomenon of our investigations.

Of course, none of this throws any general insight on the process of retroductive inference, whereby we might move from (an account of) a given phenomenon to a (hypothesis about) an underlying cause. The problem of deciding how to make this move remains a matter of context. But there is no difficulty that arises with retroduction in the context of contrast explanation that does not arise in all other causal-explanatory situations as well. The move from phenomenon to cause rests on a logic of analogy and metaphor, luck and ingenuity, here as everywhere else. Any problems of retroductive inference are not specific to non-experimental situations.

Actually, it may be the case that the surprise or shock of an unexpected contrast encourages us to examine our current understandings and realise that we already have an explanation of it. We (and our situations) are usually characterised by tensions and inconsistencies of sorts, and a development which shocks or surprises or otherwise interests us may (whatever the precise cause) lead first and foremost to introspection or self-reflection, and thus to a resolution by way of understandings already (if only tacitly) possessed. These are stages in the knowledge process that Clive Lawson (2000) describes as 'epistemically significant moments'. Lawson suggests that 'The main feature of these moments is some form of transition, crisis or rupture in the structural conditions of practice, that prompt a "reclaiming" of knowledge that the agent already has, but is not discursively aware of' (189).[10] Such processes of 'recovery' clearly deserve attention in social theoretical research.[11] The point here, though, is that whatever the mechanism whereby specific knowledge claims come to be formulated or 'reclaimed', contrasts of surprise or interest provide seemingly appropriate conditions, and so opportunities, for causal hypotheses to be meaningfully formulated.

Discriminating between causal hypotheses

Finally there is the question of how the third component of the earlier noted three-part problem of openness is (or might be) met. This is the problem of determining, in the absence of event regularities of the sort produced in experimental laboratories, a type of evidence that might usefully be brought to bear in selecting amongst any competing hypotheses. This problem arises most clearly in a situation where we believe a hitherto unaccounted for causal mechanism is responsible for some surprising contrast. And one sort of evidence we might meaningfully seek is precisely sets of contrasts on which our competing hypotheses bear.

Consider again the example of the farmer surprised by higher crop yields at one end of the field. If a river passing by is hypothesised to be the cause, then it may be sensible to check whether, in other fields through which the river passes, crop yields are higher in regions closest to it. If the hypothesis entertained is that shade from trees causes the higher yields, it may be possible to examine other fields to assess whether yields are higher where there is shade. And so on. In the case of each hypothesis in contention, inferences are drawn concerning contrasts that we might expect to find. In each case it is inferred that if the hypothesis is correct, yields will mostly be higher in the region of the contrast space closest to the hypothesised mechanism in question. The hypothesis that performs best in terms of empirical adequacy in this sense over the widest range of relevant conditions can, with reason, be accepted as the better grounded.

Of course, because the world is open, things will rarely, if ever, be clear cut. Even where a river usually brings positive benefits there may be countervailing factors (such as floods or upstream spillage of industrial pollution). The rational course of action is to persevere with the hypothesis that has the greater explanatory power, that accommodates the widest range of evidence, and to see if its explanatory failures, where they exist, can be accounted for by countervailing factors, and so on. If they cannot be, the response which is most appropriate will depend on the context. Science everywhere is a messy business. But there is no difficulty here that is insuperable in principle.

Facilitating explanatory research in the social domain

Now the central thesis I want to defend, of course, is that the conditions for contrast explanation hold for the social realm in particular. Fundamental here is the general point, noted throughout, that a condition for contrast explanation is a *rational judgement*, or a knowledgeable assessment, that the contrast space is sufficiently homogeneous (or, more precisely, that events throughout it share a similar causal history). For it is only on the basis of an informed judgement about the nature of a contrast space that a contrast can be recognised or interpreted as significant.

Contrast spaces are underpinned by expectations of continuity in social life, by expectations that causal processes are such that regularities (strict or particular) of the form 'what happens here happens there' are justified. We saw in Chapter 2 that in fact such regularities abound in social life. They underpin all observations of continuity: that prices of stamps, television licences, etc., are (currently mostly) everywhere the same in the UK; that the school curriculum is identical throughout schools in England; that most English pubs (currently) stop serving at 11:00 pm; that goods everywhere are bought and sold; and so forth. There are definite bounds to all such regularities of continuity, and most are partial within their bounds. But their nature is often of a sort that an expectation of continuity is knowledgeably formed, that a contrast space is rationally delineated.

As I have emphasised, it may turn out that we were wrong from the outset in formulating a contrast space in a particular way. That is, it may often turn out that a surprising *a posteriori* contrast is the result not of a change in circumstances, say the emergence of a new causal factor, but of an error in our previous understanding of the nature of the contrast space. But if so, on examining the cause of the contrast we may well learn that, and how, our original judgement was wrong.[12]

How specifically might this discussion bear on practices of social-explanatory research? Very often, in our day-to-day encounters, observed discrepancies between our best judgements and what happens give rise to a sense of surprise (or even shock) as I have noted. This will be the case, for example, when an acquaintance breaks accepted conventions of polite behaviour, or the UK high street shop does not open on Monday morning as usual, etc. And it will be the case, too, when people travel further afield. For example, a first trip by a British person to Naples brings the 'surprise' that almost no one stops at most red traffic lights.

However, for the social researcher alive to the conditions of contrast explanation, the relevant orientation may well be an informed curiosity more often than *a posteriori* surprise or shock. In particular, through recognising both, first, that actual or expected event regularities (of whatever degree of strictness) can, and eventually regularly do, break down, yet nevertheless, second, that existing (fallible) knowledge of certain specific or local conditions (contrast spaces) often suggests uniformity (similarity of causal histories) as our most grounded assessment, the social researcher may search out such scientifically significant contrast spaces just to see if noteworthy contrasts after all occur. In a sense, the social researcher will often be knowledgeably seeking out situations in which either they are surprised, or they know it would have been reasonable (given existing knowledge claims) to have been (and that others probably will be) surprised at the sorts of observations recorded.

For example, by exploring whether changes in given structures (e.g. the introduction of minimum wage legislation, or the legalisation of Sunday trading) impact in a uniform way throughout a given region such as the UK, it may be possible, where discontinuities or differences are observed, to uncover previously insufficiently understood differences in specific social mechanisms (for example the employment process), reflecting, in particular, the nature of their internal relationality to local context, and so obtain a less partial account than hitherto of the mechanisms at work.

In other words, in such situations it is not that a researcher necessarily expects the legislation to impact in the same way in all areas, merely that their prior knowledge is such as to have no specific reason to expect of any two sub-regions that the impact will be greater in one than in the other. If after the event a significant difference is observed it is likely that something of note can be determined by pursuing the explanation.

Similarly, by focusing on movements in specific phenomena, say house prices or productivity growth rates, or whatever, it may be found that there are marked differences in outcomes over two (or more) regions, where current understanding would have led the researcher to expect greater homogeneity.

On occasion such a development may lead to the uncovering of a previously unrecognised causal factor. For example, recent increases in house prices in Cambridge, England, appear to have been significantly higher in the south of the city. The implicit contrast involved here seems to have been caused by the phenomenon of an increase in the number of house buyers wanting to live in Cambridge, but work in, and so commute to, London. This is an option recently made feasible by the speeding up of the rail link between the two cities, with the railway station situated in the south of Cambridge.

On other occasions, the knowledge acquired may be of factors already recognised but insufficiently understood. For example, differences in productivity growth rates may reflect the fact not of a new causal factor coming into play (such as a faster railway system) but of new developments in technology being assimilated differently according to the different existing systems of industrial relations (or local levels of technical knowledge, or forms of support industries, etc.) throughout the regions of the contrast space.

A further possible basis for contrast explanation arises where a researcher's understanding of the conditions of recent developments, say trend growth rates or whatever, leads them to the view that identified trends are likely to continue unabated (or from understandings possessed could with reason have been expected so to continue). A marked downturn (or upturn) would then constitute a contrast with extrapolated outcomes, suggesting a *prima facie* case of a new and identifiable causal factor having come into play.

An example of the latter is, in effect, provided in a study by Goldin and Katz (forthcoming). They observe that just after 1970 in the United States there was a dramatic increase both in the fraction of women college graduates entering professional programmes, and in the age of all college graduate women at first marriage. For example, the percentage of first-year law students who were women rose from 10 per cent in 1970 to 36 per cent in 1980. And whilst almost 50 per cent of a cohort of women college graduates born in 1950 were married before they were twenty-three years of age, of a cohort born seven years later, fewer than 30 per cent were married by this age. These authors also provide other related data suggesting that something was affecting the life styles of (certain groups of) US women at about 1970.

The contrastive phenomenon here, then, is the trend in developments before and after the early 1970s. The explanation provided (whose correctness need not detain us here, but which anyway is carefully and convincingly defended by Goldin and Katz) is that these changes resulted in some significant part from both the introduction of 'the pill' in the 1960s along with the change in the legal environment that enabled young unmarried women to obtain it.[13]

In short, it is through recognising that generalisations about concrete social circumstances and processes will usually have limits, and through exploring how specific generalisations break down in areas where our current understanding suggests (most reason for supposing) they could nevertheless have held, that we can learn, by way of contrast explanation, of hitherto unknown or insufficiently understood factors that make the difference.

In a world that is open and complex, unforseen developments are always occurring. But by starting from a (knowledgeable) position where specific changes or developments are not foreseen, those changes such as occur provide points from which it seems feasible to initiate an explanatory investigation, and concerning which, explanatory successes seem likely.[14]

And so it is with the examples of everyday (contrast) questions listed at the outset, questions to which responses were felt to be feasible: Why are my keys not in my pocket as usual? Why does my bicycle not work as well as it did yesterday? Why did the students do so much worse/better in the exams this year compared with other years? And so forth. It is not necessarily the case that my keys have not been misplaced before, or that the cycle has never before worked badly, etc. It is merely that I had reason for supposing that matters would be other than they are currently found to be.

In truth, indeed, we are confronted with noteworthy contrasts of this nature almost everywhere. Is it not significant, for example, that in the modern day UK girls perform significantly better in single-sex schools than in mixed ones; that in all schools, girls are beginning to outperform boys academically, when until very recently boys performed significantly better than girls; that teenage pregnancy rates at the start of the twenty-first century are reported to be significantly higher than elsewhere in Europe; that men usually get paid more than women for identical work; and so on. In all such cases, the prior expectation need not have been that conditions are everywhere exactly the same, merely rather more similar (throughout the relevant contrast space) than is found to be the case. All that is required for the explanatory process to be initiated is that the contrasts observed are striking enough to suggest that something systematic is going on, given the contrast spaces involved, and that the causes of the contrasts are identifiable. I conclude from all this that contrast explanation holds out the promise for an adequate causalist approach to social science even accepting the social ontology I defend, including an absence of conditions to facilitate experimental enquiry.

The essence of the method set out, clearly, is that we learn by getting things knowledgably wrong. Thus I am here rejecting positivistic or, more generally, monistic accounts of knowledge, i.e. accounts wherein knowledge is the accumulation of incorrigible facts. And I am reaffirming the familiar realist insight that knowledge, although concerned with an at least partly independent reality or intransitive 'object', is a two-way process. Through confronting 'objects' of study we learn not only about them but simultaneously about ourselves, including, in particular, the errors of our current thinking (as well, no doubt, as something of our social-cultural situations, values, and so forth). Knowledge, as I have already stressed, is intrinsically a transformational process. And it is a process of transformation in which the continuous absenting of errors of various sorts is fundamental. Although the analytical moment, the elaboration and utilisation of surface patterns, has a role to play in explanatory research, it does not exhaust the latter. Rather the knowledge process is fundamentally dialectical.

A seemingly general explanatory model

The various explanatory scenarios referred to throughout have all been found to be open to investigation via a reasonably general (if abstractly formulated) approach that I have referred to as contrast explanation.[15] This is an approach that certainly uses such partial patterns in events as can be determined. But unlike deductivism, it seeks neither to stylise such demi-regs as are found nor to utilise any such regularities solely for purposes of deducing consequences. Rather, event patterns are but a moment in the causal process which goes beyond them.

Now, not only does contrast explanation not reduce to the sort of deductivist reasoning aspired to in modern economics, but we can at this point see that deductivist 'explanation' is actually a special case of the former. In fact, I want briefly to indicate that a variety of explanatory approaches appear to be (or perhaps more accurately can be interpreted as) special cases of contrast explanation too.

I start, though, with the sort of controlled experimental set-up associated with much of natural science, in which all but one (set of) factor(s) is held constant or at bay. This is the set-up presupposed by deductivists, and in particular economic modellers, including econometricians, even though it represents the configuration that seems least likely (and *a posteriori* least often) to obtain in the social realm.

From the perspective set out it is now possible to recognise this scenario as a very special case of contrast explanation in which two conditions hold in particular. The first is that the contrast space is regarded as enduring (it is at least expected that the experimental conditions can usually be re-established). The second condition is that causal factors operating throughout the contrast space are more than uniform in their action over the space: they are actually constant or reduced to zero. If, in an experimental set-up of this sort, a mechanism is triggered and its effect recorded, the contrast is implicitly between that which takes place prior to the mechanism being triggered and that which occurs after the mechanism is triggered. However, because in the experimental set-up of this sort, there will often be a way of viewing matters to suggest that 'nothing' is going on before the mechanism is triggered, there will be a sense in which it seems that the effect of the mechanism is being read straight off. In truth, though, the effect is determined as the change in outcomes in situations before and after the triggering of the mechanism. This is the contrastive observation. And the change can, with reason, be attributed to the mechanism so triggered. It is this special case, with all background factors held constant or at bay (or, in a statistical set-up, rendered orthogonal to the explicitly included factors), that is erroneously generalised in the economic modelling practices of the modern day.

So contrast explanation ultimately lies behind causal explanation of the sort facilitated even in the most controlled of controlled experimental situations. The latter is but a very special case of the former. Indeed, we can now see that closures of the causal sequence sort presuppose closures (or regions) of continuity (i.e. the intended objects of contrast spaces). However, whilst causal analysis in general requires only that the outcomes of contrast spaces stand in a given relation to each other, the controlled experiment, and exercises in economic modelling, require that they are also held constant.

Actually, there is a more generalised contrastive phenomenon in play here. Behind this discussion of the controlled experiment it is recognised that event regularities of the causal sequence sort can often be produced under experimental conditions but rarely under others. Now an 'interested' philosophical orientation that asks 'Why do they often occur under experimental conditions but not in general?' stimulates an ontological (explanatory) investigation and arrives at the specific ontology of critical realism. That is, by addressing this latter contrast, in explaining it, we uncover something about the basic nature of reality: that it is open, structured and differentiated. For it is only the latter (critical realist theory of) ontology that can render intelligible the result that, by way of experimental manipulation, event regularities of the sort in question are sometimes achieved that would not have occurred otherwise. It is just because relatively strict event regularities of the sought-after sort occur mostly (if not only) under the restrictive conditions noted that they are significant in science. Each experimentally produced event regularity is a measure of the difference between the experimental and non-experimental situations. In the former situation, but not the latter, a (stable) mechanism is both triggered and isolated from countervailing forces so that its effects are correlated with the triggering conditions. Critical realism identifies the ontological conception wherein such a scenario is possible.

So we can now see that contrast explanation has a field of application that is wider in scope than the sorts of examples used to motivate the discussion. For if a specific contrastive phenomenon, restricted to a specific contrast space, allows the identification of a specific mechanism, the systematic contrast between (typically experimental) conditions where strict and stable event regularities of the causal sequence sort are produced (and often reproduced) and others where they are not, allows the inference to the ontology of critical realism (that reality is generally open, but also structured in a way that localised closures are possible, and correspond to, or allow, the empirical identification of underlying mechanisms). Specific contrasts to scientific hypotheses of specific mechanisms; generalised contrasts to philosophical ontologies. Each is an example of contrast explanation.

A further example of contrast explanation is provided, I think, by the situation wherein, despite the context being open, some event in and of itself is so surprising or interesting that we are moved to ask how or why it happened. In such situations there is also an implicit contrast being addressed, this being between the event happening, and its not happening. In this case the straight negation of the event is the foil. For an outcome x, the contrastive question is 'why x rather than not x'. Now at first sight this might seem to render all outcomes open to contrast explanation, and thereby perhaps to trivialise the explanatory approach being elaborated. But this is not so. For an essential condition of contrast explanation is surprise, interest or doubt, etc., in the contrast. We need a situation where our existing knowledge is such that we expected 'not x' (or might have expected 'not x' if we had thought about it) but x did occur. To learn that the outside of person P's house is not white is hardly going to occasion surprise if we have no reason to expect it to be white. But if we learn that a sports team acknowledged as outstanding has failed to beat a team regarded as very poor, we may well be surprised. The explanation may be complacency, bribes, tiredness or whatever. Although the foil or contrast is the opposite of that which came about, our background knowledge is such that we still have reason, under such conditions, to suppose it likely that an identifiable mechanism is at work. In the final chapter of this book I ask the question why the mainstream formalistic modelling project remains so dominant in modern economics, despite its limited (absolute or relative) successes in illuminating the world in which we live. Clearly I am 'surprised' at this outcome, given there are other potentially more fruitful projects in place. Or at least I find this outcome sufficiently interesting and curious and even regrettable, as to question why it, rather than a more varied or pluralistic academic situation, has not emerged in modern economics.[16]

As a final consideration, we might note that a Kuhnian paradigm shift also in effect invokes the idea of contrast explanation. According to the Kuhnian view, any attempt at understanding presupposes a broad framework or paradigm, which is largely taken as given. This is certainly so in much of natural science. However, results are often obtained that cannot be explained within the accepted framework or paradigm, and indeed seem rather problematic in the light of it. When this happens these results are often put aside as anomalies. These anomalies are in effect surprising contrasts, divergencies between the (sorts of) outcomes the paradigm leads us to expect, and what actually is found. Eventually the set of anomalies builds up. At some point the set of anomalies becomes of central focus. In a sense the contrast question is asked: 'why this set of anomalies rather than outcomes consistent with the basic framework?'. A paradigm shift occurs when a new framework is derived and accepted which is at least as explanatorily powerful as the previous one but can avoid, and perhaps make sense of, the recognised anomalous outcomes of the earlier one.[17]

Demi-regularities

In the light of the foregoing discussion it is possible, and I suspect useful, to clarify the notion and role of demi-regularities or demi-regs. Some commentators on *Economics and Reality* have (erroneously) interpreted my account of demi-regularities there as expressing one type of situation only. This is the case where a relationship (of causal sequence) holds between measurable economic variables, and does so with sufficient strictness as to facilitate the successful application of standard techniques of econometrics, albeit only within a limited span of time and space. The scenario imagined is one in which correlations between economic variables do occur behind our backs, but only over limited intervals.

For example, an econometric model of aggregate consumption (with consumption expressed as a fixed function of measured disposable income) estimated on UK data over the last twenty years (say) and found to 'forecast' sufficiently accurately within this twenty-year period but not outside it might be said to be underpinned by a demi-regularity so interpreted.

Not surprisingly, once my account of demi-regularities has been reformulated in this fashion, and this fashion only, it has been 'found' that the approach I defend is not essentially different to that of the deductivist mainstream after all.

Now any such uncovered event regularity that is both of the sort presupposed by the use of standard procedures of econometrics and partial merely in the sense of being (sufficiently) strict (for such methods to be applied) but only within limits, is actually a restricted closed system. Even experimental closures are of this form (being restricted to the experimental conditions). In the example just noted it is effectively being claimed that 'within a specific twenty-year period then whenever x then y' (or a stochastic near equivalent is being expressed).

But still, whether or not such a pattern constitutes a restricted closure, is not the latter (assuming it were to occur) an example of a demi-reg as I have conceived it? The answer is that 'it all depends', and that if or when the pattern in question constitutes a demi-reg, it is but a degenerate special case.

On what does it 'all depend'? Central here is the conception of the 'system' being addressed. The notion of a system in the given context carries no independent meaning. It merely signifies the stretch of conditions, or the space, in which the event pattern in question is taken to hold (or not). In the just noted econometric example an event regularity is taken to hold over a twenty-year period. This period and context is a restricted closed system. Now let us extend the 'system' by ten years. In the later ten-year period it is found that, unlike in the first twenty years, when the antecedent x is instantiated the expected consequent y does not (always) occur. This is definitional of an open system. Should we describe the system as closed at first and then open, or is it open throughout the period? Nothing hangs on the answer. It depends on how the system is defined. If the first twenty years are considered separately as a system the latter is closed. If the system comprises the thirty-year period it is open.

It is from the perspective of the thirty-year system (and from others containing, but not reducing to, the twenty-year one) that the patterning of events in question, being partial, can be said to take the form of a demi-reg. Strictly speaking, of course, the content of any restricted closure is then a demi-reg when viewed from the perspective of any wider or encompassing system which both contains the restricted closure and also includes at least one occasion when the antecedent event occurs but is not followed by the usual consequent. But a scenario such as the latter is clearly, at best, a special or degenerate case of a demi-reg, one wherein over a continuous sub-period the regularity holds quite strictly. It is a special case for which a closure is a sub-system.

Now in *Economics and Reality* I certainly did not envisage the category of demi-regularity reducing to the case just discussed. Indeed, the latter represents a configuration of a sort of which I questioned the *a posteriori* relevance. My assessment there was that most observed regularities are not uniform or without exception even within limited stretches of space-time.

Moreover, in *Economics and Reality* I indicated my view that the types of demi-reg that both abound and are of some relevance to social scientific advance are very often those which express surprising or significant contrastive patterns (observed over certain contrast spaces as conceptualised above).[18] In short, I maintained (and maintain) that most such interesting and partial patterns have taken the form of contrastive demi-regs.

Enduring or widespread social processes

With this discussion in mind, it is clearly of interest to social research to seek out those scenarios where

(i)   the contrast space is relatively wide (i.e. to seek conditions in which *a priori* it might be expected that a wide stretch of outcomes [over time or space] share a similar causal history), and

(ii) a resulting (unexpected or otherwise interesting or significant) contrast turns out to be, if less than regular, nevertheless frequently apparent throughout significant stretches of this space.

In other words, an interesting case to contemplate or seek out is where the contrast of interest (if partial) makes an appearance over a wide stretch of time and/or space.

An example of this sort, to which I gave a good deal of attention in *Economics and Reality* (and which I also touched upon briefly above), relates to contrasting rates of measured productivity growth. I noted that, for a given period of time in recent history, measured productivity growth is observed to have been significantly less in the UK than in certain otherwise comparable industrial countries on the continent of Europe. Of course, such a contrast is only surprising or significant if our theories or current understandings lead us to conclude that the contrasted phenomena stand *a posteriori* in a different relation than might reasonably have been expected. In the discussion above (when comparing different contrasts involving productivity performance) I focused only on the immediate postwar period. But actually, a surprising or noteworthy feature of the contrastive phenomenon discussed here, is that up until about 1980 it held, on and off, throughout much of the preceding hundred years or more (when many economic theories would lead us to expect roughly the same performance throughout). And it is the surprising longevity that gives hope of uncovering a mechanism with a degree of space-time endurance.[19] Contrastive demi-regs, then, may be surprising, and so become the object of study, not just because a contrast is involved, but because the contrast in some form makes a somewhat frequent appearance, because it is also a demi-reg with a significant presence over time.

A further example of an enduring contrastive demi-reg of this sort is the relative movement in the prices of primary products relative to those of produced goods over the last hundred years (see Pinkstone, 2002, on this).

Other candidates include the significantly high proportion of senior posts in the academy and industry, or indeed anywhere in most modern societies, which are occupied by men, or the differential in pay for men and women doing comparable work, and so on.

Ultimately, even the sorts of contrasts which involve well controlled laboratory experimentation are forms of widely experienced (often repeated) demi-regs. Experiments, including repetitions of previously successful ones, do often fail, due to bad luck, or through being inexpertly or otherwise poorly performed. And if the results of individual experiments are demi-regs, so too is the contrast between experimental and non-experimental results that ultimately helps ground the ontology defended in this book.

The feasibility of social explanation

To sum up, it is a widely observed phenomenon that in our daily lives we are often somewhat taken aback, or at least find that our interest is aroused, when two (or more) sets of outcomes are discovered to stand in a relation to each other which is significantly contrary to expectation, or at least contrary to the situation which, on reflection, we might have expected in the light of the theories we currently hold. A precondition for this to happen, clearly, is that we have felt able to form expectations concerning the relation between (or, more precisely, to take a reasoned view about the commonality of the causal history of) the sets of outcomes over a domain that I have called the contrast space (and that these expectations have been disappointed). Further, in such situations we are often able to detect the reasons for our errors. It may turn out that a new causal factor has come into play or, and somewhat significantly, that our understanding of the nature of the contrast space, specifically of the relation between causes operating within it, has been faulty all along.

A recognition and understanding of this daily explanatory activity can inform research methodology for open systems quite widely. For if background knowledge of the sort identified can facilitate day-to-day knowledgeable human interactions, it can (and does) facilitate scientific (and philosophical) advance as well.

The explanatory process so facilitated is necessarily backward looking. The essentially open nature of reality, both natural and social, necessitates that we very often start our explanatory endeavour from situations that have turned out to surprise, occasion a feeling of doubt, or otherwise interest us in some way (the failed experiment, the unusual reaction from mixing chemical compounds, the differing *a posteriori* experiences of apparently similar economies, the accumulation of anomalies, etc.). But so long as surprising contrasts are to be had, this is not a handicap for explanatory endeavour.

It does follow that successful social science will be highly context- (contrast space) dependent. And it follows, too, that science can benefit from drawing on contributors with a range of experiences, capable of being differentially surprised, interested or concerned. So scientific positions and resources should be accessible to people from all backgrounds on methodological grounds, in addition to those stemming from considerations of fairness or democracy.

But whatever else follows it is not the impossibility of a successful explanatory social science (that does not depend on closing or otherwise [knowingly] distorting an open social reality). To the contrary, if we simply transfer the successful social-theoretical practices of our everyday lives into our social-theoretical research activities, albeit, perhaps, with the aim of pursuing these practices in more systematic, explicitly formulated, critically examined and self-reflexive ways, there is every reason to anticipate a more successful performance of our discipline.

Needless to say, there are further issues bearing on all this that I cannot consider here, although I have dealt with many of them elsewhere (e.g. Lawson 1997a: ch. 15; also see Chapter 6 below; and see as well C. Lawson 2000; Runde 1998). In the current chapter I have sought to draw out and systematise those matters I think will often be central to the process of explanatory endeavour in open systems, but overlooked in the modern economics academy. The concrete details will doubtless be significantly dependent on the context of explanatory study. But progress in knowledge is, in the face of an open social system, certainly possible. For it to be actualised, it should by now be clear, we need to reorient our explanatory approach. I have suggested that contrast explanation, as I have elaborated it, appears capable of being especially useful. But this is merely an illustration of the more general insight already noted that, given the open, processual and highly internally related nature of social reality, we need to be not only analytical in our reasoning, but also, and I suspect primarily, dialectical.

5

AN EVOLUTIONARY
ECONOMICS?

On borrowing from evolutionary biology

The allure of an evolutionary economics

The idea of an evolutionary economics based on insights from evolutionary biology is clearly enticing to many modern economists. In the last few years especially, the number of economists attracted to it appears to be significantly on the increase (see, for example, Dopfer 2001; Dugger and Sherman 2000; Hodgson 1997, 1998c, 1999b; Laurent and Nightingale 2001; Loasby 1999; Louçã and Perlman 2000; Magnussen and Ottoson 1997; Nicita and Pagano 2001; Potts 2000; Reijnders 1997; amongst numerous others; and see Witt 2001, for an interpretive survey).

The idea is not a new one. Marshall once famously concluded that 'the Mecca of the economist lies in economic biology rather than economic dynamics' (Marshall 1961: xii). And Veblen inspired many in asking 'Why is economics not an evolutionary science?'. Furthermore the issue has been frequently examined throughout the last century, not least in Nelson and Winter's (1982) *An Evolutionary Theory of Economic Change*.

Even so, many contributors have continued to urge caution, whilst debating the merits of borrowing from biology. For example, Penrose concludes a piece on biological analogies by arguing:

> But in seeking the fundamental explanations of economic and social phenomena in human affairs the economist, and the social scientist in general, would be well advised to attack his problems directly and in their own terms rather than indirectly by imposing sweeping biological models upon them.
>
> (1952: 819)

And Schumpeter (in a passage that has been interpreted as supporting the view that economics should eschew *all* metaphors from physical and natural sciences)[1] writes:

> it may be ... that certain aspects of the individual-enterprise system are correctly described as a struggle for existence, and

that a concept of survival of the fittest in this struggle can be defined in a non-tautological manner. But if this be so, then these aspects would have to be analyzed with reference to economic facts alone and no appeal to biology would be of slightest use.

(Schumpeter 1954: 789)

Others have been more obviously positive, although even amongst protagonists there is often an explicit recognition that borrowing from others, including biology, is not a panacea (e.g. Hodgson 1993). All in all, I think, the jury is still out as to whether a fruitful evolutionary economics based on principles drawn from evolutionary biology is a viable proposition.

The problem with the literature as it stands, it seems to me, is that too little progress has been made on the question of what would justify drawing on evolutionary biology (or indeed on any models first formulated outside the social domain). And the reason appears to be not so much a lack of attention to the details of evolutionary models (though there is often room for improvement here) as an insufficient attention paid to questioning the nature of the social realm to which it is intended that the evolutionary models be applied. Determining the nature of social material does matter, however. The nature of the object of study always bears implications for how it can be studied.

Though seemingly obvious, even trite, this latter insight flies in the face of much, if not most, of modern economics with its continual neglect of explicit ontological analysis. Indeed, modern economics is marked by a widespread committal of the epistemic fallacy. This consists in the view that questions about being can always be reduced to questions about our knowledge (of being), that matters of ontology can always be translated into epistemological terms. This fallacy assumes the form of an expectation that methods can be adopted from any sphere, and/or be of any kind – mathematical, evolutionary or whatever – and successfully applied irrespective of the nature of the object of study (see Lawson 1997a).

Even in the more insightful discussions bearing upon the possibility of an evolutionary economics, questions of ontology have tended to be obscured by a concentration on other matters. The latter have included such issues as whether Darwin consistently proposed one sort of evolutionary theory or mechanism only, the proper interpretation and relevance of the contributions of Lamarck, the nature of frontier modelling in modern biology, and so forth. Whilst these sorts of inquiries have their interest, they easily distract from those more relevant to the question of whether it is feasible in any useful way at all to abduct from biology into social theory.

In any case, whatever the reason for it, questions of ontology have been largely neglected in discussions of borrowing from others, and here my purpose is to help rectify this situation. It is the case that ontological considerations of some sort do already creep in here and there. However, they rarely do so in a sufficiently explicit and systematic fashion.[2] My limited aim here, as I say, is to contribute to helping redress this situation.

Perhaps it is useful if I anticipate at this point the conclusion I reach below on the worth of borrowing from biology. First let me say that by the term evolutionary I mean not any type of change, but the genealogical connection of all organisms along with an account of life and society regulated by descent with modification (essentially cumulative causation). Thus on my understanding, natural selection is but one evolutionary mechanism. However, by the term evolutionary many economists do seem to mean processes of natural selection. With this in mind, the specific thesis defended in this chapter, and developed on the basis of ontological reasoning, is that there is no legitimate basis for an evolutionary economics as such if

(i)   the term evolutionary (in 'evolutionary economics') is interpreted (as economists interested in borrowing from evolutionary biology tend to interpret the term) as denoting a process that in some way conforms to the natural selection model that derives from (Darwinian) evolutionary biology, *and* if

(ii) the phrase 'evolutionary economics' is intended to signal a universal approach to economic analysis (implying that all economic phenomena can be treated as resulting from evolutionary [natural selection] processes).

Rather my thesis is simply that the social world is such that certain social phenomena *can* result from evolutionary processes of this sort, specifically from processes that manifest evolutionary natural selection aspects. Where this is so, an evolutionary explanation of the type in question, in part at least, is clearly called for. But this particular socio-evolutionary model ought not to be universalised *a priori*. Even Darwin thought that natural selection was but one mechanism amongst many regulating life on earth, albeit, in his view, the most important one. Thus in the final edition of *The Origin of Species*, Darwin (1872) writes:

> But as my conclusions have lately been much misrepresented, and it has been stated that I attribute the modification of species exclusively to natural selection, I may be permitted to remark that in the first edition of this work and subsequently, I placed in a most conspicuous position – namely at the close of the Introduction – the following words: 'I am convinced that natural selection has been the main but not the exclusive means of modification'. This has been of no avail. Great is the power of steady misrepresentation.
>
> (Darwin 1872: 421)

As we shall see, in the social realm there is even greater reason to adopt such an open or pluralistic orientation in explanatory endeavour.

In truth, to insist on an 'evolutionary economics' modelled on the natural selection paradigm prior even to identifying the phenomenon to be understood and/or explained is ultimately no better than the modern mainstream's *a priori* insistence upon a deductivist or formalistic economics, that all phenomena be addressed using closed-systems deductivist modelling. The relevance of this particular evolutionary model, as with all other methods or epistemological principles, can be determined only *a posteriori*. And the evidence is that the domain of relevance of this evolutionary model within the social realm is certainly not unbounded. Let me now briefly run through the argument.

The biological and social connection

As I say, recent years have witnessed something of a surge of interest in (the possibility at least of) borrowing from biology. But what explains the phenomenon that some, especially (but not exclusively) heterodox economists appear so optimistic about gaining insight from biological writing, and in particular from theories of biological evolution? Much of the appeal seems intuitive. Certainly, I do not find this optimism well articulated even amongst the best of economic commentators. Although the formulation I proposed above, turning on the matching of evolutionary model or method to social ontological insight, seems simple enough, even the better parts of the literature do not always recognise that the relevant matter to be determined is indeed whether biological achievements provide a useful model for the social realm, given the latter's nature.

Actually, a study of the relevant literature reveals that very frequently several different lines of reasoning are run together. There is, in reality, not one type of connection of the biological to the social but three:

1   the biological as an *existential basis* for social phenomena;
2   the biological in *causal interaction* with social phenomena; and
3   the biological as the source of a *model* for the understanding of social phenomena.

Our understanding of capable human behaviour at any level requires an understanding of biological/social connections along the lines of types 1 and 2. But our primary concern here is actually with connections of type 3. The problem with much of the existing literature, it seems to me, is that these different forms of connection are rarely distinguished, with the consequence that support for type 3 is sometimes thought to be achieved by emphasising connections along the lines of type 1 and/or type 2. This is invalid. After all, whilst social phenomena and processes are, or include, an emergent surplus from the interactions of human beings (as opposed to being reducible to human beings themselves), it is the case that the physical realm (just like the biological) also provides an existential basis for, and exists in causal interaction with, social phenomena. Certainly if it is thought that connections of types 1 and 2 justify those of type 3, some argumentation is required. This, so far, is noticeably missing.

Evolutionary theory and metaphor

In order to assess the relevance of biological models for understanding social phenomena it is necessary to examine the nature of both social and biological modes of determination explicitly and in some detail. Before doing so, however, it is useful to consider the nature and role of metaphor. Discussions of borrowing from evolutionary biology are, as I say, usually couched in terms of the natural selection metaphor, and I think it is necessary, before going further, to unpack how such applications relate to the current discussion.

Economists' discussions of metaphors, as with the practice of borrowing from other domains more generally, often include a good deal of suspect, if not clearly fallacious, reasoning. I am aware of economists arguing that if we borrow from biology we must take the latest aspect of that theory just because it is the latest. The same is often said to be the case if we borrow from physics. In order for economics to thrive, the claim runs, it is essential to copy from the cutting edge of the hard sciences.

This attitude reflects an error I shall term the *abductionist fallacy*. This is the notion that insights, methods, or theories of one domain of science or human reasoning, let me call the latter the source domain, can be abducted into another, the target domain, without prior consideration of the nature of the latter. The basic fact of the matter is that a particular theory of physics or biology or whatever, even if cutting-edge stuff, has no clear relevance for the social domain if it presupposes a type of material or configuration that is entirely absent from the social realm. If, for example, certain regions of the social realm are not in any way atomistic then no matter how hard-nosed may be recent developments in atomic physics, they have no obvious automatic bearing on the regions of the social domain in question.[3]

For a metaphor or other form of abduction to be recognised as appropriate, something must be known about the target domain. This much is clear. And if the use of a metaphor is to prove successful as a means of illuminating the target domain it must generate new lines of analogous, and other forms of, reasoning in this domain. It will be expected, then, that once the categories in question have been abducted, they will take on their own meanings in the new context, i.e. meanings that are not wholly the same as those they carried in the source domain.

How exactly does metaphor work? I think we now know enough about the primary workings of metaphor (see e.g. Boyd 1993; Lewis 1996; 2000b; Soskice 1985; Soskice and Harré 1982) to appreciate how they facilitate understanding and knowledge development. They do so, in essence, by making connections between two domains which hitherto may not have been recognised as having parallels. And they do so, in effect, by way of revealing that an object or feature in the source domain (the vehicle of the metaphor) and an object or feature in the target domain (the tenor) are both tokens of the same type, or each a concretisation of the same more abstract object.[4]

If, for example, we say John is a pig, we are suggesting there is a more general or abstract class of objects of which John and a pig are both tokens or particular sub-types. In this example the class may be of all creatures disposed to eating in a particular fashion. If we say that Jane is a donkey, we may in fact be meaning to suggest that Jane, like the donkey, is a special case of objects that are slow moving.

In these brief illustrations I use the qualifier 'may' in giving the noted interpretations just because the exact meaning will depend on context. The person formulating the metaphor for Jane may be wishing to imply not that Jane is slow like a donkey but stubborn in the manner that donkeys very often are. When John is described as a pig it may be because he has been sun-bathing and is (like certain varieties of pig at least) pink all over (although for this, references to strawberries and lobsters seem more common). In this particular case the relevant type-class is all pink objects. Use of metaphor capturing one token of this type, i.e. a pink object, signals that the tenor or target object of this metaphor is also a token of this type i.e. is something that is pink. The particular nature of intended abstract conception or type, though, is something which can be determined only from context.

Often, of course, the context will be a general one, so that a wide body of people can interpret the metaphor in the manner its formulator intended. If, for example, it is said that trading is stagnant the general class is presumably that of all things where movement of activity is feasible but hardly happening. If it is said that prices have reached their ceiling the general class is presumably anything that has an upper limit and has reached it.

Metaphor works, then, by connecting objects or aspects, etc., previously regarded as unconnected, by showing them both to be special cases of the same general thing, to be tokens of the same type.

In making this connection, metaphor can indicate a possible model for the target object based on the object in the source domain. It allows us to set up a generic system, using insights from the source domain, which possesses the potential to provide lines of development in the target domain.

If we turn to the category of evolution, specifically, the first thing we can note is that were we to understand evolution quite generally as a form of change or development (as some do seem to) it need not be a metaphor for social processes at all. On this conception social processes simply are evolutionary.[5]

Rather, biology becomes a more interesting source of ideas or resources, including metaphors, once we contemplate the suggestion that some social processes are evolutionary in a more particular sense, and specifically in accord with the idea of natural selection. Here, as we will see in due course, the idea of natural selection *is* a metaphor. The implicit intuition or hypothesis is that certain 'natural selection' mechanisms in the source or biological domain, and aspects of processes in the target or social domain, are indeed both tokens of the same more abstract type.

But here we are jumping ahead of ourselves. My purpose with this slight detour was merely to clarify the role played by metaphor (or what I take to be its primary role). Metaphor as with any form of abduction from one realm to another requires appropriate conditions. As indicated earlier, in order to borrow usefully from biology in social theory, we need to ensure sufficient commonalities between biological and social material. Our discussion of metaphor enables us to reinterpret that need as one for a general model of which there are both social and biological sub-types or tokens.

Advantages of the evolutionary model for social understanding: a preliminary orientation

Now, in embarking on the task of identifying relevant commonalities between the nature of biological and social materials, if any, we do not start from a position of complete ignorance of course. One very obvious (if rarely explicitly elaborated) reason for the prevailing optimism that the study of the biological realm can provide insights of relevance for analysing the social, is that both worlds comprise open (i.e. highly unpredictable) and dynamic systems. In other words, there is a very general class of systems, namely those that are open and dynamic, of which the social and the biological are both immediately recognised as tokens. Let me elaborate.

The nature of social material

Certainly the social world can be recognised as an open, dynamic process. Indeed, according to the transformational model of social activity which I have defended at length elsewhere (Lawson 1997a: esp. chs 12 and 13; and see Chapter 2 above), social reality is found to be not only open and dynamic or processual, but an emergent realm, dependent upon, but irreducible to, transformative human agency, and comprising material that is structured and highly internally related, amongst other things.

More specifically, according to the transformational model, human agency, practice and social structures (including social rules, relationships, positions, etc.) are interdependent, but ontologically distinct, types of things. The social world turns on practice. In acting we both draw upon structures given to us, and contribute to reproducing and/or transforming them. Just as we usually do not acknowledge the structures we draw upon, so their reproduction or transformation is often unintended. Thus we usually speak with a purpose in mind, which is typically to convey a thought or message to someone. But the rules of grammar we draw upon are unacknowledged, and their reproduction, depending as it does upon our collective speech acts, is usually unintended.

How do social structure and agency interconnect in this transformative process? Key categories here are social positions and social relations, especially internal ones. Two objects are said to be internally related when they are what they are, and do what they do, in virtue of this relation in which they stand to one another. Examples include teacher and student, employer and employee, landlord and tenant, etc.

Now it is typically not individuals *per se* that are internally related but the positions in which they stand. The crew members of a passenger airplane have a range of duties and perks, etc. But they are not attached to the crew members personally. If one resigned and a second person were to take their place the second person would acquire access to the same positioned obligations and so forth as the first possessed. The same is even more clearly true of the passengers. As passengers they have rights and obligations. But as soon as others take their place these rights and obligations, etc., transfer. They do so because they are attached to positions the passengers occupy. All of us, choose, or (perhaps more typically) are allocated to, a multitude of positions (teacher, student, employer, employee, parent, child, European, Asian, old, young, male, female, salesperson, customer) each associated with a range of rule-conditioned obligations, rights, duties and prerogatives, etc., and related to other positions to which our practices are oriented. It is in virtue of our being slotted into social positions that we access social structures, and through acting according to position-related rights, obligations and interests that the social world is continually reproduced and/or transformed.

On this conception, then, the social world emerges as an interrelated network of dynamic totalities, of internally related processes. Practice, as I say, is the key to social being. Social structure depends on human agency, and it is through human practice that specific structures are continually reproduced and transformed. This inherently dynamic and totalising human agency-dependent process, wherein social structure is both condition and consequence of action, I repeat, is the 'transformational model of social activity'. The central point for the moment, though, is that the social system is found to be intrinsically dynamic and open.

The biological model and mainstream economics

The same, of course, can be said of the biological realm. Indeed, a factor that spurred the development of evolutionary biology was precisely an acknowledgement that the biological realm too comprises dynamic and open systems. Such an assessment did not always prevail.[6] But the view that life on earth is a continuous process of transformation is by now sufficiently widely accepted that I shall not defend it here. Rather, my point is simply that the recognised successes of biological evolutionary models in addressing open and dynamic systems gives some immediate credibility to the idea that biological models can prove of relevance in some way in facilitating the analysis of social phenomena.

Certainly biological models are seen to have an immediate *prima facie* advantage over the competing mechanistic models of modern mainstream economics. For the latter are concerned with basically static or stationary scenarios. At best, these mechanistic models conceptualise change as exogenous shocks to systems (albeit to systems which respond by tending to re-equilibrate), or some such. Mostly, modern mainstream economics concerns itself with identifying positions and set-ups in which agents lack any incentive to change what they do. In comparison, as I say, evolutionary theory was developed to explain an intrinsically dynamic order, to account for processes of relatively continuous change. It is an explanatory theory with a potential purchase on any system recognised as being fundamentally open to the future.

If I appear to be labouring the point here, it is because these parallels between the two spheres, the social and the biological, seem to be less than always fully recognised. Rosenberg, for example, concludes 'that Darwinian theory is a remarkably inappropriate model, metaphor, inspiration, or theoretical framework for economic theory' (1994b: 384). And his reservations boil down basically to one: evolutionary models in biology do not predict well:

> My pessimistic conclusions reflect a concern shared with economists who have sought comfort or inspiration from biological theory. The concern is to vindicate received theory or to underwrite new theory against a reasonable standard of predictive success. Few of these economists have noticed what the oppo-

nents of such a standard for economic theory have seen, that evolutionary theory is itself bereft of strong predictive power.

(Rosenberg 1994b: 384)

Once we take a serious look at the nature of social material, however, we can see that evolutionary theory's lack of predictive power is no objection at all. Successful prediction presupposes closure, whereas the social system is found to be, like the biological realm, open and seemingly insusceptible to many, if any, scientifically interesting local closures, at least of the causal sequence sort. If the nature of the social realm is such that the successful prediction of social outcomes is unlikely, then to adopt methods premised on the necessity of achieving predictive accuracy is to abandon or ignore insights from ontology, to commit the epistemic fallacy. *Prima facie* the biological model gives *a posteriori* grounds for hope just because the social system is an open, mostly non-teleological, system of the sort with which evolutionary methods can in principle cope. In fact, I suspect it is this particular feature of the biological model that, implicitly at least, accounts for its current attractiveness to heterodox economists.

Natural selection

But this shared concern of the two sciences with open dynamic systems cannot be all of the story if the biological evolutionary model is to prove useful to social science. After all, we already have the transformational model of social activity in modern economics and social theory more widely. Biological evolutionary theory must provide something more if it is to enable social theorising to go further in some context.

As already signalled, that 'something more' with which many economists are interested appears to be bound up with the metaphor of natural selection. In economics there are already plenty of contributions claiming to show how order of sorts in society could come about (solely) by way of conscious (human) intervention or design. Biology deals with situations that equally are ordered in some sense, but where the form of order in question has not been brought about intentionally, i.e. by conscious design. This is a radical achievement undermining the idea of a benevolent prior design in history. And it is this insight, I suspect, that provides the relevant motivation for, and context of, seeking to apply the biological evolutionary metaphor in modern economics.

Actually this is not quite correct. I detect two motivations (at least) to the quest for borrowing from others. The first, the one I am myself inter-ested in here, is a desire to understand and explain social reality, to be realistic, to seek for truth. But I cannot deny (and indeed have already acknowledged) that some contributors give a higher priority to drawing on the theories and practices of cutting-edge naturalistic sciences just because they are revered for being more naturalistic and/or 'cutting edge'. I return to this motivation towards the end of the chapter. For the time being I concentrate on the issues before us, accepting that the primary goal is social understanding including explanation. This, of course, is something I take largely for granted in arguing for an ontological turn throughout this book.

To return to the central argument, I am concerned here specifically with the relevance to the social realm of the specific Darwinian model of 'natural selection'. Although the task of demonstrating that the characteristics of openness and dynamics are common to biological and social domains is fairly straightforward, that of determining whether insights systematised as the natural selection mechanism in evolutionary biology have parallels in the social realm requires a good deal more work.

A clear route to addressing such matters is to retroduce an appropriate (see below) general model of which the biological natural selection conception can be seen as a token, a general model which can in due course be examined for its applicability to social phenomena. In truth, however, there is no need to defer to a general model at all (even if this is the way metaphor works). All that is necessary is that the essential components are distilled from any biological natural selection example. The question I need to pose is merely whether these essential elements carry over to the socio-economic realm. However, by viewing them as features of a general model of which any biological example is viewed as a token, there is, I believe, less scope for confusion as to what is going on. In any case this will be my strategy here. I will consider a biological example, distil out the components essential to a natural selection mechanism and interpret these as features of a general model of which the specific (biological) example considered is a token. I will examine whether economic tokens of it are also feasible.

As a first step on this path, then, let me very briefly now consider a particular example of the biological model. I know that such examples are familiar enough to many modern economists, especially those working in the (old) institutionalist tradition. But I go through one here anyway partly for completeness, partly to convey my understanding of a natural selection process (there are of course competing understandings and emphases) and partly to keep the discussion focused not only on abstract models but also real-world processes.[7]

A biological example: the beaks of Darwin's finches

A well documented example that will serve my purposes concerns 'Darwin's finches' (so called because they were originally studied by Darwin), a group of finches inhabiting the relatively isolated Galápagos islands (visited by Darwin for five weeks during his voyage on HMS

Beagle). I focus, in particular, on a relatively recent episode in the process of evolution in sizes of their beaks.

The evolutionary episode in question took place on the specific island of Daphne Major between 1973 and 1978. It is an episode that has been documented by various scientific observers living on the island at the time (see e.g. Weiner 1994). Conditions were such that just about all the finches on the island were individually 'known' to these observers.

In the first four years of this period, fairly lush environmental conditions prevailed on Daphne Major. In particular, the rains fell in the early part of each year allowing seed-bearing plants to grow and attendant insects to flourish. There was thus a plentiful supply of food for birds produced in the early part of each year, and most of the finches were observed to survive the remainder of the year, whatever the conditions.[8] However, after the first week of January 1977 little rain fell for the rest of that year. Throughout this period the total mass of seeds on the island declined, and the average size and hardness of the seeds that remained uneaten increased steadily.[9] Hundreds of finches died.[10] Notably, those finches which survived were the bigger-beaked birds capable of cracking open the larger harder seeds that remained.[11] Mostly these were males, the average female beak (and body) having been smaller. In any case, following the drought the birds which survived and were able to mate were those birds which were distinguished within the original population by having larger beaks. And subsequently the offspring of the survivors were found also to possess big or deep beaks, typically about 4 or 5 per cent larger than those of their ancestors in the population of a few years earlier.[12]

In short, the result was evolution by way of a process of natural selection. The period saw a shift in the environment that 'favoured' (in a relative sense) those finches with larger beaks. Larger beaked finches survived the environmental shift, and because their offspring inherited their parents' (larger) beak size, an evolutionary change was observed in the space of just a few years.[13]

Towards a general evolutionary model

So what are the essential features of the natural selection story here? What components are essential to this biological explanation of the mechanism of change or evolution via natural selection? Alternatively put, which abstract model(s) lies behind and systematises this specific illustration and others like it? What is essential to any (class of) model(s) for which the natural selection process whereby the beaks of finches evolved is a token example? Clearly there are several essential components to include.

A first feature of the explanation to retain is that it deals, at some level, with a *population* of individuals of a particular type (finches) and an aspect of the finch's environment or situation (food). Notice that the latter is indeed only an aspect. Finches need water, air, warmth and a host of other factors to survive. The environmental factor of selective causal influence here is food in the form of seeds in a context where substitutes are hard to come by.

The existence of *variety* of some sort within the relevant population is a second essential feature of this form of explanation. In the case of Darwin's finches the variety included size of beak. For, trivially, in order that finches with larger-than-average beaks were able to perform in a relatively successful manner, there clearly had to be finches with larger-than-average beaks present in the original population. Notice, then, that for a natural selection evolution story, the individuals of the population possess both traits that are essential to their qualifying as members of the relevant populations, and traits which differentiate them within that population.

A third essential feature of the explanation is that a mechanism of *reproduction* (or replication or inheritance) is included as part of the explanation. The story told could not count as an evolutionary one, as an explanation of the rise to prominence of the bigger-beaked finch in successive generations, if size of beak was something that the finches did not reproduce through their offspring. Relatedly, we have a conception of lineage here, a spatio-temporal sequence of entities in which later ones are in some sense descended from, and causally produced by, earlier ones.[14] Although over the period in question earlier generations of finches on the island had smaller beaks on average than later ones, they were still finches. There is a sense in which the bigger-beaked finches evolved out of, and constituted an evolution of, finches.

The specification of a mechanism whereby there is interaction between individual and environment is a fourth essential feature of the explanation. This is a mechanism whereby certain members of the population (with specific features) are *selected*. Following Hull (1981), I shall use the term *interactors* to refer to the entities in which interaction between the environment and the individual occurs. This will typically be a different entity to that which passes on its structure in replication. The latter, following Dawkins (1976; 1978), I refer to as a *replicator*. If a mechanism of gene replication is responsible for the reproduction or replication of finches with certain features, this is insufficient to explain the rise to prominence of birds with that gene. The interaction of the whole organism with its environment is an essential feature of the causal evolutionary process. In particular, the need for the finch to eat (in an environment of seeds as food) is an essential aspect of the story. (In biology the genetic constitution of the replicating individual is referred to as the genotype, the nature of the individual or organism the phenotype.)

A fifth relevant feature of the explanatory sketch is the fact of a degree of independence between the process whereby the variety of traits is produced and the manner in which the environmental mechanism doing the selecting has come about. Such independence is essential if the model is to explain the appearance of order or 'fit' (of beak size and seed size) in the absence of design. Otherwise there is nothing that necessarily distinguishes the explanatory schema from any other as found, for example, in modern economics. Specifically, without independence it can be argued that either trait or environment is produced in order to match the other, so that the puzzle of order in the absence of design is not, after all, addressed.

Notice further that evolutionary change in line with natural selection can come about over a period of time because either, first, a new trait emerges within a relevant population, one that is found to be favoured by the existing environment, or, second, the environment shifts in a way such as to favour a trait that has long been in existence (or through a combination of these two types of development). In each such scenario, however, the *possibilities* turn on the processes generating the traits or variety, and the contribution of the environment lies in its 'selecting' amongst the particular set of features in evidence.

The PVRS model

Given that these identified elements are each essential to a natural selection story (such as illustrated by the evolving size of the beaks of Darwin's finches), all will be part of any abstract model of which the biological natural selection model can, *qua* natural selection model, be viewed as a manifestation or token.

Let me refer to any model that contains these components as a Population-Variety-Reproduction-Selection, or a PVRS, model or system. We must keep in mind that for a process captured by a PVRS model to be one of natural selection, V (variety generation) and S (selection) conditions must be to a significant extent independent. The question is, how independent? In particular, should these conditions be strictly independent of each other, or is something weaker sufficient?

To clarify matters, let me briefly consider three versions of the PVRS model distinguished according to the manner of the relation, if any, between the conditions of variety generation and those of environmental selection.

A PVRS model with variety and selection conditions strictly independent

Consider first a PVRS model in which the mechanisms influencing the variety of traits (V) and selection conditions or mechanisms (S) are strictly independent. This can be termed the polar, or neo-, or strict Darwinian version of the model.[15] This is the form of PVRS model often thought to have most relevance in modern biology.

In the case of Darwin's finches, the presumption is that the conditions which select out the bigger-beaked finches (the availability of food only in the form of difficult-to-open seeds) are strictly independent of the (genetic mutation) mechanisms bearing on the process whereby a finch with a larger beak first emerged.

The advantage of distinguishing this version of the PVRS model is that it illustrates rather clearly that, and how, a mechanism, the natural selection mechanism, can bring about the appearance of order even in the complete absence of conscious design.

A feed-backward PVRS model

Second, we can distinguish a PVRS model that allows S to feed back to, or causally influence, V. Let me refer to this version of the PVRS model as a feed-backward or S-to-V model. A biological token of this feed-backward version is the Lamarckian model,[16] a conception which (according to the manner in which it is most commonly interpreted) allows the inheritance of acquired characteristics. It proposes that acquisitions or losses, wrought through the influence of the environment, can feed back into the evolutionary process, being capable, in certain circumstances of being preserved in the 'species' (or whatever) through reproduction.

To claim Lamarckian features for the evolutionary development of Darwin's finches, would be to suppose the finches somehow acquired the advantageous feature of a larger beak directly in the process of interacting with their environment, and also somehow passed this characteristic on to its offspring.[17]

A feed-forward PVRS model

Finally we can distinguish a PVRS model which allows V to feed forward and causally affect S. Let me refer to this as a feed-forward or V-to-S version of the PVRS model.

To suppose such a model has relevance to the example of Darwin's finches would be to maintain the mutation conditions giving rise to the larger beaks somehow affected the environment of selection, i.e. the nature, or causes, of the finches' food.

As the example of the beaks of Darwin's finches perhaps illustrates, the feed-backward and feed-forward forms of the PVRS model may have comparatively little application relative to the neo-Darwinian version in the biological realm. Or at least this was conceivably so prior to human intervention. With human manipulation via genetic modification we certainly find scope for the feed-backward model. And with the intervention of humans to ensure an environment prevails in which a particular desired variety of some species thrives, the feed-forward model also has some force.

But in other realms of the biological world, the polar or neo-Darwinian model is often thought to have most relevance. Variety and selection conditions, as in the case of Darwin's finches, are frequently found to be more or less strictly independent.

The natural selection mechanism

So with which version of the PVRS model are we concerned here? Notice that although in the case of the Darwin's finches V and S conditions appear strictly independent, the degree or extent to which the strict or polar Darwinian model holds in biology is actually contested. More to the point, all we need here are the insights that relate to the natural selection mechanism. Clearly, the strict Darwinian version best illustrates the workings of the natural selection mechanism. However, the openness of the social system means that even where a Darwinian mechanism is operative it is likely to be but one mechanism amongst many affecting the outcome. Remember we are motivated here by the recognition that in an open changing world, mechanisms can exist (and in the biological realm clearly do exist) that ensure the appearance of order, the matching of part and whole, of individual and environment, even when this outcome is not the product of conscious design. All we need consider here is whether there are 'natural selection' tendencies of this sort at play in the social realm. It is no more necessary that natural selection tendencies be the whole story on any occasion of change or persistence in the social realm than in the biological realm. The question is whether such an evolutionary mechanism is ever in play, whether there exists a tendency for certain selection conditions which are broadly independent of variety-producing mechanisms to bear in any significant way upon the (sorts of) individuals of the population which come (via replication or reproduction) to dominate. The most relevant, or potentially useful version of the PVRS model to investigate further, then, just is any version in which the V and S conditions are at least relatively independent. So the strict or polar or neo-Darwinian version of the PVRS model qualifies as a special case.

Back to social processes

The task awaiting us at this point is precisely to determine whether the biological evolutionary model as conceived here does, or could, have relevance to social analysis. If we accept that the PVRS model with S and V largely independent, expresses a process which generalises the biological evolutionary model of natural selection in a manner that captures its essential features, we need now to assess whether there is any way in which it is able to be concretised usefully, i.e. be given a meaningful specific interpretation, in the social domain.

In fact, we can again be more definite here. Having accepted the (already elaborated) transformational model of social activity as capturing essential features of social reality, the specific questions we need to address are

(i)   how, if at all, does this version of the PVRS model tie in with the transformational model?; and (supposing that it does tie in)
(ii) what might this PVRS model achieve that the transformational model does not already?

The PVRS evolutionary model as a transformational model of social activity

Although the relevance of the latter question presupposes a positive answer to the former, it is nevertheless possible here to address it first. For it is already clear that *if* a PVRS model can add anything to social analysis whilst remaining consistent with the transformational model, this is because the latter, more or less by 'design', is sufficiently abstract as to encompass all (so far) observed aspects of social reproduction/transformation. The latter was determined in the course of developing a general social ontology. But if this transformational model allows that both transformation and reproduction occur, it says little about either the conditions wherein one or the other is likely to dominate, or the specifics of any processes of social reproduction/transformation. The 'natural selection' model then, if appropriate at all, will presumably indicate one specification of the transformational model. It will provide a more concrete account of how reproduction and/or transformation of specific aspects of social structure can happen.

The more fundamental question here, though, is the former one. Given what we already know about social reality, as expressed in particular by the transformational conception elaborated above, does the PVRS model, constrained to conform to the transformational model, carry the potential to illuminate the social realm at all?

As an initial orienting strategy, let me briefly recall the sort of model we are seeking. For a social-evolutionary story we require, at a minimum, some conception of a population of social individuals each with traits rendering them members of that population; a variety generation process giving rise to additional traits which differentiate members within the population; a notion of a relevant environment; a mechanism whereby individuals with various differentiated aspects are, or can be, reproduced or replicated; a mechanism whereby individuals of the population interact with their environment with different degrees of success; and an account of the process as a whole that conforms to the transformational model of social activity.

Consider, first, some likely candidates for social interactors (the social entities that interact with their environments). What sorts of individuals, if any, are various in their aspects, compete with others in social life, and ultimately are selected by the environment in which they occur? In particular, what answer to this question can be formulated that is in keeping with the transformational model of social activity? Of course, there may be many social scientific tokens. Any evolutionary framework developed here is very unlikely to be unique. Even so, it seems to me that a certain category of social phenomena does stand out more than others as a promising candidate for the set of social interactors we are looking for here. I refer to *social practices*.

Consider, for example, language use, including speech acts. Think of an international conference of academics. Although numerous languages will be spoken by the participants, especially in local restaurants and other off-conference meeting places, in the conference lecture room the practice of speaking English invariably comes to dominate (at least currently). Some participants from countries where English is not the first language, often try valiantly to get the discussion going in their own language, or in a different one to English, in some of the attendant seminars or even the main forum. But for various reasons, including, usually, the sheer number of native English speakers, and because non-native English speakers tend to speak English well, and native English speakers tend to speak other languages very poorly, the practice of speaking in English usually comes to dominate.

Notice that it is specific practices (in this case speaking in various languages) that are the individuals in competition here, not the human individuals *per se*. In my experience, the participants whose first language is not English are often in the majority at both international conferences, as well as in the power echelons of the economics profession, including in the UK and North America. It is not individuals *per se* whose first language is other than English that are squeezed out but the practice of speaking a language other than English in the public forum.

Of course, many young scholars going to an international conference for the first time will recognise this situation, and may, if their first language is not English or if their English is poor, perhaps take actions to acquire competency in speaking it. As such there is likely to be a feed-backwards aspect to the process. But in the main, language-speaking competencies are acquired independently of the constraining influences of international academic conference practices. Or at least, to the extent that this is so, the development of language practices in these conferences might be interpreted as conforming to the evolutionary 'natural selection' model.[18]

I think this example also indicates a further likely aspect of the most promising social-evolutionary framework of the relevant sort: that the environment of social selection will usually include, and often perhaps consist mainly in, the sum total of other related, including competing, social practices.

In keeping with the transformational model, then, I would suggest that the most promising, or anyway one conceivable, candidate for the social interactor is social practice, and the environment of selection includes all other social practices that are in some way related or connected to that population of practices that constitutes our primary focus. Interaction with the environment just is human interaction.

What sort of thing or aspect might be interpreted as a social replicator, the entity that passes on its structure in replication? The answer that fits most easily with the transformational conception of social activity, I suggest, is social structure, and especially social rules including norms and conventions.

Think again of the practice of language use, say of French. This is governed by the structure of rules, etc., that make up the French langauge. These govern (though do not determine) speech acts. They are also reproduced just through people speaking French. In a manner characteristic of many social practices, this drawing on rules of language in speech acts is sooner or later performed habitually.

Consider as a further example the (methodological) practices which dominate the modern economics discipline. Elsewhere (see Chapter 10) I argue that the twentieth-century rise to prominence of the practices of formalistic-deductivist economics warrants a social-evolutionary explanation along the lines of the PVRS model. Attempts to mathematise the discipline had been in place long before mathematical economics rose to dominance. The interactor here is the practice of attempting to render the study of social phenomena mathematical. The replicator just is the belief or (as some view it) 'convention' or 'cultural norm' (see Chapter 10) that mathematics is a fundamental component of all science and serious study. The rise to prominence of mathematical economics did not reflect any obvious breakthrough in terms of its relative explanatory performance (compared to that of other approaches). Rather, it reflected a shift in the environment of academic practices more widely. Prior to the period in question, realisticness was a goal of all mathematical enquiry. With the turn of the twentieth century, mathematics became disconnected from models of sciences like physics (the mechanics model). Indeed, the need for any kind of interpretative orientation to mathematics became much reduced as the idea of 'mathematics for its own sake' became widely accepted. This removed the constraint (earlier strongly felt by Walras and others) that mathematical models in economics needed to be realistic, and allowed the mathematisation tendency in economics fuller sway. This change in the academic environment removed factors that previously were selecting against scientific research practices underpinned by the belief or convention that mathematics is an essential component. The shift in question thus allowed the latter mathematical practices more scope to become pervasive and even (as it eventually turned out) dominant. Of course, this evolutionary mechanism was never the whole story (and others are discussed in Chapter 10), but it appears to have been an important element of the relevant historical process nonetheless.

The above example, explored in some depth in Chapter 10, focuses on the mathematising tendency in economics as one set of practices within the population of all research practices. Because the explanatory puzzle is the varying fortunes, and indeed survival, of the mathematising tendency (whatever its form), the emphasis there is on environmental selection.

I might note, however, that if we narrow our perspective, the wide-ranging set of mathematising practices within economics can be construed as a population in its own right. And if we were to focus on this population as a candidate example of a selection process in the social realm, the interest would likely fall more on processes of incremental adaption, i.e. on the question of how this project has evolved over time. The likely or candidate replicators now appear to be (or to include) the enduring or core concepts, theories or methods (e.g. supply and demand analysis, general equilibrium, econometric method) underpinning the array of competing substantive contributions that are manifest. Such a hypothesis, though, is not something I shall explore further here.[19]

Disanalogies between evolutionary biology and evolutionary social science

If the above considerations are suggestive of the possibility that, and perhaps indicative as to how, the natural selection PVRS model may be concretised in the social domain, the transformational model is also especially useful as an aid to identifying some significant disanalogies between the biological and social realms.

Most obviously, it is only through the medium of human agency that variation is produced in the social realm, and that reproduction/replication and selection occur. Aspects of social structure may be reproduced by (collections of) individuals both over time, through these individuals repeatedly drawing on them (and adopting practises which presuppose and indeed manifest them), and also across people at a point of time, through (possibly sub-conscious) imitation, and so forth. Social systems are neither naturally reproduced nor self-reproducing. Rather such reproduction or transformation as occurs is the result of capable human beings purposefully going about their daily lives and tasks, interpreting themselves, their purposes and the social order in very definite ways, and continually interacting with (including copying) others. Although much of what occurs is unintended and perhaps misunderstood, intentionality is far more significant in the social than the natural domains. Human intentional activity is always the medium of both social reproduction and transformation.

The distinctiveness of the natural selection or biological evolutionary model

A further obvious difference between the social and the biological is that, whatever may be the precise relation between variety generation (V) and selection conditions (S) in the biological realm, these sets of conditions are likely more often to be interdependent or connected in the social (if and where they occur in the social realm at all). We need only think of the impact of market research, or indeed of almost any form of forward thinking or planning, to recognise that feed-backward linkages will have some force in the social domain, that selection conditions affect the variety produced. And we need only think of advertising, and then any form of persuasion, including use of power relations, to recognise the relevance of the feed-forward model in the social domain, to see how variety generation conditions can come to affect the environment of selection.

Indeed, and as I have already emphasised, it is precisely because of this contrast between conditions in the biological and those in social domains that reflection on the biological realm, and specifically the natural selection model, proves so useful to social explanation. For such reflection helps clarify the nature of a mechanism whereby order can be produced, whereby a matching of individual and environment (or part and whole) can emerge, that is not at all the result of conscious design.

Of course, just as social processes will rarely conform to the strict or neo-Darwinian model (which would mean that human practices were entirely autonomous of human intentionality – though see the discussion on 'memes' below) so they will not be purely or strictly Lamarckian or backwards-determining (the functionalist-deterministic mistake of modern mainstream economics) nor conforming to a polar feed-forward or forwards determining model (the voluntarist or perhaps environment-as-putty model).

Nor should we expect that, if and where evolutionary features of a social process are identified, they are bound, or necessarily likely, to persist. Even where V and S conditions exist in a social process and are found at some point to be to a degree independent, it cannot be presumed that one and the same relation between V and S must hold throughout. That is, although environmental selection may have made a difference to the structure of the population over a period of space-time, this in itself is no guarantee that such a selection process will continue. Indeed, the past effects of any such mechanism in the social realm will likely provide a spur to power struggles, or to developments in technology, etc., designed purely to bring such a process under increased conscious control. It all depends on the situation.

Such considerations, then, lead us to anticipate that the natural selection biological model may well prove useful to social analysis. But if so, we can also anticipate that anything which can reasonably count as social-evolutionary explanation of the relevant (natural selection) sort will typically identify modes of interaction or influence between conditions of variety generation and of selection that are only relatively independent. In order to understand a social process adequately it will likely also be necessary to identify patterns of accommodation and rejection, of harmonious reinforcement and tension, between 'individuals' and the environment. The strict separation of both modes of replication and interaction, and modes of mutation and selection, often thought to characterise the biological realm, give way, in the social realm, to processes of greater or more obvious causal interdependency and interpenetration. Indeed, in the end the contrast between the evolutionary and many other social explanatory scenarios may be one largely of degree rather than kind.

Evolutionary explanation as a limited epistemological case

Having, I think, found qualified support for the thesis that borrowing from evolutionary biology carries the potential to be of some use in the social realm, depending on context, I want (like many before me, if not necessarily for the same reasons) also to sound a note of caution. For if there is reason for supposing that successful social-evolutionary explanation remains always a possibility, depending on context, the transformational model which helps us properly to see this also indicates that the evolutionary model is unlikely ever to be the whole story. It may even be a rather small aspect of the total picture.

A fuller story (at the relevant level of abstraction) is provided precisely by the realist transformational model of social activity. Its scope of coverage includes merely developmental (including wholly planned) forms of change, forms of emergence, acts of whim, and so on. Indeed it includes forms of change where, amongst other things, there is either no variety in a population, or no meaningful concept of an identifiable environment playing a selecting role.

One difference between the transformational model and specific versions of the PVRS model is of vital significance here. This is a contrast not between their particular specifications but in the ways in which, in the social domain, the two explanatory models are derived or supported. The transformational model (unlike the PVRS model) has been derived in an *a posteriori* manner to explain highly generalised features of social experience (e.g. the prevalence of routinised forms of behaviour, segmentation of practices followed by different types of individuals, and so forth – see Chapter 2). It has been derived by inferring (by way of transcendental argument) what the world must be like for generalised social phenomena to be in evidence. In other words it has been derived by considering the social realm directly. This contrasts with the manner in which the PVRS model has been derived, which is by way of abstracting from the natural selection model found to achieve explanatory successes in biological science. The relevance of the PVRS model to social analysis is thus always open to question, a matter to be assessed in context. In other words, the sustainable reason for focusing on the 'natural selection' model in the social domain is the possession of some *a posteriori* ground (turning, I have argued, on our understanding of the nature of social reality and seeing parallels between it and the material of the biological realm) for suspecting there *may* be some scope for its successful application to social phenomena.

The danger for 'natural selection' thinking which draws on insights from biology, then, is of universalising *a priori* what is but a particular insight, a set of principles, whose relevance in the social realm is found *a posteriori* to be highly dependent on context. I am not suggesting the PVRS model cannot have relevance in the social domain; indeed I have suggested some likely applications above. Obvious further cases to study for purposes of uncovering an evolutionary story are social processes where structures and practices are found *a posteriori* to be relatively enduring but wherein the outcome is not obviously a success story by any absolute, or even necessarily very wide, set of criteria. Possible candidates for social-evolutionary explanations of this sort are (aspects of) some institutions (i.e. of structured processes of interaction that reveal a degree of space-time durability and are recognised as doing so – see Lawson 1997a: 165, 317–18; this volume, Chapter 8 below), as well as, or including, certain routines and habits, as well as some seemingly locked-in (additional, including technological) structures that will likely be bound up with the development of institutions and/or habits.

However, here I want to emphasise that, promising though such candidates may seem, we have not uncovered grounds for any insistence on, or universalisation of, the 'natural selection' evolutionary model. I repeat that to insist without investigation or argumentation that such an approach is everywhere relevant is to promulgate a reductionist *a priori* methodological injunction, on a par with methodological individualism, or deductivism.

My concern here, of course, is to urge the abandoning of all *a priori* injunctions where this is feasible, and to turn, instead, to trial-and-error experimentation as seems reasonable, but also to any approach which includes, as an essential element, the endeavour to fashion methodological principles in the light of social ontological insights obtained *a posteriori*.

Economics and metaphor

Why are reductionist tendencies of the sort I have just noted as prominent as they are in economics? One possible reason for them is the earlier noted belief, seemingly growing in popularity in some quarters, that economics, or the study of social phenomena in general, must borrow wholeheartedly from some other discipline, and, in particular, that it must draw wholesale on metaphors which connect it to other more naturalistic (and especially 'cutting edge' or anyway currently fashionable) developments. This belief is apparently supported by a perception that economics has historically been driven by an attraction for the mechanistic metaphor. The coupling of this latter perception with an assessment that the discipline needs to be brought up to date encourages the idea that the immediate task is to replace the mechanics metaphor with another drawn perhaps from biological, cyborg, or some other science.

Actually, I believe the historical conception of economics as having been driven by mechanistic ideals or the metaphor of mechanics (an orientation often disparagingly attributed in turn to 'physics envy') is largely misleading. The drive to mathematise has always been the more dominant concern (see Chapter 10). It just so happens that the sorts of mathematical methods economists have pursued rest on an implicit mechanistic (essentially atomistic) ontology, thus encouraging mechanistic substantive conceptions.

Further, I think it is important to recognise that when the likes of Marshall, Penrose and Schumpeter make reference to biological models they are concerned not with any necessity to adopt metaphors *per se*, but with the possibility of achieving the goal of a more realistic account of social reality thereby.

Of course, if I am suggesting that it is inaccurate to portray the competition over metaphors as essential to the history or the scientificity of economics, I do not deny that the employment of metaphor has often been, and will continue to be, useful. Rather I maintain only that the usefulness of any particular metaphor to any science is something to be determined empirically, and relates to its appropriateness to the nature of the material under analysis.

Memes and memetics

Still there is undeniably, at present, a wish on the part of some economists to be seen to be abreast of state-of-the art science, or of branches of it most recently in fashion. Now as it happens there appears to be a somewhat imperialistic tendency emanating from elsewhere, and specifically evolutionary psychology, ready to embrace this particular disposition. I refer to the project of memetics. Indeed some readers may wonder why the discussion so far has made (almost) no reference to it. One reason is simply that it is not clear from the literature that very many economists are aware of memetics anyway. So if achieving a short cut in my argument were the goal it is not obvious that reference to memetics would help.

But there are other reasons why I have not connected with the relevant literature before this point. Whilst I believe there may be value in the category at the centre of this project, namely the *meme*, memetics is seemingly most ardently promoted by those who give the appearance (whatever qualifying asides are also tagged on) of seeking to achieve two questionable forms of reduction. The first is a reduction of the natural selection mechanism to the achievements of the 'selfish replicator'. The second is a reduction of the study of society and culture to (aspects of) evolutionary biology or psychology. If this assessment is at all accurate, I do indeed wish to maintain a critical distance. For these tendencies, and particularly the latter, are of just the sort that I have been cautioning against throughout. Let me quickly elaborate.

The term meme derives from the writings of the evolutionary biologist Richard Dawkins, in particular *The Selfish Gene* (Dawkins 1976) and *The Blind Watchmaker* (Dawkins 1986). Having introduced the idea of a *replicator* as anything of which copies are made, i.e. a feature which passes on its structure in replication, and accepting that genes are the replicators of biology, Dawkins asks if there are replicators in other domains. He suggests there are. These are units of cultural transmission or imitation:

> We need a name for the new replicator, a noun that conveys the idea of a unit of cultural transmission, or a unit of imitation. 'Mimeme' comes from a suitable Greek root, but I want a monosyllable that sounds a bit like 'gene'. I hope my classicist friends will forgive me if I abbreviate mimene to *meme*.
>
> (Dawkins 1976: 192)

Memes then are social replicators. In fact they are bits of information which replicate between minds as individuals communicate. Dawkins writes of 'tunes, ideas, catch-phases, clothes-fashions, ways of making pots or of building arches' (1976: 192).

One specific item that may appear to qualify as a meme, so understood, is the already discussed cultural wisdom or belief that for research work to count as scientific (or substantial or serious) it must take a mathematical form. 'Mathematics is essential to science'. This idea, though false as a claim about reality (see Chapter 1), is one that is nevertheless easy to grasp and to believe (especially given the remarkable and continuing achievements of mathematics more widely). Many people (especially those who labour under the two-part impression that mathematics is merely a language, and any language is somehow neutral in scientific work) view the idea (that mathematical methods be always used in science) simply as a (scientific) convention. And as we shall see in Chapter 10, this apprehension of the role of mathematics has long been an element of Western culture.[20]

Of course the idea (or convention) that science requires mathematics is sufficiently abstract to have high fidelity, where accepted. And it is replicated as the practices, methods and theories it conditions are reproduced and transformed over time (and is implicit in, and grounding, the content of textbooks, research papers, lectures and the like). The basic belief or convention involved does not literally copy itself. Certainly it is not copied unaided by human beings. But then nor do genes replicate themselves unaided, certainly not outside the laboratory.[21] Moreover, if replication does depend on human agency, continuity of the kind achieved is not a matter of simple individual volition. The options available to economists are both informed and constrained by the current practices of the academy, as well as accepted canons of knowledge, and curricula. And for mathematical economists the goal is not to reproduce the basic convention as such; mostly the latter is an implicitly accepted belief serving as a means to an end. The perceived goal is a new theorem, or a stable econometric relationship, or some such. But in doing such work and displaying it, the relevant 'copy me' message is communicated to all would-be academic economists nevertheless.

As I say, it is conceivable that we have here an example of a meme. But I am not sure, and I leave it for memeticists to decide. My hesitation in embracing memetics stems, first of all, from a perception that its proponents mostly employ a rhetoric which implies acceptance of the view that the replicator is the prime mover in all that happens. Environmental selection (if it is to happen) 'requires' some reproduced entities to work on. In the case of the finches, for example, reproduction and selection are clearly influenced in an essential way by the nature of the birds themselves (the phenotypes). It is not just down to their genes *per se* (the genotypes or replicators). Dawkins, however, appears often to suggest that, because there is always a genetic contribution to the form, behaviour and reproduction of any phenotype and because the contribution is inherited, the gene is therefore the unit on which selection must act. Dawkins includes numerous qualifications to such an interpretation in his writings. But the thrust of the argument is clearly that everything of functional importance and complexity is an adaptation fashioned by natural selection working only for the benefit of selfish replicators, that is, in the biological realm, for the 'selfish gene'.

Transposed to the social realm, the selfish replicator become the selfish meme. To quote Dawkins again:

> When we look to the evolution of cultural traits, and at their survival value, we must be clear whose survival we are talking about. ... A cultural trait may have evolved in the way it has, *simply because it is advantageous to itself.* ... Once the genes have provided their survival machines with brains that are capable of rapid imitation, the memes will automatically take over. We do not even have to posit a genetic advantage in imitation.
>
> (Dawkins 1976: 214–15, emphasis added)

Contributors to memetics appear mostly to accept this perspective, and write of people being victimised by 'viruses of the mind' (Dawkins 1993; Brodie 1996). Thoughts think themselves.[22] Just as, for Dawkins, our bodies are lumbering robots for our genes, so our brains become lumbering robots for our memes, the latter being an evolutionary agent that evolves in accordance solely with its own interests.

Now, on the account defended throughout this book human beings are, amongst other things, intentional subjects. But further, the social realm is not just the result of mental processing by humans. Society is not even made up of people. Rather it is a realm of emergent phenomena comprising social relations of powers, institutions, positions, rules, processes and much more. Culture does not exist only in human minds. What many memeticists appear to lack is serious insight into real social processes, and of how human (intentional) agency and structure interact.

Above (and in Chapter 10) I suggest that the enduring dominance of formalistic deductive economics may involve natural selection tendencies. Here, then, I am acknowledging the possibility that this process (specifically the selection of practices which presuppose the replicator belief or convention 'mathematics is essential to science') constitutes an example of memetics. But if this is indeed thought to be the case, I must emphasise that in attempting to explain how the convention in question is reproduced I do not enquire (or write of) what this convention does for itself, or even what we do for it (which is seemingly the set of questions posed, or stance taken, by most memeticists). Rather I take for granted that, amongst those individuals who seek to mathematise the study of social phenomena, a central motivation is the attainment of improved understanding or scientific advance, or at least gratification in the form of scientific status. In other words, my argument is that the pursuance of mathematical economics is caused *not* by a self-interested, or selfish, parasite in our minds, but by (understandably) mistaken assessments of the nature and goals of science on the part of its human protagonists. It is because the proponents of mathematical economics are often mistaken in their views concerning the necessity of mathematics, and can be shown to be so, that it is worth engaging with them in order to effect a change (or at least to influence those thinking of joining in with the mainstream project).

Herein, then, lies one reason why I have not linked into the literature on memes from the outset (and am still cautious about doing so). If I have misinterpreted the intentions of memeticists here (and I do acknowledge the numerous tagged-on qualifications that are to be found in the relevant literature, here and there), I suspect the problem lies as much in the way the project is mostly presented as in this reading.[23]

But actually, there is a yet stronger reason for my hesitancy here. This is the universalising and reductionist orientation taken (and even trumpeted) by many of those who contribute to the memetics programme. Whatever insight there is in the literature on memes, and I believe there is a good deal[24] (and I do not accept all the criticisms made of it),[25] a major problem is the propensity of many of its proponents to treat the approach from the outset as one that has universal bearing (even prior to any agreement amongst those working in the area over whether memes have been shown to exist – see for example the competing views of Robert Aunger and Susan Blackmore, both found in Aunger 2000 [chs 11 and 2 respectively]).

Darwin coped with abstract units of inheritance because he had a phenomenon to explain. But modern memeticists are not in the same situation. They lack not only a clear account of details of any proposed memetic explanation, but seemingly also a developed sustainable understanding of the nature of society and culture which they wish to account for. Certainly, nowhere do I find anything closely resembling the transformational model discussed above. Nor are social-ontological elaborations much in evidence at all. The driving force of the project, rather, is an apparent desire to reduce the whole of the social sciences and cultural studies (whatever the nature of the 'objects' the latter do study) to a form of evolutionary thinking.

Perhaps it is not surprising, then, to find of the contributors to a much heralded edited volume on memes (Aunger 2000), that those most committed to the memetics project turn out to be biological in inclination, whilst those most opposed to it have a background of working more in psychology and/or social theory. It is certainly noteworthy that the quest for evolutionary understanding of the social world through using the category of memes has been systematised (by Dawkins) as 'Universal Darwinism', a heading that readily conveys the impression (whatever may be the strict definition)[26] that the endeavour is not modal, i.e. concerned with seeking *a posteriori* successes, but categorical, signalling an *a priori* thesis about the scope of relevance of the model. It is in this fashion, too, that we can appreciate Dennett's idea of 'universal acid'. It is formulated in his *Darwin's Dangerous Idea* (Dennett 1995), a book which has contributed significantly to a diffusion of the memetics idea. The 'dangerous idea' in question is an abstract algorithm, sometimes called a replicator dynamic. It consists in repeated iterations of selection from among randomly mutating replicators. Couched in such terms, a specific Darwinian evolutionary process, that of natural selection, is interpreted as an entirely general phenomenon characterising not just biological material (such as DNA) but any other kind as well, allowing application of the Dennett's algorithm to anything:

> Darwin's dangerous idea is reductionism incarnate, promising to unite and explain just about everything in one magnificent vision. Its being the idea of an algorithmic process makes it all the more powerful, since the substrate neutrality it thereby possesses permits us to consider its application to just about anything.
>
> (Dennett 1995: 82)

If memetics, at least as perceived by these contributors and others, evades the charge of genetic determinism, it does so only by embracing a universalist stance on socio-cultural evolution. That is, in (correctly) rejecting the idea that evolutionary biology or genetics can explain everything, memeticists encourage the view that biology can explain the natural world and memetics can explain the rest.

As Susan Blackmore, who has perhaps contributed more than anyone to popularising the memetics project (see for example Blackmore 1999a; 1999b; 1999c; 2000a; 2000b), observes:

> The new vision is stunning ... because now one simple theory encompasses all of human culture and creativity as well as biological evolution.
>
> (Blackmore 2000b)

In the end, it is difficult to avoid gaining the impression that, so far at least, this 'stunning' feature, this potential to facilitate a theory of everything, is actually the central drive of, and dominant explanation of much of the growing support for, the current memetics project.

My own position, defended throughout this book, is that a surer path to understanding turns on an avoidance of *a priori* universalising, where feasible, and the determining of relevance *a posteriori*. Certainly I welcome cooperative interdisciplinary endeavour concerned to explore the *scope* of evolutionary, including natural selection, mechanisms. But this is quite different from agreeing in advance that socio-cultural study, including economics, should be reduced to evolutionary psychology and/or biology.[27]

Tailoring to context

To draw the chapter to a conclusion, and to return to its central argument, the basic thesis I defend is that the borrowing by economists from others can benefit from a turn to ontology. Once ontology is brought into the picture it is conceivable that little disagreement of substance will be found to remain amongst many of the imputed protagonists to the debate over the legitimacy of borrowing from evolutionary biology.

When Schumpeter argues that social phenomena 'would have to be analyzed with reference to economic facts alone and no appeal to biology would be of slightest use' (1954: 789), we can interpret him as saying that the relevance to the social realm of the (abstract PVRS model which generalises the) biological-evolutionary model can be determined only by examining directly the nature of (the relevant aspects of) the social phenomena in which we are interested. If so Schumpeter's remark need not after all involve him in the view that economics should eschew all metaphors from physical and natural sciences.

And when Penrose writes that

> in seeking the fundamental explanations of economic and social phenomena in human affairs the economist, and the social scientist in general, would be well advised to attack his problems directly and in their own terms rather than indirectly by imposing sweeping biological models upon them.
>
> (1952: 819)

this again need not be at odds with borrowing from biology. For the point being made here is merely that the external imposition of models and metaphors, without any consideration of their potential relevance to the social domain, is likely to be unhelpful.

The evolutionary natural selection model is merely a construct that carries (now *a posteriori* grounded) potential for insightful social analysis. The call to look to such evolutionary processes, where appropriate, has modal status only. The reasoned stance is to determine the relevance of any specific evolutionary claim by examining it in context. Where the interest is with natural selection mechanisms specifically, it is important to recognise that the PVRS model (i.e. the PVRS model with S and V conditions significantly independent) is not the biological natural selection model *per se*, but an abstract conception of which the biological model is a token. However, the manner of its *a posteriori* usefulness in the biological realm (i.e. the fashion of its success as a biological token) can, given what we know of the model and of the nature of the social domain, be suggestive of leads to be followed and investigated, but never imposed, in the social realm.

Two contentions are central to my argument. The more specific one is that borrowing from evolutionary biology, or indeed from anywhere, needs to be carried through in a manner informed by the perspective on the transformational model of social activity. The more general contention (of which the former is a special case) is that, in borrowing from other disciplines, economists can benefit from a commitment continually to shaping and reshaping theories or models in the light of insights obtained (and continually updated) concerning the *nature* of social reality. Indeed, I conjecture that problems of the sort that sometimes plague the discussion in question will mostly be seen quickly to dissolve once an ontological turn is effected in economics, with a greater take-up of the realist social theorising.

6

ECONOMICS AS A DISTINCT SOCIAL SCIENCE?

The nature, scope and method of economics[1]

What is economics? Specifically, what is it about, and, can it legitimately be regarded as a distinct social science? These are my questions here. They are prompted by two observations. The first is that competing, yet enduring definitions of the subject matter or goals of the discipline abound. The second is that while conceptions of the discipline of economics as a distinctive, even separate, science of social phenomena are widely held, they are rarely examined leaving any supposed basis for such conceptions unelaborated. My primary reason for pursuing these issues at this juncture is a conviction that recent developments of a broadly philosophical nature allow them to be considered afresh, and in a way that promises to be fruitful.

A background of competing conceptions of economics

A study of the contributions of those who have offered a delineation of the subject-matter and/or goals of economics reveals that (at least) three broad and enduring conceptions compete for acceptance. In the main, the object of economics, broadly conceived, is held to be the study of

1   the causes of wealth, or
2   human daily activity, or
3   the optimising decisions of human beings.

In the latter conception, optimising refers, of course, to the allocating of 'scarce resources' between competing 'ends'. Perhaps the best known representatives of each position are, respectively, Mill, Marshall (who to some degree spans the first two conceptions) and Robbins. Representative statements provided by each of these three contributors run, in order, as follows:

> The conception … of Political Economy as a branch of science, is extremely modern; but the subject with which its enquiries are

conversant has in all ages necessarily constituted one of the chief practical interests of mankind, and, in some, a most unduly engrossing one.

That subject is Wealth. Writers on Political Economy profess to teach, or to investigate, the nature of Wealth, and the laws of its production and distribution: including, directly or remotely, the operation of all the causes by which the condition of mankind, or of any society of human beings, in respect of this universal object of human desire, is made prosperous or the reverse. Not that any treatise on Political Economy can discuss or even enumerate all these causes; but it undertakes to set forth as much as is known of the laws and principles according to which they operate.

(Mill 1900: 13)

Political Economy or Economics is a study of mankind in the ordinary business of life; it examines that part of individual and social action which is most closely connected with the attainment and with the use of the material requisites of well-being.

Thus it is on the one side a study of wealth; and on the other, and more important side, a part of the study of man.

(Marshall 1986: 1)

Economics is the science which studies human behaviour as a relationship between ends and scarce means which have alternative uses.

(Robbins 1940: 16)

A surprising feature of the situation is that, at least to my knowledge, little attempt has been made in any serious fashion to reconcile such conceptions. Most especially, the third conception, focusing on the allocating of scarce resources, is regularly counterposed to the former two conceptions. This situation is particularly curious in that some overlap of the noted conceptions is immediately apparent, whilst *prima facie* all carry a degree of intuitive appeal. Yet, those economists who have elaborated a position explicitly have tended to do so by contrasting their own orientation with one or other of the alternatives rather than attempting a reconciliation or synthesis; the apparently incompatible aspects of the conceptions, rather than their complementary features, are emphasised (see e.g. Robbins 1940; Hirshleifer 1985; Hodgson 1996).[2]

My intention here, in contrast to all such approaches, is a reconciliation or synthesis of the noted three main broad conceptions held to be in competition (or to the extent that, as with Marshall, the first two conceptions are accepted as compatible, to elaborate the nature of their connection).[3] My strategy in this is briefly stated. As is well known, a striking aspect of the contemporary discipline is its significant disarray and failure by the criteria it sets itself.[4] This is a state of affairs that, in recent years, has been addressed and rendered intelligible by analyses drawing upon insights from the philosophy of social science. My goal here is simply to examine whether these same philosophical insights can in some way be brought to bear in determining a sustainable assessment of the subject-matter of economics and identifying where, if anywhere, the limits of the discipline might lie. In consequence, I turn first, in the following section of this chapter, to review briefly some of the philosophical/methodological results I have in mind before explicitly addressing in the third section the questions posed at the outset.

A conception of science: previous results

The results to which I refer are those achieved via a project systematised in the social context as *critical realism*.[5] The basic insight sustained is that, in contradistinction to the assessments and implicit premises of mainstream economics, science is first and foremost concerned not with patterns in, or with correlations of, surface phenomena but with the latter's underlying causes. In other words, science is primarily concerned not with deductivist explanation oriented to event prediction[6] but with causal explanation. The continuing problems of the contemporary discipline turn on a failure to appreciate this.[7] The reliance on 'deductivist' explanation/prediction, with its presupposition of a ubiquity of strict (including probabilistic) event regularities, or closures, is an error in that the world in general is found to be open: closures of interest to science are rare even in the natural realm, and more or less non-existent in the social domain (Lawson 1997a).

The critical realist critique of mainstream economics acknowledges the general openness of the world but demonstrates that reality is also structured, i.e. it is irreducible to (it consists in more than) the actual course of events and possible phenomena of experience. In particular, critical realism draws attention to the generalised fact of experience that event regularities of causal sequence that are known and of interest to science are mainly restricted to the natural realm, and in particular to conditions of experimental control. And it demonstrates that this observation is explicable once it is recognised that the experimental set-up is designed to insulate, and thereby empirically identify, non-empirical structures and mechanisms that (like, say, gravity) can operate in both experimental and non-experimental situations alike. In consequence, it supports a conception of science in which the search for ever stricter patterns at the level of events need not figure at all. Rather the essential move (one which is as available to social as to natural science – see below) is from the observation of manifest phenomena at any one level to the identification of the underlying structured aspects of reality by way of which the phenomena of interest are produced (see Lawson 1997a).

Some elaboration of the structured ontology thus defended in critical realism can be briefly made. The basic view is of a world composed in part of complex things and situations which, by virtue of their *structures*, possess certain *powers* – potentials, capacities, or abilities to act in certain ways. A bicycle, in virtue of its constitution or structure has the capability of facilitating a ride; gunpowder of causing an explosion; a language system of facilitating speech acts. Such powers exist whether or not they are exercised. The bike can facilitate a ride even though it always sits in the back of the shed; the gunpowder has the power to cause damage even if it is never ignited; the language system makes a conversation possible even where people choose not to speak. In many cases we can infer something of a thing's potential from a knowledge of its structure. Certainly a good deal about the powers or capabilities of rockets, planes, bridges and parachutes are inferred before any particular one is built and subsequently 'tried out'. Complex things, then, have powers in virtue of their structures, and we can investigate their structures and in some instances thereby infer something of their powers.

A *mechanism* is basically a way of acting of a structured thing. Bicycles and rockets work in certain ways. Of course they cannot act in these ways without possessing the power to do so. Mechanisms then exist as causal powers of things. Powers of structured things are usually exercised only as a result of some input: the striking of a match, the lifting and wielding of the hammer, the switching on of a computer or interacting with it, the flexing of vocal chords, the arrival of teachers and children at school or employees at the workplace. And mechanisms when triggered (where relevant) have effects. Structured things, then, possess causal powers which, when triggered or released, act as generative mechanisms to determine the actual phenomena of the world.[8]

Now, because actual events or states of affairs may be co-determined by numerous, often countervailing mechanisms, the action of any one mechanism, though real and perhaps expressing necessity in nature, may not be precisely manifest or 'actualised'. Characteristic ways of acting or effects of mechanisms which, because of the openness of the relevant system, may not be actualised, are conceptualised here as *tendencies*. It is the idea of *continuing activity* (as distinct from enduring power *per se*) that the notion of tendency is designed to capture. Tendencies, in short, are potentialities which may be exercised or in play without being straightforwardly realised or manifest in any particular outcome.

It should be clear, then, that the way in which I am employing the term tendency differs from many of its interpretations in the economics literature. A statement of a tendency, according to its primary usage here, is not about long-run, 'normal', usual, or average outcomes at the level of events.

Nor is it reducible to a counterfactual claim about events or states of affairs that would occur if the world were different. Indeed, it is not a claim about anything at the level of the actual course of events at all. Rather it is a *transfactual* statement about the typically non-empirical activity of a structured thing or agent; here transfactuals are not counterfactuals, but take us to the level at which things are going on irrespective of the actual outcome. A statement of a tendency, in other words, is not a conditional statement about something actual or empirical but an unconditional statement about something non-actual and non-empirical. It is not a statement of logical necessity subject to *ceteris paribus* restrictions, but a statement of natural necessity without qualifications attached. It is not about events that would occur if things were different but about *a power that is being exercised whatever events ensue*. It is, for example, about the gravitational field which acts on the pen in my hand and continues to do so irrespective of whether I toss the pen in the air, continue to write with it, or drop it in a vacuum.

Retroduction

It follows that the essential mode of inference drawn upon in science is neither induction nor deduction. Rather it is one that can be styled *retroduction* or *abduction* or 'as if' reasoning. This consists in the movement, on the basis of analogy and metaphor amongst other things, from a conception of some phenomenon of interest to a conception of some totally different type of thing, mechanism, structure or condition that is responsible for the given phenomenon. If deduction is illustrated by the move from the *general* claim that 'all ravens are black' to the *particular* inference that the next one seen will be black, and induction by the move from the *particular* observation of numerous black ravens to the *general* claim that 'all ravens are black', retroductive or abductive reasoning is indicated by a move from the observation of numerous black ravens to a theory of a mechanism intrinsic (and perhaps also extrinsic) to ravens which disposes them being black. It is a movement, paradigmatically, from a 'surface phenomenon' to some 'deeper' causal thing.

According to the results I am here reviewing, then, science aims at uncovering causal laws. It is concerned with identifying structures, mechanisms and the tendencies they ground, which produce, govern or facilitate phenomena at a different level. And, if the aim of science is to illuminate structures that govern surface phenomena, then *laws*, or *law-statements* are neither empirical statements (statements about experiences) nor statements about events or their regularities (whether unqualified or subject to *ceteris paribus* restrictions), but precisely statements elucidating structures and their characteristic modes of activity. From this perspective, moreover, there can be no *a priori* presumption that in the scientific explanatory endeavour there is any end to the process of revealing deeper levels of reality. If, for example, the phenomenon to be explained is copper's ability to conduct electricity well, and we locate the reason in copper's atomic structure, the latter then marks the next phenomenon to be explained, and so on. Of course, as deeper layers of reality are revealed and understood this acquired knowledge may lead us to revise our previous conceptions of any phenomenon which the deeper level explains. Thus science, in this framework, is seen to proceed via a continuing spiral of discovery and understanding, further discovery and revised, more adequate, understanding.

Different aspects of science

I turn at this juncture to elaborate a particular feature of the perspective I am reviewing, one that will prove to be significant in due course: that the scientific endeavour can be resolved into three basic components or moments. In the above brief overview I have essentially concentrated upon describing science under its *pure* or *abstract explanatory* aspect. That is, I have been considering that most fundamental aspect of science concerned with identifying hitherto unknown causal mechanisms and structures. This moment, of course, does presuppose partial regularities, elsewhere styled as *demi-regularities* or *demi-regs* (Lawson 1997a; Chapter 4 above), as its point of departure. Although strict event regularities of interest do not seem to occur in the social realm, rough and ready patterns are occasionally in evidence suggesting that *prima facie* an explanation is called for. These, typically contrastive (Lawson 1997a; Lipton 1991) demi-regs are essential if previously unknown causal factors are to be identified. The object, though, is not to stretch such demi-regs into strict regularities but to elicit their underlying causes.

The point I wish to emphasise here, however, is that there is (of course) more to scientific inference, even broadly conceived under its essential aspects, than this abstract mode of explanation. In particular there is also a second explanatory moment: the enterprise of *concrete*, or *applied explanation*. This is concerned not with the activity of identifying previously unknown causal structures, but with using knowledge (of structures and mechanisms) already obtained to explain such phenomena as have occurred. Meteorologists, for example, are widely observed to be poor at forecasting unusual weather patterns. Yet the principles underlying the relevant phenomena are well known and experimentally verified. Thus after the event these scientists are easily able to work backwards to retrodict such circumstances as must have occurred, to work out how previously identified causal mechanisms must have combined to produce the weather pattern experienced.

The third component I have in mind has more to do with practical intervention than explanation *per se*. It is immaterial for my argument whether we think of it as the practical side of science (which I shall), or of the practical application of science. Science uncovers structures, potentials and mechanisms and their modes of action, and there is plenty of scope for exploring the various aspects of these discoveries, their further hidden properties, the manner in which they can be activated, combined with other mechanisms and otherwise utilised. As indicated, this three-way partition of science into abstract explanatory, concrete explanatory and practical aspects will figure below explicitly when I come to question the nature of a science of economics.

Social science

To this point I have referred mostly to the sciences of nature. But we can be clear that the conception of science elaborated applies as much to the social realm as to the natural (Lawson 1997a). Let me note, first of all, what is understood here by the social domain designation. Quite simply I am interpreting *social* phenomena to be those which, at least in part, depend for their existence on human (intentional) agency. The social domain, then, is the realm of all such phenomena. I assume this is not contentious. Accepting this definition, the possibility of social *science* depends on their being social *structures* to uncover, i.e structures whose existence depends upon human intentional agency, underlying and influencing manifest phenomena such as human actions as well as states of affairs.

The reality of social structure, so conceived, is relatively easy to demonstrate. If we look to the conditions of human interactions, obvious candidates are rules, relationships, positions and the like, as components, and perhaps constitutive, of societies. Existing studies of all identified putative societies, whether industrial or not, couch their explanations in such terms. Such societies are *rule*-governed in language use, games, modes of exchange, etc. They are typically structured along hierarchical lines, with *positions* (kingships, tribal leaderships, teachers, studentships) occupied by specific individuals. And such positions are always defined in *relation* to others (teachers to students, tribal leaders to other tribal members, landladies/landlords to tenants); and so on. Notice that even most self-styled 'methodological individualists' do not flinch from making reference to (or at least from using the language of) social structures such as these in their contributions (see Hodgson 1988, for an assessment). Rather members of the latter group seem to be motivated by a felt need to distance themselves from others (whoever they may be) who apparently attribute emergent human properties, such as intentions and purposes, to some or other 'aggregate' or 'collectivity'.

Social structures such as rules and especially social relationships, then, figure widely in explanatory contexts. This recognition, however, is not sufficient to establish their autonomy or reality. For it may yet be suggested that such items are not real but merely 'theoretical constructs' or some such, used purely to organise our interpretations and understandings – of, say, the (routine) patterns of everyday life. In consequence, for the possibility of naturalism to be established, i.e. that the study of social phenomena can be scientific in the sense of natural science, it is necessary to demonstrate that such putative objects of scientific investigation are both irreducible and real.

An essential point here is that science employs not only a perceptual but also a causal criterion for the ascription of reality to a posited object. The latter turns on the ability of an entity whose existence is in doubt to bring about changes in material things. It is this causal criterion, and not perceiv-ability, that is satisfied by magnetic and gravitational fields. The task at hand, then, is to demonstrate that, but for society, or at least for various social structures, certain physical conditions, including actions, would not be performed. To the extent that this conditionality holds, we are justified in accepting such structures as real. And this demonstration is easily achieved. Such (intentional) human activities as speaking, writing, driving on public roadways, cashing cheques, playing games and giving lectures would be impossible without rules of language, highway codes, banking systems, rules of play and teacher/student relationships. The latter are all structures which pre-exist and make a difference to (constrain as well as enable) the sorts of activities, including their physical manifestation, which take place. Their pre-existence establishes their autonomy, just as their making a difference establishes their reality. Commons (1934) captures this property of social structures as follows:

> The business man who declines to use the banking system which has grown up in the past, the labourer who refuses to come to work when others come, may be industrious, but he cannot live in industrialised society. This is familiar enough. ... But when customs change, or when judges and arbitrators enforce a custom by deciding a dispute, or when labourers or farmers strike in order to modify a custom of business, or when a revolu-tion confiscates slaves or other property of capitalists, or when a statute prohibits a customary mode of living, or when a holding company extends an old custom into new fields – then it is realised that the compulsion of custom has been there all along, but unquestioned and undisturbed.
>
> (1934: 701)

To repeat, if it is the dependency of such structures upon human agency that marks them out as being social, it is their ability, in turn, to make a difference to (to enable as well as to constrain) physical states, or actions, that (just as with non-perceivable objects of the natural realm such as gravitational and magnetic fields) establishes that they are real.

148

In the manner just elaborated, then, the real possibility of the study of social phenomena being scientific in the sense of natural science is established. It has been achieved, in the current chapter, by way of a (form[9] of) retroductive argument from intentional agency as dependent upon social material causes (so establishing the latter's existence), which are available to be drawn upon prior to any individual act (so establishing their relative autonomy and rendering them susceptible to social investigation). That is, a retroductive argument from intentional agency establishes the *sui generis* reality and the temporal pre-existence of forms of social structure, as its necessary condition and means.

The study of social phenomena as a distinct science?

If the possibility of social science is sustained, I must immediately acknowledge that investigations of social objects will require very different methods, techniques and criteria to those employed in the natural sciences. This turns on the aspect of social structure that, unlike natural structure, it depends for its existence on human intentional agency. Thus, in the social domain, human practice and structure are interdependent. If human action is the form of social events, social structure, including rules and especially social relations, is amongst its conditions. But all social structure is in turn produced, reproduced and transformed through human practice, necessitating that structure and practice be conceived somewhat holistically as two essential, if distinct, aspects of the same process. And this particular internal-relationality[10] of social life necessitates, for its study, methods or approaches distinctive to social science.

Thus, if specific social structures acted upon are found to be enduring to a degree, the fact that such structures are dependent upon inherently transformative human agency suggests that they will be only relatively so, being faster, or more temporal-spatially restricted, than (most of) the objects of natural science. Social science, then, in a more obvious way than natural science perhaps, is necessarily historical-geographical. In addition, if by virtue of their dependency upon human agency social structures must be continually reproduced, it follows that economics is concerned with inherently dynamic matters. The terminology of *process* is thus fundamental to social science. By this I do not mean (as some do, see e.g. Langlois 1986) merely a sequence of events. Rather, process denotes here the genesis, reproduction and decline of some structure mechanism or thing, the formation, reformation and decay of some entity in time. Clearly, if society is intrinsically dynamic, social science must be alert, and its methods tailored, to this condition. Furthermore, the dependence of social structure upon intentional human agency also entails an inescapable hermeneutic moment in social science, one that may be of consequence more frequently in social science than is any comparable moment in natural science (see Collier 1994;

Lawson 1997a). In addition, the structure/agency relation signals the impossibility, in any meaningful way, of experimentally engineering closed social systems. This condition, in the absence of spontaneously occurring closed systems, necessitates a reliance upon non-predictive, purely explanatory criteria of theory development and assessment in the social sciences.

Considerations such as these clearly suggest that many social scientific methods and ways of proceeding will be irreducible to those of the sciences of nature. Thus although the possibility of naturalism (that the study of social phenomena can be scientific in the sense of natural science) has been established, the investigations of society may qualify as a separate science nonetheless (i.e. as a science with its own methods fashioned according to the nature of its specific objects). It is the first part of the preceding sentence that is most significant here, however. That is, despite peculiarities of social phenomena, the (knowable) structured and open conditions of the social realm do allow a project of investigating social forms that can be scientific in the sense of natural science. However, whether or not, or the degree to which, a successful social science is achieved, of course, is down to the local conditions and the activities of those who remain concerned with investigating substantive social issues.

To summarise, recent developments in realist social theorising have shown the 'deductivist' framework of mainstream economics, with its ultimate recourse to positing correlations of events or actualities (whether real or fictitious), to be unsustainable as a universalising orientation for social research and basically responsible for the contemporary failings and disarray of the economics discipline. The perspective, stylised here as elsewhere as *critical realism* gives reason to resist any insistance upon always pursuing (strict) event regularities of the sort in question. Rather it construes science as a fallible social process which is primarily concerned to identify and understand structures, powers, mechanisms and their tendencies that have produced, or contributed in a significant way to the production of, some identified (real) phenomenon of interest – mechanisms, etc., which, if triggered, are operative in open and closed systems alike. It is a conception in which science is characterised by its *retroductive* mode of inference, by the move from knowledge of some phenomenon existing at any one level of reality, to a knowledge of mechanisms, at a deeper level or stratum of reality, by which the original phenomenon of interest was generated.

The nature and scope of economics?: Towards a synthesis

The remainder of this chapter addresses the questions posed at the outset. Specifically, I am concerned with the nature and scope of economics and whether there are grounds for postulating a *separate* social science of economics. In pursuing these matters I draw upon the results reviewed above.

150

I noted earlier that amongst the various definitions of the nature and scope of economics which figure prominently in the literature, those formulated by Mill, Marshall and Robbins are arguably the best known and have been (and continue to be) the most influential. Certainly they are among the most considered and extensively justified formulations in the history of the subject. More importantly they seem to typify, and collectively span, the broad categories of conceptions or definitions on offer. In consequence, it seems not unreasonable to start with an examination and reconsideration of them here. They can be briefly restated. While Mill emphasises the causes of wealth, Marshall puts the focus on everyday human life and action, and Robbins emphasises scarce resources and their competing uses. All, of course, are features which fall within our conception of the social (as the domain of those phenomena whose existence depends in some part on human agency). Thus economics, if a science, is clearly a social science. The immediate question to pursue is what the discipline aims to achieve. Let me, then, consider the three formulations in question in the light of the perspective on social science established above, with a view to effecting some kind of synthesis.

In fact, formulations of the sort sustained by Mill and Marshall are easily reconciled. I have argued above that a science is concerned to explain or understand surface phenomena in terms of their underlying causes, i.e. in terms of the structures, mechanisms, powers and tendencies which produce or facilitate them. In the social realm this amounts to identifying the structural conditions, and especially social relations, that govern the surface phenomena of human activities or practice. With Mill emphasising the conditions or causes of wealth, i.e. the *explanans*, and Marshall stressing social action bound up with wealth production and use, i.e. the *explanandum*, a possible synthesis is clear, and can be formulated as follows:

> *Economics is the identification and study of the factors, and in particular social relations, governing those aspects of human action most closely connected to the production, distribution and use of wealth.*

Let this be my working definition. It can be adjusted, if necessary, in due course. Specifically, I will need to revise it when I come to enquire below into the meaning of wealth. For the time being, though, I note that the formulation derived encompasses the basic concerns of both Mill and Marshall. Marshall's emphasis is *human action*, especially that concerned with producing and using, etc., the conditions of wealth or well-being. To *explain* such action, which is Mill's emphasis, is to bring that action under new concepts, to illuminate it. From the perspective of our expanded ontology of structures and actions there is no clash or contradiction of purpose in examining both the phenomenon and its conditions. Rather, in the social context, as I have noted, each is essential to the other, so that an understanding of either requires an understanding of the whole.[11]

What of Robbins' 'economising' conception which makes no clear reference to wealth at all? Let me at this point briefly assert the manner in which I believe Robbins' notion is reconciled with the formulation derived above. With my position up front I then examine Robbins' conception in detail to indicate why I consider my reconciliation to be legitimate.

Recall, first of all, that science has been found to have several moments or aspects. Perhaps the most important is that which I have referred to as *pure* or *abstract* explanation. It arises in situations where the occurrences of partial regularities or demi-regs allow us to identify hitherto unknown causal factors. Not all events are patterned, however, and an important moment in science, one which I have termed *applied* or *concrete* explanation, consists in attempting to explain some relatively unique outcome in terms of mechanisms previously identified. The aim is not so much to identify hitherto unknown mechanisms but to understand the manner of joint articulation of known mechanisms in producing phenomena warranting explanation. It is easy enough to see that our formulation of economic science above can encompass both the pure and applied forms or aspects of explanation.

But there is a further more practical moment that is not inherently explanatory at all. This is the study of the uses to which the discoveries of science can be put. Whether we refer to this study as *practical science* or as the *application of science*, as I have already noted, is largely immaterial; either way the activity is clearly of significance. Now in the social sphere, such practical study amounts to the analysis of alternative plans or policies. It deals with alternative possibilities for action within existing structures, or the consideration of possibilities under achievable alternative structures. *And it is the examination of real possibilities for those actions concerned with the conditions of wealth or well-being, I want to argue, that is the concern of Robbins formulation.* Thus, to the extent that we wish such activities to be captured within our conception of economics *as science*, our working definition can be adjusted as follows:

> *Economics is the identification and study of the factors, and in particular social relations, governing those aspects of human action most closely connected to the production, distribution and use of wealth, along with the assessment of alternative really possible scenarios.*

A reassessment of Robbins' essay on the *Nature and Significance of Economic Science*

Now I am aware that my interpretation (or the manner of my incorporation) of Robbins' formulation will be strenuously resisted in some quarters. There are at least three reasons for this anticipation. First of all, that strand of economics which constitutes the spectacularly dominant contemporary mainstream professes very often to subscribe to Robbins' conception. Yet, in contrast to my interpretation of the formulation (which limits its scope of relevance to non-explanatory, largely pragmatic endeavours), the mainstream project (or anyway a prominent strand of it) views Robbins' definition as a cornerstone of its avowedly explanatory science of choice or rational action. Second, and perhaps more significantly, Robbins himself does not formally restrict his economising[12] conception of economics to the set of practical activities I have associated with it, but explicitly indicates an explanatory role for economics based on identifying scientific generalities. Third, in identifying this explanatory role for economics, Robbins expressly opposes any 'materialist' conception concerned with wealth creation and use, which he explicitly associates with the likes of Marshall. For each such reason my assessment or treatment of Robbins' position here may seem *prima facie* implausible or unwarranted. Let me then address the three features just identified explicitly, and indicate why they do not lead me to abandon my assessment of the import of Robbins' formulation. I tackle them in the reverse order, starting with Robbins' apparent opposition to any conception concerned explicitly with the causes of wealth.

Robbins' opposition to the 'materialist' or wealth-based formulations

There is no doubt that Robbins does view his formulation as one in opposition, rather than as a practical complement, to conceptions along the lines of those of Mill and Marshall. Indeed, even before setting out his own 'economising' conception of economics, Robbins informs the reader that it is intended as an alternative to the originally more dominant 'materialist' version concerned with the causes of wealth.

As is perhaps to be anticipated from Robbins' referencing of the alternative as 'materialist', his assessment turns on the word 'material' in his specific formulation of it. According to Robbins this definition precludes from the scope of economic study such items as the wages of musicians:

> the wages of the members of an orchestra, for instance, are paid
> for work which has not the remotest bearing on material welfare'
> (Robbins 1940: 6).

In Robbins' opinion economics is rightly concerned with the 'theory of wages' and its 'elucidations are not limited to wages which are paid for work ministering to the "more material" side of human well-being – whatever that may be' (6).

Now Robbins may indeed enquire into the meaning of 'material welfare' or the 'material side of well-being'. In fact, if we look back at the formulations of Mill and Marshall (the latter being explicitly referred to by Robbins, and quoted by him in a footnote), we see that the expression 'material welfare' is not used.[13] Rather, whereas Mill refers in general terms to wealth and its causes, Marshall makes reference only to the material *requisites* of well-being. Clearly, in the case of Marshall it is the notion of well-being that most closely resembles Robbins' notion of welfare. But, to repeat, Marshall is concerned with its material requisites, and this surely is reasonable. Even if we allow Robbins the view that playing in an orchestra constitutes 'work which has not the remotest bearing on material welfare', it is nevertheless the case that this work itself inevitably has a material aspect (including, of course, the development of the human capacities of musicianship), as does the provisioning of means for (some) people to enjoy it.

Mill, for his part, conceives wealth as 'all useful or agreeable things which possess exchange value; or, in other words, all useful or agreeable things except those which can be obtained, in the quantity desired, without labour or sacrifice' (Mill 1900: 18). This notion of sacrifice is significant here in that it resonates with Robbins' notion of scarce resources. And indeed, I think this is the key. Mill, if not always consistent, seems to be suggesting that economics is concerned with the causes of all useful or agreeable things to the extent that labour or sacrifice is involved. In other words, it is concerned with understanding the causes of the conditions of well-being once more, i.e. the means whereby ends are satisfied.

Robbins is interested with possible alternative uses of these means. There is no (inevitable) conflict here. Indeed, Mill considers defining wealth in terms of means or 'instruments' at one stage but, whilst viewing such a formulation as 'philosophically correct', shies away from it only because it 'departs too much from the custom of language'.[14] Note that although Robbins does include non-exchangeable ends in his conception of wealth, this should not confuse matters. Even if the term *wealth* is used differently by the various contributors, no party is wishing to suggest that all ends be regarded as material, let alone that it is their materiality that constitutes the subject-matter of economics. To avoid confusion, however, I adapt my own working definition of the subject to replace the term 'wealth' by 'material conditions of well-being'. My suggested formulation, then, is as follows:

> *Economics is the identification and study of the factors, and in particular social relations, governing those aspects of human action most closely connected to the production, distribution and use of the material conditions of well-being, along with the assessment of alternative really possible scenarios.*

Robbins and scientific generalisations

Even if Robbins' opposition to formulations based on the causes of wealth are misconceived, it must be acknowledged that Robbins does recognise the possibility of uncovering economic generalisations, and so of assigning to economics an explanatory role. And he connects this explanatory role to his conception of economics as concerned merely with the allocating of scarce resources. How, then, is this feature reconciled with my claim that Robbins' formulation mainly serves to ascribe to economics a practical role, that it mainly covers the practice of assessing competing possibilities? The answer to this question has several components, and is best elaborated in a sequence of steps.

First, it should be noted that Robbins, like so many economists both before him and since,[15] adopts the view that scientific generalisations take the 'event regularity' form and that scientific explanation must follow along deductivist lines. He is quite explicit about this. Thus he opens a chapter entitled 'The nature of economic generalisations' as follows:

> We have now sufficiently discussed the subject-matter of Economics and the fundamental conceptions associated therewith. But we have not yet discussed the nature of the generalisations whereby these conceptions are related. We have not yet discussed the nature and derivation of economic laws. This, therefore, is the purpose of the present chapter.
>
> (Robbins 1940: 72)

And by the end of the chapter this position is sufficiently developed to be summarised:

> In the light of all that has been said the nature of economic analysis should now be plain. It consists of deductions from a series of postulates, the chief of which are almost universal facts of experience present whenever human activity has an economic aspect, the rest being assumptions of a more limited nature based upon the general features of particular situations or types of situations which the theory is to be used to explain.
>
> (*ibid.*: 99, 100)

It must be admitted that Robbins is aware that mere correlation is insufficient to constitute a law: 'In the absence of rational grounds for supposing intimate connection, there would be no sufficient reason for supposing that history 'would repeat itself' (*ibid.*: 74). However, Robbins does not elaborate an ontology adequate for addressing the question of when such rational grounds are in place. Specifically, he does not explicitly acknowledge that natural necessity connects mechanisms *to effects which may be realised only when the mechanism acts in isolation*, which in the social realm may be not at all. In short, once we acknowledge the structured and open nature of social being it follows that this conception of scientific explanation, however qualified, is, as a general claim, misconceived.

But how does this recognition help ground my assessment that Robbins' formulation restricts economics to an essentially practical role of examining alternative social arrangements? A key factor is implicit in the very observation that the social world is open, and hardly susceptible to local closure. In other words, on this conception there are few if any scientifically interesting event regularities or laws being found.

Of course, having set out his deductivist conception Robbins cannot then easily or absolutely deny the possibility of uncovering event regularities. As is well known, most modern economists respond to the absence of such 'laws' with fictitious 'stand-ins' combined with injunctions to 'dig deeper' for invariant event regularities. But Robbins' essentially twofold response is different. On the one hand he conjectures that the only event regularities conceivable, are of a highly general nature indeed. Second, he implies that in any case most of the generalisations of economics are already known. Singly or in combination, these presumptions serve in effect to close off any (further) explanatory role for economics conceived as the science of choice or resource allocation. Let me substantiate these two claims.

Robbins and the generalisations of economics

First we can observe that Robbins is quite explicit in suggesting that scientific propositions bearing on the act of economising are all of a rather general sort. He writes:

> At the same time it must be admitted that the propositions which have hitherto been established are very general in character. If a certain good is scarce, then we know that its disposal must conform to certain laws. If its demand schedule is of a certain order, then we know that with alterations of supply its price must move in a certain way. But ... there is nothing in this conception of scarcity which warrants us in attaching it to any particular commodity. Our deductions do not provide any justification for saying that caviare is an economic good and carrion a disutility. Still less do they inform us concerning the intensity of the demand for caviare or the demand to be rid of carrion. From the point of view of pure Economics these things are conditioned on the one side by individual valuations, and on the other by the technical facts of the given situation. And both individual valuations and technical facts are outside the sphere of economic uniformity.
>
> (*ibid.*: 106)

156

In truth it is evident that Robbins is already here taking too much for granted concerning the possible generalities of social life. But he does recognise that the social realm *is* essentially open, that very little can be anticipated at a concrete level. Robbins allows that there would be some use to 'quantitative laws of demand and supply' if they were a real possibility, but recognises that such uniformities do not constitute a realistic presumption:

> No doubt such knowledge would be useful. But a moment's reflection should make it plain that we are here entering upon a field of investigation *where there is no reason to suppose that uniformities are to be discovered*. The 'causes' which bring it about that the ultimate valuations prevailing at any moment are what they are, are heterogeneous in nature: there is no ground for supposing that the resultant effects should exhibit significant uniformity over time and space.
>
> (*ibid.*: 107)

Second, if these passages indicate that, for Robbins, such regularities as might be discovered are only of a highly general nature, there are others which convey the view that the generalities of the subject, or at least (and most significantly) those which constitute its central propositions, are believed to be already known, and known with certainty. This, in fact, is the general impression given by his writing as a whole, but in places is an assessment that is borne out fairly explicitly. Consider the following statements:

> The efforts of economists during the last hundred and fifty years have resulted in the establishment of a body of generalisations whose substantial accuracy and importance are open to question only by the ignorant or the perverse.
>
> (*ibid.*: 1)

> The most fundamental propositions of economic analysis are propositions of the general theory of value. ... It would be premature to say that the theory of this part of the subject is complete. But it is clear that enough has been done to warrant our taking the central propositions as established.
>
> (*ibid.*: 73)

> The propositions of economic theory, like all scientific theory, are obviously deductions from a series of postulates. And the chief of these postulates are all assumptions involving in some way simple and indisputable facts of experience relating to the way in which

the scarcity of goods which is the subject-matter of our science actually shows itself in the world of reality. The main postulate of the theory of value is the fact that individuals can arrange their preferences in an order, and in fact do so. The main postulate of the theory of production is the fact that there are more than one factor of production. The main postulate of the theory of dynamics is the fact that we are not certain regarding future scarcities. These are not postulates the existence of whose counterpart in reality admits of extensive dispute once their nature is fully realised. We do not need controlled experiments to establish their validity: they are so much the stuff of our everyday experience that they have only to be stated to be recognised as obvious. Indeed, the danger is that they may be thought to be so obvious that nothing signifi-cant can be derived from their further examination.

(*ibid.*: 78, 79)

It may be admitted that our knowledge of the facts which are the basis of economic deductions is different in important respects from our knowledge of the facts which are the basis of the deductions of the natural sciences. ... Indeed, it may be urged that ... there is less reason to doubt their real bearing than that of the generalisations of the natural sciences. In Economics ... the ultimate constituents of our fundamental generalisations are known to us by immediate acquaintance. In the natural sciences they are known only inferentially. There is much less reason to doubt the counterpart in reality of the assumption of individual preferences than that of the assumption of the electron.

(*ibid.*: 104, 105)

To repeat, I am suggesting that although Robbins acknowledges a role for economic science to uncover generalities broadly in tune with his economising conception of economics, his erroneous acceptance of the deductivist model leads him to indicate reasons for playing down this role in practice, if not entirely abandoning it.

Robbins' conception and its mainstream interpretation as 'the science of choice or rational action'

What, finally, about the 'theory of the rational agent'? Surely this is the basis on which Robbins' conception can be rendered explanatory at a concrete level, and my interpretation thereby discarded? This is bound to be the response of many. It will be supposed that if economics is about economising, and specifically if it is about examining how scarce resources might be allocated optimally relative to given evaluations, Robbins' position can be made operational as an explanatory science just by postulating that people always do so optimise; that people are in this, or some related sense, rational. This contention constitutes the third issue mentioned above and must now be examined in detail.

It can be admitted, first of all, that there are those who, in setting out a conception of economics, clearly both are influenced by Robbins' formulation and have explicitly tied into it a presumption of rationality in action. Consider, for example, Posner's conception of economics, which is obviously influenced by the formulation adopted by Robbins:

> Economics, the science of human choice in a world in which resources are limited in relation to human wants, explores and tests the implications of assuming that man is a rational maximiser of his ends in life, his satisfactions – what we call his 'self-interest'.
>
> (Posner 1977: 3)

And in his recent study entitled *The Inexact and Separate Science of Economics*, Hausman (1992) conceives mainstream economics in the following manner:

> Economic phenomena are the consequences of rational choices that are governed predominantly by some variant consumerism and profit maximisation. In other words, *economics studies the consequences of rational greed*.
>
> (1992: 95, original emphasis)

But what is the status of any such rationality claims, and how essential are they to a Robbins-type formulation? In fact Robbins discusses this issue at length. Although considerations of rationality are ruled out entirely *if* rational action is to involve the idea of 'ethically appropriate action', he recognises the importance of rationality interpreted as *consistent action* for 'certain analytical constructions':

> But in so far as the term rational is taken to mean merely 'consistent', then it is true that an assumption of this sort does enter into certain analytical constructions. The celebrated generalisation that in a state of equilibrium the relative significance of divisible commodities is equal to their price does involve the assumption that each final choice is consistent with every other.
>
> (Robbins 1940: 91, 92)

More significantly, though, he recognises it as one hypothesis among many:

It is perfectly true that the assumption of perfect rationality figures in constructions of this sort. But it is not true that the generalisations of economics are limited to the explanation of situations in which action is perfectly consistent. Means may be scarce in relation to ends, even though the ends may be inconsistent.

(*ibid.*: 92)

His viewpoint on this comes through most strongly in a chapter entitled 'The significance of economic science', where, on the basis of his deliberations, he comes to examine the subject's practical worth. And here, finally, Robbins seems to leave little doubt that economics is not about understanding action as it occurs, whether the latter be rational or otherwise, *but about facilitating a tool or technique of rational action.* He writes:

Economics brings the solvent of knowledge. It enables us to conceive the far-reaching implications of alternative possibilities of policy. It does not, and cannot, enable us to evade the necessity of choosing between alternatives. But it does make it possible for us to bring our different choices into harmony. It cannot remove the ultimate limitations on human action. But it does make it possible within these limitations to act consistently. It serves for the inhabitant of the modern world with its endless interconnections and relationships as an extension of his perceptive apparatus. It provides a technique of rational action.

This, then, is a further sense in which Economics can be truly said to assume rationality in human society. It makes no pretence, as has been alleged so often, that action is necessarily rational in the sense that ends pursued are not mutually inconsistent. There is nothing in its generalisations which necessarily implies reflective deliberation in ultimate evaluation. It relies upon no assumption that individuals will always act rationally. But it does depend for its practical *raison d'être* upon the assumption that it is desirable that they should do so. It does assume that, within the bounds of necessity, it is desirable to choose ends which can be achieved harmoniously.

And thus in the last analysis Economics does depend, if not for its existence, at least for its significance, on an ultimate valuation – the affirmation that rationality and ability to choose with knowledge is desirable. If irrationality, if the surrender to the blind force of external stimuli and uncoordinated impulse at every moment is a good to be preferred above all others, then it is true the *raison d'être* of Economics disappears.

(*ibid.*: 156, 157)

160

In short, while accepting (erroneously) a deductivist framework, but recognising that the economising aspect of day-to-day action (as with all other aspects) is not subject to deductivist/predictionist logic (i.e. recognising that the world is open), Robbins in effect reduces economics to a technique for assessing the rationality of alternative courses of action.

Once, however, we acknowledge the further insight, one neglected by Robbins, that reality, social as well as natural, is not only open but also structured, it follows that economics need not in practice be limited to this essentially practical side of it. The latter, practical side, of course, is not unimportant. The activity of weighing different strategies, indeed, can be vital (for considering possibilities under existing structures *and under alternatives*). But this practical contribution can now be complemented by an explanatory science of economics, appropriately conceived.

Economics as a separate or distinct social science?

In order to assess, finally, whether economics can, with justification, be appropriately conceived as a *separate* social science, it is useful to elaborate explicitly upon the strategy utilised earlier to establish the separateness of social science itself, i.e. to establish the possibility (and indeed existence) of a science of social phenomena that is distinct from the sciences of nature. Here it is important to recognise that the latter result has been established, in effect, by demonstrating that the social phenomena are emergent and possess emergent properties. Now an entity or aspect found at some level of organisation is said to be emergent if there is a sense in which it has arisen out of some 'lower' level, being conditioned by and dependent upon, but not predictable from, the properties found at the lower level. In principle it is possible that the mechanism by which the higher-order entity or aspect emerged can be reconstructed and explained in terms of principles operative at the lower level. But if powers located at the higher-order level are genuinely emergent, their explanatory reduction is proscribed.

The analysis of a genuinely emergent realm may commit either (or both) of two forms of ontological error. Not only is it possible to misinterpret emergent phenomena as reducible (in principal, if with time and effort) to certain elements and governing principles lying at some lower level of organisation, but equally it is possible to forget that higher-order phenomena are always dependent upon, and conditioned by, principles which operate at the lower level from which they emerged. And it is just as important to avoid the latter error as it is the former. Just as social structure cannot be understood independently of considerations of human powers, the natural order in which both the social and the psychological are embedded, and upon which they can act back, must be recognised as a condition for social action and thus as an object of social analysis.

161

The social domain, then, is an emergent realm that is dependent upon human agency but irreducible to it. The structures of language, for example, have powers which facilitate speech acts but which are irreducible to human agency or these acts. Have we identified an emergent realm of specifically *economic* phenomena, necessitating relatively distinct methods for their analysis? Clearly not. And it is not obvious that such is feasible. The social world, in all its aspects, turns upon human practice, the primary *explanandum* of social enquiry. And, whatever the practices of interest, amongst the *explanans* of social explanations are structures, positions, mechanisms, processes and the like. In other words, there is no obvious basis for distinguishing economics according to the nature of its object, i.e. as a *separate* science. Nor does it have its own domain. I cannot think of a single sphere of human activity – from lending support to a football team, to listening to music, or even to making love – that does not (or could not) have an economic aspect (given the interpretation of economics set out above.). These and all other activities take place in space and time, both of which can have alternative uses. All human activities require material conditions and are, for example, influenced by property relations, the length and structure of the working 'day' or 'week', opportunities forgone, and so on. But at the same time very few activities, if any, have *merely* an economic aspect, including those of labouring on the shop floor or in an office or doing shopping. Activities such as the latter can involve wearing the colours of, and so signalling support for, a particular football team, or, say, being on the lookout for an interesting companion or just being part of a crowd/community, amongst many other things.

On this conception economics must take its place as a *branch* of social science, much as high-energy physics, low-temperature physics and radio astronomy each constitutes a branch of physics, or as inorganic chemistry is but a branch of chemistry. Its *raison d'être* is not a separate *domain* of distinct phenomena with their own properties, but a particular aspect of *all* social life.[16] In consequence, the modern (forced) separation of the discipline of economics from other social sciences must be recognised as quite misguided. Indeed, this separation merely makes it difficult for economics to advance in pace with other branches of social science, and must at least be a contributory factor to the discipline's continuing tradition of adopting methods of formalistic modelling that have been found to be rarely relevant to social scientific understanding and illumination.

A final argument for separation

Now, standing against the assessment that economics is but a branch of social science, lacking a domain of its own (as opposed to a concern for all social phenomena viewed under a particular aspect) are the various attempts to delimit a separate sphere for economics. Most economists who argue for this position explicitly pursue a conception which (erroneously) supposes economics to be a deductivist project concerned with expressing social phenomena as the outcome of optimising decisions (see e.g. Hausman 1992; 1994). This conception has already been dealt with above and need not be considered further. But there is a further enterprise, one that is not of necessity inconsistent with the conceptions of science and economics sustained above, which nevertheless endeavours to separate off a domain of the social world as the proper object, or sphere of focus, of the discipline of economics. I refer to the strategy of tying economics to the analysis of (aspects of) the *exchange economy*.

Now it is certainly the case that the explanatory aspect of economics, as I have conceived it, acquires a more taxing, and so interesting, role in the context of studying exchange economies. In emphasising that all social life turns on human practice, and by allocating to economics the role of identifying those factors concerned with the material conditions of well-being, I have effectively accepted that economics is the study of all the factors (including, of course, culture, social relations, rules, positions, etc.) governing human social action conceived as work. And it is clear that while work occurs under slave, feudal and also perhaps post-capitalist societies, the task of uncovering the mechanisms of social reproduction is likely to be more straightforward in such contexts. In an exchange economy, in contrast, or more generally, in a situation where coordination is undesigned and happens 'behind the backs' of people, albeit as an unintended aspect of their everyday interactions, the explanatory task is *prima facie* of a different nature and order of complexity. Moreover, if Marx is correct that the study of work regulation under capitalism involves the study of production relations which acquire a material form, as commodities, the explanatory task is an interesting and complex one indeed.

But it is one thing to contend that economic analysis may be more interesting and useful with regard to one object; it is another to claim that it should be limited to any such object. At best the partition of focus between exchange and non-exchange economies can represent a division of labour within economics. Moreover, once we turn to the more practical, economising aspect of economics, an interesting irony is evident. For I conjecture that those most concerned with uncovering the basic real mechanisms of capitalism have tended, politically, to be to the left of those who have mainly occupied themselves with questions of alternatives for resource allocation. Yet if a truly socialist or emancipatory transformation were ever achieved, whereupon real needs are revealed in science and people decide on some collective democratic basis how (presumably always scarce) resources should be allocated in order that some subset at least of these revealed needs be satisfied, it is clear that the economising aspect of economics must necessarily come to the fore. It is easy to imagine that, under such conditions, those with the temperament of current mainstream economists will find themselves gainfully employed at last, whilst those more interested in the process of discovery and explanation, today's left-wingers or radicals, may not take to economics at all.

Be that as it may, none of these considerations and speculations undermine the thesis here being sustained. And to the point, it does not follow that if an aspect of economic scientific practice has most utility with regard to particular phenomena, it must be restricted to their study. The preceding considerations imply only that the various components of economic science, its theoretical and applied explanatory roles and its more practical 'economising' side, will assume different degrees of (relative) importance according to the particular focus of study. But, in all conditions of social activity, where individuals live together and interact, the conditions of well-being will (need to) be actively produced and perhaps reproduced. In short, in human society behaviour will always have an economic aspect and social scientific study will always include a role (if no more than a role) for economics.

A conception of economics

To summarise, I have argued that certain prominent, if supposedly competing, conceptions of the subject-matter of economics are after all easily reconciled. This result has been achieved by way of clarifying the nature of (social) science. All human well-being has a material basis of some sort. And all human action involves the production, allocation and/or usage of such material conditions. Thus under some aspect all human *activity* is economic in this sense. This is the focus of Marshall. Under its explanatory aspect, economics aims to identify and understand the *conditions* of human activity concerned with the production and use of the material conditions of well-being. This is the focus of Mill. Under its practical aspect economics explores through trial-and-error and imagination how the conditions identified at the explanatory stage might, with advantage, be *utilised* or (at least as significantly) transformed. This is the emphasis of Robbins. Because economics is concerned with an aspect of all action, where the conditions of action are features of explanatory interest common to all branches of social science, then any science of economics cannot be considered separate from the others, but more a division of labour within social science.

Part III

HETERODOX TRADITIONS OF MODERN ECONOMICS

The term heterodox qualifies those who systematically oppose a set of doctrines currently held to be true and in some sense fundamental by majority or dominant opinion within a particular community. I have argued throughout that the one enduring 'truth' and fundamental feature of the orthodox or mainstream group within modern economics is that its methods of mathematical-deductivist modelling are essential to all serious theorising whatever the context, and ought to be everywhere employed in economics. Heterodox economists are united in persistently rejecting this 'truth', arguing that formalistic methods are often inappropriate for social theorising. A central contention of this third part of the book is that in rejecting the presumption that methods of mathematical-deductivist modelling are universally valid in the social realm (and in seeking alternatives), heterodox economists, implicitly at least, are taking a view on the nature of social reality. So the heterodox rejection of the mainstream position, in the end, presupposes an ontological assessment, whether or not the latter is recognised and acknowledged. Very often it is not.

Now there is more than one way that an opposition to such an orthodoxy can be manifest. And different manifestations are only to be expected in practice, especially where the ontological motivation for their opposition (if such it is) is mostly only implicit and unacknowledged.

One such is to draw attention to features of social life that do not easily fit with (the implicit ontology of) deductivism, and to develop a constructive programme based on assessments and categories that in effect reveal the universalist presuppositions of deductivism to be invalid. This is an emphasis of post Keynesianism that I discuss in Chapter 7, and of a stream of Veblenian or 'old' institutionalism I consider in Chapter 8.

A second way an opposition to the mainstream project's 'truth' can be manifest is by way of criticising ungrounded universalising tendencies per se. It is through observing that any approach which involves universalising in an a priori *fashion is suspect at best. This is an emphasis of* feminist economics *that I discuss in Chapter 9, and also of a stream of old institutionalism I discuss in Chapter 8.*

These two types of response are not inherently oppositional or mutually exclusive. Indeed, if I am correct about their ontological underpinnings they ultimately presuppose each other. And, to a degree they both are manifest within each of the numerous heterodox traditions. However, to the extent that their grounding in ontology is not appreciated or systematised, these responses may develop in isolated, and even inconsistent, ways (both across and within specific traditions or projects).

For example, in the absence of an explicit ontological perspective (and especially where ontological presuppositions not only go unrecognised but are thought actually to be avoidable) a questioning of undefended universalising tendencies of any given project can easily metamorphose into a rejection of generalising endeavour per se. *Such an outcome can also arise where ontological presuppositions are after all recognised as inevitable but regarded as being beyond critical evaluation. Such an (unsustainable) resistance to all generalising endeavour, in turn, can lead to a relativism not just in knowledge (epistemological relativism) but also in judgement (judgemental relativism), to the view that no two competing projects or other claims can ever be assessed in terms of relative worth or comparative performance. In the end no basis remains for meaningful projects in epistemology or ethics. Tendencies of this sort are certainly present in various strands of modern heterodox economics. Below I touch upon them as they appear in aspects of old institutionalism (Chapter 8) and feminist economics (Chapter 9). These tendencies, and the difficulties to which they give rise, are significantly offset once ontological commitments are not only acknowledged but rendered explicit, systematic and open to criticism.*

Now, a conclusion I draw from the chapters included in this part of the book and from assessments made elsewhere (e.g. Lawson 1994b) is that the particular ontological commitments which drive the different heterodox traditions are reasonably similar to each other. Or at least, this is so for those strands of these traditions that do embrace the possibility of, and concern themselves with, pursuing constructive programmes. For this reason there are likely numerous advantages to a uniting or a joining of (these strands of) the heterodox traditions in a programme of linked or co-development, as I have frequently suggested.

A problem that arises here, though, is that once the assessment of (a rough) similarity of ontological presuppositions across (at least some of the) heterodox traditions is accepted, we are left wondering what, if anything, differentiates these heterodox projects from each other. On what sorts of features might delineations turn? Are distinguishing features, for example, of the form of methodological approaches adopted, preferred units of analysis, specific substantive theories accepted, or something else? I offer my own answer to this question in Chapter 7.

The form of each chapter in this part of the book is significantly determined by the nature of discussions prominent in the relevant heterodox tradition at the time of my writing. Chapter 7 examines the contention of some post Keynesians and others that post Keynesianism is not, and even could not be, a coherent (constructive) project in economics, given the sorts of results it produces. Chapter 8 addresses recent suggestions by some institutionalists that Veblen's legacy could not be a constructive programme in evolutionary economics, because the very idea of a constructive project is something Veblen disavows. And Chapter 9, an essay reprinted from Feminist Economics, joins with ongoing feminist discussion as to how it is possible to resist the ungrounded universalising tendencies that proliferate in modern social theory without at the same time giving up on progressive epistemological and emancipatory projects.

Because feminist social theorists often play down the need for ontological discussion, Chapter 9 does include argumentation that ontology is efficacious and matters. As such there is repetition here of reasoning found in Parts I and II above. However, in that this previously published essay also addresses issues not covered elsewhere in this book and which are relevant in the current section and of some import, I have included the essay as it stands anyway. Perhaps it can also serve as a sort of summary and reiteration of the material that has gone before.

The most notable omissions from this part of the book are discussions concerning the Marxian and Austrian traditions. But whilst theorising in connection with the former is widely covered by others taking an explicit realist orientation, especially in other disciplines, I have on several occasions addressed aspects of Austrianism elsewhere (e.g. Lawson 1994a; 1997a: chps. 9 and 10; 1997d). Thus it has seemed reasonable at this point to concentrate on the three traditions noted.

THE NATURE OF POST KEYNESIANISM AND THE PROBLEM OF DELINEATING THE VARIOUS HETERODOX TRADITIONS[1]

Although the formalistic modelling project does to a remarkable extent dominate the modern economics academy, it has yet to displace all alternatives. Indeed, a number of heterodox research traditions survive and endeavour to reorient the discipline in various directions. These tend to be thinly spread, but nevertheless make a significant contribution. One such is that systematised as post Keynesianism. This is a tradition that over the last thirty years or so has proven (as with most other heterodox traditions) to be highly productive indeed.[2]

However, post Keynesianism also has had its problems. In particular, in recent years a number of contributors have started questioning whether it actually constitutes a coherent project (see Arestis 1996; Arestis *et al.* 1999a; 1999b; Lee 1998; Dunn 2000). Some of this scepticism has emanated from within post Keynesianism itself (see Hamouda and Harcourt 1988).

Two observations are central to this worry over coherence. The first is that the more prominent and enduring, if fairly abstract, features of the project appear not to fit together in any essentially related, or mutually reinforcing or supportive manner, as might be expected of a coherent project. Rather they seem, to some critics at least, to constitute at best a disparate set of features which just happen to coexist. The second observation is that the more substantive or concrete theoretical claims advanced by individuals who accept the post Keynesian label are actually frequently inconsistent with each other, and indeed often in mutual competition. Moreover, these more substantive or concrete theories and policy positions are continually being revised, some in significant ways. In the face of such observations there appears to be a growing feeling in some quarters that the project is rather less than coherent, with some commentators regarding coherence as a near impossibility (again see Hamouda and Harcourt 1988).

My assessment, to the contrary, is that there is after all a cohesion to the project of post Keynesianism which renders its output a valuable and systematic contribution to social theory. To appreciate that this is so, though, requires adopting the perspective of realist social theorising. For it is my view that the basis of the project's coherence is bound up with its (mostly implicit) ontological commitments. Here I want briefly to run through and defend this suggestion and draw out some of its more significant implications for post Keynesianism.

I mentioned that post Keynesianism is but one amongst several heterodox traditions. The latter group includes Austrianism, feminist economics, evolutionary economics, (old) institutionalism, Marxian economics and social economics, amongst others. The sorts of argument I make here concerning the role of ontological preconceptions could be applied to most if not all of these traditions, or at least to definite strands within them. Specifically, I think the coherence of most heterodox traditions basically rests on their particular ontological commitments. I am also of the view that the ontological preconceptions of post Keynesians are not significantly different from those of the other heterodox traditions. To the extent that this is so, the question obviously arises as to how, if at all, these projects are to be rendered distinct from each other in any coherent and useful way. I address this issue towards the end of the chapter.

The question of coherence

I start with the perceived problems of coherence in post Keynesianism. As already indicated there are two difficulties in particular that must be addressed. The one to which I turn first is that of showing that the most prominent and enduring broad features of the project tie together in some straightforward and integral way. Note that the relevant task here requires more than demonstrating that the relevant features are not mutually inconsistent. It is easy enough to lay them side by side like different commodities in a supermarket. Rather, the task is to demonstrate that the features in question are related in a more essential fashion, like pieces of a jigsaw puzzle, or, perhaps better, as different manifestations of a single coherent core position.

The more prominent features of post Keynesianism

In a previous paper (Lawson 1994b) I identified the following as the set of most prominent, enduring and widely agreed manifestations of post Keynesian writing:

(i) a persistent opposition to mainstream contributions (see e.g. Eichner 1985; Sawyer 1988; Harcourt and Hamouda 1988; Hodgson 1989; Arestis 1990; Dow 1992; Lavoie 1992; Dunn 2000);[3]

(ii) a significant emphasis on methodological or philosophical reasoning (Arestis 1990; Dow 1990; 1992; Dunn 2000);[4]

(iii) a persistent emphasis upon the notion of fundamental uncertainty in particular, but also upon the fact of historical processes, institutions and real human choice (Davidson 1980);[5] and also

(iv) a particular lineage, most obviously running through Keynes, but also taking in Marx, and some classicists including Adam Smith (Dow 1992[6]).[7]

Towards coherence

Let me briefly indicate how these features can be viewed as not only compatible with one another but also as essentially related manifestations of a cohering core position. That core position, I want to suggest, is ontological in nature.

As an entry point for my argument it is useful (though not essential) to start with the post Keynesian opposition to mainstream contributions. Two preliminary remarks are relevant here.

First it is important to recall that the mainstream project of modern economics cannot reasonably be characterised in terms of any of its various substantive claims. Certainly there is an extraordinarily dominant mainstream tradition which is widely recognised as enduring over time. But it supports numerous and often competing substantive claims and frequently experiences rapid changes in substantive fashions (see especially Lawson 1997a; and Chapter 1 above). The only acknowledged aspect of that project which remains intact throughout the project's numerous transformations, an aspect not shared by the various heterodox traditions, is an adherence at all times to formalistic deductivist modelling. It is this feature I have elsewhere argued (e.g. Chapter 1 above) that must be recognised as the essence of the mainstream project, a feature motivated not by a conception of reality but by an *a priori* belief that the formalistic method must be everywhere used if research output is to be counted as serious or scientific.

Second, it warrants emphasis that the post Keynesian opposition to the mainstream project is not perfunctory, but pervasive and sustained. Post Keynesians are found opposing the mainstream project both in its various manifestations at a period in time, as well as in its numerous reformulations over time. Indeed, although post Keynesianism is primarily a constructive project in economics, so sustained is its opposition to the mainstream that it sometimes appears that the latter is the project's most dominant and unifying feature (see Arestis 1990; Dunn 2000).

The extent and persistence of this opposition, then, in itself tells us a good deal about the nature of post Keynesianism as a project in economics. For the persistent nature of its criticism reveals this project as standing opposed not to some contingent factors of a subset of main-stream applications, but seemingly to its essential nature, to features common and fundamental to all the mainstream's output.

In other words, one thing we can reasonably infer about post Keynesian-ism is that it rejects the mainstream *emphasis* on methods of formalistic deductivist modelling. Certainly it stands opposed to the notion that these methods are appropriate for all social situations. Let us consider what is involved in this rejection.

First of all it renders the post Keynesian position unavoidably method-ological. For the essence of the mainstream endeavour against which post Keynesians stand opposed is its particular stance on method. Already, then, we can see that two broad features of the post Keynesian project, its opposi-tion to the mainstream orientation and its methodological emphasis, are necessarily related.

How might we explain the rejection of the mainstream deductivist approach? As I argue in Chapter 1, it is essential to deductivism that regu-larities of events standing in causal sequence are ubiquitous. And this latter requirement in turn presupposes an ontology of social atomism (that social reality consists of isolated atoms – as I also demonstrate in Chapter 1).[8] It is fair to say, then, that, in opposing deductivism, post Keynesians, if implicitly, are recognising that closures of the relevant sort are not ubiqui-tous and social atomism is not sustainable as a universal thesis.

Already, then, we can see that the post Keynesian opposition to the mainstream, its attention to methodology, its denial that social reality is everywhere in a certain sense closed, as well as its rejection of social atomism with its foreclosing of the possibility of choice, are intrinsically related. They are aspects that are not merely consistent with each other but mutually reinforcing, if not determining.

What must post Keynesians be supposing about the nature of social reality in rejecting the (implicit) mainstream ontology? A preconception which, if held, is sufficient to ground this stance, is that social reality is fundamentally open in the sense sustained in throughout this book. The adoption of such a perspective does not necessitate any denial of the possi-bility of local or restricted closures (of whatever sort). It only entails a rejection of the presumption that they are ubiquitous and universal. Such a stance is quite compatible with acknowledging a pervasion of demi-regu-larities, for example. But if the noted ontological orientation is indeed being accepted in post Keynesianism, its methodologically informed resis-tance to mainstream economics (with its presuppositions of atomism and closure) quickly follows.

Once post Keynesianism is interpreted in this manner, other prominent features also soon fall into place. In particular, if events are not everywhere predictable, if openness is indeed a fundamental feature of social life, then so will be the fact of (fundamental) uncertainty (as opposed to calculable risk). Hence, on the assumption that post Keynesians implicitly adhere to an open-systems ontology, we find that at least one further post Keynesian feature is essentially related to the others already noted.

It should by now be apparent how I am suggesting that post Keynesianism, a tradition that is indeed concerned with advancing a constructive project in economics, can be interpreted as coherent. Basically I am arguing that its numerous prominent features are specific manifestations of an ontological preconception, and, more particularly of an open-systems ontology of the sort systematised within critical realism.

Given that my basic thesis is now clear, let me at this point quicken the pace of the discussion and indicate how, on the basis of maintaining the sort of overall (and I believe coherent) perspective systematised as critical realism, the remaining prominent features of post Keynesianism (leaving aside for the moment the question of post Keynesian lineage) are seen to connect intrinsically with the features already addressed.

At this point I need to tie in specifically the post Keynesian emphasis on historical processes, institutions and human choice. This is easily achieved accepting the realist perspective in question. For historical processes presuppose a transformational process ontology such as developed in critical realism, just as institutions presuppose a structured ontology and an emphasis on internal-relationality and intrinsic dynamism. Human choice, finally, is compatible with a world of structures that facilitate human acts but do not determine them. For example, the structures of language facilitate speech acts without controlling what is said.

So the more prominent and enduring features of post Keynesianism can be recognised as aspects of a coherent whole. This is achieved by recognising the project as implicitly ontologically oriented, with, first, its more enduring aspects being manifestations of the sort of ontology defended in critical realism, and second, its criticisms of the mainstream turning, in effect, on the latter's insistence on the universalisation of a specific (scientific) ontology (this latter being necessitated by the project's deductivist emphasis, and found to be an infrequently occurring special case *a posteriori*).

However, if its ontological commitments do render post Keynesianism coherent as a heterodox tradition, it has to be accepted that post Keynesians have not always expressed their contributions in explicitly ontological terms. Rather, at least until recently,[9] post Keynesian critiques of mainstream contributions, as well as elaborations of alternatives, have usually (with one or two notable exceptions such as Paul Davidson's emphasis on non-ergodic social processes)[10] been set at the level of substantive formulations.

However, it is easy to see that these post Keynesian contributions usually provide alternative formulations that are not just different from those of the mainstream, but mostly informed by a vision consistent with an open-systems ontology. Thus theories in which agents can exercise real choice are posited against each mainstream version of the passive (ever-instrumentally optimising) atoms. And an emphasis upon real-world fundamental uncertainty is regularly contrasted with the incredible knowledge claims that the closures of modern mainstream economics encourage if not necessitate, and so on.

So upon examination the project's ontological orientation is in the end found to be everywhere evident. If its ontological presuppositions have not always been explicitly acknowledged, this helps to explain the failure of some to recognise the degree to which the project does ultimately cohere. Rendering the project more ontologically explicit not only clarifies its own nature but also the nature of its criticisms of the mainstream, thereby making them more difficult to evade. The point here, though, is that once we recognise the project's ontological orientation, its various prominent and enduring features are comprehensible as manifestations of a coherent programme.

Keynes' realist orientation

Actually, this is not quite the end of the present story. For there is one prominent feature of post Keynesianism still to be considered. It remains for me to indicate that this account of the inherent core of post Keynesianism is consistent with that project's attachment to the likes of Keynes. As noted above, the claimed lineage of post Keynesianism is often held to include Marx and various classical economists especially Smith (see Dow 1992). However, on the nature of the contributions of Marx and the classicals I refer the reader to other papers where the relevant connections are made at length (Lawson 1994b; Brown *et al.* 2002a; Montes 2003). Here I concentrate on Keynes, who is the central figure after all, lending his name to the tradition. My remaining task at this point, then, is to indicate that Keynes does bring ontological considerations to bear, and that his revealed ontological commitments are indeed sufficiently similar to those underpinning modern post Keynesianism (i.e. they are something like those systematised within critical realism).

In actual fact Keynes' approach to social theory was an ontologically oriented one even before he turned to economics. This is clear from his early opposition to G. E. Moore's moral principle that certain rules (such as 'in conversation tell the truth') should always be followed. Moore reasoned that rule-following action of this sort would, over time, result in (moral) good being achieved more often than not. Keynes rejected this reasoning because it implicitly rests upon a relative frequency theory of probability, a theory which Keynes recognised presupposes a closed universe (see e.g. Lawson 1993; 1999b). In fact, this opposition to Moore's reasoning ultimately resulted in Keynes writing his *A Treatise on Probability*

(Keynes 1973b), a book concerned to demonstrate that probability judgements always have conditions of satisfaction, and conditions which, in the social realm especially, are mostly never met.

It is, then, not surprising to find that this *Treatise* is often explicitly ontological in orientation. Most obviously this is so where Keynes examines whether the inductive reasoning presupposed in probabilistic inference can be justified. Thus he seeks at one point to determine the implicit ontological presuppositions of contemporary natural scientists who use induction. And we can see that he is most unusual amongst economists in questioning the ontological presumptions of the methods of science explicitly:

> The kind of fundamental assumption about the character of material laws, on which scientists appear commonly to act, seems to me to be much less simple than the bare principle of uniformity. They appear to assume something much more like what mathematicians call the principle of the superposition of small effects, or, as I prefer to call it, in this connection, the *atomic* character of natural law. The system of the material universe must consist, if this kind of assumption is warranted, of bodies which we may term (without any implication as to their size being conveyed thereby) *legal atoms*, such that each of them exercises its own separate, independent, and invariable effect, a change of the total state being compounded of a number of separate changes each of which is solely due to a separate portion of the preceding state. We do not have an invariable relation between particular bodies, but nevertheless each has on the others its own separate and invariable effect, which does not change with changing circumstances, although, of course, the total effect may be changed to almost any extent if all the other accompanying causes are different. Each atom can, according to this theory, be treated as a separate cause and does not enter into different organic combinations in each of which it is regulated by different laws.
>
> (Keynes 1973b: 276, 277)

Note that in drawing attention to this assumption of atomic character of natural law, Keynes is simultaneously raising the logical possibility that not all natural phenomena need be atomic:

> The scientist wishes, in fact, to assume that the occurrence of a phenomenon which has appeared as part of a more complex phenomenon, may be *some* reason for expecting it to be associated on another occasion with part of the same complex. Yet if different wholes were subject to different laws *qua* wholes

and not simply on account of and in proportion to the differences of their parts, knowledge of a part could not lead, it would seem, even to presumptive or probable knowledge as to its association with other parts. Given, on the other hand, a number of legally atomic units and the laws connecting them, it would be possible to deduce their effects *pro tanto* without an exhaustive knowledge of all the coexisting circumstances.

(Keynes 1973b: 277, 278)[11]

To the extent that some phenomena are not atomic, then clearly the methods of natural scientists which presuppose atomicity cannot be accepted as universally applicable.

What is Keynes' conception of social ontology in particular? We can observe that although in the early years of the twentieth century Keynes seems somewhat non-committal regarding the extent to which the material of the natural world can be regarded as atomic, by the mid-1920s he is reasonably definite in his view that social phenomena cannot be regarded as atomic entities. Thus in his 1926 biography of Edgeworth, Keynes writes:

The atomic hypothesis which has worked so splendidly in Physics breaks down in Psychics. We are faced at every turn with the problems of Organic Unity, of Discreteness, of Discontinuity – the whole is not equal to the sum of the parts, comparisons of quantity fail us, small changes produce large effects, the assumption of a uniform and homogeneous continuum are not satisfied.

(Keynes 1933: 286)

Keynes' views on social ontology are most apparent when he criticises Tinbergen's project of econometrics. The latter enterprise is regarded as ill founded precisely because it assumes (i) a complete list (i.e. an effectively isolated set) of (ii) atomic factors, i.e. because it assumes the social world is closed in the relevant sense when in fact we know it is not.

The context in which Keynes makes this ontologically based criticism is in a response to an invitation from the League of Nations in the 1930s to review Tinbergen's early econometric work on business cycles. Here Keynes clearly expresses a view that the material of economics is of a nature such that the natural scientific practices and formulae in question are inappropriate to its analysis:

unlike typical natural science, the material to which [economics] is applied is, in too many respects, not homogeneous through time.

(Keynes 1973c: 296)

175

This ontological appraisal, as I say, is at the heart of Keynes' assessment of the potential usefulness of econometrics. In an initial response to the League of Nations' invitation, Keynes writes:

> There is first of all the central question of methodology, – the logic of applying the method of multiple correlation to unanalysed economic material, which we know to be non-homogeneous through time. If we are dealing with the action of numerically measurable, independent forces, adequately analysed so that we knew we were dealing with independent atomic factors and between them completely comprehensive, acting with fluctuating relative strength on material constant and homogeneous through time, we might be able to use the method of multiple correlation with some confidence for disentangling the laws of their action ...
>
> In fact we know that every one of these conditions is far from being satisfied by the economic material under investigation ...
>
> To proceed to some more detailed comments. The coefficients arrived at are apparently assumed to be constant for 10 years or for a larger period. Yet, surely we know that they are not constant. There is no reason at all why they should not be different every year.
>
> (1973: 285–6)

These sorts of comments are repeated throughout the late 1930s and come to a head in 1939 in Keynes' eventual review of Tinbergen's book:

> Put broadly, the most important condition is that the environment in all relevant respects, other than the fluctuations in those factors of which we take particular account, should be uniform and homogeneous over a period of time. We cannot be sure that such conditions will persist in the future, even if we find them in the past. But if we find them in the past, we have at any rate some basis for an inductive argument.

and he adds

> [The] main *prima facie* objection to the application of the method of multiple correlation to complex economic problems lies in the apparent lack of any adequate degree of uniformity in the environment.
>
> (1973c: 316)

So post Keynesianism as interpreted above is indeed very much in line with the approach of Keynes. Keynes, of course, was very keen to reorient modern economics in the direction of relevance. And post Keynesians have maintained not only that goal but, implicitly at least, Keynes' inherently ontological orientation, especially in opposing the deductivist reductionism of the modern mainstream. So the post Keynesian project can claim historical or developmental coherence too.

Competing theories and policies within post Keynesianism

It can be argued, then, that the enduring prominent features of post Keynesianism do after all tie together in a non-contingent manner. But even if this is so, it is often observed that the more substantive or concrete theoretical or policy contributions of post Keynesians turn out to be inconsistent with each other, and indeed in competition (as post Keynesians themselves acknowledge, see e.g. Arestis 1990; Dow 1990).[12] This is the second observation noted at the outset that appears to threaten the possibility of post Keynesian coherence. My aim here is to suggest that this state of affairs too can be rendered compatible with the idea of a post Keynesian project that coheres.

Now it is a matter of some significance that critical realism, being a philosophically oriented project with results pitched at a high level of abstraction, does not itself carry any direct substantive claims or concrete policy implications. It is essentially an underlabourer for science including social science. It cannot act as a substitute for scientific enquiry.

In critical realism arguments are made, for example, for supposing that social reality is an emergent realm that is structured, open, differentiated, dynamic and constituted to a significant degree by internally related totalities. However, it is not a part of the critical realist project to uncover or investigate the specific structures, including totalities or processes, that emerge, or the manner in which they combine in producing the actual course of events. Such work is down to the individual sciences themselves.

Of course, many who have contributed to, or who are informed by, the project of critical realism, also do social theory of a more concrete sort. However, any resulting substantive positions and policy orientations are reasonably associated with critical realism only by observing that they are produced by researchers acting on the basis of the critical realist understanding of the nature of science, nature and society.

In fact, once we accept the open, dynamic and holistic nature of features of reality uncovered in critical realism, it comes as little surprise to find that different social scientists informed by this realist perspective regularly produce competing explanations of given concrete phenomenon. And where this is the case it is obviously inappropriate to refer to any one explanation as *the* critical realist account of the phenomenon in question. The aim remains the pursuit of truth, and it is to be hoped that by way of subjecting competing hypotheses to empirical and other forms of assessment, an account emerges that is seen to outperform the others in terms of explanatory power, etc., and thereby to gain widespread acceptance. But even if and where agreement of this sort is reached, there can be no supposition that the account in question will not be revised or displaced in due course. It is a frequently reaffirmed realist insight that all knowledge is fallible, partial and liable to be transient. And, if progress is to be achieved, continuous transformations, even in our currently most explanatorily powerful accounts, are to be encouraged. Thus at no stage can a substantive theory be said to qualify as *the* critical realist one.

Now a parallel argument, I believe, holds concerning the output of theories produced by post Keynesians.[13] I do not wish to impute an underlabourer role for post Keynesianism. But just as critical realists can produce amongst themselves a range of substantive theories and political orientations without compromising the possibility that theirs is a coherent overall project, so it seems can post Keynesians. For the basis of coherence in post Keynesianism is found to turn on its (often implicit) ontological orientation, which is consistent with a variety of highly concrete substantive claims. In other words, substantive claims and policy results can be said to be produced or held by post Keynesians without constituting essential features *per se* of the post Keynesian position. They do not constitute *the* post Keynesian theories of anything.

Parenthetically, there is a related point to be made here concerning method. Some commentators have interpreted critical realist opposition to the mainstream project's *a priori* universalisation of formalistic modelling methods as an opposition to all attempts at formalistic modelling, whatever the context. From this understanding the inference has been made that if post Keynesians do draw on critical realist results, this somehow constrains them from engaging in formalistic methods such as econometrics (see e.g. Walters and Young 1999).

But there is a misunderstanding here. Just as critical realism *per se* can have nothing to say about which specific social processes will operate in any context, or about how different ones will combine to produce the course of actual events, so it cannot determine in advance the sorts of methods in any context that will or will not be appropriate. Thus a blanket rejection of econometrics, or indeed of any other method, is not a stance that is, or could be, sponsored in critical realism. It is certainly true that this realist project gives good reason to oppose the *reduction* of economics to formalistic analysis. And it does emphasise that any useful social scientific application of formalistic methods requires certain (closure) conditions constituting special configurations of social reality that (unsurprisingly from the perspective sustained) have turned out to be rather rare. But it cannot (and does not) rule out the possibility of these conditions occurring in certain contexts. It has in fact shown that closures of the sort in question themselves presuppose, and indeed are a special configuration of, an open and structured system, i.e. a special case of the sort of system that does widely obtain (see e.g. Lawson 1997a). Critical realism thus cannot and does not rule out *a priori* their limited occurrence.

This realist project, rather, adopts, as far as is feasible, an essentially *a posteriori* orientation. And if its primary concern is to bring ontological considerations (back) into the picture and to indicate real possibilities in the social realm especially, it cannot determine *a priori* which possibilities will be actualised in any local context. It can explain why *a posteriori* closures of the relevant sort do not seem to occur very often in the social realm (given the latter's human-agency dependent, intrinsically dynamic and highly internally related nature), and it can and does indicate ways of proceeding in their absence (e.g. forms of contrast explanation – see Chapter 4 above; or Lawson 1997a: ch. 15). But that is as far as it goes on such matters. In short, critical realism can accommodate, and *a priori* does not rule out any of, a range of phenomenal situations, and thus is quite consistent with its support for methodological pluralism.

So the opponent of critical realism is not the post Keynesian or whoever seriously attempting to find out if (or demonstrate that) in certain conditions some formalistic-deductivist methods or whatever could contribute to enlightenment. Rather, the opponent is the advocate of any form of *a priori* dogma. In the context of modern economics specifically, the primary target is (as it is for post Keynesians) the current mainstream *a priori* insistence that formalistic modelling is the only proper, and a universally valid, method for modern economics, along with its effective prohibition on alternative approaches.

In short, post Keynesianism under just about all of its aspects can be rendered coherent by seeing it as advancing claims or adopting practices or orientations which are either concrete manifestations of, or presuppose for their legitimacy, a social ontology of the (seemingly coherent) sort defended in critical realism.[14]

Implications of the sort of coherence found

However, this latter recognition may appear to be a double-edged sword for post Keynesians, which brings me to the question of distinctions between post Keynesianism and critical realism. For if coherence in post Keynesianism is achieved through linking this project to critical realism in the manner suggested,[15] we are bound to raise the question of whether post Keynesianism, so interpreted, is ultimately anything more than a philosophical position. Is it indeed just a version or precursor of critical realism? I suspect many post Keynesians presuppose, and prefer to believe, otherwise.

If, however, post Keynesianism is indeed to be regarded as not merely consistent with, but also distinct from, and indeed irreducible to, critical realism, it seems to follow that there must be some assessments or other aspects or concerns shared by all post Keynesians, but not necessarily all those who accept the broad perspective of critical realism. I speculated in an earlier piece (Lawson 1994b) that these will lie at a level of generality below that of ontology but above that of most specific substantive claims. A question raised but left unanswered in that earlier paper is to what extent is this the case? I suggest an answer below.

The range of heterodox traditions: commonality and distinctions

There is a further and related potentially problematic implication of the above discussion. For it can be argued that other heterodox traditions, like (old) institutionalism, Austrianism, and so forth, implicitly also subscribe to something like the critical realist ontology and general perspective. If this is so, if critical realism is indeed a framework that connects and potentially unites the various competing heterodox traditions (and most do perceive connections in relevant features,[16] though not all),[17] the question also arises as to what distinguishes these latter traditions from each other.[18]

By raising these questions I do not wish to imply that broadly philosophical heterodox traditions in economics cannot themselves make a contribution to critical realism. On philosophical matters the flow of insights can be, and doubtless is, both ways between critical realism and heterodox traditions. But I believe it is fair to suggest that critical realism does offer far more, and better developed, philosophical resources. The heterodox traditions in economics, it seems to me, still need to distinguish themselves primarily at a more concrete or substantive level of analysis.

I might mention, parenthetically, that certain (old) institutionalists make the empirical claim that the institution constitutes the category (of social structure) that (in some sense) matters most in economics. It is sometimes even held that the institution should replace the atomistic individual of mainstream economics as the main unit of analysis. Whether or not this claim (if more fully elaborated) is correct, and/or is accepted by the wide body of (old) institutionalists, it seems to me that it is precisely of the sort of generalised, yet reasonably concrete and empirical, nature that we are looking for. Certainly this premise is not an ingredient of critical realism *per se*. A further question I posed in my 1994b paper is whether any premise of a similar sort is, or can be, accepted within post Keynesianism.

A suggested basis for distinguishing amongst the heterodox traditions

In previous papers I have refrained from suggesting answers to the questions raised concerning how post Keynesianism might be identified, or how the various heterodox traditions might be distinguished from each other and from critical realism. At least I refrained from going beyond conjecturing that the defining characteristics of each heterodox tradition will likely lie at a level of abstraction below that of social ontology but above that of relatively concrete social-scientific explanations of highly specific phenomena. Here, though, I do want to take the matter somewhat further. Specifically, I float the suggestion that the heterodox traditions are most appropriately identified and distinguished from each other (and from critical realism) not according to any specific theories or policy proposals favoured and defended, nor in terms of any features of the economy held to constitute the most basic units of analysis, nor according to any other specific substantive or methodological claims. Rather I think the most tenable basis for drawing distinctions is according to questions raised or problems or aspects of the socio-economic world thought sufficiently important or interesting or of concern as to warrant sustained and systematic examination. That is, I suggest that the separate projects be characterised according to the features of socio-economic life upon which they find reason to continually focus their study.

In other words, if ontology can account for the distinctions between the heterodox traditions and the modern mainstream, i.e. if ontological commitments identify post Keynesians and others as heterodox, it is their particular substantive orientations and concerns, not answers or principles, that distinguish the heterodox traditions from each other.

The place of economics in social science

It may be useful to set this suggestion against the realist theory of science I defend in Chapter 6. According to the latter, the different sciences are identified (and distinguished from each other) according to the nature of the material with which they are concerned. Thus physicists study certain physical principles, biologists study life processes, and so on. Now it is a claim defended in Chapter 2 that the material of the social realm comprises such features as social rules, relations, positions, processes, practices, totalities, and so forth.[19] And it is relevant to observe that this ontology is appropriate not only to economics, but equally to sociology, politics, anthropology, human geography, and to all other disciplines concerned with the study of social life. So accepting the realist perspective here defended there is no obvious basis for distinguishing a separate science of economics. Rather, economics is best viewed as at most a division of labour within a single social science. Indeed, for historical reasons, economics is perhaps best characterised as the division of social theory or science primarily concerned with studying all social structures and processes bearing upon the material conditions of well-being (see Chapter 6). But whether or not the specifics of the latter suggestion are accepted, the broader point of relevance here is that if economics is to be distinguished as a strand of social research it cannot be according to its own ontology, methodological principles or substantive claims, but in terms only of its particular focus of interest.

The place of the heterodox traditions within economics

It is in a similar fashion that I am proposing that the various heterodox traditions might also be considered as divisions of labour, albeit as divisions now within economics. Thus (and I include the following characterisation merely to give some illustrative suggestions), post Keynesians, given their previous emphases, might be identified according to their concern with the fact of fundamental uncertainty stemming from the openness of social reality. Such a focus could take in the implications of uncertainty or openness for the development of certain sorts of institutions including money, for processes of decision making, and so forth. At the level of policy the concern may well include the analysis of contingencies which recognise the fact of pervasive uncertainty, given the openness of the social reality in the present and to the future, etc. For those influenced by Keynes especially, a likely focus is how these matters give rise to collective or macro outcomes, and how the latter in turn impact back on individual acts and pressures for structural transformation, etc.

By similar reasoning it may be best to distinguish institutionalists too, not according to claims about the main units of analysis but, given that project's traditional concern with evolutionary issues, in terms of its interest in examining how social items change and/or endure over time. From such a perspective, those aspects of social life that are most enduring, such as institutions and habits, are particularly significant. So too are the interactions of factors like institutions and technology in the process of reproduction and change. And a yet further likely related focus of interest is the manner in which the institutional shaping and reshaping of specific individual identities can be explanatorily consequential in given contexts.

Austrians may perhaps be best identified according to their emphasis on studying the market process and entrepreneurship in particular, or perhaps in line with the attention given by this project to the production and role of intersubjective meaning in social life, and so on.

It is not really for me to be too specific here. The above, I repeat, are suggestions made primarily for sake of illustration.

Such suggestions, however, do tie in with the way, for example, that some feminist economists already tend to identify their own project, namely as one that (in addition to proceeding very differently to the mainstream)[20] concerns itself with women as subjects (which may include, for example, giving attention to differences amongst women, as well as between genders) and takes a particular orientation or focus, namely on the position of women (and other marginalised groups) within society and economy. The latter focus includes an attention to the social causes at work in the oppression of, or in discrimination against, women (and others), the opportunities for progressive transformation or emancipation, questions of power and strategy, and so forth. This orientation has inevitably meant a significant attention, within feminist economics, to issues which historically have been gender-related, such as caring, especially for children, and indeed the nature of family structures in specific locations. But in principle there is no area of social life that is excluded. It is the sorts of question pursued that seem most to distinguish an approach within the heterodox traditions as feminist, not specific substantive claims or methodological principles.[21]

I might emphasise that in suggesting that heterodox economic traditions be identified and distinguished in the manner described, i.e. as divisions of labour within economics, I do not suppose any separation of subject-matter. There can be no strict partitioning of topics. The social world seems to be a highly internally related (emergent) totality. My suggestion is merely that the various heterodox projects can be seen as approaching the same totality from different perspectives, each with their own set of questions, immediate motivating interests, emphases, and so forth, and each achieving results warranting of synthesis[22] with all others.

I repeat again, however, that all this is intended to be merely suggestive. It does fly in the face of certain claims or orientations of some heterodox economists. But in that the noted set of proposals allows, without any obvious tension, a coherent way of distinguishing the various heterodox traditions not only from each other but also from critical realism, and in a manner that does not compromise their coherence and commonalities (rooted in ontology) as traditions distinct from (and transcending the errors of) the current mainstream project, it does have something to commend it.

8

INSTITUTIONAL ECONOMICS AND REALIST SOCIAL THEORISING

Over one hundred years ago Thorstein Veblen formulated possibly the most famous question in the history of economics: 'Why is economics not an evolutionary science?'. In an essay acknowledging Veblen 'as the founding father and guiding spirit of American institutionalism', Clarence Ayres concludes that it is precisely the sorts of questions he asked that 'reveal the significance of Veblen's legacy' (Ayres 1963: 62).

But what is the feature of Veblen's legacy whose significance is revealed by a largely philosophy-of-science question such as this? My thesis is that in matters philosophical at least, a fundamental legacy of Veblen's is

(i)   a constructive programme,
(ii) grounded in an ontological conception comprising features similar to those defended throughout this book.

This thesis appears contentious. I acknowledge, of course, that Veblen gives primary emphasis not to ontology at all but to a specific method or form of science, namely the evolutionary method or science. And it is this emphasis that has been noted and continually reproduced by institution-alist economists since. Moreover, whilst (old) institutionalists claiming the tradition of Veblen have repeatedly concerned themselves with (re)evalu-ating the nature of Veblen's contribution, the category of ontology barely figures anywhere, at least until relatively recently.[1]

Further, even my associating a constructive programme with Veblen will seem problematic to some. Veblen, I readily acknowledge, is some-what hesitant about revealing a commitment to any constructive programme, as a study of his methodological contributions reveals. And some recent rather compelling contributions maintain that Veblen's primary philosophical project is, contrary to my thesis, actually

(i)   a 'deconstructive' venture in
(ii) epistemology, one similar in some ways to that of modern day post-modernists (Hoksbergen 1994; Peukert 2001; Samuels 1990; 1998).

Helge Peukert (2001), for example, suggests that:

> Veblen deviates fundamentally from the common assumption that he endeavored to develop a constructive research program in the Lakatosian sense. ... He did not, and did not want to unfold a positive, new, and evolutionary approach which could practically be applied to the analysis of economic processes. He did not pretend to uncover any developmental logic of economic history or institutions.
>
> (Peukert 2001: 544)

Peukert's contention is that Veblen 'had only one scientific aim', and this was 'a radical and deconstructive critique of what he called prevailing habits of thought' (2001: 544). Alternatively put, 'Veblen's basic intention [was] to disclose scientific preconceptions', a goal which reflects the influence upon him of his early reading of Kant. The upshot is that Veblen is interpreted as having 'formulated a postmodern epistemology at the turn of the century' (551) or as coming 'close to so-called postmodern thinkers like Richard Rorty' (550).[2]

Clearly, with ontology hardly emphasised in the institutionalist tradition, and with the very idea of a Veblenian constructive programme recently expressly rejected, it seems I have a good deal of work to do if I am to defend my thesis as plausible. However, if I am correct in my contention we can view Veblen as laying a basis for a project in realist social theorising. This I believe is Veblen's particular legacy to modern economics and specifically to modern (old) institutionalism. The details of it are something I explore towards the end of the chapter.

Evolutionary science and ontology

I start with the question of ontology. Now although the ideas of an evolutionary method or of evolutionary science figure prominently in institutionalist writings and are more or less universally associated with Veblen, the question of Veblen's understanding of them is not always made clear.[3] In any case, I want to re-examine Veblen's meaning here. For it is part of my contention that in referring to evolutionary method and science, Veblen, in effect, is advancing a thesis that is largely ontological in nature. Once this is demonstrated I can more easily address the question of whether or not a constructive programme is a part of Veblen's philosophical legacy.

The passage of Veblen's famous 'evolutionary essay' in which he explicitly seeks to clarify his conception of an evolutionary science runs as follows:

The difference between the evolutionary and the pre-evolutionary sciences. … is a difference of spiritual attitude or point of
view in the two contrasted generations of scientists. To put the
matter in other words, it is a difference in the basis of valuation of
the facts for the scientific purpose, or in the interest from which
the facts are appreciated. With the earlier as with the later generation the basis of valuation of the facts handled is, in matters of
detail, the causal relation which is apprehended to subsist
between them. This is true to the greatest extent for the natural
sciences. But in their handling of the more comprehensive
schemes of sequence and relation – in their definitive formulation
of the results – the two generations differ. The modern scientist is
unwilling to depart from the test of causal relation or quantitative
sequence. When he asks the question, Why? he insists on an
answer in terms of cause and effect. … [This] recourse has in our
time been made available for the handling of schemes of development and theories of a comprehensive process by the notion of a
cumulative causation.

(Veblen 1898: 59–60)

Several features of Veblen's idea of evolutionary science contained in this
passage are worth distinguishing. It is most apparent that the discussion is
couched first of all in epistemological (or even psychological) terms. It rests
on categories such as 'spiritual attitude', 'point of view', 'basis of valuation
of the facts', 'scientific purpose', and 'the interest from which the facts are
appreciated'. Veblen is focusing in the first instance on the transitive
domain, on ways or forms of knowing rather than on the nature of what is
known.

However all methods, frameworks and points of view carry ontological presuppositions. And a striking feature of this passage (and of others
like it included throughout his contributions)[4] is that the ontological
commitments are up front and more or less built into the descriptions of
the ways or forms of knowing under discussion. Specifically evolutionary
sciences are concerned with cumulative causation. Veblen's terminology
is variable. He writes (throughout his contributions) of causal relations,
causal sequences, cause and effect, etc. However, Veblen not only understands all such features as part of a process, but considers an evolutionary
science to be concerned precisely with the nature of such (cumulative)
processes (rather than, say, with any outcomes that may at some stage
come about).[5]

A further notable feature of the extract reproduced above is Veblen's
view that an evolutionary science is distinguished in part by what is
excluded from its associated scientific ontology. Certainly the modern or
evolutionary scientist is concerned with causal processes. But in addition

any such scientist 'is unwilling to *depart* from the test of causal relation' (emphasis added). If earlier generations of scientists used causal ideas, they also imported some additional notions of 'natural law' or normality or teleology. For pre-evolutionary scientists, it was never regarded as sufficient to conceptualise reality in terms of cause and effect alone.[6] However, for the evolutionary scientist, according to Veblen, cause and effect are the only explanatory norms. Thus (continuing the last noted extract from Veblen's evolutionary essay) Veblen insists that if the evolutionary leaders are to be praised, the merit lies

> in their refusal to go back of the colorless sequence of phenomena and seek higher ground for their ultimate syntheses, and ... in their having shown that this colorless impersonal sequence of cause and effect can be made use of for theory proper, by virtue of its cumulative character.
>
> (Veblen 1898: 61)

Veblen, then, holds the view that if a science is to count as evolutionary it is illegitimate to talk of any situation that comes about as being predetermined, and thereby laudatory or 'legitimate' in any sense. These are pre- or non-evolutionary categories:

> The notion of a legitimate trend in a course of events is an extra evolutionary preconception, and lies outside the scope of an inquiry into the causal sequence in any process.
>
> (Veblen 1898: 76)

Rather, Veblen describes any course of events appropriate for evolutionary analysis as conforming to something like 'impersonal or mechanical sequence' (Veblen 1898: 62), and any process in which such an impersonal sequence is produced as one of 'dispassionate cumulate causation' (64). All such phrases are employed to indicate the non-predetermined non-teleological nature of what occurs. And this is an integral part of his thesis of cumulative causation.

I think it is clear enough, then, that Veblen's notion of an evolutionary science is conceived directly in terms of its appropriateness for addressing a specific ontology. This latter ontology is one of non-teleological causal processes, of cumulative causal sequence. Indeed, on some occasions Veblen is explicit about this:

> The prime postulate of evolutionary science, the preconception constantly underlying the inquiry, is the notion of a cumulative causal sequence.
>
> (Veblen 1900: 176)

With this understanding of Veblen's conception of evolutionary science in mind I turn, now, to my larger thesis that Veblen's legacy is a constructive thesis in which ontology figures centrally.

Method, theory of knowledge and judgemental orientation

So does Veblen's contribution include a constructive programme? An obvious issue to pursue in seeking an answer to this question, is Veblen's intention in formulating his famous question. Specifically, is he *advocating* an evolutionary economics? And if so, is he thereby setting out how it might be achieved? Or is he adopting, instead, a more disinterested stance, perhaps wishing merely to explain or predict developments without having an opinion as to their relative scientific advantage or worth?

To proceed quickly to the heart of this matter, it is my assessment that there are, in the literature, two competing basic interpretations of Veblen's concerns in posing his famous question. I want to add a third.

In order to systematise the commonalties and differences in these interpretations, it is useful to distinguish three separate orientations that a commentator may take regarding different aspects of any process whereby a method or approach may become dominant in science. These are, first, the method of science under discussion (X); second, the process itself (Y) by which method X has, or is expected to, become influential; and, finally, the evaluative stance (Z) taken towards this method (X) becoming dominant.

With these three aspects distinguished, the traditional or more common interpretation of Veblen on these matters can be represented schematically as model A in Table 8.1 below.

Table 8.1 Model A

	X	Y	Z
	Method or science under discussion	*Process whereby X is expected to become widely accepted*	*Evaluative orientation towards X*
Model A (Ayres and most institutionalists)	Evolutionary	Constructive research programme with evolutionary science of economics the goal	Non-neutral

188

I suspect the contention that model A captures the interpretation of many institutionalists is not especially controversial. As Ayres expresses matters:

> In his essay entitled 'Why is Economics Not an Evolutionary Science?' … Veblen raised a question which has been thrown up to institutionalists as a challenge ever since: If the law of supply and demand, the theory of price equilibrium, marginal analysis, and all that, are to be cast aside, what has institutionalism to put in its place?
>
> (Ayres 1963: 54)

Ayres portrays Veblen as seeking an alternative approach to the dominant one, an approach more able to facilitate understanding. Veblen's starting point is a 'rejection of the traditional conception of the economy' (Ayres 1963: 55) and the 'challenge' set by Veblen is to replace it with something that better enables the 'economic life process … [to] be understood' (Ayres 1963: 55). As Mayhew (1998a) reports, Ayres' concern was 'to hasten evolution, now clearly stated as a path toward progress' (Mayhew 1998a: 459).

In similar fashion, Malcolm Rutherford (1998) writes of Veblen's 'call for the reconstruction of economics along modern, evolutionary lines' (463) (see also Hodgson 1998b; Twomey 1998; and most others who have addressed the nature of Veblen's overall contribution). As Peukert (2001) recently finds of most of the relevant literature:

> Positive or negative interpretations, with either a neoclassical, a new, or an old institutionalist bias, *all* have one point in common; they suppose that Veblen developed, or tried to develop a positive heuristic and a constructive alternative research program.
>
> (Peukert 2001: 543)

Veblen's evolutionary epistemology

Although interpretative contributions conforming to model A usually carry significant insight, in the end, I believe, most such accounts also, to a degree, mislead. For Veblen is very clearly of the opinion that economics will fall into line as an evolutionary science independently of any consideration of the latter's likely intrinsic worth as a cognitive device, i.e. irrespective of any potential an evolutionary economic science may possess to contribute to human understanding. And with this being the case, Veblen regards a constructive programme (whether or not desired or desirable) as unnecessary. For economics will become an evolutionary science anyway:

The later [evolutionary] method of apprehending and assimilating facts and handling them for the purposes of knowledge
may be better or worse, more or less worthy or adequate, than
the earlier; it may be of greater or less ceremonial or aesthetic
effect; we may be moved to regret the incursion of underbred
habits of thought into the scholar's domain. But all that is beside
the present point. Under the stress of modern technological
exigencies, men's everyday habits of thought are falling into the
lines that in the sciences constitute the evolutionary method; and
knowledge which proceeds on a higher, more archaic plain is
becoming alien and meaningless to them. The social and political
sciences must follow the drift, for they are already caught in it.

(Veblen 1898: 81)

Veblen as a thoroughgoing evolutionist

Economics, argues Veblen, is becoming an evolutionary science, whether
anyone is happy about this or not. There is, in consequence, no point to
considering how to bring such a situation about. I think, then, that the
model A interpretation of Veblen's understanding of how the evolutionary
method (X) will come to be accepted, has to be rejected. But what is to be
put in its place? Warren Samuels (1990) provides an excellent contribution
that in effect opposes model A. On the basis of providing a wealth of
textual evidence, Samuels concludes:

Indeed [Veblen] was a *true* (may I say it that way?) evolutionary
economist: He applied his evolutionary thinking to his own
thinking, even to evolutionary thinking itself.

(Samuels 1990: 707)

In this:

Veblen adopts … the position … that interpretation is interpreta-
tion-system specific, that there are no meta-criteria on which to
chose between alternative preconceptions, et cetera, with any
serious degree of conclusivity, except by selecting the premise on
which rests the preconception thereby chosen, that there is no
independent interpretative or evaluative standpoint.

(Samuels 1990: 703–4)

Here, I take it, Samuels is acknowledging Veblen's view that the take-up
of the evolutionary method or of 'evolutionary thinking' is itself something that can be analysed by the evolutionary method or is subject to
evolutionary thinking. Samuels also reads into Veblen a belief that there is

Table 8.2 Models A and B

	X	Y	Z
	Method or science under discussion	*Process whereby X is expected to become widely accepted*	*Evaluative orientation towards X*
Model A (Ayres and most institutionalists)	Evolutionary	Constructive research programme with evolutionary science of economics the goal	Non-neutral
Model B (Samuels and postmodernists)	Evolutionary	Evolutionary	Evolutionist or neutral

no standpoint from which evolutionary thinking can be meaningfully evaluated in terms of relative worth compared to other approaches. Thus Samuel's position, and others like it, it seems to me, can be schematised as (a version of) model B in Table 8.2.

In Table 8.2 the term evolutionary, in the first column, denotes the method (X) under discussion whilst, in the second column, it indicates a process (Y) analysed in terms of the evolutionary method.[7] By describing, in the third column, an evaluative orientation (Z) as evolutionist, I simply mean a perspective according to which any outcome (and here, specifically, the relevant [anticipated] outcome is the widespread acceptance of the evolutionary method) is regarded as merely fortuitous or 'impersonal'. Its being caused or 'selected' does not thereby make it normal, good, or lauda- tory, etc.

I believe model B is a fair representation of Samuel's interpretation (as well as of other accounts which portray Veblen in postmodernist terms or along similar lines). And there is indeed reason for concluding that model B, in part at least, represents an advance over model A, as I have already noted. However, there is also a sense in which I think model B goes too far. An interpretation that I think better represents Veblen's position, and which below I want to defend, is systematised as model C in Table 8.3 on page 192.

Why do I suppose model C is the better representation of Veblen's posi- tion? There are several reasons. Let me list them before attempting to substantiate them. First, it can be shown that the passages drawn upon by Samuels and others to support model B mostly count only against the idea that Veblen was arguing explicitly that a constructive programme be taken up. In criticising an aspect of model A it is being taken for granted that model B is the only viable alternative. However, once model C is brought into contention we can see that rather more argumentation is required if model B is to be maintained. In my view, the passages noted by Samuels

Table 8.3 Models A, B and C

	X	Y	Z
	Method or science under discussion	*Process whereby X is expected to become widely accepted*	*Evaluative orientation towards X*
Model A (Ayres and most institutionalists)	Evolutionary	Constructive research programme with evolutionary science of economics the goal	Non-neutral
Model B (Samuels and postmodernists)	Evolutionary	Evolutionary	Evolutionist or neutral
Model C	Evolutionary	Evolutionary	Non-neutral

lend themselves at least as much to model C as to model B. Second, Veblen is seen to engage explicitly in the practice of ontological critique (or determinate negation)[8] in support of a particular ontological conception associated with the evolutionary approach or method. Third, Veblen does after all reveal a view that the evolutionary method is more worthy in relevant respects than considered alternatives. Taken together, these claims provide an interpretation of Veblen whereby he does not insist that we are all trapped in our current epistemological or interpretative frameworks. If substantiated, we shall see that they move us some way towards supporting the composite thesis here in contention, that a significant philosophical legacy of Veblen is a constructive programme of an essentially ontological nature. Before taking the argument further, though, I need to justify the claims just made.

The textual evidence for the claim that Veblen is a thoroughgoing evolutionist

To see that model C fares at least as well as model B in the light of the passages to which Samuels refers, let me consider some of the latter. I have already noted, for example, that Veblen writes:

> The later [evolutionary] method of apprehending and assimilating facts and handling them for the purposes of knowledge may be better or worse, more or less worthy or adequate, than the earlier. … But all that is beside the present point.
>
> (Veblen 1898: 81)

We can see, though, that this passage (and I contend the same is true of others like it reproduced by Samuels) establishes not that Veblen denies the possibility of intrinsic merit to any methods of science, but only that he considers such matters irrelevant to the process of whether or not any specific method is taken up. The point, according to Veblen, is only that the evolutionary method will come to be dominant in economics irrespective of whether it carries any intrinsic merit. The question of worth is laid aside in such passages as this, rather than dismissed as indeterminate.

A further passage, regarded by Samuels as fundamental to his argument runs as follows:

> In the modern culture, industry, industrial processes and industrial products … have become the *chief* force in *shaping* men's daily life, and therefore the *chief* factor in *shaping* men's habits of thought. Hence men have learned to think in the terms in which the technological processes act. This is *particularly* true of those men who by virtue of a *peculiarly strong susceptibility* in this direction become addicted to that habit of matter-of-fact inquiry that constitutes scientific research.
>
> (Veblen 1906: 17, emphasis added)

This passage is interpreted by Samuels as revealing Veblen's acceptance that all thinking is system-specific, that we are effectively without choice in our epistemological frameworks.

Now in arguing for model C, I do not wish to deny that industrial processes and products can have a significant influence on community habits, etc., even perhaps affecting the processes of science. All of us are in some ways shaped by our social conditions. But to accept this is not to deny all space for critical evaluative thought. In particular, to be significantly causally affected by specific social forces does not prevent us investigating and knowing these forces. As Evanthia Sofianou put it (in an extremely insightful assessment of postmodernism):

> one *need* not get outside social structures in order to study them. It is true, of course that one cannot adopt a God's eye view of the world, but that does not mean that one can only adopt a child's eye view.
>
> (Sofianou 1995: 384)

My claim at this point is only that the noted influences are not all determining, and that Veblen recognises this. I have italicised words and phrases from the quoted passage of Veblen's just because, it seems to me, they allow a critical distance to remain. Habits of thought are shaped but not determined. And if it is 'particularly true' of some that they have learned to think in the ways described, the point of emphasising this is presumably just because it is not particularly true of everyone else. Once more, though, the focus is really on the column 2 entry. And the evidence is that Veblen thinks the process of change to be broadly evolutionary, but not completely. Not everyone is totally susceptible.

Such qualified statements are found in other passages reproduced by Samuels. I cannot include all such extracts here, but consider, for example, the following. I draw the reader's attention not just to the main thrust of the comment, but equally to the qualifications (which again I have italicised):

> the point of view of economists has always been *in large part* the point of view of the enlightened common sense of their time. The spiritual attitude of a given generation of economists is therefore *in good part* a special outgrowth of the ideals and preconceptions current in the world about them.
>
> (Veblen 1899b: 86, emphasis added)

A further passage central to Samuel's assessment runs as follows:

> A discussion of the scientific point of view which avowedly proceeds from this point of view itself has necessarily the appearance of an argument in a circle; and such in *great part* is the character of what here follows. It is in *large part* an attempt to explain the scientific point of view in terms of itself, *but not altogether*.
>
> (Veblen 1908: 32, emphasis added)

Samuels is correct that this reveals Veblen's recognition of the need to be self-referential, or to situate oneself within one's own analysis. In this Veblen certainly reveals himself to be a leading thinker of his time. But the italicised words serve to qualify the extent to which Veblen sees himself arguing 'in a circle'. His next sentence, explaining his qualifications, reads:

> This inquiry does not presume to deal with the origin or the *legitimation* of the postulates of science, but only with the growth of the habitual use of these postulates, and the manner of using them.
>
> (Veblen 1908: 32, emphasis added)

Here I take Veblen to be saying that he deals only with the evolutionary process whereby the evolutionary postulates come quite widely to be habitually used. The question of their legitimisation, though, is expressly not considered. Veblen is not going as far as to suggest that the question of the legitimacy of these postulates is beyond being addressed. He is indicating only that making any such assessment is not any part of his basic objective.

So far, then, I have suggested that even textual evidence of the sort noted by Samuels does not clinch the model B interpretation of Veblen. It does count against an aspect of model A, namely the idea that Veblen was advocating the take-up of a constructive programme. But a defence of model B requires more. For proponents of model B to establish the evolutionist justificatory stance, it is essential they also demonstrate that, for Veblen, these evolutionary forces are all determining, whilst the evolutionary method itself is beyond evaluation. Samuels does seem happy to attribute to Veblen a 'cultural determinism of habits of mind and habits of behaviour' (Samuels 1990: 711), but I do not think the passages taken from Veblen can sustain such an attribution. Indeed, the various (noted) qualifications in the passages reproduced by Samuels do not really make sense on model B, and already suggest that model C is the more adequate representation. In any case, it is possible to produce further textual and other evidence that can be sustained only by model C.

Veblen's evaluative orientation

I have noted that, for Veblen, the evolutionary method is more or less defined as one that is appropriate to a causalist ontology. I am suggesting that although Veblen anticipates the evolutionary method taking hold via an evolutionary process, he actually evaluates this development positively. If this interpretation is correct we might expect to find concrete evidence to support it. Specifically, we might expect to find indications in Veblen's writings that he does indeed believe the evolutionary method to be not only worthy or realistic as a scientific aid, but also more so than are the other approaches to which he refers. Further, because the evolutionary method is conceived in terms of its appropriateness to a specific causalist ontology, we might also expect to find evidence not only of Veblen's attachment to this ontology, but also of a belief that an ontological position such as this (or indeed any that is supported) can be defended directly (rather than viewing ontological presuppositions as always, for everyone, a by-product of their current habits of thought, and being not open to question).

It is of course precisely these two implications of model C that those inclined to model B deny. The latter contributors interpret Veblen as arguing that we are more or less determined by our cultural frameworks (Samuels 1990; Peukert 2001). From this perspective, Veblen's position is that 'There is no truth beyond alternative and often opposing frames (scientific or otherwise)' (Peukert 2001: 551), so that Veblen's causalist preconceptions must be 'derivative' of his views on method, not insights rendering the former appropriate (Samuels 1990).

Now, I believe both that Veblen does defend a causalist ontology directly, and also that he is seen to evaluate the evolutionary method in both absolute and relative terms. Let me consider the former part of this contention first.[9]

Critical ontology and determinate negation

Elsewhere (Lawson 1997a: 50–1), I have defended (amongst other forms of argument) the method of *determinate negation* for discriminating between competing ontological conceptions. The aim is to search out common ground with an opponent holding an alternative conception, and then to show that this common ground presupposes (ontological and other) conditions consistent with the maintained position but not with the opponent's alternative. It is effectively such a determinate negation, I believe, that Veblen seeks to supply in support of the ontology of cumulative causation.[10] Let me briefly elaborate.

Veblen recognises that some modern scientists (especially those concerned to apply mathematical formalism) reject the metaphysical idea of cumulative causation, with its cognate categories of continuity, efficiency and activity.[11] This particular group of scientists, observes Veblen, attempts to avoid the metaphysical notion of causality by focusing only on the observable 'concomitance of variation':

> The concept of causation is recognized to be a metaphysical postulate, a matter of imputation, not of observation; whereas it is claimed that scientific inquiry neither does nor can legitimately, nor, indeed, currently, make use of a postulate more metaphysical than the concept of an idle concomitance of variation, such as is adequately expressed in terms of mathematical function.
>
> (Veblen 1908: 33)

Veblen seems to accept the contention that, at least for some (statistical) materials, concomitance of variation has a role in science, that it is possible to 'make use' of it. This is a shared premise, which Veblen accepts as 'sound' (1908: 33).[12] But in accepting this premise, Veblen argues that, by their holding to it, his opponents presuppose precisely what they seek to deny. According to Veblen, these very scientists cannot help but 'impute' causal sequence to the facts, even as they profess not to do so:

> The claim [not to impute causality], indeed, carries its own refutation. In making such a claim, both in rejecting the imputation of metaphysical postulates and in defending their position against their critics, the arguments put forward by the scientists run in causal terms. For the polemical purposes, where their antagonists are to be scientifically confuted, the defenders of the non-committal postulate of concomitance find that postulate inadequate. They are not content, in this precarious conjuncture, simply to attest a relation of idle quantitative concomitance (mathematical function) between the allegations of their critics, on the one hand, and their own controversial exposition of these

matters on the other hand. They argue that they do not 'make use of' such a postulate as 'efficiency', whereas they claim to 'make use of' the concept of function. But 'make use of' is not a notion of functional variation but of causal efficiency in a somewhat gross and highly anthropomorphic form. The relation between their own thinking and the 'principles' which they 'apply' or the experiments and calculations which they 'institute' in their 'search' for facts, is not held to be of this non-committal kind.

(Veblen 1908: 34)

The matter of primary relevance, here, is not whether Veblen's ontological argument is correct or even whether it is compelling, but that he endeavours to make it at all. Rather than accept any ontological commitments uncritically, Veblen is very clearly seeking to demonstrate that one set, specifically that which he closely associates with the evolutionary method, is explanatorily superior to another.

Notice, too, that Veblen is not just 'deconstructing' the position of scientists who reject a causalist ontology. He is not merely revealing that their premises presuppose a causalist ontology. In signalling an acceptance of their premise, he is simultaneously committing himself to its revealed presuppositions.

Further, at one point Veblen attempts a version of an argument familiar in critical realism. Elsewhere (Lawson 1997a; Chapter 1 above) I argue that although empirical realists (those who reduce reality to events and their correlations) extol the controlled experiment as the exemplar of science on the grounds that it is where event regularities are mostly found to occur, they lack the means of explaining why event regularities are mostly restricted to these experimental conditions. Or rather they can explain the latter phenomenon only by admitting that which they wish to deny. For in order to make sense of the situation it must be recognised that event regularities are so restricted precisely because it is mostly in controlled experiments that underlying causal mechanisms can be insulated (from countervailing mechanisms) and empirically identified. Veblen is surely getting at the same insight when (in the same footnote from which the previous passages have been extracted) he makes the following observation:

Least of all is the masterly experimentalist himself in a position to deny that his intelligence counts for something more efficient than idle concomitance in such a case. The connection between his premises, hypotheses, and experiments, on the one hand, and his theoretical results, on the other hand, is not felt to be of the nature of mathematical function. Consistently adhered to, the principle of 'function' or concomitant variation precludes recourse to experiment, hypotheses or inquiry – indeed it precludes 'recourse' to anything whatever. Its notation does not comprise anything so anthropomorphic.

(Veblen 1908: 35)[13]

Veblen's support for the evolutionary method

If Veblen defends a causalist ontology (albeit only in footnotes) and characterises the evolutionary method as one that is appropriate to it (more so than are the earlier deductive methods of taxonomy, and so on), it is to be expected, as I say, that he would reveal some positive inclination towards the evolutionary approach as scientific method. And so he does. In line with his revealed support for the ontology of cumulative causation, Veblen is seen to support the evolutionary method in both absolute and relative terms.

First, he most definitely sees the evolutionary habit of mind as realistic:

> But in the hands of the later classical writers the [economic] science ... was ... out of touch with that realistic or evolutionary habit of mind which got under way about the middle of the century in the natural sciences.
>
> (Veblen 1898: 69)

Second, he makes a comparative assessment. Veblen interprets the changes in habits of thought he is discussing not as epistemically neutral but as a movement in a realistic direction:

> In modern times, and particularly in the industrial countries, this coercive guidance of men's habits of thought in the realistic direction has been especially pronounced; and the effect shows itself in a somewhat reluctant but cumulative departure from the archaic point of view. The departure is most visible and has gone farthest in those homely branches of knowledge that have to do immediately with modern mechanical processes, such as engineering designs and technological contrivances generally.
>
> (Veblen 1898: 63–4)

Let me immeadiately emphasise that I am *not* interpreting Veblen as arguing that the reason habits of thought are moving in the noted (realistic) direction is the quality or desirability of their being realistic. This feature of the observed movement is not its own explanation. Rather, Veblen implies that the relevant habits of thought are taking hold for independent reasons rooted in the nature of the machine process. Technology is developing in a way that encourages changes in community-wide habits of thought. These in turn do affect the scientific habits of thought of even economists. But there is no suggestion by Veblen that the particular developments in technology are somehow being induced with the intention of facilitating changes in habits of thought in the realistic direction. The latter is but an (unintended) by-product of a process that is governed by different goals. Developments in industrial processes have not always encouraged the more realistic or evolutionary habit of thought. However, it is the case that modern changes in technological processes, whatever their particular causes, are of a nature as to produce this effect at this current time:

> As time goes on … the circumstances which condition men's systematisation of facts change in such a way as to throw the impersonal character of the sequence of events more and more into the foreground. The penalties for failure to apprehend facts in dispassionate terms fall surer and swifter. The sweep of events is forced home more consistently on men's minds. The guiding hand of a spiritual agency or a propensity in events becomes less readily traceable as men's knowledge of things grows ampler and more searching. In modern times, and particularly in the industrial countries, this coercive guidance of men's habits of thought in the realistic direction has been especially pronounced; and the effect shows itself in a somewhat reluctant but cumulative departure from the archaic point of view. The departure is most visible and has gone farthest in those homely branches of knowledge that have to do immediately with modern mechanical processes, such as engineering designs and technological contrivances generally.
>
> (Veblen 1898: 63–4)

In short, Veblen does reveal his evaluation that the evolutionary method is the more realistic, but without ever suggesting that this latter quality is the reason he expected the evolutionary habit of thought to be taking the ascendency.

I might emphasise that in defending this interpretation of Veblen's position it does not follow that I am necessarily in agreement with all of his argument. Veblen is suggesting that the spread of the machine process necessarily encourages a widespread acceptance of 'matter-of-fact' habits of thought presupposing a non-teleological causalist ontology. It is this movement that was predicted eventually to lead to the widespread acceptance of the evolutionary method, even in the economics academy. We know this latter speculation to be in large part wrong. My purpose is only to identify aspects of Veblen's basic position. Whether we entirely accept Veblen's account of how the machine process comes to affect community habits is something else again.

The puzzle of Veblen's reticence about supporting the evolutionary approach

Once the features of Veblen's writings just considered are brought into explicit focus, I think we can see that model C provides a better grounded explanation of Veblen's position than the contending alternatives. However, before we can rest content with the model C interpretation of Veblen I believe there is a challenge thrown up by it that has to be met. This is to explain Veblen's apparent reluctance to emphasise his support for the evolutionary approach. For, although Veblen's acceptance of the superior cognitive worth of the evolutionary method is apparent (at least upon close scrutiny of his contributions), it has to be admitted that it is not overly stated. Indeed, Veblen mostly plays down the sorts of factors identified and discussed above. Even the noted determinate negations, demonstrating relative support for the preconceptions of Veblen's preferred method, are wholly relegated to footnotes Although an ontological perspective which contrasts significantly with that presupposed by the (then and current) mainstream project is a distinctive and fundamental feature of Veblen's writing, it cannot be said that Veblen ever contributed significantly to explicit and sustained ontological elaboration or argumentation. Moreover, when Veblen does reveal explicit support for the evolutionary method over rivals in the main body of a text, there is little doubt that it is couched mostly in terms of the merely pragmatic criteria of being 'more up-to-date', or some such (see e.g. Veblen 1898: 57). Why, then, this apparent reluctance on Veblen's part to emphasise his (on close examination clear) relative support for the evolutionary method, and for economics becoming an evolutionary science?

I believe this reticence, if such it is, is explained precisely by Veblen's wariness of being (mis)interpreted as suggesting that the evolutionary method will catch on merely because it is in some sense the most realistic. This is not his message. As proponents of model B correctly emphasise, Veblen himself is presenting an evolutionary story. He is providing an evolutionary account of the rise to dominance of a specific (as it happens: the evolutionary) method. He is advancing an evolutionary analysis consistent with his interpretation of the evolutionary method.

I earlier noted Veblen's assessment that the mark of a modern evolutionary scientist is that he or she is '*unwilling to depart* from the test of causal relation or quantitative sequence', that he or she *refuses* 'to go back of the colourless sequence of phenomena and seek higher ground for their syntheses'. Hence if Veblen's own account is to qualify as being evolutionary according to his own conception of this category, it is essential that he too does *not depart* from 'the test of causal relation or quantitative sequence'. In consequence, any belief that Veblen also has in the greater adequacy or realisticness of the method must clearly *not* figure (and be recognised as not figuring) in his evolutionary story.

In short, it is precisely in order to emphasise his view that the evolutionary model is (he believed) rising to dominance on evolutionary grounds that Veblen is somewhat hesitant about disclosing his own evaluation of the evolutionary method too often. According to Veblen's conception, the question of worth is irrelevant to evolutionary analysis. And with ongoing developments being conceived as evolutionary, his own evaluations are treated as an irrelevancy to his argument.

However, there is nothing *per se* in the evolutionary model as conceived by Veblen that rules out the possibility of a situation wherein 'impersonal' forces do work to bring about a scientific orientation that can be judged best or worthy or more realistic than alternatives, but where this latter outcome is but an unintended by-product of the process, bearing no directional influence at all on the causal process itself. Nor is there anything in the evolutionary model which necessitates that it is impossible for some (or even many) observers of the evolutionary process to be both situated within it and yet retain something of a critical distance.[14] Even when he is most non-committal, Veblen does not deny the possibility of the evolutionary method being evaluated, or of its having intrinsic worth in given contexts. And we have further seen, indeed, that there are various arguments and statements made by Veblen which reveal he does consider the evolutionary method to be realistic, and its ontological presuppositions the more sustainable.

Coherence of meaning

Let me be clear on the nature of my argument here. Implicitly I am acting on a principle of charity. According to it, when there are conflicting interpretations of an author's meaning, it is charitable to accept that interpretation which renders the author most coherent. By this I do not mean it is best to seek out the interpretation that makes the author (most) correct from the point of view of our latest understandings.[15] On that criterion the likes of Aristotle, Newton and Einstein, for example, would not always fare especially well. Rather, I mean it is best to seek that interpretation which renders each contribution by an author most coherent in the sense of being internally (developmentally) consistent and contributing to the knowledge of her or his time.

Whilst model C can accommodate the evidence adduced in favour of model B (and, I think, can also accommodate it in a more satisfactory manner), the relation cannot be reversed: model B cannot accommodate Veblen's clear support for the ('realistic') evolutionary method underpinned by his appraisal that cumulative causation is a more sustainable ontology than others considered.

I might emphasise that the tensions I am suggesting for the model B interpretation have not gone previously unnoted. Thus at one point Samuels writes of his conclusion in favour of (in effect) model B:

> This does not negate Veblen's affection for and endorsement of matter-of-factness, evolutionary science, and technology as an imperative force. But it does enable us to perceive and to understand the tension within Veblen's work between doing his own work as an objective, evolutionary economic scientist, and recognizing the subjective and normative limits of his work, that is, its self-referentiable quality ... Veblen was comfortable with the indeterminate and the ambiguous.
>
> (Samuels 1990: 707)

My claim is that from the perspective of model C we can recognise the same objective and subjective aspects in science, and indeed in all knowledge, but without needing to attribute to Veblen the tension and ambiguity that Samuels' interpretation cannot avoid finding.[16]

If model B were the correct interpretation of Veblen it would mean he ended up in a situation wherein he can advance little beyond agreeing that whatever is selected is selected. This is a *judgemental relativism*. When in reply to Hoksbergen (1994), Samuels (1998) says that he does not know of any 'extreme relativists who upon the discovery that there is no objectively certain foundations' in epistemology or ethics 'jump to the conclusion that nothing matters' (823), he ignores the fact that this is more or less where his interpretation ultimately leaves Veblen. For on the interpretation of model B, what real basis would Veblen have for concluding otherwise (on all this see especially Sofianou 1995)?

A commitment to *epistemological relativism* is something else. Postmodernists and modern (critical) realists alike share it. Such a relativism recognises the situatedness of us all and the relativity (to our positions and experiences, etc.) of the (partial, fallible and transient) conceptions we form. This sort of relativism, though, can be coupled with an ontological realism to prevent the slide to the (judgemental relativist) position that Samuels too wants to avoid.[17] And this means acknowledging the possibility, and need, of an (explicitly realist) orientation wherein competing claims at any level are open to comparative evaluation.

The legacy of a constructive programme

So where does all this take us? My argument is that Veblen, in effect, has at least two concerns in formulating his famous question. The first is his desire that economics become more realistic, underpinning his belief that economics ought to be an evolutionary science. The second is his interest in explaining why it has not happened yet, and in announcing that, whatever the obstacle, it inevitably will do so soon.

Now it is highly significant that, in terms of implications for practice, there is a clear sense in which the presuppositions behind his second concern dominate those implicated in the first. After all if something is thought bound to happen, the question of 'what should be done' (to make it happen) becomes effectively a non-issue. This is why a constructive programme is never explicitly formulated or actively developed by Veblen.

However, Veblen has proven to be wrong (so far) in his assessment of the inevitability of economics becoming an evolutionary science. He advanced an evolutionary epistemology, and in the precise predictive form it is specified at least, it has proven to be erroneous. Indeed, Veblen's account of how the machine process would impinge on habits of thought is especially suspect. And further along in the process, there is no inevitability about what happens in the academy. The very fact that so many (old) institutionalists currently survive amidst the modern dominant group, the latter with their deductivist habits of thought, is testament to this.

The upshot is that the former of Veblen's two concerns in formulating his famous question, and the practical implications of accepting it, are no longer superfluous to the situation of economics. In other words, in the circumstances in which we find ourselves, an impetus, at least, to develop an evolutionary science can, after all, be said to be a component of Veblen's legacy. Even if model A is not a correct interpretation of his contribution, the activist programme it highlights is nevertheless something to which we might reasonably have expected Veblen to turn in the circumstances. It is unlikely that the failure of his specific evolutionary theory would have undermined his (revealed) preference for economics becoming an evolutionary science. Thus Ayres and others can, after all, be said to be developing a Veblenian programme.

In fact, we can, with some legitimacy, infer more than this. Veblen at one point in his 'evolutionary essay' indicates his view that if economics is to succeed in becoming an evolutionary science, 'the way is plain so far as regards the general direction in which the move will be made' (Veblen 1898: 72). Of course, Veblen thought that the outcome in question was inevitable. And this may, in large part, explain Veblen's relative neglect of sustained ontological elaboration. But with the failure of his predictions to be realised, we might reasonably treat his projection of how an evolutionary economics will turn out as indicative of his assessment of how it should turn out. Thus we might, after all, interpret Veblen's contributions on such matters as providing not only support, but also a suggestive basis, for a Veblenian constructivist programme. To the extent that Veblen elaborates the form he believed an evolutionary economic science was likely to take, and to the extent the elaborated account is viable, I think we can accept, after all, that a constructive programme (and not just an impetus to such a programme) is indeed a feature of Veblen's legacy. This, I quickly want to indicate, is indeed the case (for a more detailed discussion from a perspective similar to that defended here, see especially Mayhew 1998a; Hodgson 2001b).

The nature of Veblen's contribution

I am arguing that Veblen's contribution, is, in effect, a manifestation of an ontological thesis, one significantly at odds with that of our modern-day deductivist mainstream, and one, in various aspects, reasonably in line with that defended in this book.[18] Moreover, if I am correct in this it follows that the sort of constructivist programme towards which modern-day Veblenians might, with reason, be working (if concerned to develop Veblen's own contribution) is one that also involves an ontological turn, in short, a project in realist social theorising.

Simply put, my claim here is that a central philosophical thesis held by Veblen is that reality, natural and social, includes at least some aspects that can be conceived only in terms of non-teleological cumulative causation. Now, it is clear that Veblen supposes this ontology characterises many if not all the sciences, for he talks of them all falling in line with the evolutionary method. But this does not mean that he believes social processes either to be reducible to natural ones, or to lack a distinctive economics aspect. In fact, Veblen's various elaborations give reason to suspect that, in his under-standing of the social domain, he was in effect edging towards a special case of the realist transformational model of social activity that I have defended throughout this book and elsewhere (Lawson 1997a; Chapter 2 above). Let me at this point very briefly elaborate and support this claim.

A transformational social ontology

According to the transformational model, let me recall, all aspects of social life are fluid to varying degrees, with each aspect being reproduced and/or transformed through human social activity. Thus, for example, social structure[19] is conceptualised as neither fixed nor created. Rather, it both pre-exists and conditions action, and through human action in total, is itself reproduced and/or transformed. Social being is a process of becoming.

Further, this transformational conception is found also to apply to many aspects of human individuals. Human beings, like society, are structured. And with this being so each human individual also undergoes, or rather is, a process of transformation. For if our species-level being, although not ahistorical, seems *a posteriori* to be relatively enduring, this is much less the case for the cultural and individual expressions of our nature. Individuals are born into society and exist and develop through it in a way such that their very capacities and personalities, including psychological and other dispositions, are to an extent moulded, shaped, formed and continually transformed by the societal conditions.

Put differently, social and other structures that enable and constrain at a point in time, can, where they endure, facilitate a moulding or transformation of individuals affected by them. Indeed, we might say that structures constrain and enable synchronically and facilitate a continuous transformation of agency diachronically (on all this see e.g. Lawson 1997a: esp. ch. 13; Chapter 2 above).

Human practice is the key. A central plank of the conception of a social world defended above and elsewhere, is of a process in motion, which turns on human action or practice. Through human action all the social structures that make up society are reproduced and/or transformed. And so too, through this same activity, human beings themselves are, under many aspects at least, reproduced and/or transformed. The essential conception defended, in short, is of a highly structured and interactive process in motion, whose various aspects – the individual, structure and context – each presuppose, and condition, but remain irreducible to, one another. Each is an element in the social process, both as a condition of the reproduction and/or transformation of the others and as an outcome; everything is reproduced and/or transformed through practice.

Veblen's evolutionary economics

Let me now consider the bearing of all this for what I am suggesting is Veblen's implicit vision of an evolutionary economics. Because Veblen's comment that 'the way is plain so far as regards the general direction on which the move [towards an evolutionary science of economics] will be made' is found in his (more famous) 'evolutionary essay', I confine myself in the first instance to the vision as found there .

Now, as we have seen, it is Veblen's understanding that the evolutionary sciences are concerned with (non-teleological) processes of cumulative change and causation. In consequence we should not be surprised to find that Veblen focuses on processes of precisely this sort when contemplating material suitable for an evolutionary economics:

> There is the economic life process still in great measure awaiting theoretical formulation. The active material in which the economic process goes on is the human material of the industrial community. For the purpose of [an evolutionary] economic science the process of cumulative change that is to be accounted for is the sequence of change in the methods of doing things – the methods of dealing with the material means of life.
>
> (Veblen 1898: 70–1)

Several features of this passage are worth noting. Observe, first of all, that Veblen makes reference from the outset to the economic 'life process'. By this expression I take Veblen to be concerned with the way human society and culture, and human beings in society and in culture, develop or change overtime. Just as Darwin was interested in the history of all life regulated by 'descent with modification', so I think Veblen takes the goal of evolutionary social theory to be human socio-cultural history regulated through descent with modification.

Of course, Veblen is focusing on economics. So his primary concern is with one aspect of this life process, namely the economic aspect (though we shall see below that he recognises that all socio-cultural development has an economic aspect). By 'economic' Veblen means that aspect of the life process concerned with methods for dealing with the 'material means of life'. So Veblen is concerned with socio-cultural evolution primarily as it connects to changes in the methods of dealing with the material means of life, basically technology.

Now a problem of most existing writings on this subject, according to Veblen, is that the 'ways and means of turning material objects and circumstances to account' have been viewed only under their aspect of being inert (basically conceived as a mass of material objects serviceable for human use). Such a perspective is fine for purposes of taxonomy, but not for considering them as elements of a process of cumulative change or development.[20]

But how are these material means to be viewed or treated as items in such a process? Veblen's answer is as facts of human knowledge, skill and predilection. Viewed under these aspects the material means of life take the form of (or they condition) 'substantially, prevalent habits of thought, and it is as such that they enter into the process of industrial development' (1898: 71). Habits both endure and adapt, in line with 'changes in material facts'. However, the physical properties of the available materials, which Veblen associates with the taxonomic interest, are all constants. It is first and foremost the human agent that displays continuity-in-development:

> The changes that take place in the mechanical contrivances are an expression of changes in the human factor. Changes in the material facts breed further change only through the human factor. It is in the human material that the continuity of development is to be looked for; and it is here, therefore, that the motor forces of the process of economic development must be studied if they are to be studied in action at all. Economic action must be the subject-matter of the science if the science is to fall into line as an evolutionary science.

> (Veblen 1898: 71–2)

This extract, in essence, expresses Veblen's conception of the core subject-matter of economics. He develops this outline further, as we shall see. But already we have a rudimentary transformational model of social activity in which methods for dealing for the material means of life, construed as material facts, are both condition and consequence of action. It is through changes in the 'human factor' that we achieve changes in 'mechanical contrivances'.

However, Veblen, as I say, is concerned with the broader economic life process. In this much else is reproduced and transformed besides mechanical contrivances, including not only the individual (as the preceding extract already suggests) but also the group of which any individual is a part, and wider society and culture too. Veblen motivates this part of his discussion by criticising the Austrian tradition, not so much for treating the material means of production as inert (which, in his judgement, is the failing of the 'classical trend' and, for the most part, also of the Historical School [1898: 72]), but for maintaining a faulty conception of human nature. It is a conception whereby human beings are viewed mostly under the aspect of suffering pleasures and pains through the impact of particular forces. Veblen, drawing in contrast on 'later psychology, re-enforced by modern anthropological research' (1898; 73), defends an alternative conception of human nature whereby it is the characteristic of human beings to *do* something. Even in experiencing or desiring things, activity is always involved in an non-incidental way. Human activity is central to everything:

> According to this view, human activity, and economic activity among the rest, is not apprehended as something incidental to the process of saturating given desires. The activity is itself the substantial fact of the process, and the desires under whose guidance the action takes place are circumstances of temperament which determine the specific direction in which the activity will unfold itself in the given case.
>
> (Veblen 1898: 74)

Veblen here accepts that individual actions are guided by circumstances of temperament. He also acknowledges that these

> are ultimate and definitive for the individual who acts under them, so far as regards his attitude as agent in the particular action in which he is engaged.
>
> (Veblen 1898: 74)

However, from the broader perspective with which he is concerned, namely that of evolutionary science, these circumstances of temperament are but transient features, being a product of the past and a condition of the next phase of development; they 'but afford the point of departure for the next step in the process.'(Veblen 1898: 74)[21]

Here, then, we have a process of cumulative causation as it affects the methods of life, the individual's habits of thought, attitudes, circumstances of temperament, and so forth. And such a process of cumulative causation also characterises the group in which the individual lives:

> What is true of the individual in this respect is true of the group in which he lives. All economic change is a change in the economic community, – a change in the community's methods of turning material things to account. The change is always in the last resort a change in habits of thought. This is true even of changes in the mechanical processes of industry. A given contrivance for effecting certain material ends becomes a circumstance which affects the further growth of habits of thought – habitual methods of procedure – and so becomes a point of departure for further development of the methods of compassing the ends sought and for the further variation of ends that are sought to be compassed.
>
> (Veblen 1898: 75)

So the central component of Veblen's account of cumulative causation as the subject-matter of an evolutionary economics is essentially a rudimentary transformational model of social activity, in which methods of production and individual human attributes are both condition and consequence of the process, both being continually transformed within it.

The place of the evolutionary method within economics

Notice that Veblen does not seek to reduce all of economics to evolutionary science. Specifically, he does not rule out the idea of teleological processes constituting legitimate objects of economic study. In particular, Veblen accepts that individual action is teleological, so that its understanding requires methods other than those which Veblen is considering:

> Economic action is teleological, in the sense that men always and everywhere seek to do something. What, in specific detail they seek, is not to be answered except by a scrutiny of the details of their activity; but, so long as we have to do with their life as members of the economic community, there remains the generic fact that their life is an unfolding activity of a teleological kind.
>
> It may or may not be a teleological process in the sense that it tends or should tend to any end that is conceived to be worthy or adequate by the inquirer or by the consensus of inquirers. Whether it is or is a not, is a question with which the present

inquiry is not concerned; and it is also a question of which an evolutionary economics need take no account.

(Veblen 1898: 75–6)

He himself is concerned with the wider sweep of events. Further Veblen recognises that the realm of economics is not isolatable from all others.[22] In particular the economic interest, and its consequences, impact on all other spheres. It is in developing this contention that Veblen mentions institutions. And the economic interest bears on the formation and cumulative growth of these, whether or not they can be perceived as primarily economic. Notice that Veblen now couches his discussion in terms of (economic) life history:

The economic life history of any community is its life history in so far as it is shaped by men's interest in the material means of life. This economic interest has counted for much in shaping the cultural growth of all communities. Primarily and most obviously, it has guided the formation, the cumulative growth, of that range of conventionalities and methods of life that are currently recognized as economic institutions; but the same interest has also pervaded the community's life and its cultural growth at points where the resulting structural features are not chiefly and most immediately of an economic bearing. The economic interest goes with men through life, and it goes with the race throughout its process of cultural development. It affects the cultural structure at all points, so that all institutions may be said to be in some measure economic institutions. This is necessarily the case, since the base of action – the point of departure – at any step in the process is the entire organic complex of habits of thought that have been shaped by the past process.

(Veblen 1898: 76–7)

Putting all this together Veblen, in effect, contends that an evolutionary economics must be a theory of a process of cumulative causation which centres on human activity influenced by the economic interest, a process which accounts for the development (reproduction and transformation) of everything from traits of all individuals, their habits, especially habits of thought, to cultural aspects of society at large and (or including) institutions. In a word, an evolutionary economics must concern itself with the economic aspects of the life *process*:

From what has been said it appears that an evolutionary economics must be the theory of a process of cultural growth as determined by the economic interest, a theory of a cumulative sequence of economic institutions stated in terms of the process itself. ... It is necessarily the aim of such an economics to trace the cumulative working out of the economic interest in the cultural sequence. It must be a theory of the economic life process of the race or the community.

(Veblen 1898: 77–8)

I believe we do get a clear insight from all this into Veblen's vision of an evolutionary economics. As I say, Veblen was under the impression that the realisation of this imagined conception was inevitable. With the advantage of hindsight we can see that it was not, and is not, inevitable at all, but requires active support and development. In this light I think it not unreasonable to treat Veblen's vision as the basis for a modern day (Veblenian) constructive programme.

Evolutionary science, institutions and natural selection

Before finally considering the implications of all this for any modern Veblenian strand of old institutionalism, there is an aspect of Veblen's contribution as found in the 'evolutionary essay' (and elsewhere) which I think it is important briefly to address. For it has implications for any modern Veblenian programme. The feature I have in mind is actually an absence. Despite numerous references to Darwin in his writings, and Veblen's likely interpretation of himself as Darwinian, it is a noticeable feature of the 'evolutionary essay' that it contains no mention at all of Darwinian mechanisms of 'natural selection' (or the associated category of selective adaptation). In fact, as far as I can see the term 'natural selection' appears only once in the methodological essays that make up *The Place of Science in Modern Civilisation*, and even then seemingly only in passing.[23] It figures prominently in one chapter of his first book, *The Theory of the Leisure Class*. But this book is primarily a substantive, not a methodological, text. In any case it remains a most noticeable feature of Veblen's methodological papers that, although references to evolutionary method and evolutionary (or modern) science are prominent throughout, there is much less concern (to put it mildly) for Darwinian processes of natural selection.

What are we to make of this? Some commentators who have observed the sparse use of the expression 'natural selection' worry that this might be taken by some readers to compromise the interpretation of Veblen as Darwinian. Seeking to avoid this inference, explanations are offered which portray Veblen as motivated, in making these omissions, by a desire to avoid confusing readers, or some such.[24]

My own explanation of Veblen's limited use of the phrase 'natural selection' is somewhat different. As already noted I do accept that Veblen likely interpreted himself as Darwinian. But I think it wrong to suppose that to be Darwinian means to reduce evolutionary science to a concern with processes of natural selection. I suspect that Veblen, eventually at least, appreciated this. Let me briefly elaborate the claim that Darwinian evolution does not reduce to natural selection.

For Darwin, evolution is a history of life, positing the connection of all organisms, and viewing the life process as regulated by descent with modification. The relevant aspect of Darwin's account for the current discussion is that Darwin is quite explicit in his view that such mechanisms of modification as are to be found do not reduce to processes of natural selection. He even states as much explicitly in his 'Introduction' to his *On the Origin of Species*. I already noted in Chapter 5 above that in the last edition of the *Origin* Darwin complains that he has 'been much misrepresented' by those who state 'that I attribute the modification of species exclusively to natural selection' (Darwin 1872: 421). It is noteworthy, perhaps, that Darwin's complaint about being misrepresented was brought to popular attention in a famous essay by Romanes (1892–7) published at roughly the time Veblen would have been developing his ideas on Darwinian evolution. Reflecting on Darwin's complaint of misrepresentation, Romanes observes that 'In the whole range of Darwin's writings there cannot be a passage so strongly worded as this: it presents the only note of bitterness in all the thousands of pages which he has published' (1892–7: 5).

Actually Romanes is wrong in this. There is a letter that Darwin wrote to *Nature* in 1880 which is just as strongly worded. But it reinforces Romanes' point all the more. For this further passage is also concerned with the particular misrepresentation which Darwin notes in the *Origin*. This time, Darwin singles out the individual miscreant:

> I am sorry to find that Sir Wyville Thomson does not understand the principle of natural selection. ... If he had done so, he could not have written the following sentence in the introduction to the *Voyage of Challenger*: 'The Character of the abyssal fauna refuses to give the least support to the theory which refers the evolution of the species to extreme variation guided only by natural selection.' This is a standard criticism not uncommonly reached by theologians and metaphysicians when they write on scientific subjects, but is something new coming from a naturalist ... Can Sir Wyville Thomson name anyone who said that the evolution of species depends only on natural selection?
>
> (Darwin 1880: 32)

So there is no necessary puzzle in the realisation that Veblen makes frequent reference to Darwin but sparse use of the expression natural selection and associated terms such as selective adaption. It does not follow from the interpretation of Veblen's emphasis here advanced that he did not believe such mechanisms to be operative (or even pervasive) in social life (or the contrary). It merely was not essential that his analysis descend to the level of concreteness of specific mechanisms, whatever they were, for his conception to constitute a potential framework for an evolutionary economics in the Darwinian mould. For this it was enough that Veblen identified non-teleological processes of cumulative causation. The precise mechanisms in play in any context are a matter of detailed concrete, empirical analysis.

It is tempting to suppose that this explains why explicit references to processes of 'natural selection' are mostly restricted to Veblen's *Theory of the Leisure Class*. For this, as I say, is a less philosophical or abstract, more substantive, work. If this *is* the explanation, we must still note that Veblen's claims there made are somewhat stronger than a substantive study can license. Indeed, references made in the *Leisure Class* to such processes of natural selection (of institutions and habits of thought especially) are seemingly almost universalising in nature.[25] The fact that Veblen thereafter (as far as I can discern) drops such universalising claims about processes of natural selection, suggests, I think, that he came, in due course, to think better of holding to such a methodological (reductionist) stance.[26]

Habits, institutions and the transformational model

Let me also, at this point, say something about Veblen's conception of habits and institutions and how they relate to the transformational conception of social activity.

Actually, the just discussed chapter of the *Leisure Class* does in several ways seem clearly preliminary. There are times when institutions are regarded as distinct from habits of thought, and others where the two features appear almost to be conflated. And even in this chapter, Veblen implies he is not actually concerned how the adaptive process (of natural selection) operates. His basic point, rather, is to emphasise the view that institutions change and develop, and that their doing so is essential to the development of activity:

> For the present purposes, however, the question as to the nature of the adaptive process – whether it is chiefly a selection between stable types of temperament and character, or chiefly an adaptation of men's habits of thought to changing circumstances – is of less importance than the fact that, by one method or another, institutions change and develop. ... The development of these institutions is the development of society.
>
> (Veblen 1899a: 190)

Once we turn to his later (and in some ways more mature) methodological works, I think a more coherent position on the relation between institutions and habits is to be found in particular. Consider, for example, Veblen's *The Limitations of Marginal Utility* (1909). Here, as in the early 'evolutionary essay', Veblen interprets 'modern science' as 'occupied about questions of genesis and cumulative change, and it converges upon a theoretical formulation in the shape of a life-history drawn in causal terms' (1909: 240). And his conception of the tasks of economic science is much the same as it was ten years before.[27] But his conception of an institution has developed. There is now no tendency to conflate institutions with habits.[28] And more to the point, the manner whereby institutions and habits arise and develop is expressed in terms very similar to the transformational model of social activity. Thus Veblen writes:

> The growth and mutations of the institutional fabric are an outcome of the conduct of the individual members of the group, since it is out of the experience of the individuals, through the habituation of individuals, that institutions arise; and it is in this same experience that these institutions act to direct and define the aims and end of conduct. It is, of course, on individuals that the system of institutions imposes those conventional standards, ideals, and canons of conduct that make up the community's scheme of life.
>
> (Veblen 1909: 243)

There is, of course, a notable difference between Veblen's conception, as expressed in such a passage, and the formulation of the transformational model defended throughout this book. Whilst I have been focusing on social structure and agency in general, and how they condition each other, Veblen edges towards a special case of the transformational conception wherein institutions are the primary form of social structure considered, and habits the primary form of human practice,[29] with each being both condition and consequence of the other.

But I think these differences largely reflect the contrasting ambitions of our respective projects. My own goal is to derive as general a social ontology as is sustainable, whilst Veblen's is to anticipate those features of social reality that most readily lend themselves to a genetic account of cumulative causation. Thus whilst I am concerned with developing an ontology which covers (i.e. can accommodate) all aspects of social structure, and all the various modes of their being reproduced and/or transformed through all forms of practice, including (where appropriate) more or less teleological ones, Veblen's emphasis is very much on the evolutionary special case. And it seems to be Veblen's view that it is features like institutions and their conditions and consequences that best serve the purposes of a genetic account of the sort with which he is concerned:

Scientific inquiry in this field, therefore, must deal with individual conduct and must formulate its theoretical results in terms of individual conduct. But such an inquiry can serve the purposes of a genetic theory only if and in so far as this individual conduct is attended to in those respects in which it counts toward habituation, and so toward change (or stability) of the institutional fabric, on the one hand, and in those respects in which it is prompted and guided by the received institutional conceptions and ideals on the other hand.

(Veblen 1909: 243)

Implications for modern old institutionalism

What, then, follows for the modern project of old institutionalism concerned to preserve its Veblenian pedigree? My contention is that in Veblen's writings we find the basis for a constructive programme of institutionalist or evolutionary economics. The project anticipated is one concerned with processes of change and specifically cumulative causation, with institutions and habits featuring centrally as condition and consequence of each other, and considered under their economic aspects.

So interpreted, the anticipated project is broadly ontological in its basic conception. By this I mean that it is a project conditioned (and, as it happens, differentiated from the current mainstream programme) by an ontological assessment. Institutionalists, I acknowledge, have not overly emphasised matters of ontology, and certainly there is a case for rendering the ontological presuppositions of the modern-day institutionalist project more explicit and systematic. Even so, ontological considerations have, since Veblen, effectively driven many of the institutionalist tradition's insights and legitimate concerns (albeit, as with Veblen himself, mostly in implicit and unacknowledged ways). And ontological concerns remain relevant, especially in directing research. For example, they give indications of likely limits to research approaches, and of questions or projects whose pursuit promises to be fruitful. And they are suggestive too at the level of methodology. Let me consider some examples for a Veblenian programme that fall under these three heads.

Clear *limits* are suggested by the fact that Veblen's ontological conception is not a broad philosophical one covering the social domain, but a specific scientific one, of non-teleological processes of cumulative causation. Thus, and following Veblen himself, it is reasonable not to seek to universalise this evolutionary emphasis *a priori*. Specifically, if evolutionary science is concerned with non-teleological processes of cumulative causation, the teleological aspects of economic life are a sufficient reason not to reduce the whole of economics to evolutionary thinking.

Just as significantly, and again in keeping with Veblen's contributions, at least when considered as a whole, it is important not to reduce evolutionary science itself to the study of processes of natural selection. Rather, the latter are but specific mechanisms within (or examples of) non-teleological processes of cumulative causation. The question of their relevance to the social realm is something to be determined *a posteriori*.

These cautionary considerations are themselves indicative of *questions* or *projects* that it is potentially fruitful to pursue. Certainly, the task of determining the potential scope (or limits to the usefulness) of the evolutionary method in economics is now seen to be an appropriate one for this project. So is that of examining whether institutions, habits and the like are indeed the most relevant features of an evolutionary focus concerned with genetic accounts of cumulative causation, and of investigating how institutions and habits interconnect and condition each other over time. A further useful endeavour that fits in here is investigating the relevance of accounts of natural selection mechanisms to the social realm. And relevant here, too, is the question of how human subjectivity is affected or shaped by the institutional process. This latter line of inquiry will involve a focus on matters of anthropology in particular (see especially Mayhew 1998a; 1998b).

Turning to *method*, it is sometimes suggested that Veblen's contributions carry no methodological implications for substantive economics. But I think we can now see that this is incorrect. Of course, in advance of a particular investigation it is rarely, if ever, feasible to determine which precise methods will prove to be the most useful in any given context. But it is often possible to throw light on the sorts of methodological orientations or approaches that will be required. In focusing on non-teleological processes of cumulative causation, Veblen is not concerning himself with phenomena (if any) that can be usefully analysed with self-contained or ahistorical systems of economic theory.[31] Indeed, he is rejecting the idea that social processes can typically be represented as tendencies to normal or predetermined outcomes, or 'natural states', such as are presumed by such self-contained schemes or theories. Even though individual activities are intentional and in that sense teleological, what actually comes about in most situations can be determined only after the event. So substantive research, to accord with Veblen's vision and interest, will mostly be backwards-looking. It will clearly involve detailed empirical investigation of what has taken place, and appraisal of particular processes going forward. It requires of researchers that they seek to uncover what has been, and is, actually going on. Indeed, twenty-five years into the twentieth century Veblen was confident (if mistaken[31]) that this was how 'the current generation of economists' were already proceeding:

> Self-contained systems of economic theory, balanced and compendious, are no longer at the focal centre of attention; nor is there a felt need of such. ... Meantime, detailed monographic and item-

215

ised inquiry, description, analysis, and appraisal of particular processes going forward in industry and business, are engaging the best attention of economists; instead of that meticulous reconstruction and canvasing of schematic theories that once was of great moment and that brought comfort and assurance to its adepts and their disciples. There is little prospect that the current generation of economists will work out a compendious system of economic theory at large.

(Veblen 1954 [1928]: 8)

If there are general principles involved, continues Veblen, they are mostly:

principles of common sense and common information prevalent in this opening quarter of the century [which] are of an evolutionary, or genetic complexion, in that they hold the attention to the changes that are going forward, rather than focus it on that 'Natural State of Man', as Nassau Senior calls it, to which the movement of history was believed inevitably to tend. The question now before the body of economists is not how things stabilise themselves in a 'static state,' but how they endlessly grow and change.

(Veblen 1925 [1954]: 8)

If Veblen was mistaken in his assessment of the extent to which the methodological orientation described was being taken up, the latter nevertheless has been adopted by small groups of institutionalists and others in various locations here and there.[32] Veblen provides a grounding that renders endeavour of the sort described not as anti- or a-theoretical, as critics mostly interpret it,[33] and as even some sympathisers have worried,[34] but as theoretical in the sense of according with (the broader conceptual framework of) an evolutionary approach concerned with processes of cumulative causation.

I am suggesting, then, that the real modern-day import of Veblen's focus is that it coherently marks the site of a specific (evolutionary) project *within* economics, one that can with reason be interpreted as Veblen's legacy. And the project is surely one that warrants being regarded as, or at least as a central component of, that (old) institutionalist tradition which, in Ayres' words (noted at the outset of the current chapter), recognises Veblen as its 'founding father and guiding spirit'.

If, as I have argued, this project is closely identified with the analysis of economic change and development, and more particularly the study of material processes of cumulative causation couched in terms of institutions, habits and the like, it can be viewed as one in realist social theorising with a specific focus. An advantage of such a delineation is that it provides a coherent way of distinguishing the project that does not reduce it to an insistence on any (transient) current results or (reductionist) methodological stipulations (concerning units of analysis and the like). It also grounds this social-theoretical project in a manner that renders it consistent with the realist project defended throughout this book but without reducing it to the latter. Most importantly, it encumbers the project with a set of tasks whose pursuit is both urgent and promising of being fruitful.

Making the most of Veblen

In conclusion, Veblen did not advance a conception of evolutionary science as a constructive programme. He believed that there was little reason to do so, for he anticipated that economics was becoming an evolutionary science anyway. Moreover he thought the reasons for the impending dominance of the evolutionary method had no direct bearing on the worth of the evolutionary method. Indeed, he thought the process whereby this method would rise to dominance could itself be interpreted as evolutionary according to his non-teleological understanding of the concept. Thus Veblen was at pains to avoid implying that his anticipation that economics would become an evolutionary science was at all connected with any judgements he might make regarding the worth of the evolutionary method. That is, he was keen to apply the evolutionary method, as he understood it, in a consistent manner, to be an early evolutionary epistemologist.

But Veblen did make comparative appraisals. He did favour (and, at least in footnotes, defend) the evolutionary method or its preconditions. Moreover, Veblen's specific version of evolutionary epistemology turned out to be wrong. His prediction that economics would soon become an evolutionary science was confounded by events.

In the circumstances, Veblen's normative stance and its practical implications can reasonably be called into play. Specifically, Veblen's enduring insights as to how an evolutionary economics might take shape can legitimately be considered a basis for a Veblenian constructive programme.

Veblen's specific vision regarding an evolutionary economics, I have suggested, closely reflects his holding to a different social ontology from that presupposed by the current mainstream. It is an ontology of (non-teleological) cumulative causation. And if we are to make the most of Veblen's insights it is essential to recognise this, to render the ontological insights of the tradition more explicit, sustained and systematic.

Veblen adjudged that economics not only was, but also ought to be, falling in line as an evolutionary science. I am in effect suggesting that an appropriate modern-day restatement of this assessment is that the tradition of modern (old) institutionalism may be, and also seemingly ought to be, seeking to realise its evident potential not just as a constructive project, but as a specific (evolutionary) project within that strand of economics most concerned with realist social theorising.

9

FEMINISM, REALISM AND UNIVERSALISM[1]

The practice of *a priori* universalising

Feminist contributions can claim a good deal of the credit for modern social theory displaying increasing sensitivity to the dangers of overgeneralising. Fundamental here is the recognition that values, experiences, objectives and common-sense interpretations of dominant groups may be merely that; there is nothing especially natural or necessarily universal about them. All claims, whether made from within the academy or without, whether cautiously or boldly formulated, etc., are made from particular positions by interested parties. No person or group can reasonably profess a neutral, detached, unbiased perspective; all under- standings achieved are partial (as well as fallible and likely to be transient). The practice of universalising *a priori*, of merely asserting/ assuming the widespread validity/relevance of some position, is now widely recognised as, at best, a methodological mistake, and one that can carry significant political consequences.[2]

As is well known, however, it has proven all too easy to slide from a position of opposing the practice of *a priori* universalising to one of more or less opposing the endeavour of generalising altogether. In particular, once the basis for treating a dominant stance or approach as universally legitimate has been successfully called into question it has often proven difficult to avoid concluding that all approaches or stances are as legiti-mate as each other.

With regard to some issues this sort of reaction is unproblematic, even facilitating. But this is not the case with all matters, and especially, I think, with respect to broader projects of illumination and human emancipation. In particular, theorists have found it difficult to defend a notion of objectivity or progress in knowledge, or to sustain any basis for an emancipatory politics, where these objectives are of central concern to many feminists. The conclusion too often drawn is that, even in matters such as these, all we can safely say is that there are differences.

My limited objective here is to argue that, in addressing these latter sorts of difficulties, there are possible advantages to feminist explanatory and emancipatory projects from engaging (or engaging more fully) in the sort of explicit ontological analysis associated with modern versions (at least) of scientific realism.

In encouraging this sort of stance I do not wish to suggest that scientific realism or ontological considerations are entirely absent from feminist thought. Indeed, I think it is impossible that they could be. But I think it possible that ontological commitments are too rarely rendered explicit. And when the question of realism is raised (in whatever form) at all, the latter, it seems to me, is mostly treated in an overly guarded way in much feminist thought, as if accepting that any explicitly realist perspective is necessarily problematic.

I am not alone in this perception. Caroline New (1998: 2), for example, recently records that in modern feminist thought 'realism' seems 'tainted', and writes of 'realism's current resounding unpopularity among feminist theorists' (1998: 12). She also suggests that proving a reasonably, 'robust' defence of feminist standpoint theory's realism is more 'than its current proponents seem willing to risk' (1998: 6).

Others caution distance. Martha Nussbaum (whose argument for grounding ethical theory in the nature of human capacities is undoubtedly realist) finds the standing of realism to be sufficiently low as to caution 'that it would appear strategically wise for an ethical and political view that seeks broad support not to rely on the truth of metaphysical realism' (Nussbaum 1995: 69).[3]

Some feel the need to include an explicit disclaimer. Donna Haraway provides a prominent example. Despite setting out a perspective that seems so clearly to embrace scientific or ontological realism,[4] Haraway seemingly feels that credibility rests upon expressly denying that this is so: 'The approach I am recommending is not a version of "realism", which has proved a rather poor way of engaging with the world's active agency' (Haraway 1988: 260).

My worry is that this negative or distancing orientation can result in legitimate realist considerations being played down to an extent that may actually be debilitating for the feminist project, not least in preventing it from dealing as effectively as it might with the sorts of tensions or difficulties already noted. My aim here, then, is to caution against any blanket rejection of realist-type analysis as ultimately unnecessarily constraining of feminist thinking and advance.

I start, though, by defining some of my terms. Following this I move, in the main part of the paper, to indicate the sorts of differences that I think explicit realist/ontological analysis can make.

Feminism and realism

There are in fact numerous interpretations or types of realism. In the broadest philosophical sense of the term relevant here, any position can be designated a realism that asserts the existence of some (possibly disputed) kind of entity (such as black holes, quarks, gender relations, Loch Ness monsters, utilities, probabilities, men, women, truth, tables, chairs, etc.) As such I think it is clear there are very many conceivable realisms of this sort and all of us are realists of some kind or other.

In science, a realist position, i.e. *scientific realism*, asserts that the ultimate objects of enquiry exist for the most part independently of, or at least prior to, their investigation. (My primary concern here is indeed with scientific realism. But significant amongst other types of realism relevant here are *perceptual realism* maintaining the existence of material objects in space and time independently of their perception, and *predicative realism* maintaining the existence of universals either independently of particular material things, as in *Platonic realism*, or as their properties, as in *Aristotelian realism*. Clearly, scientific realism reduces to perceptual or predicative realism if the objects of scientific knowledge just are material objects or Platonic [or Aristotelian] forms.)

Realism so interpreted is inherently bound up with ontology, with (the study of) the nature of existence or being. And, indeed, it is the explicit concern with ontology that I want to promote here. Not all questions traditionally of interest to scientific realists have turned on the explicit study of ontology. Indeed, until very recently discussions about realism have turned to a large extent on the epistemological question of the truth of our knowledge, rather than the ontological question of the reality of structures and things.[5] The debate, though, has moved on in recent years, and in ways that I think has relevance for feminist concerns.[6]

Of course, scientific realism, even when recognised as first and foremost a theory not of knowledge or truth, but of being, is nevertheless bound to possess epistemological implications. But it warrants emphasis that *there is nothing essential to scientific or ontological realism that supposes or requires that objects of knowledge be naturalistic or other than transient, that knowledge obtained is other than fallible, partial and itself transient, or that scientists or researchers are other than positioned, biased, interested, and practically, culturally and socially conditioned.*

I emphasise this aspect just because I suspect that it may be central to the critical orientation to realism that I detect in much feminist thought. My concern is that there is a tendency in the feminist literature for a particular and naive form of realism to be made to stand in for all (and specifically scientific) realisms. This is a version which does treat all reality as fixed, science and knowledge as somehow value- and interest-free or neutral, as well as necessarily convergent on truth regarded as objective. To the extent that scientific realism is so conceived, its rejection in feminist thought is explicable.[7]

My primary concern here, though, is not with explaining the phenomenon in question but with indicating some of its consequences. My starting point remains the perception that, for whatever reasons, scientific realism, as an explicit orientation, is to a significant extent excluded from, or downplayed in, the mainstream feminist discussion, including that now occurring in economics.[8] But my intention here, the main purpose of this paper, is to suggest that this situation, whatever its explanation, is unfortunate. A rehabilitation of explicit realist reasoning in feminist thinking not only does not necessitate a slide into absolutism, but actually carries the potential to make a constructive difference, to serve to advance the feminist epistemological and emancipatory project.[9]

An indication that realism/ontology matters

In the remainder of the paper I want to give a set of schematic illustrations to help ground my claim that realist thought, and in particular explicit ontological analysis, can be beneficial to, and is probably indispensable for, any would-be explanatory and emancipatory projects. In particular, I want to indicate that such analysis is most likely essential to sustaining revelatory and emancipatory projects in the face of problems or difficulties of the sort I noted at the outset – turning on the need to oppose ungrounded *a priori* universalising without altogether abandoning the possibility of generalist or collective endeavour.

I start with a specific issue of method confronting contemporary economics, before moving, for my second illustration, to topics more widely discussed within feminist epistemology, and, for my third, to assessing the possibility of projects of human emancipation. In the first illustration, which lays the basis for the two illustrations which follow on, I join the 'deconstructive' strand of feminist thinking by bringing ontology to bear in questioning the general relevance of certain methods of economics that have in practice been universalised in an *a priori* fashion. In the second and third illustrations, I indicate how ontological analysis can help ground projects of epistemology and emancipation of the sort pursued by feminists.

Illustration 1: the formalistic modelling of social processes

Consider first the case of method in modern economics. The dominant feature here is the widespread reliance upon the practice of formalistic modelling.[10] This approach has certainly been universalised within the economics discipline, and with little if any grounding or argument, and despite its record of failure. Feminists have also criticised it as masculinist. I think it is (albeit an approach that is also perhaps race- and class-, etc., specific). But what follows for the feminist critic? Is it that all other approaches, including any preferred by feminists, be given greater emphasis?[11] Or should more feminists do formalistic modelling?[12] Perhaps both responses follow, or are they largely incompatible? Is it, say, that the scarcity of feminist modellers entails that the set of questions currently addressed is unnecessarily limited, or is it, perhaps, that formalistic methods themselves are undesirably limited in their usefulness, and possibly even debilitating of revelatory and emancipatory progress? How do we begin to decide?

Answering such questions, questions which may or may not involve a false dichotomy, requires at the very least that the revelatory potential of formalistic methods be investigated. And this, I want to argue, necessitates an attention to ontology. Specifically, I want to indicate that by briefly examining both the nature of social material and the ontological presuppositions of the procedures of formalistic modelling, it can be demonstrated that the latter procedures are not at all well equipped for illuminating the social realm. This conclusion is easily established, but rarely is so precisely because of the widespread reluctance to engage in ontology. It is just this relucatance that I wish to call into question.

The particularity of formalistic modelling

But is formalistic modelling really so restricted in its usefulness? As I say, I think it is, *and that it can be shown to be so*. Let me briefly sketch my argument. First, consider the sorts of conditions under which formalistic modelling has relevance. Basically, such modelling attempts to relate one (measurable) set of events or states of affairs to others. It presupposes correlations in surface phenomena, that is, strict (possibly including probabilistic) regularities of the form 'whenever event (or state of affairs) x then event (or state of affairs) y'. Let me refer to situations in which such regularities occur as closed systems. Formalistic modelling, to have general relevance, presupposes the ubiquity of such closures.

Now, an observation often recorded but rarely reflected upon is that, outside astronomy, such event regularities, or at least those found to be of interest and significance in science in general, are mostly confined to situations of well controlled experiment. An additional observation is that the results of controlled experiment are regularly successfully applied outside the experimental laboratory where event regularities are not in evidence.

A recognition of this situation, then, already casts doubt on the rationality of ploughing ever more resources into producing yet additional formalistic economic models. Certainly, the failures of the econometrics project over the last fifty years or so is indicative that the social world is open, that event regularities in the social realm are far from ubiquitous. The usual response, of course, is to pronounce that we must try harder: to formulate ever more complex models using larger data sets, or to dig deeper in the expectation of finding the sought-after invariances at a more micro, or anyway different, level. However, the recognition that even in the natural realm significant event regularities are systematically restricted, and largely found only in situations of experimental control, encourages a suspicion that significant successes in the social realm may not be possible even in principle. It is clearly essential at this stage that the observed patterning of event regularities be explained.

But how *can* we make sense of the observed *confinement* of most event regularities to the experimental set-up? Notice first that this observation generates immediate tensions for any programme which insists that such event regularities are essential to science (as the indispensable objects of scientific laws including laws of nature, or some such). For it follows that science (if thought to necessitate the elaboration of event regularities) is after all not only far from universal but, outside astronomy, mostly confined to experimental set-ups; it is actually fenced off from most of the goings-on in the world. Moreover, one is bound to conclude from this that (many) laws of nature (if event regularities are essential to them) depend upon human actions (in setting up the experimental situation), which is at least counter-intuitive. But it also follows that the further familiar observation that science is efficacious outside the experiment, where event regularities do not occur, is unintelligible.

How then are we to make sense of these considerations? How is it that scientists, in their experimental activities, can (frequently) codetermine a particular pattern of events which would not have come about but for their intervention? And how can we make sense of the successful application of science outside of the experimental laboratory, and specifically in conditions where event regularities do not necessarily occur? What must the world be like for such experimental practices, results, and their successful nonexperimental application to be possible?

A structured ontology

In order to provide a satisfactory set of answers to such questions it is necessary to abandon not only the presumption, implicit in a good deal of economic modelling practice and debate, that event regularities of the sought-after sort are ubiquitous in nature, but also the equally widely held view that the scientifically significant generalisations of nature consist of event regularities. Instead, we must accept a conception of the objects of science as structured (irreducible to events) and intransitive (existing and acting independently of their being identified). That is, experimental activity and results, and the application of experimentally determined knowledge outside of experimental situations, can be made intelligible only through invoking something like an ontology of structures, powers, generative mechanisms and their tendencies that lie behind and govern the flux of events in an essentially open world.

The fall of an autumn leaf, for example, does not conform to an empirical regularity, and precisely because it is governed in complex ways by the actions of different juxtaposed and counteracting mechanisms. Not only is the path of the leaf governed by gravitational pull, but also by aerodynamic, thermal, inertial and other mechanisms. According to this conception, then, experimental activity can be understood as an attempt to intervene in order to insulate a particular mechanism of interest by holding off all other potentially counteracting forces. The aim is to engineer a system in which the actions of any mechanism being investigated are more readily identifiable. *Thus experimental activity is rendered intelligible not as the production of a rare situation in which an empirical law is put into effect, but as an intervention designed to bring about those special circumstances under which a non-empirical law, a mechanism or tendency, can be empirically identified.* The law itself (now understood as a description of the workings of an underlying tendency) is always operative; if the triggering conditions hold, the mechanism is activated and in play whatever else is going on. On this understanding, for example, a leaf is subject to the gravitational tendency even as I hold it in the palm of my hand or as it 'flies' over roof tops and chimneys. Through this sort of reasoning we can make sense of the successful application of experimentally established scientific knowledge outside experimental situations. The context in which a mechanism is operative is irrelevant to the law's specification.

Conditions for closure

If, then, we are to make sense of the largely experimental confinement of event regularities, along with the wider application of experimentally determined results, it seems that we must recognise that reality is

1   *open* (event regularities are not ubiquitous – openness is required in order that closure, the occurrence of an event regularity, is a human achievement); and
2   *structured* (constituted by underlying powers, mechanisms and so forth as well as the actual course of events and states of affairs); with
3   some features of it being both

   (i)   *separable* (allowing the experimental manipulation and insulation of some mechanisms from the effects of others) and

(ii) *intrinsically stable* or *'atomistic'* (allowing the production of definite repeatable and predictable consequences once/if the mechanism is triggered).

Under these conditions it is at least feasible that human intervention can bring about a situation in which a mechanism which can act both inside and outside the experimental laboratory, is insulated under controlled experimental conditions and triggered. In these circumstances a predictable correlation between triggering conditions and the effects of the mechanism is feasible, and a modelling strategy legitimate.

The social domain

To what extent do these ontological conditions, conditions whose regular satisfaction seems essential if we are to persevere in a generalised fashion with methods of formalistic modelling, carry over to the social realm? I pose this question, of course, merely to determine whether the methods of formalistic modelling have much relevance to the social realm at all. We shall see that this is unlikely.

First of all, what is meant by the social realm? I follow standard practice here and interpret it as the domain of phenomena whose existence depends at least in part on (intentional) human agency.

So understood, the social world is clearly structured. For example, a condition of our speech acts, but irreducible to them, are rules of grammar and other structures of language. It is easy to see that social life in general is governed or facilitated by social rules, rules which lay down rights, obligations, prerogatives and other possibilities and limits.

Although the fact of the social realm being structured seems a necessary condition for social event regularities of the sort pursued by econometricians to be guaranteed, it is not, as we have seen, sufficient for such an outcome: social structures, including mechanisms, need also to be intrinsically stable and amenable to insulation. I now want to suggest that the regular satisfaction of the latter two conditions is unlikely, and that this in large part explains the widespread failure of the econometrics project to date.

Notice, first of all, that because social structure both depends upon human agency and in turn conditions it, a switch of emphasis in social analysis is necessitated, away from those (extreme) conceptions, familiar in economics, of creation and determination, to notions of *reproduction* and *transformation*. For human intentional activity does not *create* social structure if the latter is presupposed by such activity. Instead, individual agents draw upon social structure as a condition of acting, and through the action of individuals taken in total, social structure is *reproduced* or (in part at least) *transformed*. Equally, though, social structure cannot be reified. For it is itself dependent upon always transformative human agency, and only at the moment of acting can aspects of social structure be interpreted as given to any individual. In short, through individuals drawing upon it in action, structure is continually reproduced or modified in form.[13]

Social positions and relations as integral to social reality

Social life, then, is not only structured but intrinsically dynamic. In emphasising its structured nature I have so far focused upon social rules. But this is not all there is to it. Specifically, social being is also constituted in a fundamental way by both *social relations* and *positions*. These features are essential to understanding the precise manner in which human agency and structure come together.

The significance and fact of social relations and positions are easily recognised once we take note (and inquire into the conditions) of that general feature of experience that there is a systematic disparity across individuals regarding the practices which are, and apparently can be, followed. Although most rules can be utilised by a wide group of people, it by no means follows that all rules are available, or apply equally, to everyone, even within a given culture. To the contrary, any (segment of) society is highly segmented in terms of the obligations and prerogatives that are on offer. Teachers, for example, are allowed and expected to follow different practices to students, government ministers to follow different ones to lay-people, employers to employees, men to women, landladies and landlords to tenants, and so on. Rules as resources are not equally available, or do not apply equally, to each member of the population at large.

What, then, explains the differentiated ascription of obligations, prerogatives, privileges and responsibilities? This question directs attention to the wider one of how human beings and social structure, such as rules, come together in the first place. If social structures such as rules are a different sort of thing to human beings, human agency and even action, what is the point of contact between human agency and structure? How do they interconnect? In particular, how do they come together in such a manner that different agents achieve different responsibilities and obligations and thereby call on, or are conditioned in their actions by, different social rules and so structures of power?

If it is clearly the case that teachers have different responsibilities, obligations and prerogatives to students, and government ministers face different ones to the rest of us, then it is equally apparent that these obligations and prerogatives exist independently of the particular individuals who happen, currently, to be teachers, students or ministers. If I, as a university teacher, were to move on tomorrow, someone else would take over my teaching responsibilities and enjoy the same obligations and prerogatives as I currently do. Indeed, those who occupy the positions of students are different every year. In short, society is constituted in large part by a set of *positions*, each associated with numerous obligations, rights and duties, and into which agents, as it were, slot.

Something more about this system of societal positions can be expressed if we take note of the additional observation that practices routinely followed by occupants of any type of position tend to be orientated towards some other group(s). The rights, tasks and obligations of teachers, for example, are orientated towards their interactions with students (and vice-versa), towards research-funding bodies or governing institutions, and so forth. Similarly the rights and obligations of landladies and landlords are orientated towards their interactions with tenants, and so on.

The importance of internal relations

Such considerations clearly indicate a causal role for certain forms of *relation*. Two types of relation must be distinguished: *external* and *internal*. Two objects or aspects are said to be externally related if neither is constituted by the relationship in which it stands to the other. Bread and butter, coffee and milk, barking dog and mail carrier, two passing strangers, provide examples. In contrast, two objects are said to be internally related if they are what they are by virtue of the relationship in which they stand to one other. Landlady/landlord and tenant, employer and employee, teacher and student, magnet and its field, are examples that spring easily to mind. In each case it is not possible to have the one without the other; each, in part, is what it is, and does what it does, by virtue of the relation in which it stands to the other.

Now the intelligibility of rule-governed and the rule-differentiated social situation noted above requires that we recognise 'first' the internal relationality of social life, and 'second' that the internal relationality in question is primarily not of individuals *per se* but of social positions. It is the positions that are defined in relation to others, say of teachers to students. The picture that emerges, in other words, is of a set, or network, of positions characterised by the rules and so practices associated with them, where the latter are determined in relation to other positions and their associated rules and practices. According to this conception the basic building blocks of society are *positions*, involving, depending upon, or constituted according to, social rules and associated tasks, obligations, and prerogatives, along with the practices they govern, where such positions are both defined in relation to other positions and are immediately occupied by individuals.

Notice finally that notions of social *systems* or *collectivities* can be straightforwardly developed using the conceptions of social rules, practices, relationships and positions now elaborated. Specifically, the conception of social systems and collectivities that is supported in this framework is precisely of an ensemble of networked, internally related positions with their associated rules and practices. All the familiar social systems, collectivities and organisations – the economy, the state, international and national companies, trade unions, households, schools and hospitals – can be recognised as depending upon, presupposing, or consisting in, internally-related position-rule systems of this form.

Formalistic modelling as a generalised tool of social science

What follows for the practices of economic modelling? We know that econometrics and other projects concerned with detecting social event regularities of interest have so far been rather unsuccessful. We now have an explanation: the social world is a highly internally related, intrinsically dynamic process, and one that is dependent upon, if irreducible to, transformative human agency. Certainly the experimental isolation of stable separable social structures and processes seems infeasible. Nor is it surprising that event regularities of sufficient stability to facilitate a successful practice of economic modelling, have not been found to occur spontaneously, that is behind the backs of human intentional actions. It can be admitted that there are numerous regularities which are *made* to happen but which are thereby of limited scientific interest. For example in certain parts of the world Christmas is usually celebrated on the same day each year – though even here, in specific families say, there can be exceptions due to illnesses, the need for members of the family to be away from home on 25 December, or whatever. But regularities such as this hardly constitute the sort of result that formalistic modellers seek to uncover.

In short the social realm seems to be constituted of stuff that is largely not *separable* or *intrinsically stable*, so that the lack of successes of the formalistic modelling project in economics is quite explicable, and future success seemingly improbable.

It follows, I think, that feminists may have been too cautious in their criticisms of formalistic modelling. Certainly, there are grounds for supposing that those empirically oriented feminists in economics insistent upon applying standard econometric methods in all contexts are proceeding wholly in the wrong direction.

But it may even be the case that feminists have been largely in error in identifying the primary direction of causation of the errors involved. I have in mind here the tendency of feminist economists to interpret as fundamental the disposition of male economists to portray human agents as relatively isolated self-contained individuals. The latter is seen as a peculiarly masculinist view, counterposed with the feminist emphasis on social relations. I think it is. But it may be indirectly and subconsciously achieved. For I am suggesting that the primary problem with mainstream economists, which differentiates them from other social researchers, is their largely uncritical passion for formalistic modelling. And once it is realised that, to guarantee results that take the event-regularity form, it is necessary to formulate conceptions of separable, stable (intrinsically constant) entities – basically of isolated atoms – the mainstream emphasis falls into place. For the individualistic agents of mainstream constructions are just that: individual optimising atoms set in situations where a unique optimum of sorts is feasible, guaranteeing stable predictable results. It may thus be the modelling strategy *per se* that is the chief masculinist error here, and the substantive formulations a secondary implication.[14]

In any case, ontological analysis is seen to be consequential. It reveals that formalistic modelling is not only overly partial: it may actually be misplaced.[15] Economists can pursue the same sorts of goals as the *a posteriori* successful natural sciences; that is, be concerned to identify causes of surface phenomena. But when mainstream economists insist that we should all work more or less exclusively with procedures of formalistic modelling, they succeed not only in marginalising without investigation all alternative approaches to doing economics, i.e. those that are not based on closed-systems modelling, but also in universalising a practice that even in natural science is found to be but a special case (confined mainly to the well controlled experimental situation), and a special case that, in the social realm, conceivably has no legitimate counterpart at all.

Illustration 2: positioned interests as essential to epistemic practice

If event regularities of the sort that are sometimes produced in the experimental sciences are so elusive in the social sciences, how is the systematic investigation of social phenomena possible? If ontology has helped us understand the *a posteriori* failures of the formalistic modelling approach in the social sciences, as well as the intrinsic limitations of the latter as a method for illuminating the open social system, can it take us further and also help guide us towards a more fruitful alternative way of proceeding? I want now to suggest that it can, and that in doing so it necessarily joins, and contributes to, the discussion, prominent in feminist theory, concerning the situatedness of knowing.

An epistemology for an open system

If social reality is open and complexly structured, being intrinsically dynamic and highly internally related, with a shifting mix of mechanisms lying beneath the surface phenomena of direct experience, how can we begin even to detect the separate effects of (relatively) distinct (aspects of) mechanisms or processes? This is the question I turn to address here. And it is only through ontological reflection that it is apparent that this is indeed the question that needs addressing.

In motivating my answer let me quickly take note of the fact that controlled experiments do not *all* take the form of insulating single stable mechanisms in 'repeated trials' with the intention of generating event regularities. That is, although event regularities of the sort required by mainstream modelling approaches are mostly produced in well-controlled experimental situations, not all experimental situations are concerned with producing event regularities of this form. An alternative project, illustrated, for example, by plant-breeding experiments, involves the use of control groups to help identify the effects of specific mechanisms of interest. Where, for example, crops are grown in the open there *can* be no expectation that all the causal factors affecting the yields are stable, reproducible or even identifiable. Yet progress in understanding can be achieved, through ensuring that two sets of crops receive broadly similar conditions except for one factor that is systematically applied to one set but not to the other. In this case, systematic differences in average yields of the two sets of crops can with reason be attributed to the factor in question.

In other words, experimental control frequently takes the form of comparing two different groups or populations with common or similar (if complex, irreversible and unpredictable) histories and shared (if non-constant) conditions, excepting that one group is 'treated' in some definite way that the second, control, group is not.

In the plant-breeding scenario just described, of course, the aim is to experiment with some compound that is already suspected of possessing yield-increasing causal powers. Our primary concern, however, is with detecting the effects of hitherto unknown or unrecognised mechanisms. But it is easy enough to appreciate the relevance of this scenario for a situation wherein, say, the yield of a given crop was expected *a priori* to be roughly the same in all parts of the field but discovered *a posteriori* to be systematically higher at one end. In this case an experimentalist has *not* actively treated the relevant end of the field. But it seems *prima facie* that there is an additional causal factor in operation here, even if we are as yet unaware of its identity.

The general situation I am suggesting as being relevant for social scientific explanation in open systems, then, is one in which there are two or more comparable populations involved. Our background knowledge leads us to expect a specific relation between outcomes of these populations (frequently a relationship of similarity, but not always), but wherein we are *a posteriori* surprised by the relation we actually discover. Under such conditions it is *prima facie* plausible that there is at work a previously unknown and identifiable causal mechanism, or aspects of a mechanism. Outside these conditions, however, it is difficult to see how, in an open system, projects of identifying hitherto unknown causal processes can even begin.

Contrastive explanation

The open and structured nature of social reality, then, means that we might resort to something like *contrastive explanation*, with explaining descriptive statements that take the form 'this rather than that'. Contrastive explanation, discussed at length in Chapter 4 under the heading of 'contrast explanation', is concerned not so much with such questions as 'why is the average crop yield x?', but with 'why is the average crop yield in that end of this field significantly higher than that achieved elsewhere?'. Explaining the latter is much less demanding than explaining the total yield. While accounting for the total yield requires an exhaustive list of all the causal factors bearing upon it, the contrastive question requires that we identify only the causes responsible for the difference. But the import of relatively systematic contrasts here lies not so much (or just) in the fact that the task delineated is less demanding, but in the fact that contrasts alert us to the situation that there is something of interest to be explained at all.[16]

Of course, it could have turned out that contrasts of the sort in question were nowhere to be observed. But *a posteriori* this has not been the case, they are everywhere in evidence. Women usually get worse jobs than men, or are paid less for the same contribution; a car journey from Cambridge to London is usually quicker by night than by day; currently in the UK many women wear make-up whereas most men do not; currently in the UK schoolgirls perform better academically in single-sex schools than in mixed schools; and so on.

I am suggesting, then, that, in a highly internally related, dynamic (and so typically non-separable, and non-repeatable) reality, the effects of causal mechanisms can be identified through formulating interesting contrastives at the level of actual phenomena. This means identifying differences (or surprising relations) between outcomes of two groups whose causal histories suggest that the outcomes in question ought to stand in some definite anticipated or plausible relationship (often one of rough equality or similarity) that is systematically at odds with what we observe. We do not and could not explain the complete causal conditions of any social or other phenomenon. To do so would presumably mean accounting for everything back to the 'big bang' and beyond. Rather we aim to identify single sets of causal mechanisms and structures. And these are indicated where the observed relationship between outcomes or features of different groups is other than was, or might have been, expected or at least imagined as a real possibility.

Notice, incidently, that I am not (of course) presuming that any factor or set of factors most directly responsible for a surprising contrast inevitably combines with all others in a mechanistic fashion. A causal factor present in one situation but not another may well combine with other factors in an organic or internally related fashion and so affect the manner of functioning of any, or all, causal conditions. This, is merely, is something to be determined in the course of the investigation. Here I am mainly focusing on the usefulness of contrasts of interest for getting potentially successful projects of illumination initiated.

Now it may seem that I am recommending a reasonably general approach here. And indeed I am, although I am making no claims about how generalised is its relevance. Certainly I do not wish to claim other than a partial perspective. But in truth there is no getting away from generalities. Claims that everywhere there are differences, or that differences matter, or that knowledge is situated, partial and so forth, are no less general. The relevant point is that (unlike, say, formalistic modellers in economics) I am identifying an approach for which the claim of being widely applicable seems *a posteriori* to have some grounds: there is both reason (as seen in the first illustrative example above) to suppose that the social world is not only open but intrinsically structured, and evidence that contrasts of interest abound in the social domain.

We can note, parenthetically, that the dominant approach of mainstream economics, namely formalistic modelling, is in the end a special case of that which I am defending anyway. For under certain experimental conditions, stable mechanisms can be, and often are, insulated and empirically identified. These moments are significant just because (or when) the event patterns produced within the experimental conditions *contrast* in a systematic way with those which emerge 'outside'. In other words, the experimental scientist is able to make an advance precisely by, and when, addressing the contrastive question: 'why is this event regularity achieved under these (specific experimental) conditions but not others?'. The problem which remains for mainstream economic modellers, of course, is that whilst interesting contrasts abound in the social realm, few if any seem to involve the discovery of surprising event regularities of a degree of strictness that can be regarded as satisfactory for their intended (explanatory/predictive/policy) purposes.

We might also note that the broader argument for reality being open and structured, sustained in the discussion of formalistic modelling above, is itself a further example of contrastive explanation. The contrast in question in this case is that generalised fact of experience that, outside astronomy, event regularities of interest in science are mostly confined to experimental situations. Explaining this contrastive phenomenon leads to the structured ontology I have elaborated. Thus it can be seen that if particular contrasts of interest lead to hypotheses about specific mechanisms, generalised contrasts of interest lead to philosophical ontologies. Given the *a posteriori* pervasiveness of interesting contrasts, the fact of open systems is seen to be debilitating neither for science nor for philosophy.

Situated knowing

Now all this has a bearing on the situatedness of knowledge emphasised in feminist theorising. For it follows from the emphasis upon contrastive explanation that the sorts of issues that are addressed in science, and the manner of their treatment, will necessarily reflect the perspectives, under-standings and personal-social histories, in short the 'situations', of the scientist/investigator. It is hardly a novel insight that in the process of choosing a primary phenomenon for explanatory analysis, scientific (and other) interests necessarily come to bear. But it is now apparent, once we recognise the contrastive nature of social scientific explanation, that the interests of the researcher necessarily determine which causal mechanism is pursued as well. For when phenomena in an open system are determined by a multiplicity of causes, *the particular one singled out for attention depends upon the contrast identified as puzzling, surprising, unusual, undesirable or of interest in some other way. And this in turn will reflect the interests and under-standings of the individual or group of researchers or interested onlookers involved.* It may be that it is only the interested farmer who can recognise that the animals are behaving strangely, only the parent that perceives that all is not well with the child, and only the marginalised group that appreciates the full nature or extent/effects of certain dominant structures or processes or of inequalities, and so forth.

   In this way, if amongst others, the situatedness of the investigator comes to the fore in science and explanation, in bearing upon the sorts of contrasts found surprising and warranting of explanation. It influences the direction or location of investigatory practice and so, ultimately, such discoveries or contributions to understanding as are made. In fact, I now want to suggest that insights into the situatedness of knowing achieved by reflecting on the multiple causation of phenomena serves not only to rein-force the feminist insistence on the situated nature of knowing but also to throw further light on certain related issues raised in feminist episte-mology. Let me briefly indicate a few of the ways in which contrastive explanation theory and feminist epistemology join together.

Contrastive explanation and feminist epistemology

I should emphasise, first of all, that the theory of contrastive explanation does not merely support the thesis, argued by many feminists, that inter-ested standpoints are inevitable. Certainly, the latter insight is sustained. And this insight is sufficient to undermine the conventional presumption whereby, as Sandra Harding critically summarises: 'socially situated beliefs only get to count as opinions. In order to achieve the status of knowledge, beliefs are supposed to break free of – to transcend – their original ties to local, historical interests, values and agendas' (Harding 1993: 236).

The position I am defending, however, goes further in suggesting that interested standpoints (including acquired values and prejudices) are not only unavoidable but actually indispensable *aids* to the explanatory process.[17] The task of detecting and identifying previously unknown causal mechanisms seems to require the recognition of surprising or interesting contrasts, and the latter in turn presupposes people in positions of being able to detect relevant contrasts and to perceive them as surprising or otherwise of interest and to want to act on their surprise or aroused interest. The initiation of new lines of investigation requires people predisposed, literally prejudiced, to looking in certain directions.

It follows that science, or the knowledge process more generally, can benefit if undertaken by individuals who are predisposed in different ways, who are situated differently. It is thus the case, as other feminists have already argued (for example, Seiz 1995; Harding 1995; Longino 1990), that the endeavour to attract diverse voices into the scientific community or any prominent (or other) discussion can be supported on grounds not just of democracy or fairness but also of good methodological practice.

Second, contrastive explanation theory appears capable of reinforcing the claim of standpoint theorists that marginalised positions can facilitate significant insights. Let us recall that standpoint theories or 'epistemologies' claim that certain positioned ways of knowing are in some sense or manner privileged. In early feminist standpoint formulations the emphasis was upon women's ways of knowing.[18] In more recent accounts, the viewpoint of any group that has been marginalised is regarded as privileged. My specific thesis here, is that such claims of standpoint theory can be given a good deal of backing if we see the relative advantage of the marginalised arising (in part or whole) just in their being better able to recognise contrasts of some significance.

How might being marginalised, meaning being constrained from the centre of some form of social life, confer a relative epistemic advantage? More specifically why do I suppose it can facilitate the detection of contrasts that are (in a manner yet to be explicated) highly significant? The answer, I believe, lies in that dual feature of being marginal that it denotes both an insider and outsider position. To be marginalised you are outside of the centre. But equally in order to be marginalised you first have to belong. UK women usually are, but the Hopi indians are not, marginalised in many spheres of modern UK society. Feminist economists, post Keynesians, (old) institutionalists, Austrians and Marxian economists are, but physicists and chemists are not, marginalised in modern university economics departments.

It is this duality of belonging and yet being constrained from the centre, I think, that is essential to the epistemically advantaged situation of the marginalised. It facilitates an awareness of contrasts of significance. For unlike the dominant group, the marginalised are forced both to be aware of the practices, belief systems, values and traditions of the dominant group as well as to live their own. And with this being the case there is a greater opportunity at least, for marginalised people to be aware of contrasts between the two, contrasts that can lead ultimately to the understanding of both sets of community structures, and the relevance of the two, and their interrelatedness (and so ultimately the functioning of the totality). It is in this way and sense in particular, that contrasts more readily available to the marginalised are likely to be especially significant in a given context.[19]

I cannot elaborate this thesis here. But even from the above brief sketch we can see how this thesis, and the theory of contrastive explanation more generally, can support some of the insights of 'feminist epistemology' and specifically standpoint theory, whilst avoiding many of the tensions often associated with the latter position. Specifically, contrastive explanation theory accommodates the principle, widely accepted by feminists, that all voices be admitted to the conversation, *and* can do so in a manner that *neither* supposes that marginalised voices necessarily provide truer accounts, nor that the result necessitates (a) a plethora of contradictory voices (b) possibly backed up by a judgemental relativism (i.e. a relativism in which any discrimination amongst contending claims is impossible or arbitrary). Let me briefly indicate why.

Consider first the idea that standpoint theory is supposed to give truer accounts. This appears to be an inference drawn by some of the theory's critics. Thus, for example, Jane Flax's focus of criticism is the idea of 'a feminist standpoint which is truer than previous (male) ones' (Flax 1990: 56). Alison Assiter clearly understands the same implication of standpoint theory even if opposing Flax's assessment: 'I disagree with her [Flax], however, in her claim that there is no feminist standpoint that is more true than previous male ones' (Assiter 1996: 88). Unfortunately, though, Assiter grounds her assessment in the idea that feminists have a shared set of values and that this somehow necessarily leads them on the path to truth – or at least to ' "radical" insights that can be called knowledge' (1996: 92). Why or how, or the evidence that, this occurs remains unelaborated in Assiter's account.

It follows from the preceding discussion, however, that to dismiss standpoint theory because it is supposed to give a truer account is based on a misunderstanding of the enabling aspect of a standpoint or position. The advantage that one position may have over another is that it can facilitate the detection of different contrasts and so the pursuit of alternative lines of enquiry. In any investigation of a noted contrastive phenomenon, numerous conjectured explanations may be entertained, and the ease or difficulty with which a relevant causal mechanism is identified will depend, amongst other things, on both the context as well as the skills of the investigators involved. But this *per se* has nothing to do with the nature of any standpoint implicated. Specifically, the systematic advantage of the marginalised standpoint, if there is one, lies not in the truth status of the answers obtained, but in the nature of the questions that are recognised as significant and so substance of the answers arrived at.

Here my understanding seems to cohere with many standpoint theorists themselves, who put the emphasis on achieving alternatives lines of enquiry. Consider Sandra Harding:

> the activities of those at the bottom of such social hierarchies can provide starting points for thought – for *everyone's* research and scholarship – from which humans' relations with each other and the natural world can become visible. This is because the experience and lives of marginalised peoples, as they understand them, provide particularly significant *problems to be explained* or research agendas.
>
> (Harding 1993: 240; original emphasis)

The light thrown on standpoint theory by contrastive explanation theory, then, helps dispel the idea that anyone is claiming that marginalised viewpoints are or can be privileged because they are supposed somehow to be truer. I now want to suggest that contrastive explanation theory also helps counteract the opposed inference, sometimes drawn and raised in criticism of standpoint theory, that allowing numerous, previously marginalised, voices into the conversation inevitably results in a plethora of contradictory voices. The belief that the latter must follow encourages (though clearly does not justify) the often-repeated conclusion that standpoint theorists' support for a plurality of voices betrays the acceptance of a form of judgemental relativism. Consider the reasoning of Alison Assiter once more:

> although Harding has a legitimate point in her claim that excluding representatives of certain groups cannot help the advancement of knowledge, the converse – that allowing representation to all, on grounds of democracy – leads back to the kind of [judgemental] relativism that Harding wishes to reject.
>
> (Assiter 1996: 86)

From the perspective of contrastive explanation theory, however, we can see that neither a plethora of contradictory voices nor a commitment to judgemental relativism are inevitable. The prevalence of many different voices, even if all are considering the same phenomenon, may merely reflect a focus upon different contrasts. The investigation of different contrasts can lead to a variety of causes being pursued and perhaps uncovered. For example, suppose we focus on the UK productivity record in the post-World War II period. Even if all of our observers are all economic historians, each may note a different contrast to the others and so pursue a different cause. For example, one of our economic historians may notice that the productivity record in question is better than the prewar UK record and pursue the factor responsible (perhaps the postwar expansion of demand). Another may notice that the postwar productivity performance of the UK is below that of many otherwise comparable industrialised countries over the same period, and ponder on the causal factor responsible (perhaps Britain's relatively unique system of localised industrial bargaining). And so on.

In short, it is not too far fetched to suppose that even where a similar focus is taken, on, say, the conditions of work or some aspect of human daily life of a specific group of people, different observers will draw contrasts reflecting their own situations (those of women, lesbians, immigrants, older people, 'unskilled workers', etc.,) and in doing so uncover different aspects of the underlying causal situation. But there is nothing in this assessment that entails that the discoveries made or causal theories formulated are necessarily incompatible or contradictory.

That said, it doubtless is the case that causal explanations that are produced will often be in competition. But if or when this is so there need be nothing particularly problematic about this situation either, and certainly no reason to embrace a judgemental relativism. For when competing theories are produced, each must be assessed according to its relative empirical adequacy. This is a longer story I will not go into here (see Lawson 1997a: ch. 15; and Chapter 4 above). But there is no reason to suppose that the problems involved are different in nature or degree than those confronting, say, a single scientist or investigator who has herself or himself formulated a set of competing hypotheses all consistent with a particular contrastive phenomenon and wishes to choose between them. Once we allow that theories can be selected according to their relative explanatory powers, there is no inevitable problem in dealing with competing explanations.

Illustration 3: the possibility of human emancipation

I now turn to my third and final illustration of how ontology can make a difference. Here I want to consider the feminist project of emancipation noted at the outset, and in particular the desire to empower diverse voices. Central here is the recognition by feminists that dominant values and interests need be no more than that, whereas dominant groups often presume to speak and act for, but not necessarily in the interests of, all of us. The salient fact is that in opposing the propensity of dominant groups to universalise their own perceived identity, values, interests and customs, etc., some feminist theorists have tended to give up on the possibility of shared values and concerns altogether. Specifically, in response to the criticism of earlier feminist theorising that it marginalised differences of race, ethnocentricity, culture, age and so forth, there has been a tendency to suppose that there are no unifying characteristics of women or feminists at all, or indeed of any other announced grouping.

The resulting conception, in the limit, is of a world of *only* differences, of *only* unique values, interests and experiences. Any basis for correcting ideas of shared identities, for collectively challenging the values which dominate, for progress in science, for coherent transformative projects of emancipation and so forth, are undermined, and in the process any point to a feminist, or any other collective, project evaporates.[20]

This degeneration into an extreme form of individualism, with its associated near-impotency of collective expression or other form of action, is the experience of cultural theory, for example. Here the tendency in question has encouraged the suppression of all reference to feeling or to relatively persisting and transcultural forms of sensibility grounding aesthetic judgements and accounting for their discriminations. This has culminated in a reluctance to engage with value questions in the field of cultural studies and a tendency, indeed, to collapse cultural criticism into cultural history and sociology.

Increasingly we are witnessing the same sorts of trends in economics, with the emergence of injunctions to abandon normative methodology as a hopeless project and to embrace instead methodology as history or sociology of thought (see in particular E. Roy Weintraub 1989; or various contributions to Andrea Salanti and Ernesto Screpanti 1997). The result is a deconstruction of the possibility of sustaining any form of critical engagement. The culmination of the process is the validation of anything that is and happens, an undiscriminating positivism of the actual.

There is more to reality than the course of events and states of affairs

We can see, however, that such assessments serving to destabilise the feminist emancipatory project are hardly compelling once we accept that reality is structured, that it is irreducible to experience and its direct objects. I have already argued that actualism, i.e. the thesis that reality can be reduced to the actual course of events and states of affairs, is untenable, that we must recognise in addition a realm of underlying structures, powers, mechanisms, tendencies and so forth. At least I have done so specifically in the context of considering objects of the natural sciences and society. I now want to indicate that human subjectivity is no exception, that we can and should substitute a conception of human nature as structured in place of the actual individuality of (versions of) postmodernism. Once this is achieved, contributing a fuller non-actualistic conception of the individual to that already secured for society, we have a basis for seeing clearly that, even if experiences are unique in some sense, or if each human individual has a manifest nature that is unique in some way, it in no way follows thereby that all aspects of societies or of individuals need be. There can be shared features lying at a different level. I now want to argue that the latter is indeed the case. And it is on this understanding, I also want to indicate, that the feasibility of projects of emancipatory progress mostly rests.

I have already discussed the manner in which I take society, or societies, to be so structured. Let me at this point briefly sketch something of the structure of human nature in general, as well as the distinction between human needs and wants in particular, and indicate their significance for the issues in question (for further elaboration see Lawson 1997a; 1997b).

Human nature

I must immediately emphasise that any conception of a common human nature that is sustainable here could not be ahistorical. But equally it seems rather implausible to suppose that human beings do not possess various shared characteristics and in particular *capacities* (e.g. language capabilities – as presupposed even by the postmodernist concern with discourse) which both derive from a scientifically recognised common genetic structure and serve to differentiate us from other species. When viewed under one set of aspects, or at a high level of abstraction, then, human nature can be accepted as a common attribute, one grounded in our genetic constitution and manifest in certain species-wide needs and capacities or powers (such as language use).

Of course, even a common human nature can only ever be expressed in inherently socialised, more or less historically, geographically, and culturally specific, and very highly differentiated, forms. In other words, when human nature is viewed under a different set of aspects to the above, and specifically at a lower level of abstraction, it can be understood as a historically relatively-specific nature. Its development, at this level, has its origin at the time, place and conditions of an individual's birth, and is subsequently influenced by the class, gender, occupational positions, and so forth, in which the individual stands along with her or his experiences more widely. For example we cannot just speak in the abstract, we have to speak a specific geo-historically located language. To the extent that numerous people throughout their lives are subject to identical or similar forms of determination a historically quite definite nature may thus be held in common.

Now, to accept any of this is not to deny that, in the limit, any individual will always be subject to a unique combination of experiences and modes of determination producing a particular personality. Thus from a third and rather more specific perspective, or a yet lower level of abstraction, the nature of any given human being must be seen as a more or less unique individuality. There is no reason to doubt that a person's individuality is primarily constituted by her or his social peculiarity. Each in- dividual is the product of her or his actions and experiences within the social relations and other modes of determination into which he or she is born and thereafter lives. An individual's actions, or things which happen to her or him, are comprehensible in terms of the individual's socially con-ditioned capacities, powers, liabilities and dispositions. The agency of each individual is thus conditioned by the relationships in which he or she stands or has stood, just as these relations, as with social structure in gen-eral, are in turn dependent upon the sum total of human doings.

Ultimately, then, an individual's manifest nature and experiences may be unique. But this is quite consistent with commonality or generality lying at a different level, an insight we can recognise only when we pass beyond an ontology of the actual and specifically of experience.

Needs

In accepting that the human subject is so structured we can also recognise a basis for common or shared real needs. And indeed it is essential to any emancipatory project that we can. The possibility of human freedom pre-supposes the existence of shared human objectives, i.e. real interests and motives, ultimately rooted in common needs and capabilities. If everyone's needs are merely subjective, with the possibility of being irreconcilably opposed, then projecting the goal of social emancipation is indeed likely to be question-begging from the outset. The condition of shared real interests is a presupposition of all emancipatory proposals – whether supporting (relative) change or (relative) continuity – whatever perspective is accepted. And, of course, at the very least we share in common the need to realise some or all of our capacities: to realise our potentials as human beings.

It is not difficult to see, then, that the possibility of moral theorising can, at least in part, be based on a recognised common human nature, a recog-nition grounded in our biological unity as a species. However, because, this common nature is always historically and socially mediated, human needs will be manifest in potentially many ways. It follows, accepting the perspective on society elaborated above, that the pursuit of social goals always takes place in a context of conflicting position-related interests. It is likely, for example, that most of us most of the time need our 'own' language(s) to be spoken. Certainly, conflicts centring on the interests of class positions, age, gender, nation states, regions, culture and so forth, are as real and determining as anything else. Even so, different groups may cooperate allowing different, and even opposed, interests sometimes to be met. The point remains, though, that opposed, position-related interests or developed needs exist. And it may be upon our unity as a species and the more generalised features of our social and historical experience and make-up, that the greater possibility of unambiguous and more enduring progress rests.

Of course there will often be practical problems of identifying human needs whatever their level of generality. Things are complicated, of course, by the irreducibility both of real needs to manifest wants and of wants to the means of their satisfaction.[21] But if real needs are thereby rendered unobservable, this *per se* makes their identification no more problematic than that of other unobservables in science (such as gravitational and magnetic fields and social relationships). Indeed, this is a situation in which contrastive explanation can once more prove fruitful (although justifying this assertion will have to wait a further occasion).

Grounding the possibility of human emancipation

At this point we can see that the conception of human nature, needs and interests which I am defending, when coupled with the social ontology elaborated in the first illustration set out above (that is, with the conception of social reality as intrinsically dynamic, highly internally related, and constituted by positions, amongst other things) allows us simultaneously to accept the relativity of knowledge, the uniqueness of experiences *and* the possibility of progress, including emancipatory projects. For it is now clear that there is no contradiction in recognising each of us as a unique identity or individuality, resulting (in part) from our own unique paths through life, and *also* accepting that we can nevertheless possess similar needs or interests as well as stand in the same or similar positions and relations of domination to those of others around us, including gender relations. From this perspective there is no contradiction in recognising both our different individualities and experiences as well as the possibility of common interests in transforming certain forms of social relationships. Fundamental here is the fact that human subjectivities, human experiences and social structure cannot be reduced one to another; they are each ontologically distinct, albeit highly interdependent, modes of being.

I rush to add (or re-emphasise) that, as with processes of realising human potentials, I make no presumption that any aspects of social structure, say gender relations, are other than intrinsically dynamic, or are everywhere the same. First, social structure depends upon intentional human agency for its existence. It is both condition and consequence of human practice and so is inherently dynamic, depending for its continuity on inherently transformative intentional human agency. Second, social structure is inherently geo-historical-cultural, being dependent on geo-historically rooted practices. There is no presumption that gender relations being reproduced/transformed in Cambridge in 1999 are identical to either those reproduced in Cambridge 100 years ago or those existing currently in some other parts of the UK, Japan or wherever. It all depends. My experience is that gender relations in most places (still) serve to facilitate (localised) practices in which men can (and often do) dominate/oppress women, or appear in some way advantaged.[22] But the extent of commonality/difference across time and space is something to be determined *a posteriori*.

This conception also allows that, for people from quite diverse backgrounds, it is feasible both that their individualities/personalities are quite different, and that when they arrive in the same location they are subject to, or forced to stand within, similar, i.e. local, gender (and other) relations, whether or not they are aware of this, or they learn to become locally skilful. For example, it seems that currently in parts of the UK any (person identified as a) woman going alone to a pub in the evening is likely to meet with harassment by some 'men', whatever the former's previous experiences, realised capacities, acknowledged needs, expectations, self-perceptions or understandings of the local gender relations, and so on.

By the same token, some 'men' in the UK, aware that approaching a 'woman' in a dark street can cause anxiety, will purposefully cross to other side of the road if passing or overtaking in order to minimise alarm. This can happen even if the person being overtaken does not (is sufficiently ignorant of local culture as not to) feel any alarm or anxiety, or whatever. Gender relations with a degree of space-time extension along with practices they facilitate can be *transfactually* operative irrespective of the knowledges or understandings and wishes of those affected. The existences of multiple differences in manifest identities and individual experiences is not inconsistent with this insight – any more than the unique path of each autumn leaf undermines the hypothesis that all leaves are similarly subject to the transfactual 'pull' of gravity.

In short, once a structured ontology is recognised, we can see that multiplicity in the course of actuality remains coherent with a degree of uniformity at the level of underlying causes or structure. The conception defended thus secures the basis for an emancipatory politics rooted in real needs and interests. In so doing it provides grounds, in particular, for feminist projects of transforming gender relations, in an awareness that the existence of multiculturalism or of differences in general, need not in any way undermine or contradict such emancipatory practice. It also preserves, without strain, the possibility of strategies of solidarity or meaningful affiliated action between groups. In short, it transcends the sorts of tensions that currently seem to pervade much of feminist epistemology and political theory.

What seems to have happened in certain strands of feminist theorising (or in social philosophies that have been influential) is that a form of *a priori* universalising has once more been sanctioned. By correctly emphasising differences in experiences and manifest natures, but erroneously reducing reality to experience and its direct objects, the view encouraged is of a world of only uniqueness and differences. In this way, in place of the commonalities previously unquestioningly asserted by dominant groups in treating their own specific traits as though universal, we achieve only a world of universalised difference. And it seems that an essential condition for this erroneous result maintaining any credibility or ground is the neglect of explicit ontological enquiry.

Final comments

I have observed that explicit ontological analysis is conspicuously, if erroneously, downplayed in much feminist theorising, and I have suggested that this neglect is unfortunate in that ontology matters for any would-be projects of illumination and emancipation. I have provided some illustrations to back up this claim.

Whatever the reason for the downplaying of such realist concerns, the point bears emphasising that realists are no more committed to absolutism than relativists are committed to irrealism. The relevant question, rather, is: which realist and which relativist positions are sustainable in a given context? I have argued here, in effect, for an ontological realism and an epistemological relativism, which together amount to a rejection of a judgemental relativism in favour of a judgemental rationality.[23] In this I have defended a particular social theory which preserves and endorses, indeed itself incorporates, the impulse behind the 'deconstructive' turn in feminist theory, but which simultaneously, through its emphasis on ontology, avoids the self-subversion of *total* (including a judgemental) relativism.

The particular theory of reality defended is of a structured and open world. It is a conception which recognises that in our everyday practices, all of us, as complexly structured, socially and culturally situated, purposeful and needy individuals, knowledgeably and capably negotiate complex, shifting, only partially grasped and contested, structures of power, rules, relations and other possibly relatively enduring but nevertheless transient and action-dependent social resources at our disposal. Ontological analysis provides an insight into this reality.

Thus when Deirdre McCloskey, in the manner of others, cautions against any embracing of 'material realism' on the grounds that 'What is at issue here is the philosopher's construct, Reality, a thing deeper than what is necessary for daily life' (1997: 14–15), the primary error lies in supposing there is little depth to 'daily life', that philosophy deals (or inevitably claims to deal) with a reality apart from that continually encountered by us all. The mistaken presumption, in effect, is that social reality, and specifically 'daily life', is reducible to the actual course of social events. This reduction of reality to experience and its immediate objects is a mistake that ontological analysis allows us to rectify.

Now I am aware, finally, that the above outline is rather schematic and hurried. I suspect many will remain rather unconvinced by some or all of the sketches provided. As it happens, I do find that the broad perspective elaborated currently constitutes as sustainable (explanatorily powerful) an account as any with which I am familiar (see Lawson 1997a). But I should re-emphasise that most of the preceding discussion is provided first and foremost with the intent of being illustrative. My primary objective here is not so much to persuade others to accept precisely the conceptions developed as to suggest that such conceptions, or explicit ontological analyses of the sort grounding them, do deserve consideration by more feminists. My chief purpose here is to contribute to removing what I take to be unnecessary obstacles to a particular set of debates, with the hope of transforming, or even initiating a further strand to a particular conversation. For it may just be (from where I am situated it seems likely) that if feminists, including feminist economists, allow realism, and in particular explicit ontological analysis, to come more fully out of the margin, the opportunities for advance opened up thereby will prove to be to everyone's advantage.

Part IV

A HISTORICAL PERSPECTIVE ON ECONOMIC PRACTICE

The modern discipline of economics is dominated by a mainstream project whose contributors mostly insist that methods of mathematical-deductivist modelling be everywhere utilised. Few attempts to justify this stance are made. Meanwhile, this mathematising project appears not to be especially successful, certainly not more so than rival approaches and traditions. Here, then, we have an explanatory puzzle. Why or how did economics get into this situation, and how does it persist? Specifically, how has the mathematising project managed so to dominate when we might have expected a programme with no obvious explanatory advantage over others to play a more modest role? This (contrastive) question is addressed in the final chapter of the book.

Prima facie it does seem likely that historical, political and cultural forces will bear significantly on any explanation. And I find that this is indeed the case. Unfortunately, there exists relatively little serious research into the cultural-political history of those aspects of our discipline here in consideration. This feature of the current situation is in itself somewhat curious, given that the question before us surely represents one of the most pressing and challenging in the history of modern economic thought. In any case, being mindful of the noted state of affairs, and acutely aware that there is much more to be said than I can relate here, I offer the final chapter of the book very much in the spirit of a first step. That having been admitted, I emphasise that I nevertheless believe the account set forth does identify a fundamental component (at least) of the explanation of the puzzle before us.

10

AN EXPLANATION OF THE
MATHEMATISING TENDENCY
IN MODERN ECONOMICS

The phenomenon to explain

How are we to account for the rise to, and continuing, dominance of the modern mathematising project in economics? Not, I think, in terms of its successes in illuminating the world in which we live. For the evidence is that these are few and far between. Indeed, the modern mainstream project, viewed as a scientific or explanatory endeavour, is not in too healthy a state at all, and unclear even as to its own rationale. Certainly, this is the view of many of its leading spokespersons (see e.g. Rubinstein 1995; Leamer 1983; Chapter 1 above). And away from the mainstream, even outside the economics academy, the perception that (as an explanatory endeavour) the project is faring rather poorly is widely held indeed (see e.g. Parker 1993; Howell 2000).

Perhaps this critical reception sometimes errs on the side of underestimating what has been achieved. But there are certainly no clear grounds for supposing this project has contributed more to advancing social understanding than the numerous traditions it has either displaced or with which it (nominally) competes. And this is the pertinent consideration here. I know of no argument, evidence or reason to suppose that this mainstream tradition has been more explanatorily successful than, say, the (old) institutionalist or evolutionary tradition spawned by Veblen, Commons and others, the post Keynesian tradition building on the insights of Keynes in particular, the Austrian tradition building on the likes of Menger, Mises and Hayek, the Marxian tradition, feminist economists, social economists, and so on. To the contrary, in previous chapters I have provided reason for believing the potential for successes of the heterodox traditions (and not just the level of insight so far achieved) is rather greater.

The situation, then, is somewhat puzzling. For not only is it the case that these heterodox traditions are marginalised within the economics academy, but the degree of their marginalisation is remarkable. In my experience rarely do university lecture courses or set textbooks even acknowledge the existence of alternative projects or traditions. If we look beyond economics there appears to be no other discipline with a mainstream tradition that enjoys anywhere near so great a degree of dominance (or so little relative explanatory success).

So however we look at the situation, it seems that we have here an interesting phenomenon to explain. We have a surprising contrast that we need to account for. How *has* this mathematising project risen to such a position of dominance in modern economics, and managed to maintain this position over a longish period of time, when (given its lack of relative explanatory successes in particular) it would have been reasonable to expect it to fare no better (to say the least) than other projects being pursued? This is my contrastive question here, and I want to set out at least a sketch of an answer, to identify (what I suspect is) an essential part of the total story.[1]

An explanatory first step

I have advanced a partial explanation before (which I further ground below). Specifically, I have previously identified an impetus to the noted situation, the one I believe to be the most significant (Lawson 1997a; 1997e). This is the enormous, almost uncritical, awe of mathematics in modern Western culture. This impetus is a cultural phenomenon pervasive in society at large. The idea that mathematics has a significant role in so many spheres is deeply embedded in our cultural thinking. As Morris Kline summed up his findings in the preface to his *Mathematics in Western Culture* written almost half a century ago:

> In this book we shall survey mathematics primarily to show how its ideas have helped to mold twentieth-century life and thought. The ideas will be in historical order so that our material will range from the beginnings in Babylonia and Egypt to the modern theory of relativity. Some people may question the pertinence of material belonging to earlier historical periods. Modern culture, however, is the accumulation and synthesis of contributions made by many preceding civilizations. The Greeks, who first appreciated the power of mathematical reasoning, graciously allowing the gods to use it in designing the universe, and then urging man to uncover the pattern of this design, not only gave mathematics a major place in their civilization but initiated patterns of thought that are basic in our own. As succeeding civilizations passed on their gifts to modern times, they handed on new and increasingly more significant roles for mathematics. Many of these functions and influences of mathematics are now deeply imbedded in our culture.
>
> (Kline 1964: viii)

Indeed the influence of mathematics is now so deeply ingrained within our culture that many people appear to suppose that anything stated in mathematics must be correct, whilst for things to be correct, reliable, insightful or scientific (or at least conferring of scientific status), they must be stated in mathematics. For so many people it seems to be simply an unquestioned and unquestionable matter of faith that if a field of study is to be scientific or accorded status as a knowledge-producing activity, or otherwise regarded as serious, it must take a mathematical form.

This certainly is the view that pervades modern academies of economics. In fact, in the writings of modern mainstream economists, mathematical modelling is even synonymous with the idea (it is considered to comprise the totality) of 'theory', as I detailed in Chapter 1. Further, the belief that mathematical formalism is necessary to science or serious study is accepted even by those mainstream economists aware of the failings of the project (Kirman 1989: 137) as well as by those attempting seriously to change the scope of the discipline (see Sen in *Le Monde*, 31 October 2000). Further, it appears even to seduce many of those who prefer to think of themselves as heterodox. And if for many the belief that mathematical formalism is essential is just too ingrained to be easily shaken off, the thought that formalism could actually be deleterious to understanding is beyond comprehension. Many like Hahn simply reject the latter possibility as 'a view surely not worth discussing' (Hahn 1985: 18) as we noted in Chapter 1. To most economists, mathematical formalism is simply essential to serious substantive theorising.

The point though is that economists are merely copying, borrowing and reproducing 'scientific norms' of the wider community, norms that over time, with the successes of mathematics in numerous spheres, have become embedded in our background ideas about how things work. Certainly, the evidence is compelling that the staying power of the mathematising project in economics owes something to the way mathematics is perceived in our wider culture.

Why, amongst the social disciplines, has mathematics taken such a strong hold in economics in particular? Actually there is evidence of its increasing 'encroachment' elsewhere too. But there is a widespread perception both that the measurable phenomena of the social realm mostly fall within the field of scope of economics, and also that anything that is measurable can likely be treated mathematically. If, as I am suggesting, it is a cultural norm that anything that can be treated mathematically should so be treated, it is not surprising that tendencies to mathematise have put in a stronger showing in economics than in other areas of social theorising.

I might emphasise, before going further, that in making these observations I do not wish to belittle mathematics in any way. To the contrary, I too am enthralled by its elegance and power. But it is possible to recognise the latter without thereby concluding that mathematics be promulgated uncritically and without limit. I am simply drawing attention to what I see as the current uncritical reception (or granting of scientific authority to the perpetrators) of anything mathematical. This, as I say, is an orientation that is embedded in Western culture at large, and in the habits, norms, conventions and power structures of the modern economics academy in particular.

A further puzzle

My thesis to date, then, has been that it is this culturally based idea of science (or serious study) as necessitating mathematics that drives the mathematising project on in economics. Although the fact of this widespread perception of a link between mathematics and all serious thought, does throw light on how the mathematising project persists despite its dearth of successes, it is clear that some problems remain for the thesis advanced. The account so far given is, at best, highly incomplete. For the rise to prominence of practices concerned with mathematising the study of social phenomena occurred only in the twentieth century. Yet, as Kline observes, the cultural embracing of mathematics to which I refer was evident long before this time. And this holds true in parts of the world with amongst the longest and strongest traditions in economics. In France, in particular, the cultural impact of mathematics has, since the Enlightenment at least, been very powerful. Yet even in France it is only in the twentieth century that the attempts to mathematise economics have risen to dominance.

From the viewpoint of the thesis I have been putting forward, then, an important puzzle which remains to be resolved is why, if the cultural norm I identify (that mathematics is essential to serious research) is really so significant, the mathematical project in economics did not rise to prominence at an earlier stage, at least in a country such as France. If, as I am suggesting, the idea, or scientific convention, that mathematics is essential to serious study, is so attractive or difficult to resist, and clearly so easy to copy or imitate, why is it only recently that it has met with the widespread reception it now enjoys? Why, furthermore, did the mathematising project eventually rise to dominance when (and where) it did, given there were no notable breakthroughs in its ability (relative to that of competing projects certainly) to illuminate at that time (or since). Or, to look at the puzzle from a different angle, how can my thesis account for the fact that the project of mathematising the subject does now survive as the dominant approach, given that the place of mathematics in Western culture has not always brought this result?

In short, what explains the *relative fortunes over time* of the mathematising project in economics? If belief in the power of mathematics, along with its necessity to all serious study, has long been an embedded feature of our culture, and is as important and persuasive as the evidence suggests, why have the fortunes of the project not been the same throughout? Why in particular has the mathematising project in economics fared significantly better after the start of the twentieth century, when we might have expected it to fare no differently than before? Here we clearly have a further contrastive phenomenon to account for.

The nature of the expanded explanatory thesis

I want to suggest a development of the earlier explanation that can account for the noted puzzle. In parts at least the explanatory story advanced might reasonably be construed an evolutionary one, incorporating elements analogous to a Darwinian mechanism of natural selection. Indeed, the fact that the project of mathematising economics rose to prominence and survives without at any stage demonstrating itself to be more explanatorily successful than its numerous rivals, immediately suggests that elements of a natural selection evolutionary process may be in play. For a central and great Darwinian insight is that a subset of members of a population may come to flourish relative to other members simply because they possess a feature, which others do not, that renders them relatively suited to some local environment. The question of the intrinsic worth of those who flourish most is not relevant to the story. I shall argue that natural selection mechanisms of this sort are indeed a part of the explanation of the varying fortunes of the mathematising project in economics. But at the same time I shall indicate that such evolutionary mechanisms are *no more than a part of the story*. The episode also helps indicate that borrowing from biology, where relevant, is likely to contribute only partial insights at best.

Evolutionary explanation

In order to illustrate what I understand by 'natural selection', and to indicate why survivors of a natural selection process (typically) do not warrant being regarded as laudatory in any sense, it may be useful, briefly, to recall an example from biology. Consider the case of the varying fortunes of spotted grey and dark moths against an environment of UK industrialisation. Prior to the nineteenth century the spotted grey was more common than the dark moth. When resting on the lichen covered trees in their habitat the spotted grey moth was effectively invisible to birds, unlike the dark moth which was easily spotted against the light coloured trees and eaten. With nineteenth century industrialisation, however, pollutants killed the lichen on the trees in certain areas and rendered the bark of trees in the relevant vicinities a dark colour. Both types of moth continued to rest on trees. But with the spotted grey now more easily recognisable to birds, there was a shift in the relative proportions of the two populations from the spotted grey towards the darker variety. In a sense the pollution-darkened barks protected the darker moths from the danger of the moth-seeking birds.

Darwin provides similar examples:

> When we see leaf-eating insects green, and bark-feeders mottled-grey; the alpine ptarmigan white in winter, the red-grouse the colour of heather, and the black-grouse that of peaty earth, we must believe that these tints are of service to these birds and insects in preserving them from danger.
>
> (Darwin 1859: 84)

Notice, however, that although the tints or colours in question may indeed be of service to their possessors, the main natural selection mechanism works neither by way of the variety generation (here genetic mutation) conditions affecting the environment, nor by way of the environment conditions affecting those of variety generation (mutation). Rather, the central causal mechanism in question involves certain environmental factors bearing differentially on (i.e. 'selecting' amongst) the independently produced variety at the level of the individual. In our example, the noted environmental factor selects not at that level at which mutations in types of moth are possible but rather at the level of individual moths. And through such a natural selection mechanism a matching of (surviving) individuals and environment emerges. This is a matching which is no part of anyone's design. It explains why it is so often the case that nature has the appearance of design where it puts in an appearance at all.

Now a significant feature of this process, to return us to the point of the discussion, is that certain individuals are found to fare better than others just because they are of a type, or possess a trait, relatively suited to their local environment, not because they are successful in any wider or absolute or more laudatory sense.

As I say, the explanation I want to advance of the rise to, and continuing, dominance of the modern mainstream or mathematical project in economics (in the face of the failure of the latter to provide any obvious display of relative explanatory superiority) takes much the same form. The way in which the project has been received over the last two hundred years or so, has been related to shifts in the relevant local environment in some way. Changes in the nature of its reception have had little to do with changes in the project's relative explanatory merit or performance.

The natural selection model

Put differently, the possibility I want to examine here is that there is a general process or model of change, one which is well illustrated by

252

biological examples or tokens, but which has social manifestations as well. Specifically, I want to suggest that such a general model can indeed be identified, and that one social manifestation of it is the history of modern economics, or at least of (significant aspects of) its (currently mainstream) mathematical component.

Let me then proceed, at this point, by abstracting out essential components of the more generalised natural selection evolutionary story. The argumentation here will be brief, although it should be sufficient. However, for the reader wanting more detail the basic model is elaborated at greater length in Chapter 5 above.

First of all, in any model capable of incorporating a natural selection mechanism there has to be *variety* in a relevant *population*. The natural selection evolutionary account is one in which, within a population, individuals with a particular trait come to dominate or flourish largely because either

(i) the particular trait is a newly emergent one and found to fit relatively well to the environment into which it is 'born', or
(ii) the particular trait was always present but environmental conditions shift (independently) towards those which in some relevant sense favour the trait in question.

If each individual of a population possess the exact same traits there is no basis for change as evolution via natural selection. If evolution is to be continuous, there must be a continuous source of variation within a population.

Second, if individuals with an environmentally (relatively) apt trait or characteristic are to come to dominate in a population over a period of time, there must be a mechanism whereby the characteristic in question (colour or whatever) is *reproduced* from one generation to another. Following Dawkins (1976; 1978) I shall call an item whose structure is replicated a *replicator*.

Third, there must be a mechanism whereby individuals with different aspects interact with their environments. Without such interaction there could be no mechanism whereby a particular subset of individuals is *selected* in the sense of being found to fit or survive better than others within this environment. Notice I am referring here not (or not just – if we are to capture a natural selection story) to interaction between variety generation (mutation) conditions and the environment, but to interactions between the environment and all the developed individuals within it. Following Hull (1981) I shall call the mechanism for this the *interactor*. All aspects are essential for an explanation along evolutionary lines.

The PVRS model

Let me label an abstract model which supports these features a population-variety-reproduction-selection or PVRS model (as I say, a lengthy discussion of this model is provided in Chapter 5 above). Clearly for the model to capture a natural selection story where *a posteriori* fit is not (wholly) a product of design, it must be the case that the V (variety generation) and S (environmental selection) conditions are largely independent.

Now to suggest that such a PVRS model can have relevance not only in the biological realm but also in the social, is not to suppose that all aspects of the manner in which such a model may be concretised in the biological realm carry over to the social domain. Indeed, if the model has relevance at all to the social realm, it will be concretised quite differently in the latter than in the biological realm.

Most clearly, any processes of innovation, reproduction, interaction and selection as occur in the social realm can be achieved only through the mediation of human agency. Social systems are neither self-reproducing nor naturally produced. Rather, reproduction of the social system results from capable and purposeful human beings going about their daily business, interpreting their everyday tasks and the pertaining social order in very definite ways.

A second major difference between the two realms (that will be reflected in the form of any PVRS model developed) is that any variety generation and selection conditions will be more, or more often, interconnected in the social domain than in the biological. Although much of what occurs in the social realm is unintended and perhaps misunderstood, intentionality is far more significant in the social than natural domains.

I refer to a PVRS model which constrains variety generation (or mutation) and selection conditions to be strictly independent of each other as a strict, or polar (or neo-) Darwinian version of the model. Alternatively put, it is the PVRS model with purely Darwinian features. It is this particular polar model, or close approximations to it, which are often thought to have most relevance in modern evolutionary biology. Certainly it is the version of the PVRS model which best illuminates the natural selection mechanism in which I am here interested. For this version of the model makes it clear that order, a fitting of individual and environment, or part and whole, can emerge even where variety generation and environmental conditions are totally unrelated.

Of course, it is possible to specify versions of the PVRS model that do not conform to the polar Darwinian conception. I refer to a PVRS model which allows environmental selection conditions (S) to feed back into the process of variety generation (V) as a feed-backward or S-to-V model.[2] An example conforming to such a model for the social domain is any situation in which market research and its results, or other anticipations of environmental conditions, are fed back into the variety generation process.

Further I refer to a PVRS model where (conditions or mechanisms aff-ecting) the variety of traits (V) causally influence the selection conditions (S), the feed-forward or V-to-S model. An example here is a situation in which advertising, or indeed any form of persuasion, is used to 'manipu-late' the environment of selection.

I mentioned it only briefly above, so let me emphasise that the version of the PVRS model that I refer to as the (Darwinian) natural selection conception is one in which V (variety generation) and S (environmental selection) conditions are independent, at least to a significant degree. Thus I do not restrict it to the polar-Darwinian version, but to any in which the environment, and the factors or traits on which the latter comes pivotally to bear, are to a significant extent independently determined.

In the social realm, of course, it is to be expected that to the extent that the evolutionary or PVRS model has relevance at all, it will never be purely or polar-Darwinian (which would entail that human practices and differen-tiated survival rates are autonomous of human intentionality); nor purely feed-backward, i.e. backward-*determining* (the functionalist mistake of the modern mainstream); nor purely feed-forward, i.e. forward-*determining* (voluntarism or putty-clay environment). But if it is to be expected that feed-forward and feed-backward mechanisms will each have some role, in a world that is complex, holistic and incompletely understood, such as ours, we should not be surprised if, in any PVRS situation, a Darwinian natural selection element is found to be significant on occasion.

So, to sum up this brief discussion, the Darwinian natural selection model (a PVRS model in which V [variety generation] and S [environ-mental selection] conditions are to a significant degree independent) promises to be a useful source of redress against those who would see everything that happens in terms only of intentionality or prior design or tendencies to 'normal' or otherwise predictable outcomes. It is a model which counters any other which presumes that all outcomes are optimal in some way, and that this presumed optimality (in a world of rationally calculating individuals) is effectively its own explanation.

It is worth emphasising, however, that in any social explanatory context where the PVRS model does prove appropriate, it is unlikely that a natural (or environmental) selection mechanism acting on the individuals of the analysis will ever constitute the whole of any socio-explanatory story, even if sometimes it is highly explanatorily significant. In other words, if a successful social-evolutionary explanation is possible, it will likely identify modes of interaction between only relatively independent variety genera-tion and selection conditions. Strict Darwinian separation of modes of mutation and selection seem likely to give way to processes of causal inter-dependency and interpenetration to some degree. Any such explanation, in other words, can be expected to involve shifting patterns of both harmony and tension, of accommodation and rejection, as individuals and ultimately the environment interact in a process of continuous reproduction and transformation. Certainly the possibility that evolutionary tendencies form but part of the story should not be overlooked.

But to recognise this is not to preclude the possibility of a mechanism, analogous to that of Darwinian natural selection, having a role in the social realm, and perhaps even a quite significant one. Whether such a possibility is ever actualised is something that can be determined only empirically. As it happens, I believe that the process I have in mind concerning the eventual rise to dominance and ensuing survival of the mathematising project in economics is just such a case of this kind. Let me now turn directly to the task of explaining this particular phenomenon.

Modern mainstream economics

To recap, given that the formalistic modelling approach to modern economics has not fared noticeably better than the numerous other sets of contributions with which it competes (and even in absolute terms it is hardly a resounding success story) its emergence and continuing survival as a hugely dominant mainstream tradition provides a particularly interesting phenomenon to explain.

Indeed, I believe the history of the modern mainstream, the rise to dominance of formalistic modelling practices and the manner of their 'survival' in this role, constitutes a central chapter in the history of academic economics that remains largely unwritten. The one significant exception to this of which I am aware is the excellent study of the history of general equilibrium economics by Ingrao and Israel (1990), an account that ties in very much with my own reading of the relevant episode in the history of economics. Here I can only give the briefest sketch of certain relevant developments.

Basic components of the social evolutionary story

Now what first of all might be the relevant population of the account I am proposing? What is the population of individuals with a variety of characteristics, some of which will be more favoured than others by specific environmental shifts? The population I have in mind is that of research practices undertaken by those who study social (including economic) phenomena. And the sub-group of population members whose (varying) fortunes I am particularly interested in here, is that set of practices significantly concerned with mathematising the study of social phenomena.

A fundamental component of my account is a recognition that it was not the case that one fine morning in recent times a great economist awoke with the idea of mathematising the discipline, and thereby simply went out and (aided by a culturally embedded belief in the ubiquitous relevance of formalism) quickly achieved this. If this were so, my explanatory account would already be sufficient for my purposes. However such was not the case. Instead, attempts so to formalise the study of society and economy have been under way for a rather long time. Thus such attempts should be recognised as but one set of long existing research practices amongst the variety of practices continually in competition within the population of all academic or serious research practices.

However, it is only relatively recently that practices oriented to mathematising social phenomena have caught on in a significant way, as we shall see. *Prima facie*, then, if an evolutionary explanation is appropriate here it will likely be the version which involves a (relatively autonomous) environmental shift (favouring the mathematising practices already in place). And indeed, I shall argue precisely that the varying fortunes of the mathematising project over time reflect in some significant part (autonomous) changes that occurred in the relevant environment, that we do have something of an evolutionary story of the natural selection sort.

Interactors and replicators

It will already be apparent that the interactors of the account I am proposing are the various research practices concerned with social understanding. But what are the replicators, the entities whose structure is passed on or replicated? I think they take the form of ideas, instructions, edicts or conventional norms. Behind all research practices aimed at social understanding are ideas or norms of some sort, even if they sometimes amount to little more than the notion that 'social phenomena can and should be subject to serious systematic study'. The latter idea, indeed, is obviously widely held and continuously replicated by imitation and persuasion.

Now, in being replicated such an idea can 'mutate' or be slightly modified in many ways. One feasible modification of this particular idea involves substituting the term 'mathematical' for 'serious systematic'. This, of course, is equivalent to combining the original idea with the scientific convention 'mathematics is essential to all serious research including scientific study'. It is feasible that all variations on the original norm give rise to practices concerned with pursuing social understanding. But where the noted mutation is also accepted, only mathematical forms are considered.

Notice that there is no reason to expect an exact match between conditioning norms or ideas (the replicators) and the resulting practices (the interactors). Attempts to mathematise, for example, can be conditioned by slightly varying ideas or norms. Individuals might be guided by the idea 'it is interesting or important to mathematise' rather than the more definite 'for a study to qualify as serious or scientific it is necessary to mathematise'. But given the prevalence of the latter today, and its apparent seductiveness, there is every reason to suppose that it has been equally enticing for a good while, and at least since the time of the Enlightenment.

Of course, nothing stays completely the same overtime. If it is likely that two hundred years ago, say, a motivating concern would have been to determine if, and how, the mathematical modelling of social phenomena might proceed (so that individual contributors were probably imitating each other just in exploring whether it is possible to make any headway), in modern times the practices of mathematical economists are not typically presented as being motivated by a concern to mathematise at all. Rather the mathematical form is mostly accepted in an unquestioning manner, and indeed is typically unacknowledged. And in a similar fashion the resulting exercise is usually presented simply as economics, rather than distinguished as mathematical modelling or some such. Even where individuals take issue with the contributions of others, the implicit conditioning norm 'use mathematics' is rarely challenged and more typically subconsciously copied.

Thus, under today's conditions, with formalistic practices so prominent, it is likely that the 'scientific norms' in question are far more readily (and more subconsciously) imitated and borrowed. Indeed, the mathematisation of economics is currently a rather institutionalised phenomenon. The ways in which (positioned) individuals within any forum or workplace can and do act are significantly influenced by the evolved sets of rules (including conventions) and relations which define their (equally positioned) options and obligations.[3] And so it is within the economics academy, and in particular, with regard to the convention I am here interested in. Unlike, say, two hundred years ago, the 'scientific convention' or edict that 'mathematics is to be used' has become embedded within the institutional structures of modern economics faculties, conditioning the power relations in place, the procedures operative regarding hiring, reproduction of hierarchies, allocation of resources, etc., and so significantly bearing on which practices are encouraged. In short, norms such as that in focus, currently function almost as constitutive 'rules of the game'. Setterfield (1997) makes a similar observation:

> As a profession, academic economics is populated by economists who organize their profession according to certain 'rules of the game' and interact with each other on the basis of these rules. ... At present these rules include edicts such as 'the more mathematical an explanation becomes, the better', 'the only relevant sources for citation are recent academic journal articles', 'only mainstream ... economists need be heeded', 'only publications in what are internally defined as top journals count', and so forth.
>
> (Setterfield 1997: 23)

To recognise all this is, in part, to remind ourselves that the transformational model of social activity is central to all in the social world that takes place (see Chapter 2). All relatively enduring structures, including norms and conventions, not only condition human practice but become reproduced (and transformed) through that practice. This of course, would equally have been the case in earlier times. But the nature of operative social relations, and the manner in which specific rules and conventions would have been reproduced (including imitated) and transformed (including modified) would doubtless have been very different in many respects at different points in time.

So little, if anything, stays unchanged. Even so, if the sorts of considerations here noted are matters always to keep in mind, they do not, in and of themselves, explain the contrastive puzzle earlier identified. They are no doubt relevant to understanding how the socio-cultural system has evolved and made a difference. But the specific (contrastive) question as to why mathematical economics did not reach its current dominant state at an earlier time, as we might have expected at least in certain locations, remains unaddressed. Nor, relatedly, do we have an explanation of the timing of the breakthrough which eventually happened. These and associated matters still need our attention.[4]

Here I want to suggest an explanation of the noted developments. Before I can embark on this, however, I must first ground the specific claim that practices concerned with mathematising the study of society and economy have indeed been long in place, at least in countries like France. For some may doubt that they have been. Yet if they had not then, as I have already noted, the supposed puzzle of the varying fortunes of the mathematising tendency over time would be seen to dissolve straight away. In which case I would need to go no further with this particular explanatory endeavour. Matters, though, are (unsurprisingly) not that simple.

Origins

I do not claim to know where, in the history of those research practices that ultimately gave rise to modern mainstream economics, the formalising tendency first took root. However, it is clear that an important impetus to the process was Newton's success in uniting the heavens and the earth in mathematics. Even Kant came to argue thereafter that a science of society was required, and this necessitated a social-scientific Newton or Kepler to identify the laws of society. And in the euphoria of the achievements of the Enlightenment, indeed, the 'mathematisation' of the social sciences became a major theme of contemporary Western culture.

Certainly during the period of the Enlightenment the endeavour of mathematising the study of social life was enthusiastically taken up by some. According to Ingrao and Israel (1990), in fact, the

> historiography of philosophical thought has long identified the 'mathematization' of the social sciences as one of the major themes of contemporary culture generated and molded in the rich melting pot of the Enlightenment.
>
> (34)

France was pivotal in this development, as I have already briefly noted, especially with regards to those aspects of this history that can now be recognised as the direct lineage of modern economics. Let me, then, indicate something of this French history, and thereby give concrete substance to the claim that the drive to mathematise the discipline is really something that long preceded the widespread acceptance of that project in the twentieth century. Once this is achieved, I will be able to consider the puzzle before us under perhaps its most challenging aspect: why the mathematising tendency fared poorly (in terms of take-up) relative to today's achievements, even in France.

The drive to mathematise economics in France

Most economists are aware of Walras' eventual contribution to the mathematisation of the discipline through his formulating the theory of general equilibrium. But he was neither the first nor the last significant contributor to the mathematisation of the subject, even in France. Any list of French contributors prior to Walras, and influenced by Enlightenment achievements, would include the Physiocrats or Physiocratic 'sect', especially Quesnay (1694–1774). Quesnay supposed that the political and moral basis of society is regulated by an inescapable force established by the creator, or at least taking the form of natural law, a view which underpinned his *Tableau économique* or 'arithmetical formula' of the annual reproduction of the nation's wealth.

If Quesnay is to be added to such a list, he is not the only one. There are others whose contributions were often very significant indeed. For example, Turgot (1727–81), a contributor close to the Physiocrats but not a member of the sect, developed the metaphor of blood circulation in suggesting a connection between the operation of markets and the dynamics of fluids. Dupont de Nemours (1739–1817) argued that because everything happens in the order established by the creator of nature, it is possible to apply physico-mathematical methods to the moral sciences. Condorcet (1743–94) attempted to found a *mathématique sociale*, aiming to achieve an objective science of subjective phenomena formulated in terms of the probability calculus. Achylle-Nicolas Isnard (1749–1803) produced his own table of arithmetic to demonstrate, as a departure from Physiocratic thought, that manufacturing industry, like agriculture, may also generate a surplus, one that accrues to not only landowners but also owners of scarce productive resources. Canard (1750–1833), in works on social mathematics and on political economy, provided (or anyway attempted to provide – some dispute his achievements) the first explicit formulation, and dynamic treatment, of the notion of economic equilibrium, the first application of marginal analysis, and a conception of the connection between the ideas of mechanical and economic equilibrium. Dupuit (1804–66), contributed to the development of general equilibrium theory by providing a mathematical foundation for the idea of the measurability of utility (a quality of the good depending upon the attitude of the economic individual). And Cournot (1801–77) demonstrated how to apply functional analysis to economic phenomena in a manner that required specifying only the most generalised features of the functional forms utilised. He also provided a statement of a supposed law relating the quantity of a good demanded and the latter's monetary price in a single market. And it was Cournot who introduced concepts eventually known as the elasticity of demand and marginal cost, and ideal types of market forms (perfect or unlimited competition, etc.), amongst much else.

Walras (1834–1910) remains the central figure in this early French history, of course, at least in terms of modern-day renown. But we can already see that in formulating a mathematical theory of general equilibrium, Walras was developing the work of others, most especially the contributions of Canard, Isnard and Cournot (although only the latter is explicitly acknowledged by Walras).[5]

I have no need to go into the details of Walras' contribution here, which are in any case well known. At this point I am merely concerned with identifying relevant threads in the early history of the current mainstream. I am wanting to draw attention to the fact that practices concerned with mathematising the discipline of economics have long been under way. And the driving force, the generative motor, was societal culture. This bore as heavily on Walras as on his predecessors more than a hundred years earlier. The historical analysis of Ingrao and Israel indicates well

> how deeply attached Walras was to the main trends in French culture that had inspired the application of mathematics to economics and, in particular, the early development of economic equilibrium theory. Despite his reluctance to acknowledge his precursors … there are numerous passages clearly showing his awareness of belonging to a French cultural tradition inspired by

a project of applying the Newtonian model of physical and
mathematical science to the economic and social sciences.

(Ingrao and Israel 1990: 141–2)

We might note, too, that when Walras resigned from his teaching obligations in Lausanne in 1893, he was succeeded by Pareto (1848–1923),
born in Paris but eventually raised in Italy, who was also concerned with
the mathematisation of the social world. For Pareto, at least as much as
for Walras, an understanding of mechanical equilibrium served as a
model for theorising general economic equilibrium. In attempting to
construct a rational mechanics of economic behaviour using methods of
physics and mathematics, Pareto aimed to give the former the same
analytical foundation and empirical grounding as rational mechanics.

Part of the lineage of modern economics is to be found, then, in
France's intellectual history. However, although important contributions
to the modern situation emerged during this early French episode, none
were especially well accepted in their own time (even if Walras was occasionally prone to making extravagant claims to the contrary). Of course,
as we now know, the goal of mathematising the discipline, including that
of developing a formalistic equilibrium theory, did eventually become
widely accepted, even if mathematical modelling methods have never
proven to be particularly successful or fruitful as ways of investigating
and understanding social reality (see e.g. Hahn 1985). Walras in particular, albeit long after his death, was eventually to achieve the recognition
he had, for much of his lifetime, felt he deserved. Samuelson, for
example, was to interpret him as the only economist on the level of
Newton. And Schumpeter declared him 'the greatest of all economists'.
However, before there was to be a widespread acceptance of mathematical economics in general, and of the importance of Walras' contribution
in particular, a new methodological framework was to be adopted, and
the focus of attention would veer away from France to interwar Vienna,
Britain, Sweden and ultimately the USA.

Before examining various relevant aspects of these developments,
however, there are other matters to consider. But first, let me reempha-
sise my objective here. I am proposing a socio-evolutionary explanation
of the development and persistence of modern mainstream economics
interpreted as the project concerned to formalise social/economic
phenomena. To this point I have merely indicated that amongst the
variety of practices within the population of methodological practices of
economists, endeavours to mathematise the study of social phenomena
have long been in evidence. If this, at least in part, is an evolutionary
story, I need to demonstrate how the environment has played a role in
selecting out the *a posteriori* successful practices (or equivalently, in
filtering out those which, at any point of time, were unsuccessful). I

emphasise that I do not take a deterministic stance here. Changes in the environment do not have to play such an influential role. My argument is just that, in the case of the rise of modern mainstream economics, it turned out *a posteriori* that they did.

The culture of mathematics in France

In fact, a question I ought really to address at this point is why the euphoria of the achievements of the Enlightenment gave rise to such an impulse to mathematise the social sciences in France in particular. Of central relevance here, I believe, is the Cartesian heritage of this country. Newtonianism was initially wielded as a weapon in the intellectual struggle against Cartesianism (Voltaire 1738). But, as is so often the case in a debate where each side contains insight, the outcome was a project modified very much in the light of criticisms of, and so conforming to, the other. Thus it was, that on emerging from its encounter with Cartesianism, Newtonianism (in its particular guise of a concern with elaborating laws)[6] assumed quite unique features in France, being substantially transformed in line with the opposition. In particular, whereas the empiricist orientation of England gave rise to small-scale empirical research, the French physico-mathematical approach adopted the goal of furthering the mathematical analysis of Newton's laws of physics. Moreover those who accepted this goal were quite successful in their pursuit of it. So much were they so, in fact, that (at a time when the English Royal Society was in decline) the French Académie des Sciences, very much bound up with the development of (this form of) Newtonianism, became established as the leading scientific institution in Europe.

As might be expected, this achievement of French science had knock-on effects in society at large. Science came to be seen as the most prestigious sphere of French life and thereby amongst the most influential. In its mathematical-Newtonian guise it came to be seen as an ideal for all branches of study and for culture more widely, giving an impulse to the idea of a mathematical-scientific approach to the governance of society, and, as a condition for this, to an understanding of its conditions. In their historical overview, Ingrao and Israel summarise the ensuing situation in France as follows:

> [With the successes of the 'French physico-mathematical school'] the scientific intellectual became the model intellectual and the scientific community the model for scholarly communities. In the reformist view of the values and decrepit institutions of abso-lutism, Newton's scientific philosophy and the model of the scientific intellectual established in France became points of reference for an ideal renewal of the whole of society. In its new

Newtonian garb, science put itself forward as the *center* of society and the *driving force* of reform, promising new horizons in all fields of knowledge to which the new methods of scientific thought could be applied. This scientistic (in the full and broad sense) vision was thus projected beyond the confines of traditional science, and under the urgent prompting of institutional, economic and social problems – first under the *Ancien Régime* and then during the Revolution – the question of the *scientific* government of society and economy achieved full status also in theoretical terms.

(Ingrao and Israel 1990: 35–6)

The environment: orientations to the mathematisation of social phenomena

If Western culture in general, and French post-Enlightenment culture in particular, held mathematical practice in such high esteem, it is not surprising that attempts to formalise economics took place in such conditions.

It may be thought a puzzle, then, that such practices failed to win widespread approval within the academy at an earlier time, at least in a country like France. If the culture placed a premium on the reproduction and proliferation of mathematical practices, including in economics, why did they not flourish more in that field in the immediate Enlightenment period, and on the scale they do today? After all, they have since achieved dominance without proving to be especially explanatorily fruitful, certainly not more so than other approaches. Why did widespread acceptance within the academy take so long? Why were the mathematising practices (or the scientific values, codes and norms underpinning them) not more widely copied amongst would-be social-economic theorists? Or where they were copied, why were the results not more influential? Why, most especially, did mathematical economics not become more widely accepted at a far earlier point in time in France, where the Enlightenment impulse to the mathematising ideal was accepted so quickly, and early on became deeply culturally embedded.

The answer, I now want to argue, has something to do with the specific local academic environment in which the mathematising economists were situated. Let me indicate something of the context in which the early post-Enlightenment attempts to formalise the study of social phenomena occurred in France.

In fact, in the period immediately following the Revolution, the academic climate in France was particularly open to ambitious projects of political and educational reform. At this point, the application of mathematics, as opposed to many literary activities, was interpreted as accessible to people from all backgrounds or classes, and so desirable, and social mathematics found some space in the educational system. In particular, the Academy of Moral and Political Sciences of the Institut de France concerned itself in a very significant way with the application of mathematics to the study of society.

But Enlightenment culture not only prompted attempts to mathematise all areas, it also required criteria of verification in all fields. There was a demand that descriptive or explanatory accuracy be demonstrated. From early on, even in France, there was significant opposition from the sciences at large, and from within mathematics especially, to the use of mathematics in areas for which it was considered unsuited. As the early optimism of the Revolution turned to the harsher realism, even to academic intolerance, of the Napoleonic order, there was less emphasis on encouraging certain academic practices for their own sake, or for the sake of those who prosecuted them. Greater emphasis, instead, was put on accepting academic practices for their perceived relevance.

The demand for descriptive or explanatory relevance was to prove, then as now, beyond the means of those striving to mathematise the social realm. And this was widely recognised. Laplace, in particular, came to view the attempt to mathematise the study of social phenomena as an intellectual mistake. He gave some support to the idea at the time of the Revolution. But with further study and reflection, his attitude turned to one of outright hostility. So hostile was he, in fact, that when, with the death of Lagrange, he achieved near supremacy in scientific matters in France, especially at the Institut de France's class of geometry, Laplace set about actively purging what remained of the programme of mathematising the study of society.

In this period, with Laplace's influence large, the scientific world largely lost interest in applying mathematical methods outside of physics. Only the physico-mathematical sciences were accorded any serious status. The project of mathematising the social world continued, of course. But a result of developments in the physico-mathematical sciences was the abandonment of all attempts at constructing an autonomous discipline. Instead, such attempts to mathematise social phenomena as persisted followed the official model as laid down by the physico-mathematical sciences. They became oriented to traditional mathematical tools and concepts and deterministic methods of mechanics. All traces of Condorcet's probabilistic approach, for example, for the time being disappeared.

The impact of Jean-Baptiste Say

In this climate it is perhaps not surprising that the study of social phenomena was undertaken in a largely non-mathematical way. Actually this is too neutral a description. For in resonance with Laplace's views, the study of social phenomena in the nineteenth century became dominated by those who not only mostly abstained from formalistic endeavour, but also actively discouraged it, albeit, in part, for somewhat idiosyncratic reasons.

Jean-Baptiste Say (1767–1832) and the French liberal school he in effect founded, a school that was to dominate the field of social study for most of the nineteenth century, took much the same position as Laplace. Say even made opposition to the mathematisation of social phenomena a central plank of the school's broader philosophy. It is relevant to inquire why. After all, the French liberal school was primarily concerned with particular substantive theories and policies. It is true that Say provided numerous comments as to why realisticness ought to be prioritised over 'algebraic formulas' and the like. Even so, an obvious, and sufficient, orientation to have adopted, was opposition to any dogmatism on the part of others who neglect the real world. On the face of things, there was no obvious reason to make an opposition to all mathematising tendencies a central part of the school's programme. Yet this is what happened. Indeed, as Ingrao and Israel have also observed, this 'rejection of the mathematisation of social science was pushed by Say almost to the point of the idiosyncratic rejection of mathematics *tout court*' (Ingrao and Israel 1990: 60). If the stance taken by Say and others to economics was in keeping with the views of natural scientists, and perhaps contributed something to Say's significant influence at the time, what actually was the reason for Say coming to adopt such a position in the first place?

The story is somewhat complicated, as Arena (2000a) makes especially clear. Although the period 1790–1870 saw the rise to prominence of the French classical or liberal school, with Say as the founder and figure-head, Say's initial project was not to establish a new school at all, but something rather different. His purpose was merely to disseminate the insights of Smith's *Wealth of Nations* in continental Europe, albeit with some extensions introduced for purposes of clarity (Say 1803).

But Ricardo and Malthus adopted similar projects, albeit providing different interpretations of Smith. This introduced a kind of rivalry, especially between Say and Ricardo. Over time this led Say to re-evaluate his own contribution. First he revised upwards the degree of originality of his contribution. He reinterpreted his project not merely as disseminating Smith's writings but also as advancing Say's own scientific discoveries. And eventually he came to argue explicitly for a different approach to that of Ricardo and other heirs of Smith. Although Ricardo did not use mathematics in his contributions, he did adopt a deductivist style of argument. It is a mode of argumentation that would lend itself to easy mathematisation by later mathematical economists, and suffers from the same problems of connecting with social reality as experienced with mathematical methods in economics. Say was keen to be distinguished from the Ricardians, and indeed to be viewed as providing a superior contribution. It was an opposition to Ricardo's deductivist method, in particular, that Say chose to emphasise in this, and which emerged thereby as a central plank of French classical thought. Thus commentaries on mathematics, like the following, invariably connect the mathematising tendency with economists influenced by Ricardo:

> Without referring to algebraic formulas that would obviously not apply to the political world, a couple of writers from the eighteenth century and from Quesnay's dogmatic school on the one hand, and some English economists from David Ricardo's school on the other hand, wanted to introduce a kind of argumentation which I believe, as a general argument, to be inapplicable to political economy as to all sciences that acknowledge only experience as a foundation. By that I mean the argumentation that lies on abstract ideas. Condillac has rightly noticed that abstract reasoning is nothing but a calculation with different signs. But an argument does not provide, nor does an equation, the data that is essential, as far as experimental sciences are concerned, to get to the discovery of truth. Ricardo set it in a hypothesis that cannot be attacked because, based on observations that cannot be questioned, he imposes his reasoning until he draws the last consequences from it, but he does not compare its results with experience. Reasoning never wavers, but an often unnoticed and always unpredictable vital force diverts the facts from our calculation. Ricardo's followers … considered real cases as exceptions and did not take them into account. Freed from the control of experience, they rushed into metaphysics deprived of applications; they have transformed political economy into a verbal and argumentative science. Trying to broaden it they have led only to its downfall.
>
> (Say 1971: 15)

As Arena summarises matters:

> This dissent from Ricardo's method was considered by Say as a fundamental issue and this view was then adopted by most of Say's French Liberal followers, forming therefore one of the crucial components of the liberal theoretical framework in France.
>
> (Arena 2000a: 207)

Certainly, most of Say's followers took his lead in opposing the Ricardian deductive approach, with some of them, especially Wolowski (1848), Reybaud (1862) and Baudrillart (1872) being opposed to the use of mathematics in particular.[7] According to Reybaud, for example, the Ricardians were only out 'to feed principles with equations and give political economy a false air of algebra in order to impress minds who look for deep thinking' (Reybaud 1862: 301)

The details of the rise to dominance of the French liberal school, with its fundamental opposition to mathematical methods, need not concern us here (and are well documented in Arena 2000a: esp. 215–18). The point to emphasise, rather, is that once it achieved dominance this school developed strategies to maintain its position. For example, liberals attempted to control educational institutions that played any role in the teaching of political economy. At some point or other, they carried significant and often total influence in the Athénée, the Ecole Spéciale de Commerce, the Ecole Commerciale, the Conservatoire des Arts et Métiers, and the French Grandes Ecoles, with the peak of their sway culminating, in 1871, in the creation of the Ecole Libre des Sciences Politiques. The liberals also significantly influenced the constitution of scientific societies. They created the Société d'Economie Politique in 1842, and became prominent amongst the members of Académie des Sciences Morales et Politiques after its re-establishment in 1832. And liberals also either dominated, or very significantly influenced, the major journals read by economists. These included *Le Censeur*, *Le Libre-Echange*, *L'Economiste Français*, *Le Globe*, *Le Journal des Débats*, *Le Siècle*, and most significantly *Le Journal des Economistes*. The latter, which was created by the liberals in 1841, defended the liberal viewpoint until its demise during World War II. The effect of all this on the contemporary practices of economics in France is once more well summarised by Arena:

> French liberal economists, however, were jealous of the influence of their approach. Therefore, they built and implemented a strategy for the diffusion of this message. The liberal school thus formed a homogeneous group unified by familial links, friendship and participation in common Societies and Journals. This participation strongly contributed to the diffusion of the liberal central message. It was however decisively reinforced by the strategy of control of educational institutions. This control helped French liberal economists to diffuse their views and act as if they were the only ones who could be considered 'economists', as such. Their cultural, political and social predominance was no longer questionable. Economists who did not accept the liberal views were proclaimed to be 'heretics': they became 'socialists' or 'prohibitionists'; they actually lost their right of belonging to the realm of political economy.
>
> (Arena 2000a: 219)

So important was the liberal school's influence, including its amplification of Say's rejection of attempts to mathematise the social sciences, according to Ingrao and Israel (1990), that 'Say's methodological views were long to weigh upon French culture as an impediment to any further attempt to use mathematical models in economics' (60).

Thus from the beginning of the French classical period to the time of Walras, the relevant academic environment presented difficulties for would-be mathematisers of the study of social phenomena. In French society at large the idea of mathematics as an essential feature of any respectful discipline prevailed. Yet within relevant branches of the academy (the relevant local environment) the reception afforded the would-be mathematisers of social phenomena was continually hostile. For the natural sciences and their mathematicians, this of course did not entail a demotion in the importance of mathematics *per se*, merely a recognition that economics required something different. For Say and his followers, in contrast, there likely was a rejection of the view that mathematics is an essential component of all serious processes of knowledge production. But in either case, attempts to mathematise the study of social phenomena were viewed as misguided and, more significantly, actively resisted.

Still, attempts to mathematise the social sciences continued throughout, as we have seen. Variety in social research practices was always present, and the wider cultural forces ensured that the range of practices followed included at least some of this mathematising sort. But it was always difficult for the would-be social mathematicians. The influence of Laplace, as I say, resulted mainly in a forced concentration on the strictly deterministic approach of mechanics based on methods of infinitesimal calculus. And the fact of the near-total dominance of Say's school within economics, along indeed with, in the late nineteenth century, the growing influence of historicism and institutional analysis, in addition to the scientific community's eventual near-total dissociation from the mathematisation of the social sciences project, rendered any contribution to the latter a somewhat isolating and wearisome endeavour. It was precisely these conditions that Walras himself was to encounter.

The reception of Walras

It is against a backdrop of such forces and developments, then, that we must interpret the reception of Walras' efforts. Not surprisingly, when in 1873 Walras presented his first attempts at formulating a mathematical economics at the Institut de France's Académie des Sciences Morales et Politiques, it was largely met with either disinterest or outright hostility. The economic historian Levasseur was especially critical. In particular, he ridiculed Walras' application of mathematics to social phenomena which, as he saw it, do not lend themselves to such a treatment, concluding that 'one gets a far better idea from thinking than from the author's mathematical formulae' (Levasseur in Walras 1874: 117). Levasseur also warned of the:

danger that lies in the desire to bring together, as a unit, at any cost, things that are complex by their nature, as in wishing to apply to political economy a method that is excellent for the physical sciences but could not be applied indiscriminately to an order of phenomena whose causes are so variable and complex and that above all involve one eminently variable cause that can absolutely not be reduced to algebraic formulae: human freedom.

(Levasseur in Walras 1874: 119)

Other economists proved hardly more charitable in their reception of Walras' formulations.

Thus ignored or dismissed by economists, Walras turned some of his efforts to seeking the approval of physicists and mathematicians. This is not to say that Walras no longer sought the approval of economists as well. But perceiving that mathematics was the dominant and most influential discipline, Walras reasoned that if the mathematicians could be brought on side, the economists would sooner or later follow. But persuading mathematicians that his approach had relevance was no easier than persuading economists. Although some were interested, most were not. Walras, ever the optimist, eventually claimed Poincaré as amongst the more positively inclined. But this was really an exaggeration. In a short letter he sent to Walras in 1901, commenting on the copy of *Eléments d'économie politique pure* that he had recently received from Walras, Poincaré observed:

> at the beginning of every mathematical speculation there are hypotheses and that, for this speculation to be fruitful, it is necessary (as in applications to physics for that matter) to account for these hypotheses. If one forgets this condition, then one goes beyond the correct limits.

(Poincaré 1901)

It is this realist condition, of course, that mathematical economists have been unable fully to satisfy either prior to, or since, this time.[8] Against Walras' *Eléments*, specifically, Poincaré, picking up on features that are still prominent in much modern economic theorising, observed:

> You regard men as infinitely selfish and infinitely farsighted. The first hypothesis may perhaps be admitted in a first approximation, the second may call for some reservations.

(Poincaré 1901)

In truth, after several years of self-propaganda by Walras and often fierce rejections of the idea of mathematical economics by mathematicians, the dialogue between the two groups – mathematicians and those economists keen to formalise the study of social phenomena – became severely curtailed. Ten years into the twentieth century, indeed, it seemed that the goal of extending support for the application of mathematical methods beyond the borders of physics, certainly to the social sciences, was widely (though never universally)[9] regarded as impossible.

Yet despite these setbacks, the story was, at this point, far from over. As we know the mathematisation project in general, and general equilibrium analysis specifically, were yet to rise phoenix-like from the ashes. How could this be? In particular how could this be if, amongst other things, and as I have noted all along, the project was never to achieve much success in terms of illuminating the social world?

A shifting environment: reinterpreting mathematics

A significant part of the answer lies in a shift that occurred in the relevant environment, specifically, in the environment of academic practices within which attempts to mathematise the discipline competed with others. I have already noted how the criticisms of Laplace and others led those economists who continued with the mathematisation project to adopt the model of the contemporary paradigm of physics, basically mechanics. However, at this time, this classical reductionist programme (the programme of reducing everything to the model of physics, in particular mechanics) was itself coming into disarray. With the development of relativity theory and especially quantum theory, the image of nature as continuous came to be re-examined in particular, and the role of infinitesimal calculus, which had previously been regarded as having almost ubiquitous relevance within physics, came to be re-examined even within that domain.

The outcome, in effect, was a switch away from an emphasis on mathematics as an attempt to apply the physics model, and specifically the mechanics metaphor, to an emphasis on mathematics for its own sake. As classical physics itself went into crisis, developments in mathematics were to reduce the dependency of mathematisation projects on physics altogether. Mathematics, especially through the work of Hilbert, became increasingly viewed as a discipline properly concerned with providing a pool of frameworks for *possible realities*. No longer was mathematics seen as the language of nature, abstracted from the study of nature. Rather it was conceived as a practice concerned with formulating systems comprising sets of axioms and their deductive consequences, with these systems in effect taking on a life of their own. The task of finding applications was henceforth regarded as being of secondary importance at best, and not of immediate concern.

This method, the axiomatic method, removed at a stroke various hitherto insurmountable constraints facing those who would mathematise the discipline of economics. Researchers involved with mathematical projects could, for the time being at least, postpone the day of interpreting their preferred axioms and assumptions. There was no longer any need to seek the blessing of other economists or of mathematicians and physicists who might insist that the relevance of metaphors and analogies be established at the outset. A need to match method to the nature of social reality was no longer regarded as a binding constraint, or even a matter of any relevance, at least for the time being. Nor, it seemed, was it possible for anyone to insist (with any legitimacy) that the formulations of economists conform to any specific model already found to be successful elsewhere (such as the mechanics model in physics). Indeed, the whole idea of prior models, metaphors, even interpretations, came to be rejected by some economic 'modellers' (albeit never in any really plausible manner).

If, then, there is, for many, something almost addictive, certainly seductive, about the idea that undertaking serious study requires the application of mathematical formalism, early in the twentieth century this particular 'scientific convention', as a motive for social study, was cut free from its previous leash. Economists could now indulge their mathematical desires, freed from the need to give much by way of realistic interpretation of their contributions as justification, or even (at least in principle) from the need to provide any interpretation at all.

Probably the most famous (though certainly not the only)[10] influential contribution to the formalisation of economics since Walras remains Debreu's (1959) axiomatic treatment of (the existence and uniqueness) of general equilibrium, a contribution that gained its author the Nobel Memorial Prize in economic science. Even today the language and symbolism of Debreu's *Theory of Value* is found in many axiomatic papers. And Debreu's contribution rests for its legitimacy precisely on the claim that axioms are not in need of any interpretation. As Debreu expresses these matters himself:

> *Allegiance to rigor dictates the axiomatic form of the analysis where the theory, in the strict sense, is logically entirely disconnected from its interpretations.* In order to bring out fully this disconnectedness, all the definitions, all the hypotheses, and the main results of the theory, in the strict sense, are distinguished by italics; moreover, the transition from the informal discussion of interpretations to the formal construction of the theory is often marked by one of the expressions: 'in the language of the theory,' 'for the sake of the theory,' 'formally.' Such a dichotomy reveals all the assumptions and the logical structure of the analysis. It also makes possible immediate extensions of that analysis without modification of the theory by simple reinterpretations of concepts.
>
> (Debreu 1959: viii, emphasis added)

If the decline in the classical reductionist programme and the rise of axiomatic mathematics laid the conditions for the eventual proliferation of mathematical economics, advances along these lines came only gradually. And it is perhaps significant that the project of mathematising economics received the greater stimulus at this juncture not in France, with its close links with the classical reductionist programme, but in Austria and Germany, where the new physics, a revised conception of the role of mathematics and a specific emphasis upon axiomatic mathematics, had originated and now flourished. In particular, it was here that von Neumann, Wald, Morgenstern and other mathematicians made their initial contributions. And although approaches such as those of Wald and von Neumann were different in kind, they were later reconciled in the US, where many of the early contributors emigrated under the Nazi threat.

Of course, France itself eventually witnessed significant related developments as well. I have already mentioned the contribution of Debreu. Although Debreu's *Theory of Value* was produced after his move to the US Cowles Commission in the 1950s, Debreu was very much a product of the French Bourbaki 'school' (a group of French mathematicians[11] who argued that mathematical systems should be studied as pure structures devoid of any possible interpretations). It was at the Ecole Normale Supérieure in the 1940s that Debreu came into contact with the Bourbaki teaching. And once trained in this maths, but with his interests aroused by economics, Debreu sought a suitable location to pursue an interest in reformulating economics in terms of this mathematics. It is perhaps not insignificant that his move to the Cowles Commission coincided with the latter's effective acceptance of Bourbakism.

The fine details of the latter and all other developments cannot be elaborated here.[12] My general point, though, is common to most if not all such individual pathways, and can be stated without filling in all the specific links. It is that in the Western academies at least, the constraint of social reality on mathematical modelling was at this point postponed until some 'tomorrow'. And with this being the case, the possibilities for mathematical modelling were, for the time being anyway, restrained almost solely by the ingenuity of the protagonists.[13]

The political environment

But is this shift in the way mathematics became understood and pursued a sufficient explanation of the fact that the formalising tendency in economics came to achieve such a dominant position? The factors so far discussed certainly provide some understanding as to why the cultural perception of the ubiquitous role of mathematics came to play a bigger role in influencing developments within the economics academy at a certain point in the twentieth century. They also help explain why before that time the mathematising tendency was constrained from playing a greater role, at least in France where a significant role was most to have been expected. However, it is not clear that the environmental shift described is sufficient by itself to account for the phenomenon that, from the mid-twentieth century onwards, the mathematising project has become quite so dominant in economics. Is the seductiveness of doing things mathematically sufficient to explain its successful take-up? Or did aspects of the relevant environment move in further ways that not only unleashed, or freed up, the mathematising tendency, but actually advantaged the formalising endeavour relative to other forms of research practice? I think the latter happened as well.

The post-World War II US context

This freeing up of mathematics, this removal of the burden or constraint of having to fit with reality, was indeed a reasonably generalised phenomenon. Nevertheless, to understand subsequent worldwide developments in the post-World War II period, it is necessary to appreciate that, and why, this decoupling of mathematics and (the study of) reality (allowing the promotion of the former unhindered by the constraint of conforming to the latter) enjoyed an especially warm reception in US economic faculties.[14] For it has turned out that the US has had the resources to dominate the post-World War II international academic scene in economics (as indeed it does in so many other disciplines).

Why was the US so receptive to this decoupling? A significant feature was a shift in the political environment. In particular the emergence of McCarthyite witch-hunts in the context of the Cold War significantly affected the developments in which we are interested. In this climate, the nature of the output of economics faculties became a particularly sensitive matter. And in such a context, the project of mathematising economics proved to be especially attractive. For it carried scientific pretensions but (especially when carried out in the spirit of the Bourbaki approach) was significantly devoid of any necessary empirical content. The group most feared or resented by the McCarthyites were the intellectuals (Reinert 2000). The formalising project with its technicist emphasis, often to the exclusion of almost any critical or reflexive orientation, was clearly extremely attractive to those caught up in the situation. This was especially the case not just for insecure or fearful university administrators, but also for the funding agencies of US social scientific research (who were especially important in this period – see for example Coats 1992; Goodwin 1998; Yonay 1998).

In making these observations I am not, of course, suggesting that those who contributed to the formalising project in economics did so opportunistically to pander to this demand for non-controversial stances. Indeed, it is an essential part of my thesis that this formalistic project was already long established. It had a tradition in the US as elsewhere, especially since the 1930s (see for example Yonay 1998), and most clearly after the establishment of the Econometrics Society. Those who pursued the mathematising project were no doubt motivated only to improve the project's academic performance and intellectual legitimacy. My argument, rather, is that, during this period, various relevant environments, including the political environment of the US, swung in a way that favoured the formalising project. And as always there were enough people around, or attracted by the North American situation, who were enamoured of formalising practices. These just happened to be the economists who benefited most from swings in the political environment.[15]

In fact, historians of the US have long argued that McCarthyism and the Cold War was decisive in the growth of anti-intellectualism in the US in the twentieth century[16] (see e.g. Hofstadter's [1963] *Anti-Intellectualism in American Life*; or Bloom's [1987] *The Closing of the American Mind*). My point here is simply that this environment impacted on the economics faculties as elsewhere, and was doubtless conducive to the spread of economics as mere technicist manipulation. Reinert (2000) reaches a somewhat similar conclusion:

> McCarthyism and the Cold War created a demand for a kind of economics that the mechanical versions of neo-classical economics and Austrian economics could both provide. The neo-classical utopia of market clearing harmony and factor price equalisation was an important counterweight to the communist utopia and its omnipotent state that promised to wither away.
>
> In this context the 'intellectuals' became a nuisance. The 'intellectuals' had historical and political qualifications and modifications to the clear message of an absolute superiority of the unmollified market economy. American pragmatism under the pressures of the Cold War degenerated into expediency and anti-intellectualism. History – also US history – cluttered the message of the near 'evilness' of state interventions under all circumstances and in all contexts. Removing economics' previously solid foundation in the humanities pried open for the rule and dominance of the mechanical models: clear conclusions, but conclusions which in their pure and undiluted form are only valid in a world devoid of diversity, of friction, of scale effects, and of time and ignorance. ...
>
> The pure neo-classical techniques in which economic harmony is already solidly built into the basic assumptions – providing results like Samuelson's *factor-price equalisation* – was the kind of theory that was ideologically and politically in demand. We are not suggesting that this kind of theory was created for political purposes. The theories had been there essentially since Ricardo,

but the *demand* for this kind of theorising rose considerably during the Cold War, sharpening its focus and message, but conveniently leaving aside the mitigating counter arguments of history. ... In this way the 'technicians' crowded out the 'intellectuals' of the economics profession.

(Reinert 2000: 29)

Clearly Reinert, in drawing attention to the nature of the postwar US context, is focusing as much on the content of the (sorts of) theories that thrived as on their formalistic nature. But the nature of the (potential) content is always constrained by the method. And in any case, the arguments about the environment of selection have even more bearing when we focus on the use of technique *per se*, and particularly on those instances in which the construction of (formalistic) structures were held to have no necessary interpretation whatsoever (also see Morgan and Rutherford 1998).[17]

Let me briefly take stock. I have argued that the formalising tendency has been in play long before the twentieth century, albeit meeting with little success in the area of formalising the study of society. In the early to middle twentieth century, however, that project's fortunes, in terms of approval rating, started to improve remarkably. This, however, occurred not as a result of any improved explanatory performance relative to that of any competing projects (or even in absolute terms). Rather it was the climate of its reception that shifted. Fundamental here are changes in the way mathematics became interpreted, and in the criteria according to which mathematical reasoning in any sphere is considered justified. And, in the US especially, there were relevant shifts in the political environment as well.

Of course, a multitude of factors not considered here will also have played a role in shaping eventual outcomes, or at least in shaping the manner in which things happened. No doubt, as I have already acknowledged, the life paths of specific individuals will have made differences, often fortuitously. And one especially significant development in the midst of all this was the emergence of cheap computing facilities, allowing the speedy development, initially of econometrics, and later of computer simulation models and the like. Indeed, the war effort likely induced a range of technical developments which facilitated the post-World War II mathematising project.

However, I do not need to recount the precise steps whereby, in the changed and changing, more conducive, environment, mathematical economics came to be accepted and indeed grew to become dominant. Nor do I really want to. For I am not suggesting a deterministic account, that what happened had to be. My aim is merely to indicate that, as it turned out, the environment of other relevant practices often had a very significant bearing in the determination of which practices in economics were, or were not, able to survive comfortably enough to flourish. Although there was no inevitability about anything that happened, it is clear, I think, that the changes in the environment made a significant difference, that the account of them sketched above has significant evolutionary-explanatory power. If the environmental shifts which occurred did not determine the outcome, they did serve to make what in the end happened more likely.

The drive to mathematise the study of social phenomena has for a long time been a dominant force in Western culture, a force that has been manifest in the academy. However, prior to the twentieth century, this drive was essentially constrained within the academy (or at least within parts of it that I have, with reason, focused on here) by the more dominant local view that research practices ought to be relevant to the object of study, that reality ought to constrain the analyses prosecuted. With the re-conceptualisation of mathematics in the early twentieth century, this constraint of reality on the mathematising project in the social sciences was lifted. Thus unconstrained, and aided by shifts in the political environment, a cheapening of computing power and other factors, the project came to achieve a spell of dominance, a spell that still continues.

An important point, here, from the perspective of establishing a Darwinian natural selection story, is that the conditions responsible for the noted shifts in the environment had little to do with the conditions generating the variety of research practices which economists followed. The conditions of variety generation and environmental selection are largely independent.

Feed-forward and feed-backward mechanisms

The topic of this illustration does warrant further comment at this point, however. For although the axiomatic approach allowed a postponing of the day when the axioms and assumptions were to be given a realistic interpretation, it was always expected that the day of reckoning would eventually come. Yet we are still waiting. Illuminatory successes, as noted throughout and detailed in Chapter 1, are hard to find. How, then, after more than half a century of the 'new' approach to mathematics, is modern mainstream economics managing to survive, despite its unhappy record in providing social illumination?

To this point I have focused very much on the role of the environment of all practices serving to select or reject those of mathematical economics. Of course, once any project has achieved a certain level of dominance the opportunity may well exist for its agents to affect variety and selection conditions in its favour. And if and where this occurs, we must recognise that the natural selection model is limited in its explanatory contribution, or at least that the degree of dependence between conditions of variety production and environmental selection is relatively high.

We have already seen, for example, how the dominance of Say's school made it very difficult for the early mathematising project to gain proper consideration, or even to get started, and how the influence of Laplace made it difficult for any endeavour that did not conform to the standard model(s) of physics. These are possibly best viewed as cases of the feed-backward version of the PVRS model having some relevance, of selection conditions likely affecting the variety in play.

There are also numerous historical examples whereby the feed-forward version of the PVRS model is appropriate, of variety-generating factors influencing, or at least being brought to bear on, an attempt to influence the selecting environment as well. One such is Walras' well known attempt to publicise his own approach. He appealed not just to Poincaré, but to almost any economist or (more often) physical scientist or mathematician of influence, who might find an interest in it. As Ingrao and Israel note:

> An examination of Walras's published correspondence provides confirmation of the turning point reached in 1874. It was precisely in that period that he began an intense promotional campaign largely through his letters in an attempt to open channels of scientific exchange and possibly to win pupils and create a number of 'Walrasian schools'. His method was to establish networks of correspondents in various countries (Britain, the United States, Germany, Austria, Italy, and France). His greatest efforts were, as usual, directed to his home country and now in particular to the scientists, while not neglecting his traditional relations with economists. A brief glance immediately reveals where he found listeners and where not, where interest was sometimes followed by disappointment. While the German-speaking world proved fairly indifferent to mathematical economics, greater interest was displayed in Anglo-Saxon circles, albeit only amongst economists. In this sphere, his most important exchanges were with Jevons and Edgeworth, and both brought disappointment and difficulty.
>
> (1990: 148)

And if a century ago, possibilities for new approaches to mathematising the study of social phenomena, or for influencing the environment of selection, were rendered difficult, today the boot is on the other foot. In modern times it is the traditions that maintain realisticness or social illumination as the primary goal that mostly fail to receive a sympathetic hearing.

In other words, I think it is fair to say that, within the modern economics academy, there are instances where this mathematising project, now the mainstream tradition, maintains its position of dominance by closing off lines of intellectual competition, where it manipulates conditions both of variety generation and environmental selection. During the period of the dominance of mathematical economics, for example, we have tended towards a position where university lecture courses in faculties of economics in many countries cover little more than methods of formalistic modelling (especially at the postgraduate level), where most journals regarded as prestigious have acquired gate-keepers who effectively bar non-mathematical expositions, where appointments and promotions in academic economic departments and the like are heavily biased in favour of (econometric, micro- or macro-) modellers, and so on. I do not suggest that this is done with ill intent. The ways of proceeding regarded as standard or proper, along with the reward system supported, merely reflect the values that the dominant group of the day have come to accept.[18]

In my experience mathematicians, philosophers and other social scientists who are aware of the situation of modern economics side heavily with heterodox criticisms of the (concentrated emphasis on the) mathematising tendency within economics (though this often means they [erroneously] regard it as not a serious subject, even in potential). However, the mainstream of modern economics preserves itself in a situation of significant isolation from other disciplines. And until recent times, at least, such a situation has appeared sustainable. To the uninformed, the mathematical emphasis gives an aura of technical sophistication that is perhaps intimidating, esoteric, something to be left in the hands of economist experts,[19] certainly culturally accepted and admired; whilst the degree to which the project dominates the modern discipline encourages the response that surely so many people (most mainstream economists) cannot be wrong.

Yet nothing stands still, especially in the social realm. The McCarthyite period is past. Certainly in many countries there is nothing resembling it in place. Further, the impetus gained to the mathematising project from recent advances in computer technology appears to be petering out. In these circumstances we might expect the emergence of forces working to change the academic balance in the direction of prioritising realisticness, despite the mainstream's hold on positions of power. And significant changes do seem to be happening. Whilst the heterodox groups persist in making significant contributions, other tendencies are in train. Student enrolments in economics faculties are currently in decline in many parts of the world (see for example Abelson 1996; Chote 1995; Kirman 2001; Parker 1993; Pisanie 1997). This has certainly coincided with the growth of business schools, and a reorienting of departments of human geography, sociology and the like, which now provide opportunities for people to teach and study aspects of life considered to be economic without the constraint of it all having to be carried out in a formalistic fashion. It seems likely, certainly possible, that such pressures will lead to a more pluralistic reorientation sooner or later.

Overview and further questions

I hope that I have by now covered enough ground to indicate that the rise to prominence of the mathematising project in economics conforms (or has aspects which conform) to a significant degree to the (Darwinian) evolutionary model, to the natural selection metaphor. It is indeed a success story for the practices concerned in terms of their eventual rise to, and continued, dominance. But, it does not appear to be a story of relative success by any wider or more laudatory criteria. In fact, if measured against the criterion of progress in knowledge and understanding of the social realm, many observers, as we have seen, continue to conceive modern economics as something of an unfortunate episode.

The example discussed here illustrates that any social process that does manifest evolutionary tendencies of a 'natural selection' sort will almost inevitably be one of continual accommodation and resistance, attraction and rejection, fit and mismatch, harmony and disharmony of subject and object or of 'individual' and environment, as changes in each interact with the other, as new practices emerge, and selections and selecting environments adjust. The social evolutionary process, then, will inevitably be one of shifting, slipping and sliding.

There can be no presumption that any *a posteriori* underlying direction of longer-term change is necessarily irreversible, of course. We are sometimes encouraged to think of the development of life on earth, including the emergence of human beings, or of developments in some branches of knowledge as, by and large, stories of irreversible progress. But there is no reason to suppose that all evolutionary episodes conform to such examples if so interpreted. Reversals of fortune are always possible. Such a reversal, of course, is precisely the outcome many heterodox economists are attempting to facilitate in the context of modern economics. The aim is so to reorient the discipline. It is to reinstall the goal of explanatory adequacy, even of truth, as primary once more, as part of a process of seeking a more pluralistic forum.

Of course, reversals in fortune are not unheard of even in the biological realm. Indeed they are rather common. I referred earlier to the varying fortunes of spotted grey and dark moths in the UK in the nineteenth century. In particular I noted how, with nineteenth-century industrialisation, pollutants killed the lichen on the trees in question and rendered the bark a dark colour, leaving the spotted grey at a relative disadvantage compared to dark moths because more easily recognisable to moth-eating birds. With the increase in pollution control in the twentieth century, however, lichen is again growing on trees in relevant areas, and I understand that once more the dark moth is on the decline relative to the spotted grey.

The opportunities (noted at the end of the previous section) for students to study economics without the constraint of reducing all to formalistic modelling, in business or management schools, departments of human geography, sociology and the like, and the openings equally provided for researchers more interested in social illumination, may mark an analogous case of re-switching in the environment of academic economic practices. Recently, students at some of the elite schools in France have begun a protest against the excessive mathematisation of the modern economics discipline, a protest that appears to be drawing significant support world-wide (for an overview see Kirman 2000; and especially Fullbrook 2003, forthcoming). Perhaps it will all make a difference.

However that may be, the evolutionary model does seem capable of providing a framework for understanding certain significant aspects of developments in the modern economics academy. Of course, the explanatory sketch provided here, though an extension of an argument found in previous contributions, remains (like any explanatory account) somewhat partial. Indeed (and again as with any explanation) new questions are thrown up by the answer(s) suggested. For example, why did the mathematising tendency not take off in a bigger way in the other branches of social science? Is the fact that most measurable social phenomena are regarded as 'economic' sufficient to explain this? And why in the last fifty years especially, have *specific* forms of mathematical economics (and not others) taken off, and why have they taken off when they have? For example, why has game theory risen to prominence only relatively recently, given that the basic principles were developed rather a long time ago?

What, in turn explains the explanation supported here? Specifically, what explains the *attractiveness* of conventions or edicts of the 'use mathematics' sort? Is the enduring place of mathematics in Western culture, with its very significant effect on the aspirations of modern economists in particular, solely due to the continuing successes of mathematical methods in numerous disciplines other than economics? Or is there also a deeper psychological explanation, turning, perhaps, on a fear of accepting the openness of society (and indeed of reality in general), the consequent fact of pervasive and fundamental uncertainty, and so the limited scope for predictability in life and thereby for control over what happens?[20] And, if the latter putative psychological mechanism is at all contributory, there arises the interesting supplementary question as to whether, as some suspect[21], its influence is significantly gender-differentiated.

I postpone setting out my own answers to questions such as these to a further occasion. But, whilst most answers to questions can generate yet more problems or puzzles to be resolved, the truth is that the historical documentation and explanation of the mathematising tendency in economics is a task that largely still lies in the waiting.

Here I have merely provided a sketch of what I believe is one set of explanatory ingredients in the history of modern economics. But it is an important set in that the features noted seem, in some significant part, to account in a coherent way for the varying fortunes of the mathematising project overtime, including its relatively recent rise to prominence, and indeed continuing dominance, in the absence of any obvious measure of relative success over and above the fact of its current widespread acceptance. Moreover, this explanatory coherence is achieved in a context where, currently, it is difficult to find, or easily imagine, any convincing alternative explanatory story.

NOTES

1 Four theses on the state of modern economics

1 As Baumol (1992) records:

> These days few specialised students are allowed to proceed without devoting a very considerable portion of their time to the acquisition of mathematical tools, and they often come away feeling that any piece of writing they produce will automatically be rejected as unworthy if is not liberally sprinkled with an array of algebraic symbols.
>
> (Baumol 1992: 2; see also Debreu 1991)

2 This is certainly so in the UK. But it seems to be increasingly the case everywhere.

3 As Guesnerie (1997) acknowledges:

> Mathematics now plays a controversial but decisive role in economic research. This is demonstrated, for example, by the recourse to formalization in the discussion of economic theory, and increasingly, regardless of the field. Anyone with doubts has only to skim the latest issues of the journals that are considered, for better or worse, the most prestigious and are in any case the most influential in the academic world.
>
> (Guesnerie, 1997: 88)

4 A tendency to conflate economics with mathematical methods has, of course, long been under way. For example, more than half a century ago Samuelson, speculating that economics would in some degree become, as he believed physics had, 'captured by mathematics' (1952: 63) welcomed the trend he was observing:

> Indeed, as I look back over recent years, I am struck by the fact that the species of mathematical economist pure and simple seems to be dying out and becoming extinct. Instead, as one of my older friends complained to me: 'These days you can hardly tell a mathematical economist from an ordinary economist'. I know the sense in which he meant the remark, but let me reverse its emphasis by concluding with a question: Is that bad?
>
> (Samuelson 1952: 66)

5 Thus, in his Jevons Memorial Fund Lecture entitled 'In Praise of Economic Theory', we find Hahn (1985), perhaps the most reflective mainstream economist of recent times, praising only mathematical axiomatic-deductive modelling. And in a recent *Journal of Economic Literature* article billed as 'The Young Person's Guide to Writing Economic Theory', the author considers only the elaborating of mathematical models (Thomson 1999). See also Gee 1991.

6 My own view, which I cannot elaborate here, is that mathematics is the science of operators. On this conception, although modern economics makes heavy use of the results of mathematics, in form it is at most a would-be branch of applied mathematics.

7 Always recognising that in each case there will be far more going on than can be expressed in the mathematical formalism (see especially Dennis 1994; 1995).

8 I am aware that across different literatures or disciplines (including mathematics) the category of closure is used to mean different things. Here, as I say (and state in previous contributions), I take a closed system to be one in which event regularities of the noted kind occur.

9 I might also emphasise that this conception does not preclude a number of interpretations of how models are usually, or might best be, employed. Models may be viewed as alternatives to narratives or story-telling (about the world). This is (or was) McCloskey's position (McCloskey 1990). Or story-telling may be treated as an essential aspect of the modelling process, as Mary Morgan maintains (e.g. Morgan 2001). Morgan's account perhaps best captures the practices of the majority. I believe too that it gives the most charitable interpretation of what takes place. But if, with Morgan, we accept that there can be different stories told with a given model *structure*, and allow that economists can be concerned to explore 'the full range of features and outcomes compatible with the structure' (2001: 369–70) it nevertheless remains the case, as Morgan indeed recognises, that the 'structure constrains and shapes the stories that can be told with a model' (366). Specifically, it remains always the case that the 'story is deductive because it uses the logic of the mathematics or materials … of the model to answer the question' (370).

10 I am aware, of course, that like everything else mathematics itself is, in some ways, continually changing and developing. But I see nothing in this insight that *per se* undermines my characterisation of the modern mainstream economics project or tradition. The latter changes too, of course, but not in its commitment to mathematical deductivist reasoning.

11 Modern economics is certainly subject to wide fluctuations in fashions or 'fads'. As Turnovsky notes:

> There are several aspects of economics as it is currently practised which I find to be troubling and which I hope will be reversed over the next several years. First, economics, particularly in the United States, is very much subject to fads. Certain topics become hot for a period, consuming a lot of research effort, only to become obsolete in a relatively short period of time and to be superseded by something else.
>
> (Turnovsky 1992: 143)

Fine (2001), in an excellent study of the causes and (unfortunate) consequences of the recent popularity of so-called social capital theory, even perceives a general pattern to the swings in fashion within mainstream economics:

> Yet, as already hinted … the emergence of social capital to rapid prominence is a familiar phenomenon in terms of academic fashions. It is most disturbing as evidence of a more general trend towards the popularisation and degradation of scholarship. The pattern is familiar by now. A case study or two leads to the invention of grand concepts and generalisations. These are refined in light of theoretical and empirical critiques that point to omitted theoretical variables and/or case study counter-examples. Existing and new knowledge is run through the evolving framework. Ultimately, the whole edifice becomes too complex and succumbs to the critical heretics or others who have remained or become cynical. It is then time for a new fashion to emerge.
>
> Despite this intellectual cycle, the effects are significant. Quite apart from the waste of scholarly resources, the impact of such fashions over the longer term is not necessarily negligible nor is it even across disciplines and topics.
>
> (Fine 2001: 190–1)

12 Mirowski (2000; 2001), for example, eventually views himself as somehow advancing an alternative to mainstream economics in encouraging an economics as computational science focusing on the theory of (markets as) automata (along lines seemingly anticipated by von Neumann). Mirowski does often maintain a critical distance from economists enamoured with prosecuting a computational economics. But his commitment comes through when he criticises the various approaches to computer simulation that are different to his preferred (von Neumannian) alternative.

13 Thus Richard Parker writes, on assessing the overall state of the discipline:

> [E]conomists no longer agree about what they do, or even whether it is all worth doing. Critics outside the profession long faulted economists for a host of sins: their deductive method, their formalism, their over-reliance on arcane algebra, their imperviousness to complex evidence, the bald inconsistency of different facets of the economic paradigm. What's new – after decades of steadfast resistance – is that these same concerns have begun to bother the profession too.
>
> (Parker 1993: 1)

14 *The Economist* (23 August 1997) recently carried an article entitled 'The Puzzling Failure of Economics'. According to this source the problem 'is not a failure of economics, in fact, but of modern … economics. The classical economists [provided a better understanding]'.

15 In an award-winning book the former minister Lord Howell assesses the state of modern economics as follows:

> The paradox of modern economics is that while the computers are churning out more and more figures, giving more and more spurious precision to economic pronouncements, the assumptions behind this fiesta of quantification are looking less and less safe. Economic model-making was never easier to undertake and never more disconnected from reality.
>
> (Howell 2000: 199)

He adds below:

> Somewhere along the way economics took a wrong turn. What has occurred, and what been vastly accentuated by the information revolution and its impact, is that economists have drained economic analysis both out of philosophy and out of real life, and have produced an abstract monstrosity, a world of models and assumptions increasingly disconnected from everyday experience and from discernible patterns of human behaviour, whether at the individual or the institutional level.
>
> As a result, economists have not only failed to discern, explain or predict most of the ills which beset the world economy and society, but they have actively encouraged a deformity of perception amongst policy makers and communicators, which has led in turn to a deep public bewilderment and distrust of government authorities – and this at the very time when the need is greater than ever for a bond of trust between government and society.
>
> This misleading 'black box' view of the world purveyed by the economics profession (with heroic exceptions), at all levels from the most intimate micro workings of markets to the macro level of nation states and their jurisdictions, has been vastly reinforced by compliant statisticians who have brought a spurious precision and quantification to entities and concepts which may not in fact have any existence outside economic theory, or whose validity has been sapped away by the impact of information technology.
>
> (Howell 2000: 203–4)

16 Of course, even where a contributor insists on viewing the process merely as a case of using one language rather than another, it is essential to recognise that acts of translation are rarely straightforward. Finding a way of expressing in a second language an idea previously acquired or formulated in a first one, is a creative constructive process. The structure of the expression as well as the terms used, etc., may change significantly. And new features may be brought in whilst others are de-emphasised. It is likely the case that in changing languages we are often changing in part how we present the world. We come to express features differently. But with mathematical-deductivist forms of reasoning, constraints are also placed on what can be allowed, on the sort of thing that can be said, on the sorts of worlds that can be admitted (see below). So any claim to be merely changing the language, to be translating, will likely be misleading indeed (see also Morgan, forthcoming).

17 For further discussion see Lawson 1997a: esp. chs 7 and 8.

18 In fact, Keynes (1973b: 276–7) long ago observed that atomism need not hold even for the natural realm (see Chapter 7 below).

19 Nor, once more, is this assessment especially novel. We shall see in Chapter 7 that Keynes saw the problem. And Veblen recognised it earlier still when he described a specifically hedonistic version of atomism (see Lawson 1997a: 10, 11).

20 This approach is also sometimes described as conventionalism. A good discussion of this interpretation of modern mainstream economics, as well as its critique, is found in Latsis 1976.

21 In conversation with the author.

22 For a few suggested alternatives, some more compelling than others, see Hoover (1997: 14). The real difference between Hoover's position and my own, it seems, is that Hoover sees econometricians as not really seeking constant conjunctions (or those covered by well defined probability laws), despite their rhetoric. Rather, he portrays them as pretty much practising the methods defended in Lawson (1997a). Our differences, then, stem from a claim that is open to empirical assessment. Of course I wish that Hoover's 'observation' were correct. But it certainly appears not to be in my neck of the woods, nor in most other parts of the economics academy with which I am familiar (including examples of Hoover's own recent work – see Hoover 2001b). Indeed, a moment's glance at economic journals regarded as prestigious (i.e. the mainstream ones) seems enough to douse most optimism on this score.

23 A version of this is raised by Krugman (1998), who suggests that the real reason formalism is discarded by some critics, and specifically by 'outsiders' to the economics profession, is that it often refutes pet doctrines:

> when outsiders criticise formalism in economics, their real complaint is often not about method but about content – in particular, they dislike 'formalistic' arguments not because they are formalistic, but because they refute their pet doctrines.
>
> (Krugman 1998: 1829)

Let me acknowledge straight away that if critics of formalism do oppose formalistic methods just because the substantive results achieved are unpalatable, because the critics see them as refuting pet theories or whatever, then this opposition is not soundly based. Here we must surely agree with Krugman. I do not doubt that analyses do often find favour in certain quarters just because of their results. This is a practice that is difficult to defend; ultimately, it is the relevance of the analysis that matters, not whether its results conform with our preferences.

24 Some critics hold that formalism should be banished in effect because it serves to exclude from the conversation those without the basic mathematical know-how. Krugman (1998) again draws attention to this charge, noting that in 1997 the editor of *Governing* magazine published an op-ed which asserted in particular that

> algebra could not be essential to economic understanding, because if it were this would delegitimise the opinions of people who had not studied algebra when young and were now too old to retool.
>
> (Krugman 1998: 1831)

Once more I think we must support Krugman's dismissal of the charge. *If* algebra (or any other specific research approach) is found to be essential to achieving any insight or sensibly formulated project, then it cannot be opposed just because the opinions of those without a sufficient knowledge of algebra (or of the techniques, etc. in question) cannot easily join the discussion. There certainly is a broader issue here about who is admitted to the academy; I personally am in favour of making admission as open as possible. But there is no argument here that applies merely to the mathematising of economics and not to all other branches of study where specific skills, training, experiences and/or know-how are involved.

25 An apparent charge to which modellers often respond is that economics should not even seek to be scientific or in any sense rigorous. In similar fashion modellers often see fit to defend their results as producing clarity and/or consistency. If there are those who rule out on some *a priori* basis the possibility of social science, or who think the pursuit of clarity is *necessarily* to be avoided, whatever the context, then I myself can be counted against them. Consistency is more problematic. But as long as we do not treat it in static terms, and accept that the best which we often can hope to achieve is developmental consistency, like, say, an acorn turning into an oak, or initial ideas being transformed into a thesis, then consistency can be accepted as a typically desirable and feasible goal.

26 A further criticism made of the use of formalism, or at least a charge against which modern mathematical modellers often see fit to defend themselves, is that formalists do not use empirical data and fail to draw conclusions from their models regarding matters of policy. Krugman (1998) cites some illustrious exceptions (1830). But to agree with him that the charge is untenable we need only to look at modern applied econometricians, all of whom use data, and many of whom interpret their models as bearing directly on the policy discussion.

27 Some mainstream economists have long recognised all this. Frank Hahn, I believe, is one. And it may be worth repeating some of his reactions explicitly here, if only because other mainstream economists may be encouraged thereby to examine whether there is really much point to the activities in question.

Thus, with respect to any attempts to estimate or test the formal models of economic 'theory' using measured data on actual phenomena, Hahn writes:

> The economists I have been discussing might be taken to be engaged in the following programme: to enquire how far observed events are consistent with an economy which is in continuous Walrasian equilibrium. ... [Even if this programme was successful] ... it would not be true that we understood the events. For we would not understand how continuous equilibrium is possible in a decentralised economy and we do not understand why a world with Trade Unions and monopolies behaves like a perfectly competitive one. Theorising in economics I have argued is an attempt at understanding and I now add that bad theorising is a premature claim to understand.
>
> (Hahn 1985: 15; see also Hahn 1994: 240)

And elsewhere Hahn reveals, albeit in somewhat dramatic fashion, what he thinks of the practice of using mathematical models for drawing policy implications:

> When policy conclusions are drawn from such models, it is time to reach for one's gun.
>
> (Hahn 1982: 29)

28 Those who recognise only positive or desirable aspects of mathematical methods in economics tend to neglect ontology altogether. Elsewhere (Lawson 1997c) I have examined whether assessments of the value of using formalistic

methods in economics vary according to whether or not a criterion of 'appropriateness of method to nature of the subject-matter' or 'ontological fit' is considered. Geoff Harcourt (1995) had already put together a large set of statements by a number of economists on the usefulness of mathematical modelling. Harcourt's impression was that the overall picture is mixed, that no clear conclusion follows as to what economists conclude. However, with Harcourt's sample of contributors, a clearer impression is obtained by distinguishing between those who do, and those who do not, examine whether or not formalistic methods are appropriate to the nature of social reality. Only three do. These are Marshall, Keynes and Boulding. The others, Samuelson, Debreu, Koopmans, Mirrlees, Chichilinsky, Hahn and Stone, consider only pragmatic criteria or criteria that in the context are too ambiguous to interpret (e.g. scientific advance).

So what is to be learnt from sub-dividing the contributions referred to by Harcourt in this manner? The answer is simply that a systematically different conclusion is reached concerning the relevance of mathematical formalism to economics according to whether or not ontological considerations are invoked. Specifically, while those who fail to question explicitly whether formalistic methods are capable of illuminating social material infer universally that the application of mathematical formalism to all areas of economics can only be beneficial, those who question the relevance of formalistic methods to the nature of social material (Marshall, Keynes and Boulding) draw more or less the opposite conclusion (see Lawson 1997c).

29 A similar position on all this is adopted by Nancy Cartwright (2001) (in fact Cartwright's approach and that defended here are contrasted and criticised in Hoover 1997). Recognising that 'regularities of this kind are rare indeed and the majority are hard won in a physics laboratory' (2001: 280), and mostly occur where single mechanisms are set operating on their own, Cartwright wonders if it is meaningful to expect these conditions of regularities to hold in economics? Cartwright is sceptical:

> Let us turn next to the idea of a mechanism operating *on its own*. We may conceive of the demand mechanism in terms of individual preferences, goals and constraints or as irreducibly institutional or structural. In either case on the regularity account of laws the law of demand records the regular behavior that results when the demand mechanism is set running alone. This paradigmatic case ... shows up the absurdity of trying to describe the capacities of mechanisms in terms of regularities. No behavior results from either the supply or the demand mechanism operating on its own, and that is nothing special about this case. In general it will not make sense to talk about a mechanism operating on its own.
>
> (Cartwright 2001: 280)

Another philosopher, John Dupré (2001), concludes similarly. Focusing, in effect, on the assumption that a (stable) causal mechanism, to give rise to an event regularity, must be isolated, and recognising that, in an interconnected and pluralistic social world, this amounts to an assumption of causal completeness, Dupré suggests economists might as well give up on the search for (event regularity) laws (330).

30 This claim is well illustrated by aspects of a recent debate in France. The debate was prompted by protests of French students critical of the perceived

lack of relevance of their courses. The students criticise, in particular, the fact that their courses mostly reduce to exercises in mathematical modelling. These protests have given rise to interesting interchanges in French magazines and newspapers, especially in the pages of *Le Monde*. The responses from leading (mostly French) economists seem to be openly sympathetic to many of the students' complaints, and in particular to the requests for more variety in approaches. Yet these economists nevertheless remain insistent that economics has to be scientific, where science is mostly (unquestioningly) equated with the use of mathematics. The possibility that mathematics is not essential to science is barely ever contemplated (see e.g. discussion under the head of 'Les mathématiques, condition nécessaire mais pas suffisante aux sciences économiques' in *Le Monde* of 31 October 2000).

31 Notice, though, how the conditions of experimental control and mainstream theorising differ. In the experiment, an understanding of an isolated mechanism is achieved as an explanation of an experimental regularity that is produced. In the case of mainstream economics there typically is no event regularity produced or found, rather a construct is formulated that posits an event regularity in theory.

32 We might now note, parenthetically, that to assume that event regularities (of the causal sequence sort) are ubiquitous even in the natural realm (an assumption that appears to encourage the modelling tradition of mainstream economics) is to commit one or more of a set of related errors. We have observed that such event regularities mostly correspond to the experimental actualisation and empirical identification of underlying mechanisms. Thus to treat such event regularities as existing apart from the mechanisms (and conditions under which any mechanisms can be isolated) is to commit what Whitehead (1926) refers to as the fallacy of misplaced concreteness; it is to treat something as separated from its necessary relations to other things, to treat an abstraction as though it were more concrete than it is.

This is the error of empirical realism (see Lawson 1997a: 19–20). I am not suggesting that economists necessarily commit it. But to avoid the error through acknowledging that event regularities of the relevant sort are indeed produced by underlying mechanisms, and yet to maintain that such event regularities are ubiquitous in the social realm, is to adopt an equally questionable position. It is to suppose not only that the sorts of mechanisms open to experimental investigation typify all real-world processes, but also that social mechanisms are all relatively concrete, i.e. that they exist and operate as separable, and indeed separate, entities.

The satisfaction of this latter supposition involves two further conditions. First it requires that in the way each identified mechanism works to produce its effects, it is unaffected by its relations with the rest of reality. This is the implicit assumption of atomism. And second, it is necessary that the direct actualisation of the effects of the working of each mechanism are not undercut by the effects of other countervailing factors. This is the assumption of isolationism.

To hold to this latter (isolationist) assumption for the natural (or any other) world is to render the experiment redundant. To combine it with the former assumption (of atomism) is to achieve the (implicit) ontology of modern mainstream economics. To assume the universal relevance of this latter ontology in a world that is open and complexly interrelated is to commit the fallacies of atomism and isolationism (see Lawson 1997a: chs 7 and 8) and also to help perpetuate the fictional aspect of much modern economics, as well as its record of explanatory failure. To perpetrate any of these errors is to commit the fallacy of misplaced universality (see Chapter 2 below).

33 Clearly this conception of science appears to make social (and natural) scientists of all of us. Actually, I think it only right that it should. Like so many activities, for example singing, cleaning, gardening, certain individuals are identified with one in particular only because they pursue it in a more systematic and sustained fashion than do the rest of us. To acknowledge this is not in any way to belittle such practices or the skills that the 'professionals' come to develop. So it is, I believe, in science.

34 This is not yet a unity of science thesis. I merely argue that economics can itself adopt those moves that seem to characterise the most successful aspects of natural science. An excellent contribution that explicitly challenges the thesis of scientific unity is John Dupré's *The Disorder of Things: Metaphysical Foundations of the Disunity of Science* (Dupré 1993). Actually, despite the title and orientation of this contribution, the position Dupré develops is quite close (at least in many respects) to that sustained here. The conception of order underpinning scientific unity which Dupré criticises is captured by the classical philosophical doctrines of (naive or extreme) essentialism, (regularity) determinism and (material) reductionism, all positions I also reject (see Lawson 1997a). Dupré critiques these theses mainly by way of drawing on scientific results from biology. But Dupré equally critiques scientific *dis*unity theses advanced by extreme forms of constructivism and empiricism. And he ends up maintaining a pluralistic 'promiscuous realism' which is not very different to the realist conception sustained here. For recent work where this contributor addresses the ontology of economics specifically, see Dupré (2001).

35 Although Hoover's example of such a power or disposition, namely a 'utility function', is hardly compelling.

36 In truth, the move to a conception of a rational (optimising) agent may not be a case of retroduction at all. I acknowledged above that mainstream economists will be using retroduction where novel social causes are hypothesised. The activity invoking retroduction to get at novel entities or aspects is *pure* or *abstract (causal) explanation*. Where a knowledge of causes is already held, and the understanding achieved is put to use to throw light on some concrete phenomenon, the activity is one of *applied* or *concrete explanation*. Strictly speaking the mode of inference applied here is *retrodiction* rather than retroduction. It involves working out the way in which known causes must have been triggered and interacted with one another for some concrete phenomenon to have materialised (see Lawson 1997a: 221, 244). Given that many mainstream economists start from the *prior* 'understanding' that the explanatory cause is a set of optimising human individuals, the exercise may often be best considered an explanatory endeavour of an applied sort.

37 Thus I side with Victoria Chick's (1998) recent assessment that: 'Formalism is fine, but it must know its place. Economists need to debate further the boundaries of that place' (Chick 1998: 1868). This chapter is a contribution to such endeavour.

38 The sort of methodological pluralism I am wanting to promote, though, does not negate the need for practitioners of economics critically to engage each other or to canvass reasoned change. I take it that to be a methodological pluralist does not require one to be lacking of definite views concerning, say, practices most likely to bear fruit in specific contexts. The maintenance of pluralism is not inconsistent with the use of reason. As I understand or rather defend the position, a commitment to methodological pluralism entails not a

hiding of differences but a respecting and accommodation of views and approaches alternative to one's own (in an awareness, in particular, that all assessments are fallible). To adopt such a stance is to support an environment which allows, and even encourages, competing ideas and approaches to co-exist, albeit with the hope of mutual engagement and enrichment. This, anyway, is the sort of position to which I am committed and seek here to advance.

But I see no contradiction in both accepting such an orientation and also arguing that it *is* prudent at this point in time to reorient the discipline to a significant extent. Currently, the resources of the discipline (curricula, jour-nals, new academic posts and research grants) are allocated almost exc-lusively to furthering a project that is rather unsuccessful even on its own terms, and has little apparent justification. I am suggesting that it is reason-able, in the circumstances, that a significant share of the available resources be allocated to furthering alternative approaches, especially those which can be shown to be successful at illuminating the social domain, or for which we have grounds for expecting significant success.

2 An ontological turn in economics

1 The label critical realism has been around a long time (see Lawson 1997a). The modern project systematised under this heading owes much to the contributions of Bhaskar (1978; 1979). In economics specifically, a number of economists are employing it (see for example Fleetwood 1999).

2 For it is apparent that my position is sometimes misunderstood. Although the goal, then, is to lay out an overview of the method and ontological results of *Economics and Reality*, the chapter is necessarily relatively brief compared to that book, and should be viewed only as a complement to the more devel-oped arguments of the latter.

3 Wade Hands refers to the latter as the 'shelf of scientific philosophy view of economic methodology' (1994; 2001: 2). If my presentation of developments in recent economic methodology here is broad and perhaps something of a caricature, an excellent overview of the subject, a reference for all ongoing developments, is Hands (2001). Here Hands sets out to survey recent devel-opments in both economic methodology and in contemporary science theory, and to chart how the subject of economic methodology has recently been subject to significant change. An additional and also excellent, if smaller book on developments in economic methodology, one which serves especially well as an introduction to ongoing advances, is Sheila Dow's even more recent book (Dow 2002a).

4 There is also a danger of circular reasoning. For, by starting from the economic-practice-is-rational premise, the result of the philosophical exercise will be the identification of various conditions relative to which the already accepted premise stands vindicated. But to the extent the supposed viability of the identi-fied conditions gain support only in this way, they clearly cannot by themselves provide any independent justification of the rationality of modern economics.

5 For a useful discussion see C. Lawson *et al.* 1996.

6 And instead criticism is directed mostly at critics of the mainstream and/or (or including) other methodologists.

7 In the previous chapter I argued that the deductivist methods of the modern mainstream presuppose closed systems, those in which event regularities occur. I also demonstrated that these in turn presuppose an ontology of isolated

systems of atoms. I also suggested that because social reality is found to be open and highly internally related, mainstream conceptions are likely frequently to be highly unrealistic. This is indeed what we find. Those methodological exercises which largely presume the rationality of modern economics seem destined to argue, therefore, that lack of realisticness does not (always) matter.

Of course, it is trivially true, that anything quite *in*essential to an analysis might (though need not) be given an unrealistic representation (without this making any difference to the outcome). This, though, is not the nature of the fictions of modern economics (see Chapter 1).

It is equally true that if event regularities were ubiquitous in the social domain, models could be predictively successful, irrespective of the degree of realisticness of theoretical constructions attached to them. A problem facing modern economics, though, is that social event regularities of the relevant sort are extremely rare.

It is also the case that if social reality really were atomistic/mechanical, so that the effects of omitted features could simply be added in (or subtracted out), we might consider known-to-be-fictitious claims as a methodological 'first step', to be later (hopefully) modified according to some step-wise process of successive approximation (see Lawson 1997a: chs 9 and 16). But our best accounts of social ontology lead us to reject this atomistic metaphysics for the social realm, certainly as a generalisation. This is demonstrated in the text below.

In truth, I think it is somewhat uncharitable to suppose of mainstream economists that they really prefer, and actually choose, to rely on the sorts of absurd fictions they produce (whether the latter are interpreted as irrelevant detail, instruments of prediction, or as a methodological 'first step' or whatever). Rather, mainstream economists understandably (see Chapter 10), if erroneously (see Chapter 1), choose to apply methods of mathematical modelling. It is an unhappy consequence of this prior choice that, given the nature of social phenomena, they are forced to make fictitious claims despite themselves.

In the end, of course, and despite the best efforts of methodologists to save the situation, the only sustainable defence of mainstream economics that appears to be on offer entails a moving of the goalposts; it is to claim a commitment to objectives other than (i.e. excluding) social explanation (Hahn 1985; 1994; Rosenberg 1976; 1978; 1983; 1992; 1994a).

8   It is worth emphasising that as Jochen Runde has reminded me 'standard economic methodology', as laid down in the introductory chapters of many textbooks, is not usually the methodology thereafter followed in those same textbooks.

9   In reaching this conclusion Leamer observes:

> The opinion that econometric theory is largely irrelevant is held by an embarrassingly large share of the economics profession. The wide gap between econometric theory and econometric practice might be expected to cause professional tension. In fact, a calm equilibrium permeates our journals and our meetings. We comfortably divide ourselves into a celibate priesthood of statistical theorists, on the one hand, and a legion of inveterate sinner-data analysts, on the other. The priests are empowered to draw up lists of sins and are revered for the special talents they display. Sinners are not expected to avoid sins; they need only confess their errors openly.
>
> (Leamer 1978: vi)

Hendry concludes in similar fashion:

> At present there are peculiar gaps between theory and what people actually do: I think the sinners and preacher analogy in Leamer (1978) is the correct one here. The theoretical econometrician says one thing but as a practitioner does something different. I am trying to understand why economists do that, given that they know the theory, and they are obviously trying to solve practical problems.
>
> (Hendry *et al.* 1990: 179)

10 Though this project is methodological in nature, many of its protagonists and co-researchers have been primarily heterodox economists (including Austrians, feminists, (old) institutionalists, post Keynesians, Marxians, social economists, and others unaligned), concerned not so much with methodology for its own sake as with transforming modern economics to make it a more realistic and productive endeavour (see Fleetwood 1999: esp. 127–32; also see C. Lawson *et al.* 1996).

11 Actually I have to admit that as soon as I began studying economics I quickly formed the view that modern economics, as practised, is largely inappropriate for addressing real-world problems. And when I looked for commentaries on the discipline, or to leading developments, to see how problems of the discipline's limited relevance were being addressed, I discovered that discussions of the nature of the social world, of ontology, were almost entirely absent, at least within that project I came to view as the mainstream. The activity of comparing standard accounts or 'models' of the economy was sanctioned with limited attention given to assessing methods (techniques) of evaluation. But philosophical discussions of the nature of reality itself were almost entirely neglected if not discouraged.

12 I briefly note for the moment that, in a developmentally constructive mode, ontology assists in that, if the conditions of possibility of any set of practices (i.e. conditions that render them intelligible) can be uncovered, the understanding achieved will in turn likely reveal/indicate something more widely of what, in science, is (and may not be) feasible. Just as, say, the observation of certain species of fish in a particular river indicates (presupposes as a necessary condition of their survival) that types of pollution are absent or below certain critical levels, allowing some inferences about other forms of water species whose survival is possible in such locations, so the fact of certain human activities presupposes conditions which in turn may well facilitate (and perhaps rule out) other forms of practice, including cognitive ones. My project, then, has involved pursuing this possibility amongst others.

13 This explains the frequent use of the transcendental realist label to systematise specific insights achieved in this way in considering the natural realm (see Lawson 1997a: ch. 5). Of course, Kant used the same form of argument, but asked questions about only us and the presuppositions of our knowledge of being. Hence his transcendental idealism. But there is no need to restrict transcendental argument to the individualist and idealist mode employed by Kant. See Lawson 1997e; see also Viskovatoff 2002.

14 It is important, though, to get the balance right here. If it is not necessary to examine the practices of the natural, or any other, realm to determine the possibilities for social research, there is equally no necessary harm in doing so either, and perhaps much to be gained, especially with respect to determining the sorts of questions that it is interesting to pursue (Lawson 1997a: ch. 5). Indeed, as in the widespread use of metaphor, the borrowing from

external domains is essential to all human understanding (see Chapter 5). The error or danger that lies in waiting is not *per se* in bringing insights from one (source) domain to another (target), but in imposing them into the target domain without ever assessing their relevance to it. Any such borrowing is legitimate just as long as the orientation is modal rather than injunctive. In other words, there can be little harm in abducting from one sphere to another ideas, etc., which can be held up for investigation. And in the context of modern economics (where naturalism has long been both merely asserted as true as well as inadequately formulated) there are significant strategic advantages to questioning explicitly its possibility at this time, as part of, albeit only as part of, a multifaceted or multi-pronged project.

15 One response to my strategy is to question whether it is worth the effort. Fine (forthcoming) suggests not. Four points are advanced by Fine in reaching this assessment. First the mainstream refuses to engage at the level of methodology (6). Second, the mainstream in the past has never been 'shifted by logical arguments' (7). Third, in any case 'mainstream academic economics has become so homogeneous and intolerant of alternatives that it is increasingly impossible to engage fruitfully with it as the means of establishing an alternative' (7). And finally, 'the most fertile location within which an alternative economics can prosper is currently … within other social sciences' (7). Fine concludes from all this that it is best to get on with determining alternative theory at the substantive level (and most especially Marxian political economy), and that the attention given by critical realists to methodology in modern economics is, in the circumstances, basically misguided, thus inevitably rendering the project insufficiently critical.

Two quick responses can be made. The first, and most pertinent at this point, is that although as marginalised heterodox contributors Fine and I inevitably contrast our own contributions with those of the centre or mainstream, it by no means follows that existing members of the mainstream project are the only, or even the primary audience for the sorts of discussions in which we engage. If, for example, recent entrants to economics and social theorising are usually adjudged to be the more open to (new) ideas and criticism, they too, under the barrage of assertions that mathematics means science, rigour and explanatory success in due course, need to see the case made, rather than also merely asserted, that there are errors in these dominant, essentially methodological claims. The primary problem I see facing heterodox contributions is not that their results are not insightful, but that the mainstream is all too successful in dismissing heterodox contributions entirely for not taking the appropriate (mathematical) form. It is with considerations of this sort in mind, anyway, that the methodological case for change is yet pursued here.

Second, I in no way want to imply criticism of Fine's own set of priorities, emphasis and orientation; indeed I have a very great appreciation for Fine's numerous concerns and contributions. I suspect I interpret deductivism as more central and defining of the modern mainstream group than does Fine. But, whether or not that is so, I do not suppose we should all be engaged in precisely the same task. A division of labour is usually beneficial. Fine and I, though seemingly in many ways similarly situated, cannot be expected of necessity to share identical priorities. Some realists do also travel down Fine's preferred path. Recent examples include Creaven (2000) and Brown *et al.* (2002a). But my experience is that realist economists are, at the substantive level, concerned with the *range* of contemporary and other issues, and support a range of heterodox and other projects. And this, I suspect, is how it should be.

16 My assessment clearly differs from those accounts that appear to interpret rules as merely generalised features of practices. I think the latter is Giddens' interpretation (see Giddens 1984; also see Archer 1995).

17 Of course, conflicts in practices may also lead to existing rules being transformed. But a condition of any such conflict-resolving transformations being induced is just that existing rules are having a causal impact.

18 As a corollary it is important to clarify the set of conditions required for a closure. In previous contributions (e.g. Lawson 1997a) I have implicitly focused on (or mostly made reference to) those systems wherein the supposedly correlated events are held to stand in the same causal sequence, i.e. wherein one or more of the correlated events stand in the causal history of the others. This is the sort of closure presupposed in a typical exercise in modern mainstream deductivist modelling, and encourages an atomistic ontology. It is in respect to this kind of closure that, in *Economics and Reality*, I set about identifying sufficient conditions. These are the extrinsic and intrinsic closure conditions. It is apparent, now, however, that event regularities that play a role in social life do not reduce to this sort. If the category of closure is taken to cover not only systems in which regularities of events standing in causal sequence occur, but also those where events are associated because possessing similar causal histories, we must recognise the property of sharing of causal histories as, in effect, an alternative closure condition. Clearly, the intrinsic and extrinsic closure conditions remain sufficient to guarantee a closure of the causal sequence sort. But a shared causal history will, it seems, guarantee a closure of the merely concomitant sort.

19 For a very recent and detailed challenge adopting a similar perspective, see Searle 2001.

20 I think it is also an aspect of the set of action-conditioning capacities and dispositions referred to by Searle as the 'Background' (See e.g. Faulkner 2002; Runde 2002; Searle 1995; 1999).

21 But if so, it is not the case, as Bourdieu seems sometimes to imply, that recognising the role of the habitus undermines the claim that codified rules have an ontological existence. Just as not all tacit knowledge is of a sort that could be codified (see Lawson 1997a: 177–8), not all rule following is tacitly or habitually performed. Indeed, codified rules are most likely to disappear from view, and the habitus dominate, precisely when conditions are such that a similar action is repeatedly performed. But when we are entering new territory, actually or metaphorically, we are always likely to enquire after the existence of, or be instructed in, the local rules, including conventions.

22 Note there is no necessary contradiction in (the non-dualistic position of) allowing both that consciousness is caused by brain processes and yet is an (emergent) feature of the brain.

23 And to the extent that specific action can result from numerous, even conflicting reasons, the operation of reasons (beliefs grounded in the practical interests in life) must be viewed as tendencies (see Lawson 1997a: ch. 2).

24 The fact that a terminology similar to that utilised in *Economics and Reality* is employed in contrasting ways in some other contributions has led various commentators to impute necessary differences in argument. But this is not always so. A case in point is where the conception set out in *Economics and Reality* is compared with the writings of John Searle (see e.g. Searle 1995; 1999; 2001). I suspect a sustained comparison of the two conceptions would be useful in many ways. But my own understanding of Searle leads me to suppose that where we address the same issues, our two conceptions, though not the same, may not be so far apart as has been supposed.

One problem of comparison, perhaps, is the way the term intentionality is brought into the discussion. For Searle it is always clear that the term refers to that feature of the mind that it can be directed at, or be about, or of, objects and states of affairs in the world. It is a relation between subjective states (including beliefs, desires, intentions and perceptions, loves, hates, fears and hopes) and the rest of the world. In my own usage (and that of others contributing to the same realist project) intentionality has been primarily introduced and utilised in the context of denoting that feature of some human doings that is caused by reasons, where reasons are beliefs grounded in the practical interests of life (Lawson 1997a: ch. 13). As noted in the main text above, it is the human doings caused by reasons, in this framework, that constitute actions.

Does this mean Searle and I support different conceptions of action? I am not sure it does. Although Searle seems nowhere to define action explicitly in terms of reasons, action is seemingly always treated as something to which reasons make a causal contribution. Thus there are numerous passages of the following sort:

> Reasons for action must be able to motivate an action. If the reason is given why a past action was performed, then the reason must have functioned causally in the performance of the action, because it must have been the reason the agent *acted on*.
>
> (Searle 2001: 138, original emphasis)

More tellingly, Searle argues that human beings do not 'first have beliefs, hopes, desires and intentions and then external to them introduce rational forms of assessment; rather to have the beliefs, etc., is already to have phenomena subject to these norms' (Searle 2001: 109). In other words: 'Being subject to rational criteria of assessment is internal to and constitutive of intentional phenomena' (Searle 2001: 109). But for Searle, actions are included in his list of intentional phenomena (Searle 2001: 106), where an action justification takes the form of a reply to the question 'On what reasons did you act?' In other words, in action it is the reason for the act that is subject to rational criteria of assessment. Thus, in Searle's framework, it seems that reasons are indeed internal to and constitutive of actions.

Put differently, unreasoned doings such as falling over, or breaking the light cord on pulling it, are not intentional in the sense of being directed; they are not subject to rational criteria of assessment. Behaviour is directed when it is subject to rational assessment, when oriented to some goal, when it is motivated by reasons, that is, caused by beliefs rooted in the practical interests in life. In short, Searle and I appear to arrive at the same understanding of action despite our different starting points and emphasis.

25 I have observed in effect that all understandings of aspects of human subjectivity, including psychology, vary according to the projects to which we are contributing and the conceptions we are employing (see note 24 above). Even the same terminology can be used differently in different projects. To recognise this is to acknowledge the relativity of all knowledge, to see the latter as a social construction. But an acceptance that all knowledge is socially constructed does not imply that the matter of whether or not knowledge claims are true is also open to social construction. Whether a claim is true, rather, depends on the way the world is (see Lawson 1997a: ch. 17). It is quite feasible to accept that folk or scientific psychology are social structures or 'institutions' (Kusch 1999) which depend on us, and which equally serve to

shape us, without concluding thereby that they are mere constructions, i.e. with no referents beyond the knowledge framework or 'institution'. Indeed, a central argument of this book is that modern economics is a holistic institution, one that is nested within, and criss-crosses others, whose theories are (like all theories) social constructions, where these particular constructions feed into and significantly shape what it is that they purport to be about (i.e. aspects of social reality). But none of this undermines the idea that what economists are seeking to express is a relatively independent or autonomous social reality, i.e. a social reality which does not reduce to the conceptions of economists, and which, for any given set of economists, exists as a given at the moment it is investigated (or pre-exists economists' investigations of it, even if the latter facilitate its eventual transformation). Nor does anything I have acknowledged undermine the possibility of the economists' theories in question being true or (very often) false. Though dependent on our concepts, social reality does not reduce to them. And I hold the same is true of those psychological features that we seek to capture by such (folk psychological) categories as belief, desire and action, etc., (even if some other cultures appear to grasp the same reality with quite different concepts and categories). The sort of realism I defend accepts many of the epistemological insights of social constructivists, especially in their critique of positivists, and psychological individualists. But in accepting such an epistemological relativism I see no need to abandon an ontological realism. Although objects of our analysis may (come to) be significantly affected by how we see them, it does not follow that the latter is all there is. For a very detailed and important alternative (though not always opposed) account of psychological knowledge, one that certainly takes a different emphasis, see Kusch (1999).

26 Again, although my categories are fairly standard of some recent contributions to social theory and philosophy, they are not universally adopted. Once more the terminology of Searle is slightly different (or is used differently). And again this has led observers to infer more difference between our conceptions than I think is the case. In particular, it is suggested that Searle rejects the idea that actions (intentional human doings – see note 25 above), or if the reader prefers, 'intentions in action', can be motivated or carried out at different levels of consciousness. But I am not sure this is so. An extensive presentation of (my understanding of) Searle's account on this and related issues is not appropriate here. But I can briefly note Searle's distinction between a prior intention and an intention-in-action. The former arises through reasoning on beliefs and desires (Searle 2001: 44) whilst the latter arises in the course of performing the action. Searle writes:

> Of course, not all actions are premeditated. Many of the things I do, I do quite spontaneously. In such a case I have an intention-in-action but no prior intention. For example, I sometimes just get up and walk around the room when I am thinking about a philosophical problem. My walking around the room is done intentionally, even though I had no prior intention. My bodily movements in such a case are caused by an ongoing intention-in-action, but there was no prior intention.
>
> (Searle 2001: 45)

For Searle, although deliberation causes prior intention, which causes intention-in-action, 'intention-in-action ... in turn causes bodily movement' (2001: 49). Now, such 'walking around the room' is an example of an action that, in my own terminology, is carried out at the level of practical conscious-ness. The latter (as far as I can discern) is not a terminology that Searle employs. But Searle is quite clear, in considering examples such as this, that (to adopt his own categories) 'Intentions in action may or may not be conscious' (Searle 2001: 47).

Of course there are differences here. But there seems to be further commonality as well. We both emphasise that all action presupposes (i.e. involves) some reliance on the individual agent's array of capacities, disposi-tions, abilities, and so forth. The latter Searle collects under the heading of the 'Background', and are discussed in critical realism under the structuring of the individual. But there are no *prima facie* significant differences in the two projects here, although, even if I am correct in this, it may take a good deal of work to indicate how precisely the two accounts match up.

And a further clear point of agreement between the two projects is that if reasons do function causally in the performance of an action they need not be causally sufficient. For an action to be given an adequate psychological expla-nation it is not necessary that there be causally sufficient antecedent psychological conditions. To recognise that we all act for one or more reasons is not to presuppose a sufficient (set of) antecedent cause(s). For Searle's posi-tion on all this see Searle 2001, especially chapter 3 on 'The Gap'.

27 Nor should we conclude that unconscious determinations are beyond theori-sation. For example, if we take note of the fact that we are continuously reflexive and that, as Archer (2000) has pointed out, each one of us is continu-ally in conversation with ourselves, the question arises as to why we so frequently choose to follow routines and allow habits to form. For we often do so even when they seem *prima facie* unnecessary. One possible explanation (explored in Lawson 1997a: ch. 13) is the further existence of specific uncon-scious motivations or needs, on the part of the individual, to achieve 'ontological security', to attain continuity and sameness in life, to counteract the deep psychological forces of anxiety and insecurity.

28 In short, it is not just social structure that is dependent on, and continually reshaped through, human practice. The transformational model noted above applies to aspects of the human subject too. I return to this matter below.

29 It is a curious feature of some criticism of the conception defended here and earlier elaborated in Lawson (1997a) that its (inevitable) partiality is inter-preted as evidence not only that critical realism must be fundamentally flawed in some way, but that contributors to this realist project must thereby be committed to the idea of uncaused causes in play. Thus, for example, I have seen it suggested that the 'failure' of the project to go further than it does in explaining *reasons* amounts to an acceptance that reasons are uncaused causes. The logic of such an inference is clearly questionable. But let me attempt to assuage such fears. There is clearly a need, first of all, to distinguish the capacity of reasoning from specific reasons. The former is no doubt an emergent property that has come about in the course of human evolution. If this is so, the uncovering of details of the mechanisms or processes whereby it has emerged is a project for science (including biology), not for critical realism. Specific reasons (particular beliefs grounded in the practical interests of life) will depend on specific social and psychological processes. But again these are matters for science, not critical realism, to uncover. How the brain gives rise to states of consciousness is again a matter for the specific sciences (and as far as I know is still little understood, though it seems clear enough that it does). So yes, critical realism 'fails' to address substantive or concrete issues of the sort noted. But this does not warrant the

inference that realists must accept uncaused causes here (or anywhere else where the analysis is [as it always is] partial). It merely indicates the limits of ontology or current understandings (or both). Nor *per se* does the partiality of the project's findings necessarily reflect on the relevance of such claims as are sustained.

30 Although Lachmann is perhaps the economist who has been most vocal on the importance of reasonably abstract plans, his formulation, in the end, is a form of voluntarism. He rightly criticises any conceptual schema in which the human being 'is not a bearer of active thought but a mere bundle of dispositions', especially when the latter take 'the form of a comprehensive preference field' (Lachmann 1991: 278). But in reacting to any such conception in developing his Austrian alternative, Lachmann suggests that 'In its essence Austrian economics may be said to provide a voluntaristic theory of action, not a mechanistic one' (278). From the perspective of critical realism it seems clear that there are various aspects to reconcile. Human beings and social structures both have their own sets of emergent powers (including dispositions on the parts of human beings), and the task is to assess how the two are mediated in the context of the transformational model. For Lachmann 'plans are based on, and oriented to, means available and ends freely chosen' (278). From the perspective set out above, however, the availability of means as well as the forming of ends is something dependent on context. For the realist, then, an aim is to study how people reflexively understand their projects, how the choices made are both affected by possibilities of, and lead to, the activating, transforming or avoidance of structural forms (structural enablements and constraints, like all causal powers, can remain unexercised; it is a contingent matter dependent on human agency whether or how they are activated or avoided, etc.), and how human beings continually monitor themselves in pursuing their plans or projects. In short, a transformational conception, presupposing the reality of causal social structures, as well as the continuous social reshaping of the (enduring if developing) individual, is required (for a realist perspective on these matters as they are dealt with in modern Austrian economics see Lewis 2003).

31 One area in which the project is still rapidly developing concerns the just discussed theorising of the coming together of agency and structure. I think it is fair to say that critical realism has contributed a good deal more to an understanding of this than many projects. In economics, for example, many still believe a reconciliation of macro- and micro-level analyses is the relevant question. Social structure is hardly a recognised category (see Smithin, forthcoming). Critical realism has demonstrated that structure and agency comprise different sets of emergent powers, but I must acknowledge that a good deal of the theorisation of their mediation remains to be done. Much, though, is under way in this and closely related projects (see also Davis 2001; 2002; forthcoming a; forthcoming b). Actually, within economics especially there is a good deal of developing and refining of the project going on. For very recent contributions see Brown *et al.* 2002b; Dow 2002b; Faulkner 2002; Finch and McMaster 2002; Kaul 2002; Lee 2002; Nielsen 2002; Viskovatoff 2002.

32 The error to which I refer here might indeed be described as *(mis)concretising the abstract*. To see what I mean by it consider the well controlled experiment where an event regularity is produced because a stable mechanism is successfully insulated from countervailing mechanisms and triggered (see Chapter 1). The event regularity holds between the triggering conditions and the actualised effects. Here there is indeed generality: under the specific conditions of

the experiment when this mechanism is triggered certain effects follow (an event regularity holds). For numerous mechanisms it is even found to be the case that, when they are triggered under at least some non-experimental conditions, transfactual tendencies are always in play. But it need not, and does not, follow that whenever any such mechanism is triggered, its effects are always actualised. It does not follow that the event regularity that occurs under experimental conditions holds everywhere (or anywhere) outside them. Even less does it follow that because event regularities of a certain sort are sometimes produced in controlled experimental conditions, event regularities of this sort abound everywhere else. The point here is that the experimentally produced event regularity is intrinsically related to the mechanism triggered in experimental conditions. To focus on the event regularity alone is to abstract (from the mechanism and its conditions of isolation). To treat the regularity as existing independently of the mechanism and its conditions of insulation, is to treat an abstraction as though it were concrete. It is to commit what Whitehead calls the fallacy of misplaced concreteness, a form of the fallacy of misplaced universalisation. It is to misconcretise the abstract.

33 Hodgson describes his project in the following terms:

> This book is devoted to [a] … problem. What is it? I call it the problem of historical specificity. It first acknowledges the fact that there are different types of socio-economic system, in historical time and geographical space. The problem of historical specificity addresses the limits of explanatory unification in social science: substantially different socio-economic phenomena may require theories that are in some respects different. If different socio-economic systems have features in common, then, to some extent, the different theories required to analyse different systems might reasonably share some common characteristics. But sometimes there will be important differences as well. Concepts and theoretical frameworks appropriate for one real object may not be best suited for another. The problem of historical specificity starts from a recognition of significant underlying differences between different objects of analysis. One theory may not fit all.
>
> For instance, the socio-economic system of today is very different from the systems of five hundred, one thousand or two thousand years ago. Even today, despite having some important features in common, existing socio-economic systems in different countries are substantially different from each other in key particulars. There are important variations in the structures, rules and mechanisms of production and allocation. Individual purposes and social norms also vary, relating to differences in culture.
>
> (Hodgson 2001b: 23)

34 It is for this reason that, in Chapter 6 below, I resist the idea that economics or even political economy be restricted to the study of capitalism alone. But this does not mean I fail to recognise the urgency of prioritising the study of capitalism, and with it the need for a political economy sensitive to the historical, social and cultural specificity of its relations, processes, categories and conditions. I am aware that some are impatient with social theorising that is more abstract than analyses of the specific structures of capitalism (see e.g. Fine 2001). Yet I perceive ontological endeavour such as I am pursuing as underlabouring for precisely the sort of scholarly integrity, interdisciplinarity and take up of political economy that the latter group clearly wish to effect.

35 It thus follows that researchers concerned with social life must be prepared for the eventuality that determining suitable orientations, analogies, even questions, will be a highly context-dependent and messy affair.

36 One natural reaction to the complex situation here discussed perhaps, at least in the context of social theorising (as opposed to methodology, etc.) is to search for so-called middle-range theories. These are substantive (typically not ontological) conceptions that are neither general nor merely empirical but which seek somehow to bridge the two, to fit in between. This was Merton's (1968) ambition, recently taken up in a significant way as an explicitly realist project by Pawson (1999). Also see Wright Mills (1959), Stinchcombe (1975), Boudon (1991), Layder (1993), and recently Hodgson (2001b: 21). It needs to be remembered, though, that the appropriateness of middle-range theorising in any specific context is always an empirical matter. In fact the ontological conception sustained above and elsewhere suggests that given features of reality can, under some aspects, be regarded as (reasonably) general or common, and, under others, be recognised as particular. Thus it may often be the case that an appropriate social-theoretic strategy is not to seek an attempted bridge between generality and particularity, but to develop conceptions which can accommodate features that are both general and particular (and common and unique) at one and the same time. Still, as I say, these are partly empirical matters, and not something I can say more on here.

37 Those emphasising increased integration or globalisation often focus on the changing configuration and distribution of power at a world level. It is noticed that there is a reordering of power relations between and across regions of the world in such a manner that the sites of power and of those subject to it are often continents apart. Power resides increasingly less in the locales in which it is most heavily experienced (Castells 1996; Dicken 1998; Jameson 1991). However those stressing increased interaction or internationalism argue that international developments and wielding of power do not necessarily penetrate the domestic economy. And where they do, they need not do so directly. Rather they are refracted through national policies and processes. It is argued that international and domestic policy fields tend to remain fairly separate (Sterling 1974; Dore 1995; Hirst and Thompson 1999; Kozul-Wright and Rowthorn 1998). These differences in viewpoint have recently taken on a such a significance as to constitute the 'great globalisation debate' (see e.g. Held and McGrew 2000: esp. introduction). A useful recent account raising important issues of causality in this context is Gillies and Ietto-Gillies (2002).

38 Underpinning the sorts of conceptions some have sought to systematise as collective intentionality (Searle 1995; Davis 2002).

39 The list includes, in fact, money (Ingham 1996), the firm and region (C. Lawson 1999a; 2000; 2002), institutions (Lawson 1997a); transactions (Pratten 1997a), the individual (Davis, forthcoming a, forthcoming b) social order (Fleetwood 1995; 1996), collective learning (C. Lawson 2000), causality (Fleetwood 2001; Lewis 2000a; Runde 1998a), tendencies, (Pratten 1998; Lawson 1989; 1997a; 1998), markets (O'Neill 1998), households (Ruwanpura 2002), consciousness (Faulkner 2002), timeful theorising (Rotheim 2002); uncertainty (Dunn 2000; 2001); macroeconomics (Smithin, forthcoming), space (Sayer 2000), probabilities (Runde 1996; 1998b; 2001a), trust (Layder 1997; Lawson 2000; Reed 2001), technology (C. Lawson, forthcoming), metaphor (Lewis 1996; 2000b).

40 For example, through examining the relevant author's ontological preconceptions it has proven possible to give support to (contested) assessments that Commons did hold a theoretical perspective (see C. Lawson 1994; 1995; 1996b; 1999b); that Hayek's position changed significantly over time (Lawson 1994a; Fleetwood 1995); that Keynes' rejection of econometrics was not a superficial response based on ignorance of the topic (Lawson 1997c; Chapter 8 below); that Veblen did favour an evolutionary economics and not merely because making economics evolutionary would render it up-to-date (this volume, Chapter 8 below); that neither Smith nor even Newton adopted 'Newtonian' methodology, and Smith's contribution is hardly in the mould of, or a precursor to, general equilibrium theory (Montes 2003); that Popper was ultimately not a 'Popperian' (Runde 1996); that Marx's theory (of capitalist tendencies) is not a deterministic theory (Fleetwood 2002; Collier 1989), and so on.

41 Notice, however, that the finding that reality is structured, that it includes both powers (and any structural conditions they may have) as well as the actualisation of these powers, does not carry the implication that the actualisations (or the powers themselves) are constrained to any particular level. It is clear, for instance, that events have powers, for example to be observed (when they can be) or to have effects. A war is an event, containing structures, processes and so forth. The human body is an actuality, containing powers, structures, mechanisms, including mechanisms within mechanisms, and so on. None of this is denied in critical realism. Powers themselves may be actual or possible. When actual (e.g. my capacity to speak English) they are instances of higher-order powers (e.g. the capacity to develop and speak a range of human languages). The frequent illustrating of the actual by focusing on events and states of affairs is best thought of as an initial orienting position, subject to dialectical development. The error which the category of actualism usefully captures, is that of treating *specific* powers, etc., always in terms of their exercise and actualisation. The latter sort of reduction serves to render obscure the operation of causal efficacy in the relevant domain or at the level of the specific power, encouraging the interpretation of causal efficacy in a particular and erroneous (Humean) way, namely in terms of constant conjunctions. The ontology sustained in critical realism makes it clear that explanation of phenomena at one level in terms of powers, structures and other factors at a deeper level, is always a potentially fruitful direction for research.

42 I originally included in Part II a chapter devoted to the question of the implications for positions in ethics. I eventually removed it because it grew extremely long and became, in any case, overly substantive. But let me sketch something of the argument here. In *Economics and Reality* I advocated a specific moral realist position. By moral realism I mean the doctrine that there exists an objective morality or moral reality, and that particular moral claims or judgements are true or false independently of our conceptions of them. The (cognitivist) counterpart of moral realism is that we can achieve knowledge of this objective morality, and can criticise, transform and develop moral knowledge claims through scientific and other forms of reasoning.

The specific (naturalistic) moral realist position I advanced in *Economics and Reality* is grounded in the flourishing of (especially human) being. Actions are judged morally good or worthy according to the extent to which they facilitate well-being or flourishing. The extent to which they do or not (a substantive matter always dependent on context) holds irrespective of our conceptions of whether (or how well) they do. Thus the claim that 'it is good to do x' is true (or false) independently of our beliefs about the matter.

Now the ontological discussion above reveals all human beings to be not only structured but also unique concrete individualities, with each of us being historically situated and interconnected (via social relations and other social forces) to everyone else as well as to the rest of nature.

This set of insights, it seems, must be built into our assessments of the morality of actions. Because we are each unique, but exist in society where everything we do affects others, it seems that a moral objective must be to transform society into a form that recognises our differences without our needing to suppress, or suffer for, them. Such a society is described by Marx as 'an association in which the free development of each is a condition of the free development of all' (Marx and Engels 1952 [1848]: 76). Given our best understanding of human nature, this is the only sort of conception we can justify pursuing, assuming it is feasible. For it is the formulation of society which allows that each and all of us may remain true to ourselves, as needy, socially formed human individuals. Such a configuration deserves to be labelled the *good society* or, following Aristotle the *eudaemonistic society*.

Accepting, then, the moral realist position described, the ontological insights of critical realism are found to impart a good deal of directionality into social research, this time in terms of an agenda. For if ontological reasoning raises the contention that the good society is the only scenario in which we all can flourish then, *assuming it is ultimately achievable*, the good society so conceived ought, as I say, to be built into all actions that can be interpreted as morally good. The question arises, therefore, as to whether the good society is actually realisable. For if it can be shown not to be, the claim that we should all act to bring it about may not be sustainable (depending on alternative real possibilities, etc). Actually, I think the same follows if such a society can only be shown to be unlikely. This realisation in turn encourages an examination of whether or not there is a tendency to the good society in existence. For only if there is, I think, can fears about whether such a society is reachable in practice be sufficiently allayed. As it happens I think there is such a tendency. It turns on our evolved dispositions both to care for, and also to interact with, others, along with changes to the ways in which the latter are happening (in the face of current globalising tendencies). But making the argument requires a lot of substantive work. It also involves explicitly facing up to, and taking an explicit stand on, Hume's Law, that you cannot get a value from a fact. But this is a long story, which will now have to appear in a different outlet at a later date. I include this outline here merely to provide a feel as to how ontology can further impart directionality. In the case of ethics, I have suggested, it both can serve to constrain what is possible and to encourage research into specific substantive, including anthropological, issues. (For related, but often very different positions in ethics advanced by those working within critical realism see Archer 2000; Bhaskar 1993; 1994; 2000; Bhaskar and Collier 1998, Brereton 2000; Collier 1999; 2001; Hostetler and Norrie 2000; Lawson 2000; Norrie 2001; Sayer 2000. For related contributions that do not explicitly connect themselves with critical realism also see Boyd 1988; 1993; Dupré 1999; Nussbaum and Sen 1993; Nussbaum 1995; Soper 1990; Staveran 2001).

43 On this I concur with Harold Kincaid (2001).
44 Although the amount of social theorising, including economics, that adopts an ontological orientation remains overly limited, in the last few years matters have started to improve, here and there. I briefly reference some of

this literature below, parts of which I have only had chance to glance at (it appeared only after this book was more or less finished), but much of which clearly connects with my own project in some way.

The book that most complements both the current one and *Economics and Reality* is Fleetwood 1999. A volume in press that also closely connects is Lewis (forthcoming).

Other contributions in which ontology also explicitly figures, and sometimes in a significant way, include: Ackroyd and Fleetwood 2000; Archer 2000; Archer *et al.* 1998; Archer and Tritter 2000; Bhaskar 2000; Brown *et al.* 2002a; Carter 2000; Collier 1999; 2001; Costello 2000; Creaven 2000; Danermark *et al.* 2002; Davis, forthcoming; Dow 2002; Downward, forthcoming; Chick 1998; Hamlin 2002; Hands 2001; Herrmann-Pillath 2001; Hodgson 2001b; Fullbrook 2002; C. Lawson 1999a; 1999b; 2000; 2002; Lewis 2002a; 2002b; Mäki 2001; Nell 1998; Nelson 2002; Norrie 2000; Northover 1995; Patomäki 2002; Pinkstone 2002; Pfouts 2002; Pratten 1997a; 1997b; 1998; 2001; Rotheim 1999; 2002; Runde 2001a; 2002; Sayer 2000; Siakantaris 2000; Smithin 2000; Staveren 2001; Willmott 2002; amongst others.

45 Thus although some commentators have interpreted critical realism as essentially connected to a more substantive position such as Marxism just because some contributors illustrate their arguments with examples from Marx, Fine (forthcoming) conveys a more accurate impression in noting (albeit regretting) the failure of critical realism to take the 'path towards the Marxism to which [he does] subscribe' (12). However, when Fine suggests the critical realist project as it has been developed in the context of modern economics is 'too liberal' in taking a very positive orientation to 'new feminist economics, evolutionary theory, certain path dependence literature, Austrian, Marxian, and (some) post Keynesian approaches' (4), it needs to be recognised that this support not only does not extend to the numerous substantive theory and policy stances which these (or any) projects may generate, but itself rests on the assessment that these projects are not only more pluralistic in nature than, but also presupposes a more sustainable ontology than does, the approach of the modern mainstream. The latter assessment, at least in part, is empirical in nature. For sure, it is one I, for the most part, accept (see Part III below). But it makes the interpretation of these projects an issue in the history of economic thought, not a proposition in critical realism.

3 What has realism got to do with it?

1 This chapter was originally published in *Economics and Philosophy* (1999) vol. 15, 269–82.

4 Explanatory method for social science

1 Imposing from ontology to method (i.e. the ontic fallacy of reducing epistemology to ontology) is a second 'top down' approach rejected here (see also Chapter 2). Thus the explanatory approach discussed here is but one suggested way of proceeding that carries the potential for coping with the sort of ontology defended in Chapter 2. Not surprisingly, others who accept this ontology can often be seen to advance explanatory work in related but non-identical ways (see for example, Brown *et al.* 2002b; Downward 2002; Finch and McMaster 2002; Lee 2002).

2 Some further clarification and elaboration of my understanding of causal explanation may be helpful here. According to it, to explain some phenomenon is to identify aspects of, or otherwise elucidate, its causal history. And the fundamental step, here, is the uncovering of structures, powers, mechanisms and tendencies that facilitate or produce the phenomenon to be explained. Of course, events and states of affairs are just as causal (as bearing of causal properties) as underlying structures and mechanisms, etc. Mainstream economists regularly seek to correlate variables expressing events or states of affairs, say movements in consumer expenditures with movements in disposable incomes, or movements in nominal wages with those in consumer prices, or movements in the amount of investment undertaken with changes in certain interest rates. The immediately questionable feature of such exercises lies not in the efforts of these economists to investigate whether the second component of each couple (the independent variable or antecedent event) lies in the causal history (is a causal condition of) the first component (the dependent variable or consequent event), but in the *a priori* insistence that if the two phenomena of each couple are indeed causally connected, they must be constantly conjoined (or covered by a 'well behaved' probability law).

Systems in which such strict event regularities occur are said to be *closed*. Those in which the events related are such that some (the antecedent events of 'independent variables') stand in the causal history of the others (the consequent events or 'dependent variables') can be termed *closures of causal sequence*. The primary error of the mainstream tradition is to suppose that closures of this sort are ubiquitous in the social realm. This supposition reflects the fact that the mainstream project of modern economics (modern micro-modelling, macro-modelling and econometric modelling) is not only concerned with causal conditioning, it is also deductivist. According to deductivism, to explain an event is to deduce it from a set of event regularities and initial conditions (see Chapter 1). The fact that economic events assumed to be constantly conjoined rarely are so, but that the antecedent events often causally condition the consequent events (albeit, in reality, typically via open non-atomistic human agency and in conjunction with a [changing] variety of other [often transient] causal factors), serves merely to confuse matters.

I mention such matters to acknowledge that whereas causal analysis, as I am interpreting this endeavour, constitutes a rejection of deductivism as a universal stance, it does not thereby preclude the activity of uncovering events standing in the causal history of others. More often than not, however, when we seek to explain social phenomena, the identification of antecedent conditioning events, if relevant, will not be sufficient. Even in a closed system situation of the (causal sequence) sort noted above, a knowledge merely of events and their achieved correlations, allows, at best, a very partial and limited explanation and understanding of any outcome. And in the social world, closures of this sort are in any case found to be rather rare. In fact, even in the natural realm they are found to be mostly restricted to situations of experimental control. And in the social realm meaningful controlled experiments are largely impossible. The result is that, apart from highly rule-governed routinised behaviour (to which there are in any case frequent exceptions even where the rules are reproduced), regularities of the sort in question are found to be sparse indeed. Thus, typically, causal explanation in social research will require identifying some of the structures and mechanisms, etc., which facilitate and/or produce phenomena of interest.

So in what follows, I am centrally concerned with the identification of social structures or mechanisms lying at a different level to the phenomenon

306

to be explained. This, typically, is what I intend by use of the category of causal explanation. And I am clearly interested in methods of causal analysis appropriate for conditions in which even closures of the (restricted and causal sequence) sort often achieved in the experimental laboratory are mostly absent. Ontological theorising suggests that, whatever the precise configuration of social reality at any point in time, the social theorist ought to be at least prepared for investigative endeavour in such open conditions.

I might also emphasise, here, that my primary concern in the current chapter is not with the manner in which knowledge of underlying mechanisms may be put to further explanatory use. The activity of applying such knowledge to throw light on concrete events or outcomes can be designated *applied* or *concrete explanation* (see Chapter 6 below). In contrast, the endeavour of identifying hitherto unknown, or insufficiently known, causal mechanisms (and causal conditions, etc.) can be interpreted as *pure* or *abstract explanation*. It is the latter activity that I systematise simply as causal explanation in the current chapter.

3   In accepting this I do not wish to imply that all natural sciences are experimental. As emphasised in Lawson 1997a, I differ from Bhaskar (1978; 1979) and others in viewing the lack of experiment opportunities in the social realm *not* as a limit to naturalism (i.e. as qualifying the way in which the study of social phenomena can be scientific in the sense of natural science). A limitation on experimental opportunities represents a problem or challenge to all sciences. However, this does not detract from its being a (if not the) central problem facing social scientific research (where experimental opportunities are limited indeed). What follows from this recognition, rather, is that the sort of endeavour I defend below may in some form have potential application to various natural scientific contexts as well.

4   There appear to be two central mistakes involved in reasoning of the sort in question. First the idea that a realistic analysis of a complex social reality must itself be so complex as to be impossible (thus necessitating a reliance upon simplifying fictions), presupposes a correspondence theory of truth or knowledge, that an object of analysis and the analysis of the object must stand in an isomorphic relationship. Such a conception is not sustainable (see Lawson 1997a: ch. 17). We can certainly express holistic entities, without knowingly fictionalising. It may be, for example, that in order to explain current forms of discrimination in a specific region it is necessary to focus on a totality that stretches over space and is continually reproduced and transformed over time, a totality that includes religious, cultural and biological aspects, and so forth. But there is no obvious inherent reason why we should knowingly misrepresent such a process just because it is holistic and complex. The point is that any discussion of such an explanatory causal process takes the form of words and symbols, etc. The complexity of an object is not inevitably mirrored in a similar form of complexity in the description of the object. Knowledge and its object are typically different types of 'things' with their own modes of being.

Second, the complexity of all reality does indeed mean that methods of abstraction will always be involved in explanatory work. But these do not reduce to isolationist procedures at all. In abstracting we focus on one (set of) aspect(s) of an 'object' of investigation, whilst momentarily leaving aside others or the concrete 'whole'. It is vital always to recognise that the features on which we focus are aspects of more concrete realities, as well as conditioned by, and perhaps internally related to, other aspects upon which, momentarily, we are not focusing. But as long as we seek to so abstract, there is no reason at all to suppose the unavoidably partial nature of the analysis necessitates our falling back on claims or conceptions we already believe to be fictitious. To abstract is to concentrate our focus, not to assume away aspects we do not explicitly consider, or to deny the dependency of those aspects on which we focus upon those on which we do not. In this respect abstracting is like (and of course includes) watching and comprehending a 'live' scene unfolding on the television (say a demonstration or a sports event) without supposing that anything not on our screens at any point in time is not happening, or that aspects of the situation we see are somehow isolated or isolatable from those we do not. In short, abstraction is a method or approach applicable to open (and closed) systems as they are, whereas a reliance on isolationist methods means treating all phenomena as though they were determined in closed systems, whether or not they are. Once abstractions have been achieved we can (re)construct our conception of the (more) concrete out of them via a process of synthesis (on all this see Lawson 1997a: chs 9 and 16).

5 The case that methodology does not (or does no longer) reduce to such a conception is made in Hands' recent and aptly named *Reflection Without Rules* (Hands 2001).

6 As set out this is an example of Mill's 'method of difference' (see Mill 1981: 391).

7 Or at least over adjoining sub-regions within the set of plots where the experimental contrast space turns out to be insufficiently homogeneous throughout.

8 I prefer this terminology because we are concerned with the explanation of contrasts. The term 'contrast' signifies something of the nature of the (relational) object of investigation rather than the nature of the investigative or explanatory process *per se*.

9 And if there is a sense in which the uninteresting is a condition for the interesting, it is equally the case that the unsurprising can be a condition of the surprising, the expected a condition of the unexpected, the ordinary a condition of the extraordinary, and so on.

10 Lawson goes on to argue that 'such moments are important to the researcher because they offer access to a (social) reality that is inherently interconnected and for the most part tacitly apprehended even by those agents most immediately involved' (189).

11 Clive Lawson discusses the process at length. One earlier contributor that Lawson singles out as discussing the recovery of the tacit in moments of disruption is Commons. This process figures prominently in Commons' analysis of the processes whereby disputes come about and are settled, and particularly in the contradictions that arise through the existence both of rules and routines laid down or legitimised by some central authority and those that emerge from custom and practice (on all this see C. Lawson 2000).

12 Of course, in the special case where the contrast space stretches from the current point in time into the future, and it is expected that things will continue much as they are, the *a posteriori* outcome of getting the contrast space wrong, and that of an unforseen causal mechanism coming into play may amount to the same thing.

13 Norethynodrel, a synthetic progesterone, was approved as an oral contraception for women by the US Food and Drug Administration in 1960. It was named Enovid by its manufacturers, but most people came to refer to it just as 'the pill'. Before the late 1960s a physician could not legally prescribe an oral contraceptive to an unmarried minor without the parents' consent. But

in the late 1960s legislation started to change, enabling young unmarried women to obtain contraceptive services.

14 This, of course, is more or less the opposite emphasis to that of mainstream modellers who attempt to assume away or gloss over discrepancies as 'noise'.

15 Contrast (or contrastive) explanation, much of it building on Mill's system of logic, has been widely discussed over the last twenty years of course (see for example van Fraassen 1980; Garfinkel 1981; Lewis 1986; Lipton 1991). However, whilst I think it fair to say that much of this literature has been concerned with applied explanation, with considering whether known factors can be said to constitute an (adequate) explanation, I am here concerned with a topic not covered by Mill's system, namely (the role of contrastive phenomena in) the process of identifying causes that are unknown or hitherto unrecognised.

16 Perhaps a special case of this scenario is one in which seemingly non-spurious (because relatively enduring or striking, etc.) correlations occur where they were not anticipated. Our prior expectation was that the causal factors in play were such that no systematic pattern was conceivable, yet one or more patterns emerge suggesting that prior theories or assessments may have been incorrect. Hoover (1997: 2001a) treats some observed associations between unemployment and vacancies in this way. Hoover further observes 'Even if ... the relationship of unemployment to vacancies, were to vanish ... its having been stands in need of explanation' (1997: 26). And if the relation-ship can be explained, and it does disappear, the latter change too might reflect an interesting contrastive phenomenon to pursue. A further example might be a similarity of voting patterns over regions that were expected to vote somewhat differently, and so on.

17 Of course, a paradigm change in the face of anomalies may take a longish time. Nor do I want to suggest that truth is everywhere pursued. In this chapter I am concerned only with epistemological possibilities. In modern economics, for example, the number of anomalies arising from the practices of mainstream economists is already rather large. Indeed, Richard Lipsey acknowledges:

> anomalies, particularly those that cut across the sub-disciplines and that can be studied with various technical levels of sophistication, are toler-ated on a scale that would be impossible in most natural sciences – and would be regarded as a scandal if they were.
>
> (Lipsey 2001: 173)

Furthermore alternative, more adequate paradigms to the mainstream already lie in the waiting. This, of course, is precisely the situation that, with this book, I am seeking to call to general attention. But there can be no over-looking the fact that in the knowledge process what actually happens is influenced by institutional and other constraints as well as insight (see Chapter 10 especially on this).

18 Thus at the relevant point of *Economics and Reality* I wrote:

> For example: 'women look after children more often than men do'; 'a relatively small proportion of children from poor backgrounds in the UK continue into higher education'; 'average unemployment rates in western industrial countries are higher in the 1990s than the 1960s'; 'in the 1990s UK firms are externalising or 'putting out' more parts of the

production process than twenty years ago'; 'in the late nineteenth century UK firms increasingly internalised parts of the production process'; 'an increasing proportion of the world's population lives in cities'; 'women in the UK usually wear brighter colours, use more make-up, but go alone to the pub less often than men do'; 'the proportion of the UK public that reveals an intention to vote for the Conservative party increases in run-ups to general elections'; 'government spokespersons tell more lies in war-time'; 'reported crime in the UK has increased steadily since the 1970s'; 'Cubans currently spend more time in queues than the English, who in turn spend more time in queues than Italians'; and so on. Or, at a general level, the persistence of inflationary trends in certain economies but not others, of significant variations in rates of growth or decline of area-specific manufacturing sectors, of poverty in the midst of plenty, of production primarily for exchange rather than, as previously, for immediate use, provide examples of notable space-time patterns in economic phenomena. In each such case there is not an invariable relation but repetition of such a nature, or to such a degree, that an explanation seems required all the same. In each such case it is to be expected, or anyway is *prima facie* plausible, that there are systematic and identifiable mechanisms in play which social science can uncover.

(Lawson 1997a: 206–7)

19 It is noteworthy, indeed, that the uniquely localised nature of UK collective bargaining, the explanation of the contrast I speculated upon above, is something that was in place throughout the period in question.

5 An evolutionary economics? On borrowing from evolutionary biology

1 See Hodgson 1995: xv.

2 One recent exception is Vromen (2001). However Vromen's emphasis is less with the ontological conditions of an evolutionary economics than with the ontological presuppositions of the contributions of Nelson and Winter (1982) and of 'evolutionary game theory'. A further contribution I came across just as this present volume was going to press is that by Carsten Herrmann-Pillath (2001). This is closer in orientation to the position defended here and in many ways complements it. Clearly there is a shared recognition of the need to bring ontology more explicitly into evolutionary thinking, a recognition of the openness of the world and its structured nature. Our emphases are different, however, and we do not cover the same ground. Herrmann-Pillath focuses very little on social process, being more concerned to stress that the mind has emerged from biological evolution and must be included in the acknowledged subject-matter of economics (and to demonstrate the superiority of realism over instrumentalism). Our approaches are different, too, in that Herrmann-Pillath writes as if the possibility of economics as an evolutionary economics is a forgone conclusion. And we differ most, perhaps, when Herrmann-Pillath interprets the philosophical discipline of ontology as a dogmatic one, with acceptance of one ontological 'dogma' over another being little more than a matter of taste.

3 Actually we can identify a string of related errors here. The *abductionist fallacy* is similar to the *epistemic fallacy* already mentioned, the belief that matters of ontology can be reduced to matters of epistemology, that questions about

being can be rephrased as question about knowledge (of being). The *linguistic fallacy*, denoting the error of supposing that questions of being can be reduced to questions of discourse (about being) is a further related category. We might also identify as the *moralistic fallacy* the error of reducing questions about human nature and well-being to questions of best policy and practical action (affecting well-being). This is a fallacy I intend to explore on a future occasion. All are species of the general case which might be termed the *reductionist fallacy*, the error of reducing (or misinterpreting) questions about one type of thing to (or as) questions about something quite different in nature or character.

4   Of course, metaphor like most other categories is a contested concept. Those who reject a realist orientation will no doubt disagree with the interpretation accepted here. But then they will probably take issue with the whole discussion.

5   As is well known, evolutionary ideas have moved from economics to biology as much as vice-versa.

6   For early Christians it was a matter of faith that the living world was a replica of one which God originally created; neither extinction nor transformation of species were admitted. This led early investigators to interpret fossils as patterns which coincidentally resembled shellfish and other life forms. Eventually, the organic character of fossils was recognised, however, and by the end of the eighteenth century it was acknowledged that rocks provided a compendious record of previously existing life-forms. However, and much in the way that modern day economists use their conceptions of 'exogenous shocks to the system' to explain what does not easily fit with their models, scientists of this time, wishing to avoid the blasphemous conclusion of continuous change, fell back on theories of their own exogenous shocks; in particular they invoked theories of periodic floods and other catastrophes. After each one God saw fit to replenish the world with a novel stock of living things. A difficulty for this type of explanation came with the eventual realisation that fossil levels revealed not only differences but advances in life-forms. The lowest (and oldest) strata of rocks recorded invertebrates, fish appeared on later ones, then reptiles and birds, later mammals including, finally, humans. Progressionists and other creationists argued that this merely meant that God had staggered the manner in which God's creations were introduced; there was no question of transformation or descent involved in these changes. But in so doing the various contributors were by now acknowledging that the phenomena to be explained had changed.

A variety of positions designed to preserve the traditional view were developed. But by the end of the eighteenth century, science at large was taking paths which would foster a more transformative perspective in biology. Most significantly, the earth lost its place at the centre of the universe; the closed world opened to an infinite universe as the cosmos came to be regarded as a developing, if law-governed, process. At the same time biologists recognised that many life-forms contained remnants of once, but no longer, functional organs (e.g. wings that no longer facilitated flight), undermining directly the arguments from design.

In due course, as further insights into the nature of life on earth were achieved, the notion of it as essentially unchanging became replaced by the recognition that it, like everything else, is in a state of relatively continuous transformation. It was in order to account for the mechanisms of transformation that theories of evolution were formulated.

7　It is my impression that economists and others concerned with drawing on biology give far too little attention to the nature of the biological processes themselves (as well as to social ones). Rather, arguments over models are reported as if debates can be resolved at this level independently of considering the nature of real-world processes. In other words, it is frequently the case in the philosophy of biology (and, or including, psychology) that the epistemic fallacy is evident: questions of being are here, as elsewhere, too often treated as though reducible to questions about the knowledge or modelling of being.

8　The finches on Daphne Major were studied by Peter Boag and Peter and Rosemary Grant (see e.g. Boag and Grant 1981) and their findings are well summarised in Weiner (1994):

> In the Grants' first four years on this island, they never saw the struggle for existence get … [very] intense. Those were the good years for Darwin's finches. By the end of the Grant's first season, for instance, there were about fifteen hundred *fortis* on Daphne Major. Nine out of ten of those *fortis* were still alive in December, just before the next rains came. There were also about three hundred cactus finches on the island that first April, and nineteen out of twenty of them survived the dry season and made it through to December.
>
> Their fourth year, in 1976, was especially wet and green. There were great bouts of rain in January and February, and light showers in April and May, a total of 137 millimetres of rain, which is a good year for Darwin's finches.
>
> (Weiner 1994: 71)

9　The biologists involved in the study graded the seeds on the island according to the ease with which they could be opened. This resulted in a 'struggle index', with lowest numbers denoting the seeds that are easiest to eat. In June of 1976 there had been more than 10 grams of seeds in an average square metre of lava (the islands being volcanic). By June of 1977

> there were only 6 grams of seeds per square meter. … By December there would be only 3 grams.
>
> As they always do in dry times, the birds went on looking for the easiest seeds. But now they were sharing the last of the last of the pistachio nuts. They were down to the bottom of the bowl. In June of the previous year, four out of five seeds that a finch picked up were easy, scoring less than 1 on the Struggle Index. But as the small, soft, easy seeds of *Heliotropium* and other plants disappeared, the rating climbed and climbed, peaking above 6. The birds were forced to struggle with the big tough seeds of the *Palo Santo*, and the cactus, and *Tribulus*, symbol of the struggle for existence, a seed sheathed in swords.
>
> (Weiner 1994: 73–4)

10　All through the drought the total mass of seeds on the island went down, down, down. The average size and hardness of the remaining seeds went up, up, up. The total number of finches on the island fell with the food supply: 1,400 in March 1976, 1,300 in January 1977, fewer than 300 in December.

Next they take the finches species by species. At the start of 1977 there were about 1,200 *fortis* on Daphne. By the end of the year there were 180, a loss of 85 per cent.

At the start of the year there were exactly 280 cactus finches on the island. By the end of it there were 110, a loss of 60 per cent.

Of the smallest ground finches, *fuliginosa*, there were a dozen on the island at the start of 1977, and only one of them survived the year.

(Weiner 1994: 77)

11 Weiner(1994) describes, almost with excited impatience, the process the scientists Peter Grant and Peter Boag go through in studying the data of the events of 1977. First these scientists discuss the deaths of many finches and other details.

At last ... Grant and Boag look at the beaks of the survivors. ... Among *fortis*, they already knew that the biggest birds with the deepest beaks had the best equipment for big tough seeds like *Tribulus*; and when they totted up the statistics, they saw that during the drought, when big tough seeds were all a bird could find, these big-bodied, big-beaked birds had come through the best. The surviving *fortis* were an average 5 to 6 per cent larger than the dead. The average *fortis* beak before the draught was 10.68 millimetres long and 9.42 deep. The average beak of the *fortis* that survived the drought was 11.07 millimetres long and 9.96 deep. Variations too small to see with the naked eye had helped make the difference between life and death. The mills of God grind exceedingly small.

Not only had they seen natural selection in action. It was the most intense episode of natural selection ever documented in nature.

(Weiner 1994: 78)

12 Now it became of great significance that variations of body and beak are passed on from one generation to the next with fidelity. As a result, the males' unequal luck in love helped perpetuate the effects of the drought. The male and female *fortis* that survived in 1978 were already significantly bigger birds than the average *fortis* had been before the drought. Of this group the males that became fathers were bigger than the rest. And the young birds that hatched and grew up that year turned out to be big too, and their beaks were deep. The average *fortis* beak of the new generation was 4 or 5 per cent deeper than the beak of their ancestors before the drought.

In the drought of 1977 the Finch Unit had seen natural selection in action. Now in its aftermath they saw evolution in action, in the dimensions of the birds' beaks and in other dimensions too.

After that, the watchers on Daphne Major had to keep watching. They had to keep coming back. Not only is Darwin's process in action among Darwin's finches, not only can natural selection lead to evolution among their flocks, but it leads there much more swiftly than Darwin supposed possible.

(Weiner 1994: 81)

13 This difference in beak sizes may not seem especially significant. And one can easily imagine how different unusual spells of climatic conditions can so change the environment as to (re)select in favour of smaller beaked finches.

Indeed, such occurrences are also documented amongst those who have studied Darwin's Finches. Other evolutionary changes are certainly more enduring. No doubt many of us were brought up hearing natural selection explanations of the giraffe's seemingly enduring long neck. According to the standard account, there was once a time when giraffes had necks far shorter than those observed on giraffes today. Let us suppose so. The hypothesis, often recounted, is that something eventually happened whereby a long-necked giraffe appeared. That something, by most accounts (so let's accept this account here), consisted in a mutation at the level of the individual's genes. Such a long-necked giraffe was able to eat from the higher branches of trees out of reach to others and so thrived. So did the offspring, who also had longer necks, in virtue of gene reproduction. Indeed, long-necked giraffes not only were able to cope better than others in general, they were able to survive in conditions that others could not: when available food was concentrated on the higher branches of trees. Gradually the advantage bestowed on long-necked giraffes led to their being the dominant group in the population of giraffes, and eventually indeed being the only group.

I do not know if there is evidence to support such an explanation. But whether or not there is, the nature of the process producing an evolution in the beak of the finch is much the same, if on a smaller scale, albeit with a seemingly less stable result. Indeed, it is surely a fundamental insight, one stressed by Darwin himself, that variations do not need to be large to make a difference. Small variations in some aspect of an organism can mean the difference between life and death.

14 Of course, because in biology all organisms have evolved, they contain features of their evolutionary, and typically highly path-dependent, past. In biology, as in all else, for an understanding, history matters.

15 I am not wishing to suggest that Darwin himself accepted this strict case.

16 The Lamarckian model is named after Jean Bapiste de Monet, the Chevalier de Lamarck (1744–1829). However, 'Lamarck' was far from unique in holding to the doctrine (admitting the possibility of the inheritance of acquired characteristics); nor was he its original formulator. Lamarck's acceptance of the doctrine is, though, clear when he writes:

> All the acquisitions or losses wrought by nature on individuals, through the influence of the environment in which their race has been placed, and hence through the influence of the predominant use or permanent disuse of any organ; all these are preserved by reproduction to the new individuals which arise, provided that the acquired modifications are common to both sexes, or at least to the individuals which produce the young.
>
> (Lamarck 1984 [1809]: 113)

For further discussions, see for example Burkhardt (1977; 1984) or Hodgson (1993; 2001a).

17 Of course, it is possible that where
    (i)   traits *can* be developed as a response to environmental conditions, and
    (ii)   these can be acquired only by some subset that has the capacity to develop them, and
    (iii)   these traits are helpful to 'survival',

it will appear as though we have a feed backwards mechanism when really we do not. That is, it will seem that the environment is determining genetic variation. For example, suppose a subset of finches developed a flying manoeuvre that is very helpful in avoiding predators or obtaining a type of food, or whatever. If only a subset of finches has the capacity to develop this technique (a result of genetic mutation), the environment will favour those that have this capacity *and* come to develop it. Thus it will seem that some finches are developing a trait in the environment (which they are) and passing it on through inheritance (which they are not). Rather, it is the capacity to develop the trait which is passed on through inheritance, and this capacity was (by my construction) first generated via genetic mutation not environmental selection. The point is that such examples can give the appearance of not invoking a natural selection mechanism when ultimately they may do.

18 Of course, this example merely illustrates a selective tendency in play in many aspects of perhaps most societies (even in those like France where linguistic imperialism is fiercely resisted).

19 Let me, however, briefly elaborate a little further. Several characteristics of the mathematising project are evident. Its development is cumulative. Incremental changes in mathematical forms, when coupled with the selective effects of environmental pressures, have given rise to complex, multi-functional, economic theories, practices, projects and institutions. Further mathematical forms have been adaptive without being in any obvious way optimal. They reflect an internal dynamic of change which is shaped by historical conditions rather than predestined convergence on a single, uniquely efficient form of evolutionary optimum. To see this, one need only remember how early empirical-statistical work evolved into the 'probability approach' of modern econometrics, which in turn adapted in form with the widespread introduction into universities of computers; and later how, with the widespread availability of cheap high-powered computers, computer simulation methodology rose to dominance. Further, the evolution of basic mathematical concepts and techniques has continually operated through a process somewhat analogous to inheritance in the biological sphere, which involves vertical transmission (i.e. replication over time) of stored information. More specifically, mathematical concepts and techniques store coded information about theoretical adaptations in a way which parallels the form and function of the genetic code. Replication or inheritance occurs through the replication of basic methods and concepts over time. As a study of the history of mathematical economics reveals, although the content of substantive theorising often shifts considerably from one period to another, underpinning the more substantive contributions there is a significant degree of methodological and conceptual continuity. These replicated methods and concepts are put to use by econometricians and theorists when new ideas emerge.

In short, mathematical economics might be thought of as a particular mechanism of cultural transmission which works by coding information into conceptual form, often reproduced in textbooks, research papers and lectures, etc., thereby assisting its inter-temporal dissemination. Mathematical economics discourse currently appears to possess the degree of autonomy and self-reference sufficient to provide it with the capacity for self-replication, while at the same time it is linked to wider academic and other processes through co-evolution.

315

20 I note that according to the *Oxford English Dictionary* a meme simply is 'An element of culture that may be considered passed on by non-genetic means, esp. imitation'.

21 It is sometimes said that if memes do exist, they cannot be true replicators because, unlike genes, they replicate only as a consequence of some other agent's activity. Now first I do not think that if such differences do exist they matter. Rather the claim seems to reveal a misunderstanding of the nature of metaphor and analogy. The relevant issue is to identify a process whereby order can come about in the absence of design. But I think it is in any case incorrect to view genes as somehow self-sufficient in replication. There is no self-replicating molecule in biology. For its replication DNA relies on dozens of protein enzymes, which in their turn require (for their correct synthesis) many other factors (such as coded information embedded in the combinatorial permutations of the four nucleotide bases of DNA – see e.g. Steven Rose 2001; Dover 2001).

22 For some memeticists, at least, memes are to be found only in the brain, though they are (mostly) not generated from within the brain but acquired from others. On this view units of culture or some such replicators mutate inside human minds.

23 I do not refer here to all contributions to memetics. But my reading of many resonates with the basics of the following assessment, by Dover (2001), of the writings of Dawkins in particular:

> Dawkins can often be seen to face both ways (the selfish gene: now we see it, now we don't). Dawkins' hard line is that he has opened our eyes to a dramatic new way of thinking (what he terms a 'transfiguration') about the genetic motor of natural selection; his soft line is that he is saying nothing new of major importance, for, yes, deep down, he recognises that it is the phenotype which is the prime mover, as Darwin rightly conceived. This ability to look both ways at once was likened by Dawkins himself to the visual illustration of the Necker Cube presenting two simultaneous orientations of a 3-D cube from a 2-D paper image. We should not be taken in by this edgy ambivalence; the perceived thrust of Dawkins's writing is about only one thing: everything of functional importance and complexity is an adaptation fashioned by natural selection working for the good of selfish replicators. The caveats, the qualifications, the 'ifs' and 'buts', are not part of the grand illusion.
>
> (Dover 2001: 55–6)

24 Its truth is presumably that being social creatures we often assimilate the views and values of those around us. But this does not necessitate cultural determinism.

25 For example, there is a demand that because the category of meme is created to sound like gene that the two are more closely related than they are, that a meme is a gene in more than a metaphorical way. Susan Blackmore is keen to avoid this:

> Gould seems to think that because memes and genes are related by analogy or metaphor we would somehow be doing a disservice to biological evolution by making the comparison. Again he has missed the point that both are replicators but they need not work in the same way.
>
> (Blackmore 1999a: 18)

Whether not Gould is correctly portrayed here, I think the worry which Blackmore raises is more a reason for avoiding the term meme altogether. For it immediately invites greater comparison of the meme with the gene than relations of analogy or metaphor warrant. If the term social replicator is instead used, it is then an open question whether the latter share with genes commonalities over and above those that constitute them as replicators. Relatedly, it seems to me that other commentators too (especially those sympathetic to memetics but not or not [yet] prepared to acknowledge that memes exist) want to tie the meme and gene too closely and (without reflecting on the nature of metaphorical relations) set seemingly arbitrary requirements on memes to qualify as appropriate gene analogues (see e.g. Sperber 2000; Aunger 2000). Further, Hull's (2000) observation that Blackmore's conception of a meme (her restriction of the subject-matter of memetics to 'information learned through imitation') serves to restrict this evolutionary theory to a single species, namely humans, is not a criticism at all.

26 I am aware that Universal Darwinism is defined as a project concerned only with the possibility that Darwinian principles have wide application (with auxiliary considerations specific to each domain). But if this is the stance, what a misleading label for it.

27 Worries about memetics which are in some ways similar to those discussed here are also expressed by Mary Midgley (2001).

6 Economics as a distinct social science? The nature, scope and method of economics

1 This chapter was first published in *Economie Appliquée* (1997) tome L, no. 2: 5–35.

2 Thus Robbins, for example, opposes his own conception to that concerned with the causes of wealth (or 'material welfare'). He writes:

> The definition of Economics which would probably command most adherents, at any rate in Anglo-Saxon countries, is that which relates it to the study of the causes of material welfare. This element is common to the definitions of …
>
> [However, once we 'test' this definition according to its] capacity to describe exactly the ultimate subject-matter of the main generalisations of the science … it is seen to possess deficiencies which, so far from being marginal and subsidiary, amount to nothing less than a complete failure to exhibit either the scope or the significance of the most central generalisations of all.
>
> (Robbins 1940: 4–5)

> Hirshleifer, in broadly supporting Robbins' own conception, starts out with the following intended put-down of Marshall's definition:
>
> As to Marshall, how terribly narrow, dull, bourgeois! Must we economists limit our attention to the ordinary, the crassly material business of life?
>
> (Hirshleifer 1985: 53)

`Hodgson (1996), in supporting a perspective turning on the causes and use of wealth, opposes this to the optimising framework such as propounded by Robbins.

3 Perhaps the interpretation of economics which is closest to that defended here in that it seeks to include the different conceptions, albeit arguing that they 'have nothing in common', is that of Karl Polanyi (1971: 140).

4 In particular, while econometric forecasting models do not forecast very well, the models formulated by 'economic theorists' do not explain anything of interest (see e.g. Phelps Brown 1972; Bell and Kristol 1981; Wiles and Routh 1984; Donaldson 1985; Hodgson 1988, Kirman 1989; Ormerod 1994; Lawson 1997a). Nor is it even clear where the 'theory' project is going (see e.g. Rubinstein 1995). Moreover, as numerous commentators have emphasised, the subject is strewn with inconsistencies between 'methodologies' acknowledged and practices actually followed (see e.g. Blaug 1980; McCloskey 1983; 1986; Lawson 1997a).

5 This project, which draws upon the philosophical contributions of Bhaskar (1978; 1979) amongst others, is extensively elaborated as a perspective in economics in Lawson 1997a. Recent developments of the latter are also to be found in Fleetwood 1996; Ingham 1996; C. Lawson 1996; Lewis 1996; Pratten 1996; Runde 1996. The following is an overview of certain results achieved in the project rather than their justification (for the latter the reader might consult Lawson 1997a).

6 Generally speaking, to explain some event, thing, or phenomenon, (i.e. the *explanandum*) is to provide an account (the *explanans*) whereby the initial phenomenon is rendered intelligible. According to deductivist explanation the explanandum must be deduced from a set of initial and boundary conditions plus (presumed) universal laws of the form 'whenever event (type) x then event (type) y'. Clearly on this deductivist conception, explanation and prediction amount to much the same thing (this is the so-called symmetry thesis). The former entails the deduction of an event after it has (or is known to have) occurred, the latter prior to (knowledge of) its occurrence. According to deductivism, the explanation of laws, theories and sciences similarly proceeds by deductive subsumption. Of course, it does not follow that because this model is pursued in economics, the event regularities formulated are actually borne out empirically, or indeed are always other than obvious fictions. It is the structure or form of these regularities that is the characteristic feature of deductivism.

7 This conception of science as necessitating successful prediction is accepted as much by economists who conclude that economics can *not* be scientific as by those who believe otherwise. Examples abound of explicit assertions in line with this assessment, but let me sample merely from winners of the Nobel Memorial Prize in economic science. If the list of prizewinners who suppose that a predictively successful science has actually been achieved includes not only such well known cases as Friedman but also perceived critics within orthodoxy such as Allais, the group which concludes that economic science is impossible precisely because successful prediction is not realisable includes Hicks, a former 'theorist' who seems at some stage to have abandoned the orthodox project entirely. Consider, for example, the following assessments:

> The essential condition of any science is the existence of regularities which can be analyzed and forecast. This is the case in celestial mechanics. But it is also true of many economic phenomena. Indeed, their thorough analysis displays the existence of regularities which are just as striking as those found in the physical sciences. This is why

economics is a science, and why this science rests on the same general principles and methods of physics.

(Allais 1992: 25)

A science, I would say, consists of a body of propositions, which have three distinguishing characters. (1) They are about real things, things we observe, about phenomena. (2) They are general propositions, about classes of phenomena. (3) They are propositions on which it is possible to base predictions, predictions which command some degree of belief. All of these three appear to be necessary, if the body of propositions is to be a science.

(Hicks 1986: 91)

[Economics] is no more than on the edge [of science] because the experiences that it analyses have so much that is non-repetitive about them.

(*ibid.*: 100)

8 And, in the natural sphere at least, it is in the notion of a generative mechanism at work that natural necessity (i.e. necessity independent of people and their actions) lies.

9 When the premises are general features of experience, this form of retroduction can be referred to as transcendental argument (see e.g. Lawson 1997a; chapter 2 above).

10 Two objects or features, etc., are said to be internally related if they are what they are by virtue of the relationship in which they stand to one other. Landlady/lord and tenant, employer and employee, teacher and student, magnet and its field, are examples that spring easily to mind. In each case it is not possible to have the one without the other; each, in part, is what it is, and does what it does, by virtue of the relation in which it stands to the other. This contrasts with objects or features which are externally related. Two objects or aspects are said to be externally related if neither is constituted by the relationship in which it stands to the other. Fish and chips, coffee and croissant, barking dog and post-person, two passing strangers, provide examples.

11 In putting forward this suggested synthesis I do not want to suggest that Mill necessarily adopts an identical notion of cause or causation. To the extent that he does not then Mill's conception, of course, is here being transformed. But such a step is necessitated by the results of methodological investigation reviewed above. All syntheses necessitate the transformation of aspects of any source position. The result achieved does, though, maintain Mill's fundamental claim: that the causes of wealth are a fundamental concern of economics.

12 There is no question that, for Robbins, the economic aspect of any situation *does* indeed refer to the notion of economising. This is clear from Robbins' positive arguments for his formulation, where terms like economic and Economics first appear. Robbins introduces this positive part of his thesis through discussing the lot of an isolated individual wishing to choose between work and leisure when it is necessary to engage in both:

such a division may legitimately be said to have an economic aspect. Wherein does this aspect consist?

319

The answer is to be found in the formulation of the exact conditions which make such division necessary. They are four. In the first place, isolated man wants both real income and real leisure. Secondly, he has not enough of either fully to satisfy his want of each. Thirdly, he can spend his time in augmenting his real income or he can spend it in taking more leisure. Fourthly, it may be presumed that, save in most exceptional cases, his want for the different constituents of real income and leisure will be different. Therefore he has to choose. He has to economise. The disposition of his time and his resources has a relationship to his system of wants. It has an economic aspect.

(*ibid.*: 12)

Robbins insists that this 'example is typical of the whole field of economic studies' (*ibid.*: 12), and continues a few pages below:

We have to choose between the different uses to which … [resources] may be put. The services which others put at our disposal are limited. The material means of achieving ends are limited. We have been turned out of Paradise. We have neither eternal life nor unlimited means of gratification. Everywhere we turn, if we choose one thing we must relinquish others which, in different circumstances, we would wish not to have relinquished. Scarcity of means to satisfy ends of varying importance is an almost ubiquitous condition of human behaviour.

Here, then, is the unity of subject of Economic Science, the forms assumed by human behaviour in disposing of scarce means.

(*ibid.*: 15)

13 This is not to deny that some commentators (e.g. Cannan 1903) do use this formulation. But if we are contrasting broad, supposedly competing, conceptions, it is important to consider the better examples of each.
14 Specifically, Mill writes:

It has been proposed to define wealth as signifying 'instruments': meaning not tools and machinery alone, but the whole accumulation possessed by individuals or communities, of means for the attainment of their ends. Thus, a field is an instrument, because it is a means to the attainment of corn. Corn is an instrument, being a means to the attainment of flour. Flour is an instrument, being a means to the attainment of bread. Bread is an instrument, as a means to the satisfaction of hunger and to the support of life. Here we at last arrive at things which are not instruments, being desired on their own account, and not as mere means to something beyond. This view of the subject is philosophically correct; or rather, this mode of expression may be usefully employed along with others, not as conveying a different view of the subject from the common one, but as giving more distinctness and reality to the common view. It departs, however, too widely from the custom of language, to be likely to obtain general acceptance, or to be of use for any other purpose than that of occasional illustration.

(1900: 18)

15 Including, much of the time, both Marshall and Mill.

16 Here I think we must side with Robbins (1940) against Mill and, more recently, Hausman.

7 The nature of post Keynesianism and the problem of delineating the various heterodox traditions

1 This chapter is essentially a synthesis and slight development of two previous papers (Lawson 1994b; 1999a) both published in the *Journal of Post Keynesian Economics*. Various other contributors have further developed the arguments advanced in these two papers, including Dow 1999; Lewis and Runde 1999; Pratten 1996; 1997b; McKenna and Zannoni 1999; Rotheim 1999. Some too have debated various closely connected issues (see especially Brown 2000; Dow 2000). Others express disagreement with the arguments of these papers, particularly Parsons 1995; Walters and Young 1997; 1999. Replies to these latter critics also exist; see especially McKenna and Zannoni 1999; Runde 2001b; Fleetwood 2002; Arestis *et al.* 1999b; and Dunn 2000.

2 As is revealed for example by a study of the contributions to the *Journal of Post Keynesian Economics*.

3 On this point the following remarks are typical:

> Post-Keynesian economics can be seen as covering a considerable assortment of approaches. It has sometimes been said that the unifying feature of post-Keynesians is the dislike of neoclassical economics.
>
> (Sawyer 1988: 1)

> post-Keynesian economics is often portrayed as being distinguished more by its dislike of neoclassical theory, than by any coherence or agreement on fundamentals by its contributors.
>
> (Hodgson 1989: 96)

> It is less controversial to say what post-Keynesian theory is not than to say what it is. Post-Keynesian theory is not neoclassical theory.
>
> (Eichner 1985: 151)

> post-Keynesians tend to define their program in a negative way as a reaction to neo-classical economics.
>
> (Arestis 1990: 222)

> Some have argued that what unites post-Keynesians is a negative factor: the rejection of neoclassical economics.
>
> (Dow 1992: 176)

> What seems to be striking to outsiders of post-Keynesianism and neo-Ricardianism is that these two schools of thought and their major proponents only seem to have one cementing theme, their rejection of the dominant neoclassical paradigm.
>
> (Lavoie 1992: 45)

See also Hamouda and Harcourt (1989: 2) and Harcourt (1985: 125; 1988: 924) amongst many others.

4 This emphasis is apparent from a glance at the content of any post Keynesian contribution. In addition the following explicit assessments are to be found:

> So the methodological content of post-Keynesian writing tends to be high. This contrasts with the minimal attention paid to methodological issues in [neoclassical textbooks] ... the post-Keynesian view of methodology as ranging from ideology through to technique requires that it be continually raised as an issue.
>
> (Dow 1992: 182)

> the post-Keynesian school of thought represents a positive statement of methodology, ideology and content.
>
> (Arestis 1990: 222)

> [One] approach to specifying post-Keynesian economics is a methodological one. Elsewhere ... I have attempted to define post-Keynesianism as a shared methodological approach. ...
>
> Post-Keynesianism can be understood as a subset of political economy which can in turn be understood as a general embracing of a methodology of diverse methods. An attempt will therefore be made to relate post-Keynesianism and political economy in methodological terms.
>
> (Dow 1990: 346–7)

5 A typical assessment is the following:

> The characteristics of the historical and humanistic models employed by Post Keynesians may be summarized in the following three propositions: 1) The economy is a historical process; 2) in a world where uncertainty is unavoidable, expectations have an unavoidable and significant effect on economic outcomes; 3) economic and political institutions play a significant role in shaping economic events.
>
> (Davidson 1980: 158)

Under the third heading above, Davidson explicitly notes that the 'distribution of income and power is a basic concern of Post Keynesians' (162) and spends some time discussing the post Keynesian concern for matters of democracy, policy and distributional issues more generally.

6 Consider Dow's typical (if highly abbreviated) assessment:

> As the name 'post-Keynesian' suggests, the work of John Maynard Keynes is a significant influence. But Keynes is not the sole influence on the school, and indeed the earlier writers who influenced Keynes himself are often identified by post-Keynesians as having influenced them directly. ...
>
> Post-Keynesianism has its roots in classical economics. ...

Adam Smith is regarded as the first key figure…

> As far as the content of post-Keynesian economics is concerned, the key classical figures are Malthus, Ricardo and Marx, each influencing different groups within post-Keynesian economics.
>
> (Dow 1992: 177)

7 Where other contenders for inclusion, Sraffa for example (along, indeed, with other possible nominal features of post Keynesianism not focused upon here), seem to be accepted by only a section of post Keynesians and whose inclusion would appear to be especially controversial, my strategy has been to omit them from explicit consideration here. This seems appropriate. For if coherence within post Keynesianism (the question here at issue) cannot be found amongst those features that appear to be widely agreed upon by post Keynesians, then the inclusion of controversial features is unlikely to change matters. Alternatively, if coherence can be brought to, or found within, the agreed features, it should then be that much easier to assess whether, conditional upon coherence being required, those features not considered here do, could, or should not, etc., belong.

8 Economic analyses are mostly couched in terms of atomistic individual agents. Internal stability and so passivity is usually achieved by interpreting these agents as instrumental optimisers acting in conditions where a unique optimum always exists to be uncovered.

9 The orientation of modern post Keynesianism does now seem to be changing relatively fast, however, especially in some quarters. For recent ontologically explicit contributions to post Keynesian theory and understanding see, for example, Arestis *et al.* 1999a; 1999b; Rosser Jr 2001; Dow 1997; 1999; 2000; Downward 1999; 2000; Dunn 2000; 2001; Fontana 2000; Lee 2002; McKenna and Zannoni 1999; Rotheim 1998; 1999; 2002; Setterfield 2000; Smithin, forthcoming.

10 See for example Davidson 1978, 1980, 1989, 1991, 1994, 1996.

11 If a further indication of Keynes' early realist orientation is required, let me recall the observations and reflections with which Keynes concludes his *Treatise*:

> The physicists of the nineteenth century have reduced matter to the collisions and arrangements of particles, between which the ultimate qualitative differences are very few; and the Mendelian biologists are deriving the various qualities of men from the collisions and arrangements of chromosomes. In both cases the analogy with the perfect game of chance is really present; and the validity of some current modes of inference may depend on the assumption that it is to material of this kind that we are applying them. Here, though I have complained sometimes at their want of logic, I am in fundamental sympathy with the deep underlying conceptions of the statistical theory of the day. If the contemporary doctrines of biology and physics remain tenable, we may have a remarkable, if undeserved, justification of some of the methods of the traditional calculus of probabilities. Professors of probability have been often and justly derided for arguing as if nature were an urn containing black and white balls on fixed proportions. Quetelet once declared in so many words – 'l'urne que nous interrogeons, c'est la nature'. But again in the history of science the methods of astrology may prove useful to the astronomer; and it may turn out to be true – reversing Quetelet's expression – that 'La nature que nous interrogeons, c'est une urne'.
>
> (Keynes 1973b: 468)

12 Thus Arestis (1990) admits that 'there is a substantial theoretical diversity of theoretical premises' (222), and Dow (1990) observes that an 'important feature of existing post-Keynesian literature is its apparent diversity of content' (352).

13 And, of course, those of other heterodox economists.

14 This claim receives further grounding from the number of contributors to post Keynesianism recently responding positively (accepting or at least giving serious and sympathetic consideration) to critical realist results and findings. See for example Arestis *et al.* 1999a; 1999b; Dow 1997; 1999; 2000; Downward 1999; 2000; Dunn 2000; 2001; Lee 2002; McKenna and Zannoni 1999; Rotheim 1998; 1999, 2002; Setterfield 2000; Smithin, forthcoming.

15 It remains an open question, of course, whether post Keynesians do value coherence of some sort (though problems clearly arise if they do not). I am merely concerned with how, *if* it is desired and pursued, it might best be conceptualised and achieved.

16 O'Driscoll and Rizzo (1985), for example, suggest commonalities between their own Austrian perspective and that of post Keynesianism:

> In recent years a largely American branch of the Cambridge (UK) school, known as post-Keynesian economics, has arisen to carry forth the subjectivist aspects of Keynes' system. ... Paul Davidson has conveniently summarized the post-Keynesian perspective in three propositions ... :
> 1   the economy is a process in historical (real) time;
> 2   in a world where uncertainty and surprises are unavoidable, expectations have an unavoidable and significant effect on economic outcomes;
> 3   economic and political institutions are not negligible, and, in fact, play an extremely important role in determining real world economic outcomes.
>
> The reader will be hard pressed to find any significant differences between these propositions and the argument of this chapter. What is even more surprising is that Davidson's explication of the meaning of these propositions increases, rather than reduces, the area of overlap. It is evident that there is much more common ground between post-Keynesian subjectivism and Austrian subjectivism. Cross-fertilization between the two schools is, however, exceedingly rare, although the possibilities for mutually advantageous interchange seem significant.
>
> (O'Driscoll and Rizzo 1985: 9)

In parallel fashion, common ground between Austrianism and institutionalism has also been noted (e.g. Samuels 1989; Boettke 1989). There has even been a symposium on the subject. Moreover, it is clear that the commonalities regularly highlighted here consist in the sorts of feature noted at the outset as characteristic of post Keynesianism. Thus, for example, Samuels (1989) finds of Austrianism and institutionalism that, amongst other things, 'each tends to define itself, in part, in terms of its contrast with neoclassical economics' (60); 'each is internally heterogeneous' (60); 'both schools comprise more a paradigm than a fully detailed body of particular theories' (61); 'both schools are preoccupied (relative to neoclassicism) with methodological, philosophical (including epistemological), and political economy issues and foundations' (61). And see also Dunn 2000.

17 Thus Davidson (1989) for example is quite dismissive of the specific claims of commonality between post Keynesians and Austrians noted by O'Driscoll and Rizzo, just as Miller (1989) rejects the specific claims of commonality between Austrians and institutionalists as made by Samuels (1989) and Boettke (1989).

18 I previously speculated that if there are differentiating characteristics of note, these too must be found in features lying at a level of abstraction below that of social ontology but above that of relatively concrete social-scientific explanations of highly specific phenomena.

19 From this perspective, the fact that mainstream economics distinguishes itself by its method already indicates a phenomenon that warrants explanation.

20 All heterodox traditions proceed differently to, and are critical of, the mainstream emphasis, of course. I re-emphasise the point here, in the context of referring explicitly to feminist economics, just because there is a tendency for some to characterise feminist economics as 'add women to mainstream economics and stir', and I do not want an overly quick reading of these passages, out of context, to lend themselves to such an interpretation. My position is more or less the opposite of this. I am interpreting the feminist project as one that adopts a critical response to the mainstream's (universalising) emphasis, is inclusive in orientation, informed, if implicitly, by an ontology which is more sustainable than that of the mainstream (and ultimately similar to one defended in this book) and which takes a more open-minded and critical (ethically informed, and context-sensitive) approach to how things can be done. I intend none of this to be diminished by advancing the suggestion that *within the heterodox traditions* feminist economics might be first of all distinguished by its (developing) focus and questions pursued.

21 Of course, the question 'what is feminist theory?' is highly discussed amongst feminist writers, and generates various often quite different responses. For a critical survey of the question that reaches a not dissimilar assessment to the very general suggestion advanced here, see Beasley 1999.

22 I use the word loosely. If findings are inconsistent, clearly forms of critical resolution are required.

8 Institutional economics and realist social theorising

1 See for example C. Lawson 1994; 1995; 1996b; 1999b; Hodgson 2001b; Pratten 1997a; 2001; Pagano, forthcoming.

2 Warren Samuels, too, might be interpreted as suggesting a postmodernist conception of Veblen (Hoksbergen 1994: 694). Indeed, postmodern is an ascription which Samuels seems happy to accept for himself (Samuels 1998). Further, Roland Hoksbergen (1994) assesses that this postmodern element is a growing force within institutionalism.

3 For an excellent exception which gives more detail than is included below, see Mayhew 1998a.

4 Consider for example the following passage published ten years later:

> The characteristic feature by which post-Darwinian science is contrasted with what went before is a new distribution of emphasis, whereby the process of causation, the interval of instability and transition between initial cause and definitive effect, has come to take the first place in the inquiry; instead of that consummation in which causal effect was once

presumed to come to rest. This change of the point of view ... has latterly gone so far that modern science is becoming substantially a theory of the process of consecutive change, which is taken as a sequence of cumulative change, realized to be self-continuing or self-propagating and to have no final term.

(Veblen 1908: 37)

5 As the passage reproduced in the previous footnote also makes especially clear.
6 As Veblen also formulates matters:

For the earlier natural scientists, as for the classical economists, this ground of cause and effect is not definitive. Their sense of truth and substantiality is not satisfied with a formulation of mechanical sequence. The ultimate term in their systematisation of knowledge is a 'natural law.' This natural law is felt to exercise some sort of a coercive surveillance over the sequence of events, and to give a spiritual stability and consistence to the causal relation at any given juncture. To meet the high classical requirement, a sequence – and a developmental process especially – must be apprehended in terms of a consistent propensity tending to some spiritually legitimate end. When facts and events have been reduce to these terms of fundamental truth and have been made to square with the requirements of definitive normality, the investigator rests his case. Any causal sequence which is apprehended to traverse the imputed propensity in events is a 'disturbing factor.' Logical congruity with the apprehended propensity is, in this view, adequate ground of procedure in building up a scheme of knowledge or of development. The objective point of the efforts of the scientists working under the guidance of this classical tradition, is to formulate knowledge in terms of absolute truth; and this absolute truth is a spiritual fact. It means a coincident of facts with the deliverances of an enlightened and deliberate common sense.

The development and the attenuation of this preconception of normality or of a propensity in events might be traced in detail from primitive animism down through the elaborate discipline of faith and metaphysics, overruling Providence, order of nature, natural rights, natural law, underlying principles. But all that may be necessary here is to point out that, by descent and by psychological content, this constraining normality is of a spiritual kind. It is for the scientific purpose an imputation of spiritual coherence to the facts dealt with. The question of interest is how this preconception of normality has fared at the hands of modern science, and how it has come to be superseded in the intellectual primacy by the latter day preconception of a non-spiritual sequence. This question is of interest because its answer may throw light on the question as to what chance there is for the indefinite persistence of this archaic habit of thought in the methods of economic science.

(Veblen 1898: 61)

7 Notice that Veblen mostly reserved the term 'evolutionary' for a form of method or science. But this is not always the case. He occasionally includes passages like 'the evolutionary process of cumulative causation' (Veblen 1908: 55).
8 See Lawson 1997a: ch. 5.

9 Actually, the very fact that Veblen more or less interprets evolutionary method in terms of the ontological conception for which it is considered appropriate is immediately suggestive of the likelihood that he does not consider this ontology derivative of the method. The former is not an implicit, possibly unrecognised, preconception resulting from accepting the method, but an upfront statement of the conditions under which the evolutionary method will prove useful. However, I believe an independent defence of the causalist ontology can also be found in Veblen's writing.

10 This is something that seems to have gone largely unnoticed in the institutionalist literature. I am aware that Veblen writes that in actuality metaphysical preconceptions tend to be accepted uncritically, via natural selection and selective adaptation:

> This ultimate term or ground of knowledge is always of a metaphysical character. It is something in the way of a preconception, accepted uncritically.
>
> (Veblen 1900: 149)

> [The ultimate metaphysical ground of knowledge] is subject to natural selection and selective adaptation, as are other conventions. The underlying metaphysics of scientific research and purpose, therefore, changes gradually and, of course, incompletely, much as is the case with the metaphysics underlying the common law and the schedule of civil rights.
>
> (Veblen 1900: 149)

And it is true that, at one point, in a phrase that *prima facie* is perhaps the most damaging for the account I am defending, Veblen says of the postulate that things change consecutively that this 'is an unproven and unprovable postulate – that is to say it is a metaphysical preconception' (Veblen 1908: 33). But when Veblen elaborates this remark in an attached footnote it is fairly evident that by something unprovable Veblen merely means something unobservable which has to be retroduced or transcendentally deduced or, in Veblen's words, 'imputed':

> The concept of causation is recognized [by modern scientists] to be a metaphysical postulate, a matter of imputation, not of observation.
>
> (Veblen 1908: 33)

This association of unobservable with unprovable may reflect the philosophical thinking of his time (clearly, in Veblen's case influenced by Kant's empirical realism). The point I want to stress, however, is that in the same (very long) footnote, Veblen noticeably engages in explicit ontological argument and defence of his position. As such, 'provable', as I say, seems to coincide with observable. For the significance of Veblen's emphasis seems more to reflect his view of the incorrigibility of the observable. From a modern perspective, of course, we recognise that all claims, even observational ones, are fallible. In any case, the important aspect for the thesis I am pursuing is not the precise manner in which categories such as (un)provable are used, but the very fact that Veblen attempts to argue the relative advantages of the ontology of cumulative causation. To the extent that he does, we can reject the idea that Veblen holds that our ontological commitments must be accepted uncritically.

11 Veblen writes:

> It is by no means unusual for modern scientists to deny the truth of this characterization, so far as regards this alleged recourse to the concept of causation. They deny that such a concept – of efficiency, activity, and the like – enters or can legitimately enter, into their work, whether as an instrument of research or as a means or guide to theoretical formulation. They even deny the substantial continuity of the sequence of changes that excite their scientific attention. This attitude seems particularly to commend itself to those who by preference attend to the mathematical formulations of theory and who are chiefly occupied with proving up and working out details of the system of theory which have previously been left unsettled or uncovered.
>
> (Veblen 1908: 33)

12 Thus Veblen writes

> The contention seems sound, to the extent that the materials – essentially statistical materials – with which scientific inquiry is occupied are of this non-committal character, and that the mathematical formulations of theory include no further element than that of idle variation. Such is necessarily the case because causation is a fact of imputation, not of observation, and so cannot be included among the data; and because nothing further than noncommittal variation can be expressed in mathematical terms. A bare notation of quantity can convey nothing further.
>
> (Veblen 1908: 33–4)

13 Veblen also adds a further example of what is, in effect, a determinate negation. He observes that those scientists who deny an ontology of unobservable (efficient) causality are also those who find the prevailing notion of action at a distance repugnant. Yet this very repugnance (which Veblen too can share as common ground) presupposes precisely the ontological commitment to unseen or unobservable causation that these scientists deny:

> Of the sciences which affect a non-committal attitude in respect of the concept of efficiency and which claim to get along with the notion of mathematical function alone, physics is the most outspoken and the one in which the claim has the best *prima facie* validity. At the same time latter-day physicists, for a hundred years or more, have been much occupied with explaining how phenomena which to all appearance involve action at a distance do not involve action at a distance at all. The greater theoretical achievements of physics during the past century lie within the sweep of this (metaphysical) principle that action at a distance does not take place, that apparent action at a distance must be explained by effective contact, through a continuum, or by a material transference. But this principle is nothing better than an unreasoning repugnance on the part of the physicists to admitting action at a distance. The requirement of a continuum involves a gross form of the concept of efficient causation. The 'functional' concept, concomitant variation, requires no contact

and no continuum. Concomitance at a distance is quite as simple and convincing a notion as concomitance within contact or by the intervention of a continuum, if not more so. What stands in the way of its acceptance is the irrepressible anthropomorphism of the physicists. And yet the great achievements of physics are due to the initiative of men animated with this anthropomorphic repugnance to the notion of concomitant variation at a distance. All the generalisations on undulatory motion and translation belong here. The latter-day researches in light, electrical transmission, the theory of ions, together with what is known of the obscure and late-found radiations and emanations, are to be credited to the same metaphysical preconception, which is never absent in any 'scientific' inquiry in the field of physical science.

(Veblen 1908: 35–6)

14 Of course, it is impossible to remain uninfluenced by ongoing developments, But complete submission or independence are not the only alternatives here.

15 For example, I do not share the view argued by Hodgson (1998) that Veblen held a theory of emergence.

16 Others, perhaps especially those implicitly accepting model A, seem to find even more tension than does Samuels. Samuels notes a letter to him from Paul Strassmann who concludes that on the matters discussed above Veblen is 'tongue in cheek, mischievous to baffle and infuriate his followers, mock seriousness (playing games to dislodge the preconceptions of readers, anticipating objections hence defusing them, a defensive possibly paranoid smokescreen' (Samuels 1990: 707–8). Samuels also notes the reaction of others that run along similar lines. Samuels in response basically indicates that he is not surprised that Veblen holds to competing views simultaneously. As I say, no such tensions need be imputed to Veblen if the interpretation of model C is accepted.

17 Again, see Sofianou 1995.

18 Veblen usually describes the sort of economics that prevails at the turn of the twentieth century as taxonomic. This is what he opposes. But as an explanatory endeavour it clearly encompasses enterprises like the modern deductivist programme. As Veblen observes, if a segment of an industrial field is to be investigated, a predictive scheme (referred to as normalised or teleological because predetermined) is adopted. And with

this normalised scheme as a guide, the permutations of a given segment of the apparatus are worked out according to the values assigned the several items and features comprised in the calculation; and a ceremonially consistent formula is constructed to cover that much of the industrial field. This is the deductive method. The formula is then tested by comparison with observed permutations, by the polariscopic use of the 'normal case'; and the results arrived at are thus authenticated by induction. Features of the process that do not lend themselves to interpretation in the terms of the formula are abnormal cases and are due to disturbing causes. In all this the agencies or forces causally at work in the economic life process are neatly avoided. The outcome of the method, at its best, is a body of logically consistent propositions concerning the normal relations of things – a system of economic taxonomy.

(Veblen 1898: 67)

19 This applies, for example, to social structure in all its aspects. In critical realism social structure is explicitly distinguished from human agency and

actions; indeed social structure comprises just those features of social material that are irreducible to events and other actualities. Social structure includes social rules, relationships, institutions, processes, totalities, and so forth. And the mode of being of social structure just is as expressed by the transformational model.

20 Veblen writes:

> The ways and means of turning material objects and circumstances to account lie before the investigator at any given point of time in the form of mechanical contrivances and arrangements for compassing certain mechanical ends. It has therefore been easy to accept these ways and means as items of inert matter having a given mechanical structure and thereby serving the material ends of man. As such, they have been scheduled and graded by the economists under the head of capital, this capital being conceived as a mass of material objects serviceable for human use. This is well enough for the purposes of taxonomy; but it is not an effective method of conceiving the matter for the purpose of a theory of the developmental process.
>
> (Veblen 1898: 71)

21 More expansively, Veblen writes:

> But, in the view of the science, [these circumstances of temperament] are elements of the existing frame of mind of the agent, and are the outcome of his antecedents and his life up to the point at which he stands. They are the products of his hereditary traits and his past experience, cumulatively wrought out under a given body of traditions conventionalities, and material circumstances; and they afford the point of departure for the next step in the process. The economic life history of the individual is a cumulative process of adaptation of means to ends that cumulatively change as the process goes on, both the agent and his environment being at any point the outcome of the last process. His methods of life today are enforced upon him by his habits of life carried over from yesterday and by the circumstances left as the mechanical residue of the life of yesterday.
>
> (Veblen 1898: 74–5)

22 Indeed, he adopts a view not dissimilar to that contained in Chapter 6 above:

> The economic interest does not act in isolation, for it is but one of several vaguely isolable interests on which the complex of teleological activity carried out by the individual proceeds. The individual is but a single agent in each case; and he enters into each successive action as a whole, although the specific end sought in a given action may be sought avowedly on the basis of a particular interest; as e.g., the economic, aesthetic, sexual, humanitarian, devotional interests. Since each of these passably isolable interests is a propensity of the organic agent man, with his complex of habits of thought, the expression of each is affected by habits of life formed under the guidance of all the rest. There is, therefore, no neatly isolable range of cultural phenomena that can be rigorously set apart under the head of economic institutions, although a category of 'economic institutions' may be of service as a convenient

caption, comprising those institutions in which the economic interest most immediately and consistently finds expression, and which most immediately and with the least limitation are of an economic bearing.

(Veblen 1898: 77)

23 It appears when Veblen briefly asserts that certain metaphysical grounds of knowledge, once criticised, become superseded, being 'subject to natural selection and selective adaptation, as are other conventions' (149).

24 For example, it is speculated that Veblen worried that reference to the term 'natural' would confuse readers into supposing he was either not dealing with social processes, or else was dealing with them in an overly naturalistic fashion, or even interpreting them as 'normal' in some way, and so forth. See Hodgson (1998d) for a list of speculations of this sort to support the answer 'no' being given to his own question: 'can the relatively infrequent appearance of the words "natural selection" undermine the claim that Veblen was principally an evolutionary economist in the Darwinian genre?' (185).

25 Thus Veblen boldly asserts in particular that

> The life of man in society, just like the life of other species, is a struggle for existence, and therefore it is a process of selective adaptation. The evolution of social structure has been a process of natural selection of institutions. The progress which has been and is being made in human institutions and in human character may be set down, broadly, to a natural selection of the fittest habits of thought and to a process of enforced adaptation of individuals to an environment which has progressively changed with the growth of the community and with the changing institutions under which men have lived. Institutions are not only themselves the result of a selective and adaptive process which shapes the prevailing or dominant types of spiritual attitude and aptitudes; they are at the same time special methods of life and of human relations, and are therefore in their turn efficient factors of selection. So that the changing institutions in their turn make for a further selection of individuals endowed with the fittest temperament, and a further adaptation of individual temperament and habits to the changing environment through the formation of new institutions.

(Veblen 1899a: 188)

26 Perhaps Veblen wrote the relevant chapter of the *Leisure Class* at an early stage and later read Romannes. This is mere speculation, of course. But whether or not it is correct I believe it would be unreasonable to associate too closely Veblen's significant contribution to evolutionary economics with an unsustainable feature which he himself soon apparently relinquished. As I have often argued, the most we can expect of an author is developmental consistency. With the passage of time it is to be expected that early errors are amended as new problems are tackled and resolved. Certainly, taking an overview of Veblen's writing, it would be unreasonable to associate his path-breaking contribution to evolutionary thinking in economics with one universalising position found in one chapter of an early text that appears not to have been reproduced thereafter.

27 Thus Veblen writes:

> In so far as it is a science in the current sense of the term, any science, such as economics, which has to do with human conduct, becomes a genetic inquiry into the human scheme of life; and where, as in economics, the subject of inquiry is the conduct of man in his dealings with the material means of life, the science is necessarily an inquiry into the life-history of material civilization, on a more or less extended or restricted plan.
>
> (Veblen 1909: 240–41)

28 Actually, the claim here that Veblen allows that an institution can be something other than habit will still seem questionable to some institutionalists, even when considering contributions like *The Limitations of Marginal Utility*. Indeed, although in the contribution in question Veblen is far from reducing institutions to habits (for example, he writes in this specific contribution of the 'institution of ownership' [244], the 'institution of property' [244], '[e]conomic institutions' [245], 'pecuniary institutions' [247], and so forth), it is actually an extract from *The Limitations of Marginal Utility* that is most frequently cited to support the reduction in question. However, I believe the equating of institutions with habits arises only though a (mis)reading of the relevant extract, when it is considered out of its fuller context. Let me briefly address this issue, and defend my claim.

Elsewhere (Lawson 1997a: ch. 12; Chapter 2 above) I offer an interpretation of institutions as designating those systems, or structured processes of inter-action (collecting together rules, relations and positions as well as habits and other practices), or aspects of them, which are *relatively enduring and identified as such*. An institution, on this conception, is a relatively enduring feature of social life that has become somewhat taken for granted through widespread acceptance and continual use. I think it is fairly clear that Veblen does not reduce institutions to practices such as habits when he observes (in a passage about to be noted in the text below) that it is 'through the habituation of individuals, that institutions arise' (243). A habit might well be considered an example of an institution, but institutions do not reduce to habits (for a conception of habits see note 30 below). As I say, the term institution denotes a social feature or phenomenon recognised as relatively enduring. Or as Veblen elsewhere puts it: 'An institution is of the nature of a usage which has become axiomatic and indispensable by habituation and general acceptance' (Veblen 1924 [1923]: 101).

However there is, as I say, a passage in *The Limitations of Marginal Utility*, much quoted by (old) institutionalists (see e.g. Hodgson 1998a: 179), and widely interpreted as in effect Veblen's definition of an institution. According to this interpretation, Veblen conceives institutions to be 'settled habits of thought common to the generality of men'.

But now consider a rather more extended version of the passage from which the above 'definition' is extracted. The context is Veblen's discussion of the 'premises of marginal-utility economics'. At the relevant point of the discussion, in a passage that includes the suggested definition of an institution, Veblen is arguing:

> [these premises of marginal-utility economics] … are principles of action which underlie the current, business-like scheme of economic life, and as such, as practical grounds of conduct, they are not to be called in ques-

tion without questioning the existing law and order. As a matter of course, men order their lives by these principles and, practically, entertain no question of their stability and finality. That is what is meant by calling them institutions; they are settled habits of thought common to the generality of men.

(Veblen 1909: 239)

Veblen immediately continues, however:

But it would be mere absentmindedness in any student of civilization therefore to admit that these or any other human institutions have this stability which is currently imputed to them or that they are in this way intrinsic to the nature of things. The acceptance by the economists of these or other institutional elements as given and immutable limits their inquiry in a particular and decisive way. It shuts off the inquiry at a point where the modern scientific interest sets in.

(Veblen 1909: 239–40)

It is clear from the wider passage that Veblen is not here offering a definition of an institution in terms of habits of thought at all. Rather, in the often quoted passage, the subject of the sentence is not even institutions but (certain) habits. Veblen indeed is suggesting of certain habits that they qualify as institutions. More particularly, he is suggesting that the specific habits of thought in contention, namely those bound up with the principles of marginal utility analysis, qualify as institutions, and do so just because they are 'settled' and are 'common to the generality of men'. Veblen is not offering a strict definition here, but is implicitly applying his understanding that institutions are in effect relatively enduring and widely recognised as such.

Consider, too, that part of the extract that immediately follows the familiar short excerpt. From Veblen's suggesting it would be absentmindedness to 'admit that these or any other human institutions have [the noted] stability', it is apparent that he has been referring not to institutions *per se*, but rather to particular examples of institutions, namely the habits of thought relating to the principles of marginal utility analysis. In short, the term 'they' in the sentence in which the familiar excerpt occurs refers not to institutions as such, but to these specific habits of thought. Veblen's purpose is not so much to define for us what an institution is as to indicate why certain specific habits of thought under discussion so qualify. Of course, in so doing he reveals something of what he takes an institution to be, but it does not follow that it is restricted to habits of thought or indeed to habits of any kind.

29 I am here interpreting Veblen as using the term habit to indicate certain (repeated) forms of action. This, I believe, is indeed the correct way to interpret him (and indeed the most useful way to employ the category). But as this term seems occasionally to be interpreted in other ways in modern (old) institutionalism, it is probably warranted that I also elaborate briefly on these matters at this stage. I actually do not think there is anything very significant at stake turning on which of the competing more dominant interpretations or usages is adopted. But it seems best that I be clear here about my own understanding just in case.

Veblen rarely defines his terms. But, as I say, I do find that the most plausible interpretation is that, for him, a habit is basically a settled form of action, one repeatedly carried out, in relevant conditions, without necessarily involving conscious deliberation, i.e. habitually. Thinking is a form of action of course. Thus, on the interpretation I am advancing, a habit of mind or thought is basically a settled manner of thinking. Methods or principles of analysis, if repeatedly actualised in observable forms of action, sooner or later become habits of thought, i.e. ways of thinking which in themselves hardly rely on conscious reflection. On this conception we may or may not want to concur with Commons (1934: 155) that 'Habit is repetition by one person. Custom is repetition by the continuing group of changing persons', but habit is a form of (repetitive) human action, tacitly carried out.

The main alternative interpretation of habit is as a disposition. Now clearly, to act repeatedly in a given way in certain circumstances presupposes a disposition so to do, where a disposition is a potential so structured, or (better) constrained, that it is directed to a given form of behaviour in given conditions (see Chapter 2). In turn, such a disposition itself is likely a result of the action having being frequently undertaken, albeit often in a more self-conscious fashion, in an earlier period. Reliance upon such self-actuating tendencies (in appropriate conditions) is a large part of what is meant when human actions are described as being tacitly carried out, or performed at a subconscious level (these sorts of categories relating to the structured human ontology are elaborated in Chapter 2 above).

I do recognise that, traditionally, the term habit has sometimes been used to signify (amongst other things) a settled disposition or propensity to act in a certain way, as well as a settled way of acting. And I think some modern (old) institutionalists, perhaps influenced by a reading of James, Dewey and others, opt for the former of the two interpretations at the expense of the latter.

However, I think this usage unfortunate in that we already have the category 'disposition'; we need a term to capture settled forms of action appropriate to certain conditions, and the category habit captures this nicely. But more to the point here, I do not think it is Veblen's usage. First of all, Veblen rarely employs the category dispositions anyway, and as far as I can see he never does when clarifying his understanding of habits. Moreover, Veblen regularly uses not just the noun habit but also, and in particular when detailing specific concrete instances of habits, the qualifier 'habitual'. And as far as I can discern, this latter term is always used to qualify a form of action, and in such a manner as to express its being settled or repeatedly carried out. This interpretation anyway makes most sense of his repeated references to 'habitual responses', 'habitual uses' and 'habitual resorts', etc. Thus I think that for Veblen habits are settled or repeated forms of behaviour.

But in truth, even if we were to interpret Veblen as understanding habit as disposition, little is at stake here as long as we recognise that the sorts of dispositions bound up with habits are effectively self-actuating (in appropriate conditions). Indeed, the dispositions in question and the settled forms of behaviour that are ushered in are internally related: each presupposes the other. And, however the term is understood, Veblen, when using it, is, as I say, clearly interested in the repeated-form-of-action aspect. In consequence, it can be accepted that any reference to habit necessarily entails reference to the ensuing action, even if it were held that the direct referent were just the disposition responsible.

In other words, there would be a difference of substance stemming from the competing conceptions considered only if it were the case both that, first, the term habit is used by some interpreters to indicate a disposition; and also, second, the latter disposition is treated somehow as autonomous from, rather than internally related to, the behaviour which Veblen repeatedly describes as habitual. That is, there would be something at stake only if the disposition-as-habit is interpreted not as self-activating but a matter of conscious deliberation. But, as I say, as long as this particular (and clearly erroneous) path is avoided, and there is no evidence at all that Veblen takes it (to the contrary, according to Veblen, changes in habitual ways of acting have almost to be forced on us, eventually), I do not think there is much here at issue.

However we look at it, then, I think we can accept that Veblen's use of habit involves at least reference to settled forms of behaviour, to actions repeatedly carried out (under appropriate conditions). For action is always at least entailed in his use of the term. As I say, by habit I believe Veblen means just this, i.e. a settled form of behaviour; Veblen does not develop a sophisticated conception of structured human nature. But it is enough for my purposes here if we recognise that, in Veblen's referencing of habit, a form of behaviour is always entailed. Thus, in referring to the category habit in what follows, I shall take it for granted that a form of conduct is always at least implied.

30 Which lend themselves to systems of taxonomy, which Veblen repeatedly criticised – Mayhew 1998a)

31 Indeed, the evidence suggests that the tide was going the other way from early on. See especially Mayhew (1998a), who seeks to understand why 'even as Veblen issued his call for an evolutionary economics … the evolutionary vision in the social sciences had begun to fade' (Mayhew 1998a: 452).

32 I can acknowledge that a perspective broadly of this sort underpinned a strand of economics being developed in Cambridge, when I first arrived, and proved very useful to my own development. It was most evident within research projects housed in the Cambridge Department of Applied Economics. A good example of this sort of work is reported in an excellent paper by Frank Wilkinson (1983) on productive systems. Acknowledging the similarity of his thinking to that of the 'historical and institutional schools of economic thought', Wilkinson writes:

> The cental proposition of this paper is that economic, social and political forces combine in determining how economies develop and that the result is a dynamic non-equilibrium process which can only be revealed by empirical investigation. This is not to suggest that abstract reasoning has no role to play but rather to argue that there are and can be *no* universal, pre-determined, 'true' systems to which underlying forces are tending. Nor is it argued that empirical investigation should be conducted in a vacuum: a theoretical and analytical framework is an essential guide. But it is necessary at the outset to recognise that the abandonment of conventional economic theorising requires sacrificing the formality of its modelling and the surety of its conclusions. What is proposed here as an alternative are broad guidelines formulated with the specific aim of improving our understanding of how economic systems operate in practice. This framework has been developed from empirical and historical investigation and from long discussions with others engaged on similar research. A central feature of this methodology is that the framework itself is to be tested and where necessary modified as a result of empirical findings.
>
> (Wilkinson 1983: 413–14)

If the forgoing describes Wilkinson's basic approach, his conclusions run as follows:

> What is observed in this brief sketch of the changes in productive systems is a dialectical process in which techniques of production and economic, social and political elements dynamically interact. Changes in techniques, products and power relations between capital and labour and their different factions lead to the destruction or radical modification of productive systems and the growth of new forms. The changing balance of power within and between productive systems interacts with the social and political framework and both are modified in the process. This perspective suggests an economic process radically different from that of 'equilibration' in orthodox theory, in which power relations and other imperfections merely displace the economy by some conceptually measurable distance to a 'disequilibrium'. What is implied is a *non*-equilibrium process. At one level the fittest (and best organised) survive. But such a simple evolutionary approach ignores the way in which productive systems create their own environment and how they mutate under the impact of innovation in techniques and organisational forms.
>
> (Wilkinson 1983: 426)

33 For rejections of the charge that institutional economics has been anti-theoretical, see especially C. Lawson 1994; 1996b; Pratten 1994.
34 See e.g. Hodgson 2001b: 151.

9 Feminism, realism and universalism

1 This chapter was first published in *Feminist Economics* (1999) vol. 5, no. 2.
2 Most obviously, such a universalising tendency serves to exclude alternative voices and practices. In resisting it feminists have been strategic in facilitating a stage, inside and outside the academy, for otherwise marginalised or excluded voices, a contribution that has both emancipatory and enlightening dimensions (see Susan Bordo 1993).
   Against this background of the opening-up of social theory in a variety of areas, feminists within economics have been endeavouring to achieve similar progress in a discipline which, over the last half-century at least, has become one of the least pluralistic of all. On the constructive side has been the creation of the journal *Feminist Economics*. Here the intention to include voices previously marginalised or excluded altogether is accepted as fundamental (see especially Diana Strassmann's opening editorial). On the more critical side, feminist economists have not been slow in revealing the tendency of prominent economists, mainly white, middle-class and male, to universalise their own experiences and perspectives, and, most significantly, to use the assumed, but unestablished, universal validity of their own particular methodological and other dispositions to exclude others who might wish to do things differently (see for example Paula England 1993; Nancy Folbre 1993; Ulla Grapard 1995; Julie Nelson 1993; 1996; Janet Seiz 1993; 1995; Diana Strassmann 1993a; 1993b; Diana Strassmann and Livia Polanyi 1995). Others have been concerned that implicit over generalising is avoided in feminist (substantive) economics itself (see, for example, M.V. Lee Badgett 1995).
3 Nussbaum writes 'By metaphysical realism I mean the view … that there is some determinate way the world is, apart from the interpretive workings of the cognitive faculties of living beings' (1995: 68).

4 In a reflective and critical follow-up, or response, to her own 'cyborg' paper, i.e. in her paper on 'situated knowledges', Donna Haraway acknowledges that 'feminists have both selectively and flexibly used and been trapped by two poles of a tempting dichotomy on the question of objectivity' (1988: 249). This dichotomy is between positions which Haraway refers to as feminist critical empiricism and radical constructionism. The empiricist wing is criticised for expecting too much in terms of knowing reality, the radical constructionist or postmodernist position for knowing to little. Haraway formulates her resolution as follows:

> So, I think, my problem, and 'our' problem, is how to have *simultaneously* an account of radical historical contingency for all knowledge claims and knowing subjects, a critical practice for recognizing our own 'semiotic technologies' for making meanings, *and* a no-nonsense commitment to faithful accounts of a 'real' world, one that can be partially shared and that is friendly to earth-wide projects of finite freedom, adequate material abundance, modest meaning in suffering, and limited happiness.
>
> (1988: 252)

5 Of course, all methods and epistemological positions generate implicit ontological claims of some kind. Hume's empiricism (as usually interpreted) is an example. By restricting knowledge to experience, (knowable) reality is itself in effect restricted to (atomistic) events given in experience. In consequence, any generalist claims are restricted to formulations of regularities in the succession and coexistence of these phenomena, to elaborations of Humean causal laws.

Just as empiricists in the Humean mode presuppose a (knowable) reality of atomistic events and states of affairs given in experience, so radical constructivists necessarily recognise a reality of the text (or the conversation or some such) and all its presuppositions. Even if discourse or conversation is thought only to be about discourse or conversation, the text being discussed in a particular discourse is at the level of ontology, it constitutes the referent of thought and knowledge, and the ongoing discourse-making reference is at the level of epistemic practice, the process of knowledge. There is nothing in philosophical realism that warrants that ontology is restricted to things immutable or known infallibly, etc. Certainly, any text is real and a potential object of knowledge. And this remains so even if someone voices disagreement with aspects of it, and even if the author changes her or his own view as a result, or even if the reader has not fully understood the author's intention.

6 For an introduction to some of this literature, see especially Margaret Archer *et al.* 1998.

7 I am not sure any contributor would want to put things quite so starkly as this. But it is a (polar) conception to which allusions appear sometimes to be made (or are easily interpreted as being made) even in the best of feminist writing. Helen Longino's important contributions provide a prominent example. In a statement about realism that is otherwise helpful she writes of 'the idea that there is one consistent, integrated or coherent, true theoretical treatment of all natural phenomena. ... These ideas are part of the realist tradition in the philosophy of science'. And a few lines below she adds: 'Even more, the scientific inquirer, and we with her, become passive onlookers, victims of the truth. The idea of a value-free science is integral to this view of scientific inquiry' (Helen Longino 1987: 256–7. See also Longino 1990: 29).

In similar fashion Mary Tiles (employing capital letters as a distancing device, in a manner adopted in economics for example by Deirdre McCloskey [1997]) writes:

> we see increasing numbers of philosophers of science rallying under the banner of Realism to defend the view of science as aiming at objective Truth and as possessed of methods of theory choice which, even if they do not guarantee truth, do at least ensure objectivity by preventing the intrusion of non-scientific interests or values into theory choice.
>
> (Tiles 1987: 221)

It is easy to see how influential assessments such as these (whether or not couched in terms of *scientific* realism and even allowing for their particular contexts) might encourage the view that all scientific realisms take, or at least tend towards, the narrow absolutist perspective described. My suspicion is that it is by way of universalising this very narrow version to cover the entire perspective of scientific realism, that the latter, and in particular the activity of explicit ontological elaboration closely associated with it, tends to be played down if not altogether excluded from serious discussion and debate. In this way there is a real possibility that, in feminist thinking, scientific realism is itself in effect marginalised through misrepresentation.

8 See for example McCloskey's (1997) 'You shouldn't want a Realism if you have a Rhetoric' as a recent example of attempting to play down the role of explicitly realist considerations in economics.

9 Before indicating how this constructive input might be achieved, though, I must make sure that I do not myself knowingly falsely universalise here. Specifically, I should acknowledge that there are at least some feminist theorists sensitive to, and who explicitly acknowledge, the fact that there is far more to realism than the naive or absolutist conception that some may be erroneously generalising (see, for example, Miranda Fricker 1994; Jean Grimshaw 1986; Marina Lazreg 1994; Martha Nussbaum 1995; Caroline New 1998; Janet Seiz 1993; 1995; Kate Soper 1991). However, this group does seem to constitute a relatively small minority, as some of the individuals concerned themselves observe.

10 For an indication of how dominant is the practice of formalistic modelling in modern mainstream economics, see Diana Strassmann's (1994) discussion.

11 A good preliminary discussion of alternative methods based on more qualitative approaches is provided by a set of contributions – by Günseli Berik; Joyce P. Jacobsen and Andrew A. Newman; Irene van Staveren; Simel Esim; and Jennifer C. Olmsted – collected together by Michèle Pujol (1997), for a 'special issue' of *Feminist Economics* entitled 'Expanding the Methodological Boundaries of Economics'.

12 A response that to some extent is already being realised. (See, for example, Esther Redmount 1995; Shelly Phipps and Peter S. Burton 1995; or Notburga Ott 1995.)

13 In their daily activities, then, human beings draw upon social structure which, in turn, is reproduced or transformed through human action taken in total. Although human acts may sometimes be performed with the intention of (1) reproducing structure (speaking to a child with the intention of imparting knowledge of language) or (2) transforming structure (collective attempts to change some feature of the current economic or legal system), it is likely that most structural reproduction and/or transformation arises as an

unintended product, whether or not desired or even recognised. Of course, if the reproduction/transformation of social structure is only rarely recognised by individuals or their reason for acting in the way they do, individuals usually have some motivation for, and conception of what they are doing in, their activity. Human acts are mostly if not always intentional under some description. Even if most speakers of English, say, are not intending, in their individual speech acts, to reproduce that language, its reproduction neverthe-less is the sum result of the speech acts in which English speakers engage, just as the speech acts in which individual agents engage always have their own intended objectives.

If the reproduction/transformation of social structure is rarely an intended project, it is equally the case that the individual agents are not always aware, certainly not discursively or self-consciously so, of the structures (such as language rules) upon which they are drawing. The picture that emerges, then, is one of largely unmotivated and only partially grasped social repro-duction. Individuals draw upon existing social structure as a typically unacknowledged condition for acting, and through the action of all individ-uals taken in total, social structure is typically unintentionally reproduced. Social structure in general is neither created by, nor independent of, human agency, but rather is the unmotivated condition of all our motivated produc-tions, the non-created but drawn upon and reproduced/transformed condition for our daily economic/social activities. For an elaboration on all this see Lawson 1997a: esp. chs 12 and 13.

14 Of course, both orientations are causal and have become historically associ-ated in economics. The point is that as long as economists keep to their formalistic methods they are constrained from dealing with realistic accounts, even if so inclined. But the method and the theory are currently so inter-twined that it is easy to support Michèle Pujol's conclusion:

> Can neoclassical economics be cleansed of its patriarchal bias so that it can open its eyes to the methodological flaws resulting from its ingrained sexism? ... I want to suggest that the very logic, rhetoric and symbolism of the paradigm may be inseparable from the ... sexist assumptions I have discussed here. Neoclassical economics has a *his*tory of stifling feminist approaches. We cannot wait for change. We must transcend it.
>
> (Pujol 1995: 29, 30)

See also Martha McDonald's (1995) assessment that 'economic theory and methodology both have to change if they are to serve feminist purposes, and the changes are interactive' (191).

15 Of course all reasoning is fallible, including ontological analysis of the sort presented here. On the pluralist/anti-dogmatic grounds of not wishing to foreclose any line of epistemic activity (in case it proves illuminating), there-fore, I do not conclude that we need to reject all formalistic modelling out of hand. But I do think we must accept that there are compelling grounds for expecting the dismal record of generalised failure to continue (and for effecting a substantial reallocation of economics-research resources).

16 Contrastive explanation has been widely discussed over the last twenty years, of course (see for example, Bas van Fraassen 1980; Alan Garfinkel 1981; David Lewis 1986; Peter Lipton 1991). However, whilst I think it is fair to say that much of this literature has been concerned with applied explanation,

with considering whether known factors can be said to constitute an (adequate) explanation, I am here concerned with the role of contrastive phenomena in the process of identifying causes that are unknown or hitherto unrecognised.

17 Perhaps this recognition lends support to Donna Haraway's remark that 'Feminist objectivity means quite simply *situated knowledges*' (Haraway 1988: 253).

18 These formutions, in turn, often critically built on Marx's analysis of contrasting 'class' positions in a capitalist society. A major contribution of this sort is Nancy Hartsock's (1983) 'The Feminist Standpoint: Developing the Ground for a Specifically Feminist Historical Materialism'.

19 This thesis does, I think, closely resonate with those of other standpoint theorists. It has close affinities, for example, with Nancy Hartsock's (1983) insistence that 'A standpoint is not simply an interested position (interpreted as bias) but is interested in the sense of being engaged' (218). According to Hartsock,

> like the lives of proletarians according to Marxian theory, women's lives make available a particular and privileged vantage point on male supremacy, a vantage point which can ground a powerful critique of the phallocratic institutions and ideology which constitute the capitalist form of patriarchy.
>
> (Hartsock 1983: 217)

It also fits closely with Patricia Hill Collins' (1991) discussion of the 'outsiders within' and with Dorothy Smith's (1987; 1990) notion of 'bifurcated consciousness'.

20 All we have are different voices, interests and values, and the absence of any non-arbitrary way for distinguishing between them. Each claim is as good as any other. There is no basis for progress, criticism, or any kind of engagement with our times. We have what we have; a situation to be described, perhaps, but not to be judged or criticised. As Susan Bordo summarises the situation:

> Assessing where we are now, it seems to me that feminism stands less in danger of the totalizing tendencies of feminists than of an increasingly paralysing anxiety over falling (from what grace?) into ethnocentrism or 'essentialism.' ... Do we want to delegitimate *a priori* the exploration of experimental continuity and structural common ground among women? ... If we wish to empower diverse voices, we would do better, I believe, to shift strategy from the methodological dictum that we foreswear talk of 'male' and 'female' realities ... to the messier, more slippery, practical struggle to create institutions and communities that will not permit *some* groups of people to make determinations about reality for *all*.
>
> (Bordo 1993: 465)

or as Kate Soper complains:

> the logic which challenged certain kinds of identity thinking and deconstructed specific notions of truth, progress, humanism and the like, has pushed on to question the possibility of objectivity or of making reference in language to what itself is not the effect of discourse ... Pushed to

its uttermost, the logic of difference rules out *any* holistic and objective analysis of societies of a kind which allows to define them as 'capitalist' or 'patriarchal' or indeed totalitarian, together with the transformative projects such analyses advocate. It gives us not new identities, not a better understanding of the plural and complex nature of society, but tends rather to collapse into an out and out individualism.

(Soper 1991: 45)

21 Clearly, needs and rights can be formulated as goals or wants or demands, and treated as legitimate or illegitimate, only under definite historical conditions. As such they may be poorly, and even misleadingly, formulated. Specifically, real needs can be manifest in a variety of historically contingent wants, which may then be met by any of perhaps a multitude of potential satisfiers. It follows that to assume either actual satisfiers (e.g. specific commodities purchased or perhaps acts of violence) or expressed objectives (such as owning more than others) are defining of human needs is to commit an ethical fallacy – to reduce needs to wants and wants to the conditions of their being satisfied or expressed.

I am not suggesting that wants as expressed in actions bear no relation to underlying needs, of course. Indeed, although certain activities sometimes appear quite undesirable from the point of view of facilitating human development and potential, it is often easy enough to see how they are nevertheless motivated by various real needs on the part of the perpetrators – for example, to obtain respect from others, inner security or simply a release of frustration. But it is important that real needs and expressed wants are not conflated (which is just what tends to happen in modern mainstream economics of course, a mistake that is encouraged by that project's continuing neglect of explicit ontological analysis). For a lengthier discussion of all this see Lawson (1997a).

22 Consider, for example, Kate Soper's UK-based experience. In arguing that 'there are some concrete and universal dimensions to women's lives', she illustrates with the case of solitude:

I mean that women live in a kind of alertness to the possibility of attack and must to some degree organize their lives in order to minimize its threat. In particular, I think, this has constraints – from which men are free – on our capacity to enjoy solitude. As a woman, one's reaction to the sight of a male stranger approaching on a lonely road or country walk is utterly different from one's reaction to the approach of a female stranger. In the former case there is a frisson of anxiety quite absent in the latter. This anxiety, of course, is almost always confounded by the man's perfectly friendly behaviour, but the damage to the relations between the sexes has already been done – and done not by individual men and women – but by their culture. This female fear and the constraints it places on what women can do – particularly in the way of spending time on their own – has, of course, its negative consequences for men too, most of whom doubtless deplore its impact on their own capacities for spontaneous relations with women. … But the situation all the same is not symmetrical: resentment or regret is not as disabling as fear; and importantly it does not affect the man's capacity to go about on his own.

(Soper 1990: 242)

23 This is a topic I explore more fully elsewhere (Lawson 1997a). It is also central to various contributions in Archer *et al.* 1998.

10 An explanation of the mathematising tendency in modern economics

1 Clearly this chapter will not be addressing questions of ontology. It does, though, address a set of questions that are rendered especially interesting if the perspective on ontology taken in this book is accepted.

2 A biological token being the Lamarckian model.

3 See, for example, Deakin and Wilkinson (2000) for a wider study of how conventions can operate to structure capabilities and opportunities of individuals within the labour market.

4 Differently put, the transformational model requires supplementing with concrete detail to understand its operation at relevant points in place and time.

5 In an autobiographical note Walras records how the wishes of his father convinced him to devote his career to continuing his father's work and produce a pure political economy 'in mathematical form' (Walras 1893). Though his idea for a science of mathematical economics had been clear about fifteen years earlier, it was in his *Eléments d'économie politique pure*, published between 1874 and 1879, that Walras' major contribution to the mathematising project appeared.

6 Of course even at the level of methodology there is more to Newton's contribution than this form of 'Newtonianism'. Indeed, Newton's method of analysis and synthesis was very much oriented to identifying the underlying causes of phenomena. It just so happens that some of his most spectacular findings lend themselves to mathematical representation. An unfortunate result of this has been a widespread tendency to conflate Newton's method with a way of presenting some of his results (on all this see Montes 2003, forthcoming).

7 There were, though, exceptions. Dupuit pursued the mathematisation project but supported the remainder of the liberal programme, and seems to have received some accommodation.

8 In other words, mathematical economists, in perhaps trying too hard to be scientific, whilst associating the latter in an essential way with the use of mathematics, are neglecting reality. Consider the assessment of the mathematician Kline (1964) writing a half century ago about the two centuries prior to that:

> Perhaps the severest criticism that may be levelled at the eighteenth- and nineteenth-century workers in the social sciences is that they were too mathematical and not sufficiently scientific. They wanted to find axioms or general principles from which the science of politics and economics would readily follow. But very few would, like Montesquieu, examine society itself, first to check the correctness of their axioms, and later to check their deductions.
>
> (Kline 1964: 339)

9 Gide, for example, established with Walras the *Revue d'Economie Politique*. And Colson attempted to save the mathematising project by providing a synthesis of liberalism and mathematics.

10 Contributions by the likes of Samuelson and Hicks cannot be overlooked, for example. To some extent these contributors can be viewed as attempting to

provide a general framework in which the various competing positions could be embedded and contrasted.

11 The group met in secret and took the name of a nineteenth-century French general whose name was already given to the street in which they met.

12 But see for example, Weintraub and Mirowski 1994 on the path of Debreu in particular. Or for Debreu's own account of this see especially Debreu 1984. And for an account of postwar French developments centring on the 1950s, see Arena 2000b.

13 As I say, substantive interpretations were not that constraining of what economists produced. For some, indeed, the ability of the mathematical infrastructure to stand on its own seems to have been at least as much of interest. Consider Debreu once more:

> The rigor that has been reached as a consequence is in sharp contrast to the standards of reasoning that were accepted in the late 1930's. Few of the articles published then by *Econometrica* or by the *Review of Economic Studies* would pass the acid test of removing all their economic interpretations and letting their mathematical infrastructure stand on its own. The greater logical solidity of more recent analyses has contributed to the rapid contemporary construction of economic theory. It has enabled researchers to build on the work of their predecessors and to accelerate the cumulative process in which they are participating.
>
> (Debreu 1991: 3)

14 Consider Debreu's own observations:

> As the Second World War was drawing near its resolution, economic theory entered a phase of intensive mathematization that profoundly transformed our profession. In several of its main features that phase had no precedent …
>
> While the professional journals in the field of mathematical economics grew at an unsustainably rapid rate, the *American Economic Review* underwent a radical change in identity. In 1940, less than 3 percent of the refereed pages of its 30th volume ventured to include rudimentary mathematical expressions. Fifty years later, nearly 40 percent of the refereed pages of the 80th volume display mathematics of a more elaborate type.
>
> At the same time, the mathematization of economists proceeded at an even faster pace in the 13 American departments of economics labelled by a recent assessment of research-doctorate programs in the United States (Lyle v. Jones et al. 1982) as 'distinguished' or 'strong' according to the scholarly quality of their faculties. Every year the Fellows of the *Econometric Society* (ES) certify new members by election into their international guild, which increased in size from 46 in 1940 to 422 in 1990. For those 13 departments together, the proportion of ES Fellows among professors was less than 1 percent in 1940; it is now close to 50 percent. It equals or exceeds 50 percent for six of them, which were among those assessed as the eight strongest. So mathematized a faculty expects its students to have what it considers to be minimal mathematical proficiency, and knowledge of calculus and linear algebra is required, or forcefully recommended, for admission to all 13 graduate programs.

Several scholarly recognitions lay additional emphasis on the role that mathematical culture is now playing in our profession. Of the 152 members of the economics section of the American Academy of Arts and Sciences, 87 are Fellows of the Econometric Society; and of the 40 members of the economics section of the National Academy of Sciences of the United States, 34 are ES Fellows. From 1969 to 1990, 30 economics Nobel awards were made, and 25 of the laureates are, or were, ES Fellows. Since it was first presented to Paul Samuelson in 1947, the John Bates Clark medal of the *American Economic Association* has been given to 21 economists, of whom 20 are ES Fellows; and of the 26 living past presidents of our Association, 13 are ES Fellows.

(Debreu 1991: 1–2)

15 Further, of course, the Nazi threat in Europe led to the immigration of numerous positivists or those of a scientistic disposition into the US.
16 Even if it is possible to trace the roots of this anti-intellectualism to the early European settlers or 'pioneers' (Hofstadter 1963).
17 I interpret Morgan and Rutherford as taking a similar view of the historical process (albeit seemingly conditioned by a more optimistic assessment than my own of the relevance of mathematics in economics) when they write:

The cold war enforced, if it did not create, the trend towards economists offering professionally neutral, objective expertise, which contrasted strongly with the ethical, and strongly held, advocacy of the late-nineteenth-century professional economist. Even in their 'evenhanded' mode, public statements of the late nineteenth century offered considerable political ammunition compared to the expert jargon and tool-kit style of postwar economics, which could be used to disguise theoretical content and ideology from the outside world.

Although this move to mathematics was partly a self-imposed defense undertaken by individuals ... it was also encouraged by academic institutions seeking 'safe' teachers and research institutes seeking 'acceptable' researchers.

(Morgan and Rutherford 1998: 16)

18 Consider Debreu's observations once more:

In the past two decades, economic theory has been carried away further by a seemingly irresistible current that can be explained only partly by the intellectual successes of its mathematization.

Essential to an attempt at a fuller explanation are the values imprinted on an economist by his study of mathematics. When a theorist who has been so typed judges his scholarly work, those values do not play a silent role; they may play a decisive role. The very choice of the questions to which he tries to find answers is influenced by his mathematical background. Thus, the danger is ever present that the part of economics will become secondary, if not marginal, in that judgment.

The reward system of our profession reinforces the effects of that auto-criticism. Decisions that shape the career of an economic theorist are made by his peers. Whether they are referees of a journal or of a research organization, members of an appointment or of a promotion committee, when they sit as judges in any capacity, their verdicts will not be independent of their own values. An economist who appears in their court rarely ignores his perception of those values. If he believes that they rate mathematical sophistication highly, and if he can prove that he is one of the sophisticates, the applause that he expects to receive will condition his performance.

The same effects are also amplified by the relentless pressure to publish exerted by his environment.

(Debreu 1991: 5)

19 Some mathematical economists like Debreu see this too:

The spread of mathematized economic theory was helped even by its esoteric character. Since its messages cannot be deciphered by economists who do not have the proper key, their evaluation is entrusted to those who have access to the code. But acceptance of their technical expertise also implies acceptance of their values.

(Debreu 1991: 6)

20 In Lawson (1997a: 180–6) I suggested that the nature and extensiveness of the routinisation of human behaviour is explained by a deep-seated psychological need for ontological security, for continuity, stability and sameness in daily life, the avoidance of radical disruption. The lack of stability and continuity makes us anxious. Keynes too noticed this psychological need in analysing how investors cope with uncertainty. Keynes, indeed, takes the view that the practice of assuming things will continue as they are (that the world is not open) is so deep-rooted in our behaviour that 'it continues to influence our minds even in those cases where we do have good reasons to expect a definite change' (1973c: 125); that 'the idea of the future being different from the present is so repugnant to our conventional modes of thought and behaviour that we, most of us, offer a great resistance to acting on it in practice' (1973c: 125). Perhaps this psychological need helps explain the persistence of the role of mathematics in modern culture, in that it sometimes overwhelms the recognition that the world is fundamentally open. If so, there is an irony in the fact that certain rationalistic tendencies in modern society are sustained only by ignoring the implications of reason. In any case, an investigation into the psychological need to suppose that all reality conforms to the dictates of closed-system, mathematical logic, that all outcomes are deducible or predictable, promises to be a fruitful line of enquiry.

21 Nelson (2002), for example, points to a 'feminist critique of economic methodology' which springs

from a deep analysis of the social, historical, and psychosexual meanings the traditional image of science holds for its participants. The idea that the universe may be open, in some ways fundamentally unpredictable, and intrinsically purposive – in contrast to being a closed system, ultimately distillable into formulae, controllable, and fundamentally indifferent – is not simply a reasonable alternative ontology that can be carefully weighed for its logical implications and neutrally evaluated for its relative merit. ... The idea of an open universe feels fundamentally *scary* for those who feel that not only their status as scientists set above the objects they study, but also their safety vis-à-vis chaos, their 'manhood' (whether actual, or, in the case of female scientists, symbolic), and their very own distinct selfhood are threatened unless they can keep the living, novel, relational aspects of nature safely at bay.

(Nelson 2003: 3)

See also studies on autism and Asperger's syndrome, which do indeed suggest that orientations to such matters are gender-differentiated (Baron-Cohen and Hammer 1997; Baron-Cohen *et al.* 2002; J. Lawson 2002; J. Lawson *et al.* 2002).

BIBLIOGRAPHY

Abelson, Peter (1996) 'Declining Enrolments in Economics: The Australian experience', *Royal Economic Society Newsletter*, no. 95, 19–20.

Ackroyd, Stephen and Steven Fleetwood (eds) (2000) *Realist Perspectives on Management Organisations*, London and New York: Routledge.

Allais, Maurice (1992) 'The Economic Science of Today and Global Disequilibrium', in Mario Baldassarri, John McCallum and Robert Mundell (eds) *Global Disequilibrium in the World Economy*, Basingstoke: Macmillan.

Archer, Margaret (1995) *Realist Social Theory: The Morphogenetic Approach*, Cambridge: Cambridge University Press.

——(2000) *Being Human: The Problem of Agency*, Cambridge: Cambridge University Press.

Archer, Margaret, Roy Bhaskar, Andrew Collier, Tony Lawson and Alan Norrie (1998) *Critical Realism: Essential Readings*, London: Routledge.

Archer, Margaret and Jonathan Q. Tritter (eds) (2000) *Rational Choice Theory: Resisting Colonization*, London and New York: Routledge.

Arena, Richard (2000a) 'Jean-Baptiste Say and the French Liberal School of the Nineteenth Century: Outside the Canon?', in Sandra Peart (ed.) *Reflections on the Classical Canon: Essays in Honour of Samuel Hollander*, London: Routledge.

——(2000b) 'Les économistes français en 1950', *Revue économique*, vol. 51, no. 5, September, 969–1007.

Arestis, Philip (1990) 'Post-Keynesianism: A New Approach to Economics', *Review of Social Economy*, vol. XLVIII, no. 3, fall, 222–246.

——(1996) 'Post-Keynesian Economics: Towards Coherence, Critical Survey', *Cambridge Journal of Economics*, vol. 20, 111–35.

Arestis, Philip, Stephen P. Dunn and Malcolm Sawyer (1999a) 'Post Keynesian Economics and Its Critics', *Journal of Post Keynesian Economics*, vol. 21, 527–49.

——(1999b) 'On the Coherence of Post Keynesian Economics: a comment upon Walters and Young', *Scottish Journal of Political Economy*, vol. 46, no. 3, 339–45.

Arestis, Philip, Meghnad Desai and Sheila Dow (eds) (2002) *Methodology, Microeconomics and Keynes: Essays in honour of Victoria Chick, Volume Two*, London: Routledge.

Assister, Alison (1996) *Enlightened Women: Modernist Feminism in a Postmodern Age*, London and New York: Routledge.

Aunger, Robert (ed.) (2000) *Darwinizing Culture: The Status of Memetics as a Science*, Oxford: Oxford University Press.

347

D'Autume, Antoine and Jean Cartelier (eds) (1997) *Is Economics becoming a Hard Science?*, Cheltenham: Edward Elgar.

Ayres, Clarence E. (1963) 'The Legacy of Thorstein Veblen', in J. Dorfman (ed.) *Institutional Economics: Veblen, Commons and Mitchell Reconsidered*, Berkeley and Los Angeles: University of California Press.

Badgett, M. V. Lee (1995) 'Gender, Sexuality, and Sexual Orientation: All in the Feminist Family?', *Feminist Economics*, vol. 1, no. 1, 121–39.

Baron-Cohen, Simon and Jessica Hammer (1997) 'Is Autism an Extreme Form of the Male Brain?', *Advances in Infancy Research*, vol. 11, 193–217.

Baron-Cohen, Simon, Sally Wheelwright, John Lawson, Rick Griffin and Jacqui Hill (2002) 'The Exact Mind: Empathising and Systemising in Autism Spectrum Conditions', in U. Goswami (ed.) *Handbook of Cognitive Development*, Oxford: Blackwell.

Baudrillart, Henri (1872) *Manuel d'Economie Politique*, Paris: Guillaumin.

Baumol, William J. (1992) 'Towards a Newer Economics: The Future Lies Ahead!', in John D. Hey (ed.) *The Future of Economics,* Oxford: Blackwell.

Beasley, Chris (1999) *What is Feminism?*, London: Sage.

Bell, Daniel and Irving Kristol (eds)(1981) *The Crisis in Economic Theory*, New York: Basic Books.

Berik, Günseli (1997) 'The Need for Crossing the Method Boundaries in Economics Research', *Feminist Economics*, vol. 3, no. 2, 121–6.

Bhaskar, Roy (1978) *A Realist Theory of Science*, Hemel Hempstead: Harvester Press (1st edn Leeds 1975).

——(1979) *The Possibility of Naturalism: A philosophical critique of the contemporary human sciences*, Hemel Hempstead: Harvester Press.

——(1993) *Dialectic: The Pulse of Freedom*, London and New York: Verso.

——(1994) *Plato etc. : the problems of philosophy and their resolution*, London and New York: Verso.

——(2000) *From East to West: Odyssey of a Soul*, London: Routledge.

Bhaskar, Roy and Andrew Collier (1998) 'Explanatory Critiques', in Margaret Archer, Roy Bhaskar, Andrew Collier, Tony Lawson and Alan Norrie (1998) *Critical Realism: Essential Readings*, London: Routledge.

Blackmore, Susan (1999a) *The Meme Machine*, Oxford: Oxford University Press.

——(1999b) 'Meme, Myself and I', *New Scientist*, March, 40–4.

——(1999c) 'The Forget-Meme-Not Theory', *Times Higher Educational Supplement*, February.

——(2000a) 'Can Memes Get off the Leash?', in Robert Aunger (ed.) *Darwinizing Culture: The Status of Memetics as a Science*, Oxford: Oxford University Press.

——(2000b) 'The Power of Memes', *Scientific American*, vol. 283, no. 4, 52–61.

Blaug, Mark (1980) *The Methodology of Economics: Or How Economists Explain*, Cambridge: Cambridge University Press.

——(1997) 'Ugly Currents in Modern Economics', *Options Politiques*, Vol. 18, no. 17, September, 3–8.

Bloom, Allan (1987) *The Closing of the American Mind: How Higher Education Has Failed Democracy and Impoverished the Souls of Today's Students*, New York: Simon and Schuster.

Boag, Peter T. and Peter R. Grant (1981) 'Intense Natural Selection in a Population of Darwin's Finches (*Geospizinae*) in the Galápagos', *Science*, 214: 82–5.

Boettke, Peter J. (1989) 'Evolution and Economics: Austrians as Institutionalists', *Research in the History of Economic Thought and Methodology*, 73, 91.

Bordo, Susan (1993) 'Feminism, Post Modernism and Gender Scepticism', in *Unbearable Weight: Feminism, Western Culture, and the Body*, The Regents of the University of California; reprinted in Anne C. Herrmann and Abigail Stewart (eds) (1994) *Theorizing Feminism: Parallel Trends in the Humanities and Social Sciences*, Boulder, San Francisco and Oxford: Westview Press (page references to the latter).

Boudon, Raymond (1991) 'What Middle Range Theories are', *Contemporary Sociology*, vol. 20, no. 4, 519–22.

Bourdieu, Pierre (1990) *The Logic of Practice*, trans. Richard Nice, Cambridge: Polity Press.

Boyd, Richard (1988) 'How to be a Moral Realist', in Geoffrey Sayre-McCord (ed.) *Essays on Moral Realism*, Ithaca NY and London: Cornell University Press.

——(1993) 'Metaphor and Theory Change: What is "Metaphor" a Metaphor for?', in A. Ortony (ed.) *Metaphor and Thought*, 2nd edn (1st edn 1979) Cambridge: Cambridge University Press.

Brereton, Derek (2000) 'Innate Virtue', *Alethia* vol. 3, no. 2, 21–9.

Brodie, Richard (1996) *Virus of the Mind: The New Science of the Meme*, Seattle: Integral Press.

Brown, Andrew (2000) 'A Comment on Dow's "Post Keynesianism and critical realism: what is the connection?" ', *Journal of Post Keynesian Economics*, vol. 23, no. 2, 349–55, winter.

Brown, Andrew, Steven Fleetwood and Michael Roberts (eds) (2002a) *Critical Realism and Marxism*, London and New York: Routledge.

Brown, Andrew, Gary Slater and David Spencer (2002b) 'Driven to abstraction? Critical Realism and the Search for the '"Inner Connection" of Social Phenomena", *Cambridge Journal of Economics*, vol. 26, no. 6, 773–88.

Burkhardt, Richard W. Jr (1977) *The Spirit of the System: Lamarck and Evolutionary Biology*, Cambridge: Cambridge University Press.

——(1984) 'The Zoological Philosophy of J. B. Lamarck', in J. B. de Lamarck [1809] *Zoological Philosophy: An Exposition with Regard to the Natural History of Animals*, trans. Elliot from the first (French) edition of 1809, Chicago: Chicago University Press, xv–xxxix.

Cannan, Edwin (1903) *Elementary Political Economy*, London.

Carter, Robert (2000) *Realism and Racism: Concepts of Race in Sociological Research*, London and New York: Routledge.

Cartwright, Nancy (2001) 'Ceteris paribus laws and socio-economic machines', in Uskali Mäki (ed.) (2001) *The Economic Worldview*, Cambridge: Cambridge University Press.

Castells, Manuel (1996) *The Rise of The Network Society*, Oxford: Blackwell.

Chick, Victoria (1998) 'On Knowing One's Place: The Role of Formalism in Economics', *Economic Journal*, vol. 108, no. 45, November, 1850–69.

Chote, Robert (1995) 'Decay of the Dismal Science', *Financial Times*, 28 March.

Clower, Robert W. (1999) in Brian Snowdon and Howard Vane (eds) *Conversations with Leading Economists: Interpreting Modern Macroeconomics*, Cheltenham: Edward Elgar.

Coase, Ronald (1999) 'Interview with Ronald Coase', *Newsletter of the International Society for New Institutional Economics*, vol. 2, no. 1, spring.

Coats, A. W. Bob (1992) *On the History of Economic Thought: British and American Economic Essays, Volume I*, London and New York: Routledge.

Collier, Andrew (1989) *Scientific Realism and Socialist Thought*, Hemel Hempstead: Harvester Wheatsheaf.

——(1994) *Critical Realism: An Introduction to Roy Bhaskar's Philosophy*, London: Verso.

——(1999) *Being and Worth*, London: Routledge.

——(2001) *Christianity and Marxism: A Philosophical Contribution to Their Reconciliation*, London and New York: Routledge.

Collins, Patricia Hill (1991) *Black Feminist Thought: Knowledge, Consciousness and the Politics of Empowerment*, London and New York: Routledge.

Commons, John R. (1934) *Institutional Economics: Its Place in Political Economy*, New York: Macmillan; reprinted 1990 with introduction by M. Rutherford, New Brunswick: Transaction.

Costello, Neil (2000) *Stability and Change in High-tech Enterprises: Organisational Practices and Routines*, London: Routledge.

Creaven, Sean (2000) *Marxism and Realism: A Materialistic Application of Realism in the Social Sciences*, London and New York: Routledge.

Danermark, Berth, Mats Ekström, Liselotte Jakobsen and Jan Ch. Karlson (2002) *Explaining Society: Critical Realism in the Social Sciences*, London and New York: Routledge.

Darwin, Charles (1859) *On the Origin of Species by Means of Natural Selection, or Preservation of Favoured Races in the Struggle for Life*, 1st edn, London: John Murray. Facsimile reprint 1964 with introduction by Ernst Mayr, Cambridge MA: Harvard University Press.

——(1872) *On the Origin of Species by Means of Natural Selection, or Preservation of Favoured Races in the Struggle for Life*, 6th edn, with additions and corrections, London: John Murray.

—— (1880) 'Sir Wyville Thomson and Natural Selection', *Nature*, 11 November, vol. XXIII, 32.

Davidson, Paul (1978) *Money and the Real World*, 2nd edn, London: Macmillan.

——(1980) 'Post Keynesian Economics', *The Public Interest, Special Edition*, 151–73; reprinted in D. Bell and I. Kristol (eds) *The Crisis in Economic Theory*, New York: Basic Books, 1981.

——(1989) 'The Economics of Ignorance or the Ignorance of Economics?', *Critical Review*, 3, 467, 487.

——(1991) 'Is Probability Theory Relevant for Uncertainty?', *Journal of Economic Perspectives*, vol. 5, no. 1, 129–43.

——(1994) *Post Keynesian Macroeconomic Theory*, Aldershot: Edward Elgar.

——(1996) 'Reality and Economic Theory', *Journal of Post Keynesian Economics*, vol. 18, no. 4, summer, 479–508.

Davis, John B. (2001) 'Agent Identity in Economics', in Uskali Mäki (ed.) *The Economic Worldview*, Cambridge: Cambridge University Press.

——(2002) 'Collective Intentionality and Individual Behaviour', in Edward Fullbrook (ed.) *Intersubjectivity in Economics: Agents and Structures*, London: Routledge.

——(forthcoming a) *The Theory of the Individual in Economics*, London and New York: Routledge.

——(forthcoming b) 'The Agency-Structure Model and the Embedded Individual in Heterodox Economics', in Paul Lewis (ed.) *Transforming Economics: Perspectives on the Critical Realist Project*, London and New York: Routledge.

Dawkins, Richard (1976) *The Selfish Gene*, Oxford: Oxford University Press.

——(1978) 'Replicator Selection and the Extended Phenotype', *Zeitschrift für Tierpsychologie*, vol. 47, 61–76.

Dawkins, Richard (1986) *The Blind Watchmaker,* Harlow: Longman.

——(1993) 'Viruses of the Mind', in Bo Dahlbom (ed.) *Dennett and his Critics: Demystifying Mind*, Oxford: Blackwell, 13–27.

Deakin, Simon and Frank Wilkinson (2000) 'Capabilities, Spontaneous Order and Social Rights', ESRC Centre for Business Working Paper Series, Cambridge University.

Debreu, Gerard (1959) *Theory of Value: an atiomatic treatment of economic equilibrium*, New York: Wiley.

——(1984) 'Economic Theory in the Mathematical Mode', *American Economic Review*, vol. 74, no. 3, 267–78.

——(1991) 'The Mathematization of Economic Theory', *American Economic Review*, vol. 81, no. 1, 1–7.

Dennett, Daniel (1995) *Darwin's Dangerous Idea: evolution and the meaning of life*, London: Penguin.

Dennis, Ken (1994) 'Formalism in Economics', in Geoffrey Hodgson, Warren Samuels and Mark Tool (eds) *The Elgar Companion to Institutional and Evolutionary Economics*, vol. 1, Aldershot: Edward Elgar, 251–6.

——(1995) 'A Logical Critique of Mathematical Formalism in Economics', *Journal of Economic Methodology*, vol. 2, no. 2, 181–99.

Dicken, Peter (1998) *Global Shift: Transforming the World Economy*, London: Paul Chapman.

Donaldson, Peter (1984) *Economics of the Real World*, 3rd edn, Harmondsworth: Penguin.

Dopfer, Kurt (ed.) (2001) *Evolutionary Economics: Program and Scope*, Boston MA, Dordrecht and London: Kluwer Academic Publishers.

Dore, Ronald (ed.) (1995) *Convergence or Diversity? National Modes of Production in a Global Economy*, New York: Cornell University Press.

Dover, Gabriel (2001) 'Anti-Dawkins', in Hilary Rose and Steven Rose (eds) *Alas Poor Darwin: Arguments Against Evolutionary Psychology*, London: Vintage.

Dow, Sheila C. (1990) 'Post-Keynesianism as political economy: A Methodological Discussion', *Review of Political Economy*, 2–3, 345–58.

——(1992) 'Post Keynesian School', in D. Mair and A. Miller (eds) *A Modern Guide to Economic Thought: An Introduction to Comparative Schools of Thought in Economics* , Aldershot: Edward Elgar.

——(1997) 'Mainstream Economic Methodology', *Cambridge Journal of Economics*, vol. 21, no. 1, January, 73–93.

——(1999) 'Post Keynesianism and Critical Realism: What is the Connection?', *Journal of Post Keynesian Economics*, vol. 22, no. 1, 15–33.

——(2000) 'Brown's Comment: A Reply', *Journal of Post Keynesian Economics*, vol. 23, no. 2, winter, 357–60.

——(2002a) *Economic Methodology: An Inquiry*, Oxford: Oxford University Press.

——(2002b) 'Historical Reference: Hume and Critical Realism', *Cambridge Journal of Economics*, vol. 26, no. 6, 683–695.

Downward, Paul (1999) *Pricing Theory in Post Keynesian Economics: A Realist Approach*, Aldershot: Edward Elgar.

——(2000) 'A Realist Appraisal of Post Keynesian Pricing Theory', *Cambridge Journal of Economics*, vol. 24, no. 2, 211–24.

——(2002) 'Critical Realism, Empirical Methods and Inference: A Critical Discussion', *Cambridge Journal of Economics*, vol. 26, no. 4, 481–500.

——(forthcoming) *Applied Economics and the Critical Realist Critique*, London: Routledge.

Dugger, William M. and Howard J. Sherman (2000) *Reclaiming Evolution: A Dialogue between Marxism and Institutionalism on Social Change*, London and New York: Routledge.

Dunn, Stephen P. (2000) 'Wither Post Keynesianism', *Journal of Post Keynesian Economics*, vol. 22, no. 3, spring, 343–64.

——(2001) 'Bounded Rationality Is not Fundamental Uncertainty: A Post Keynesian Perspective', *Journal of Post Keynesian Economics*, vol. 23, no. 4, summer, 567–87.

Dupré, John (1993) *The Disorder of Things: Metaphysical Foundations of the Disunity of Science*, Cambridge MA: Harvard University Press.

——(1999) 'Review of *Economics and Reality*', *Feminist Economics*, vol. 5, no. 1, 121–6.

——(2001) 'Economics without Mechanism', in Uskali Mäki (ed.) *The Economic Worldview*, Cambridge: Cambridge University Press.

Eichner, Alfred S. (1985) *Towards a New Economics: Essays in Post-Keynesian and Institutionalist Theory*, London: Macmillan.

England, Paula (1993) 'The Separative Self: Androcentric Bias in Neoclassical Assumptions', in Marianne A. Ferber and Julie A. Nelson (eds) *Beyond Economic Man: Feminist Theory and Economics*, Chicago: University of Chicago Press, 37–53.

Engle, Robert, Clive Granger, Ramu Ramanathan, Vahid-Araghi Farshid and Casey Brace (1997) 'Short-run Forecasts of Electricity Loads and Peaks', *International Journal of Forecasting*, vol. 13, 161–74.

Esim, Simel (1997) 'Can Feminist Methodology Reduce Power Hierarchies in Research Settings?', *Feminist Economics*, vol. 3, no. 2, 137–40.

Faulkner, Philip (2002) 'Some Problems with the Conception of the Human Subject in Critical Realism', *Cambridge Journal of Economics*, vol. 26, no. 6, 739–51.

Ferber, Marianne A. and Julie A. Nelson (eds) (1993) *Beyond Economic Man: Feminist Theory and Economics*, Chicago: University of Chicago Press.

Finch, John H. and Robert McMaster (2002) 'On Categorical Variables and Non-Parametric Statistical Inference in the Pursuit of Causal Explanation', *Cambridge Journal of Economics*, vol. 26, no. 6, 753–72.

Fine, Ben (2001) *Social Capital versus Social Theory: Political Economy and Social Science at the Turn of the Millennium*, London and New York: Routledge.

——(forthcoming) 'Addressing the Critical and the Real in Critical Realism', in Paul Lewis (ed.) *Transforming Economics: Perspectives on the Critical Realist Project*, London and New York: Routledge.

Flax, Jane (1990) 'Postmodernism and Gender Relations in Feminist Theory', in Linda J. Nicholson (ed.) *Feminism/Postmodernism*, New York and London: Routledge, 39–62.

Fleetwood, Steven (1995) *Hayek's Political Economy: The Socio Economics of Order*, London: Routledge.

——(1996) 'Order Without Equilibrium: A Critical Realist Interpretation of Hayek's Notion of Spontaneous Order', *Cambridge Journal of Economics*, vol. 20, no. 6, 729–47.

——(2001) 'Causal Laws, Functional Relations and Tendencies', *Review of Political Economy*, vol. 13, no. 2, 201–20; reprinted in P. Downward (forthcoming 2002) *Applied Economics and the Critical Realist Critique*, Routledge: London.

——(2002) 'A Critical Realist Reply to Walters and Young', *Review of Political Economy* (forthcoming).

Fleetwood, Steven (ed.) (1999) *Critical Realism in Economics: Development and Debate*, London: Routledge.

Folbre, Nancy (1993) 'How Does She Know? Feminist Theories of Gender Bias in Economics', *History of Political Economy*, vol. 25, no. 4, 167–84.

Fontana, Giuseppe (2000) 'Post Keynesian and Circuitists on Money and Uncertainty: An Attempt at Generality', *Journal of Post Keynesian Economics*, vol. 32, no. 1, fall, 27–48.

Fricker, Miranda (1994) 'Knowledge as Construct: Theorizing the Role of Gender in Knowledge', in Kathleen Lennon and Margaret Whitford (eds) *Knowing the Difference: Feminist Perspectives in Epistemology*, London and New York: Routledge.

Friedman, Milton (1953) *Essays in Positive Economics*, Chicago: University of Chicago Press.

——(1999) 'Conversation with Milton Friedman', in Brian Snowdon and Howard Vane (eds) *Conversations with Leading Economists: Interpreting Modern Macroeconomics*, Cheltenham: Edward Elgar, 124–44.

Fullbrook, Edward (ed.) (2002) *Intersubjectivity in Economics: Agents and Structures*, London: Routledge.

——(2003) *The Crisis in Economics: Teaching, Practice and Ethics*, London and New York: Routledge, forthcoming.

Garfinkel, Alan (1981) *Forms of Explanation: Rethinking the Questions in Social Explanation*, New Haven: Yale University Press.

Gee, J. M. Alec (1991) 'The Neoclassical School', in Douglas Mair and Anne Miller (eds) *A Modern Guide to Economic Thought: An Introduction to Comparative Schools of Thought in Economics*, Aldershot: Edward Elgar, 71–108.

Giddens, Anthony (1984) *The Constitution of Society: Outline of the Theory of Structuration*, Oxford: Basil Blackwell.

Gillies, Donald and Grazia Ietto-Gillies (2002) 'Keynes's Notion of *Causa Causans* and Its Application to the Globalisation Process', in P. Arestis, M. Desai and S. Dow (eds) *Methodology, Microeconomics and Keynes: Essays in Honour of Victoria Chick, Volume Two*, London: Routledge.

Goldin, Claudia and Lawrence F. Katz (forthcoming) 'The Power of the Pill: Oral Contraceptives and Women's Career and Marriage Decisions, *Journal of Political Economy*.

Goodwin, Crawford. D. (1998) 'The Patrons of Economics in a Time of Transformation', in Mary S. Morgan and Malcolm Rutherford (eds) *From Interwar Pluralism to Postwar Neoclassicism*, annual supplement to vol. 30, *History of Political Economy*, Duke and London: Duke University Press.

Graça Moura, Mário da (1997) *Schumpeter's Inconsistencies and Schumpeterian Exegesis: Diagnosing the Theory of Creative Destruction*, Ph.D. dissertation, University of Cambridge.

——(2002) 'Metatheory as the Key to Understanding: Schumpeter after Shionoya', *Cambridge Journal of Economics*, vol. 26, no. 6, 805–21.

Grapard, Ulla (1995) 'Robinson Crusoe: The Quintessential Economic Man?', *Feminist Economics*, vol. 1, no. 1, 33–52.

Grimshaw, Jean (1986) *Feminist Philosophers: Women's Perspectives on Philosophical Traditions*, Brighton: Wheatsheaf Books.

Guesnerie, Roger (1997) 'Modelling and Economic Theory: Evolution and Problems', in Antoine D'Autume and Jean Cartelier (eds) *Is Economics becoming a Hard Science?*, Cheltenham: Edward Elgar, 85–91.

Hahn, Frank H. (1982) *Money and Inflation*, Oxford: Blackwell.

——(1985) 'In Praise of Economic Theory', the 1984 Jevons Memorial Fund Lecture, London: University College London.

——(1992a) 'Reflections', *Royal Economics Society Newsletter*, 77.

——(1992b) 'Answer to Backhouse: Yes', *Royal Economic Society Newsletter*, vol. 78, 5.

——(1994) 'An Intellectual Retrospect', *Banca Nazionale del Lavoro Quarterly Review*, vol. XLVIII, no. 190, 245–58.

Hamlin, Cynthia L. (2002) *Beyond Relativism: Raymond Boudon, Cognitive Rationality and Critical Realism*, London: Routledge.

Hamouda, Omar F. and Harcourt, Geoffrey C. (1988) Post-Keynesianism: From Criticism to Coherence?, *Bulletin of Economic Research*, 40, January, 1–34; reprinted in J. Pheby (ed.) (1989) *New Directions in Post-Keynesian Economics*, Aldershot: Edward Elgar.

Hands, D. Wade (1994) 'Blurred Boundaries: Recent Changes in the Relationship Between Economics and the Philosophy of Natural Science', *Studies in History and Philosophy of Science*, 25: 751–72.

——(2001) *Reflection Without Rules: Economic Methodology and Contemporary Science Theory*, Cambridge: Cambridge University Press.

Haraway, Donna (1985) 'A Manifesto for Cyborgs: Science, Technology, and Socialist Feminism in the 1980s', *Socialist Review*, vol. 15, no. 2, 65–108; reprinted in Donna Haraway (1991) *Simians, Cyborgs and Women: The Reinvention of Nature*, New York: Routledge and Chapman and Hall, 149–81, 243–8; also reprinted in Anne Herrmann and Abigail Stewart (eds) (1994) *Theorizing Feminism: Parallel Trends in the Humanities and Social Sciences*, Boulder, San Francisco and Oxford: Westview Press.

——(1988) 'Situated Knowledges: The Science Question in Feminism and the Privilege of Partial Perspective', *Feminist Studies*, vol. 14, no. 3, 575–99.

Harcourt, Geoffrey C. (1985) 'Post-Keynesianism: Quite Wrong and/or Nothing New', in Philip Arestis and Thomas Skouras (eds) *Post Keynesian Economic Theory: A Challenge to Neo Classical Economics*, Brighton: Wheatsheaf.

——(1988) 'Post-Keynesian Economics', entry in John Eatwell, Murray Milgate and Peter Newman (eds) *The New Palgrave: A Dictionary of Economics*, London: Macmillan, 924, 928.

——(1995) 'On Mathematics and Economics', in *Capitalism, Socialism and Post-Keynesianism: Selected Essays of G. C. Harcourt*, Aldershot: Edward Elgar.

Harcourt, Geoffrey C. and Peter A. Riach (eds) (1997) *A 'Second Edition' of The General Theory*, 2 vols, London: Routledge.

Harding, Sandra (1993) 'Rethinking Standpoint Epistemology: What is "Strong Objectivity"?', in Linda Alcoff and Elizabeth Potter (eds) (1996) *Feminist Epistemologies*, New York: Routledge; reprinted in Evelyn Fox Keller and Helen E. Longino (eds) *Feminism and Science*, Oxford and New York: Oxford University Press (page references to the latter).

——(1995) 'Can Feminist Thought Make Economics More Objective?', *Feminist Economics*, vol. 1, no. 1, 7–32.

——(1998) *Is Science Multi-cultural?: Postcolonialisms, Feminisms and Epistemologies*, Bloomington and Indianapolis: Indiana University Press.

Hartsock, Nancy C. M. (1983) 'The Feminist Standpoint', in Sandra Harding and Merrill B. Hintikka (eds) *Discovering Reality: Feminist Perspectives on Epistemology, Metaphysics, Methodology, and Philosophy of Science*, Dordrecht: Reidel; reprinted in (for example) Linda Nicholson (ed.) *The Second Wave: A Reader in Feminist Theory*, London and New York: Routledge, 216, 40 (page references to the latter version).

Hausman, Daniel M. (1992) *The Inexact and Separate Science of Economics*, Cambridge: Cambridge University Press.

——(1994) 'Kuhn, Lakatos and the Character of Economics', in R. E. Backhouse (ed.) *New Directions in Economic Methodology*, London and New York: Routledge.

——(1998) 'Problems with Realism in Economics', *Economics and Philosophy*, vol. 14, no. 2, October, 185–213.

Hausman, Daniel M. and McPherson, Michael S. (1996) *Economic Analysis and Moral Philosophy*, Cambridge: Cambridge University Press.

Hayek, Friedrich A. (1988) *The Fatal Conceit: The Errors of Socialism*, London: Routledge.

Herrmann-Pillath, Carsten (2001) 'On the Ontological Foundations of Evolutionary Economics', in Kurt Dopfer (ed.) *Evolutionary Economics: Programme and Scope*, Boston MA, Dordrecht and London: Kluwer Academic Publishers.

Hey, John D. (ed.) (1992) *The Future of Economics*, Oxford: Blackwell.

Hicks, John (1986) 'Is Economics a Science?', in Mauro Baranzini and Roberto Scazzieri (eds) *Foundations of Economics: Structures of Inquiry and Economic Theory*, Oxford: Blackwell, 91–101.

Hirst, Paul and Grahame Thompson (1999) *Globalization in Question: The International Economy and the Possibilities of Governance*, 2nd edn, Cambridge: Polity Press.

Held, David and Anthony McGrew (eds) (2000) *The Global Transformations Reader: An Introduction to the Globalization Debate*, Cambridge: Polity Press.

Hendry, David F., Edward E. Leamer and Dale J. Poirier (1990) 'The ET dialogue; A Conversation on Econometric Methodology', *Econometric Theory*, vol. 6, No. 2, 171–261.

Hirshleifer, Jack (1985) 'The Expanding Domain of Economics', *American Economic Review*, vol. 75, no. 6, 53–68.

Hodgson, Geoffrey M. (1988) *Economics and Institutions: A Manifesto for a Modern Institutional Economics*, Cambridge: Polity Press.

——(1989) 'Post-Keynesianism and Institutionalism: The Missing Link', in J. Pheby (ed.) *New Directions in Post-Keynesian Economics*, Aldershot: Edward Elgar, 94–123.

——(1993) *Economics and Evolution: Bringing Life Back into Economics*, Cambridge and Ann Arbor: Polity Press and University of Michigan Press.

Hodgson, Geoffrey M. (ed.) (1995) 'Economics and Biology', in *The International Library of Critical Writings in Economics*, Cheltenham: Edward Elgar.

——(1996) 'Towards a Worthwhile Economics', in S. Medema and W. Samuels (eds) *Foundations of Research in Economics: How do Economists do Economics?*, Cheltenham: Edward Elgar.

——(1997) 'Economics and Evolution and the Evolution of Economics', in J. Reijnders (ed.) *Economics and Evolution*, Cheltenham: Edward Elgar.

——(1998a) 'The Approach of Institutional Economics', *Journal of Economic Literature*, vol. XXXVI, 166–92.

——(1998b) 'On the Evolution of Thorstein Veblen's Evolutionary Economics, *Cambridge Journal of Economics*, vol. 22, no. 4, 415–31.

——(ed.) (1998c) 'The Foundations of Evolutionary Economics: 1890–1973', in *The International Library of Critical Writings in Economics*, Cheltenham: Edward Elgar.

——(1998d) 'Veblen's *Theory of the Leisure Class* and the Genesis of Evolutionary Economics' in Warren J. Samuels (ed.) *The Founding of Evolutionary Economics*, London: Routledge 170–200.

——(1999a) *Economics and Utopia: Why the Learning Economy Is not the End of History*, London: Routledge.

——(1999b) *Evolution and Institutions: On Evolutionary Economics and the Evolution of Economics*, Cheltenham: Edward Elgar.

——(2001a) 'Is Social Evolution Lamarckian or Darwinian?', in John Laurent and John Nightingale (eds) *Darwinism and Evolutionary Economics*, Cheltenham: Edward Elgar, 87–118.

——(2001b) *How Economics Forgot History: The Problem of Historical Specificity in Social Science*, London and New York: Routledge.

Hofstadter, Richard (1963) *Anti-Intellectualism in American Life*, New York: Knopf.

Hoksbergen, Ronald (1994) 'Postmodernism and Institutionalism: Towards a Resolution of the Debate on Relativism', *Journal of Economic Issues*, vol. XXVIII, no. 3, September, 679–713.

Hoover, Kevin D. (1997) 'Econometrics and Reality', working paper, Department of Economics, University of California Davis.

——(2001a) *The Methodology of Empirical Macroeconomics*, Cambridge: Cambridge University Press.

——(2001b) *Causality in Macroeconomics*, Cambridge: Cambridge University Press.

Howell, David (2000) *The Edge of Now: New Questions for Democracy and the Network Age*, London: Macmillan.

Hull, David (1981) 'Units of Evolution: A Metaphysical Essay', in U. J. Jensen. and Rom Harré (eds) *The Philosophy of Evolution*, Brighton: Harvester Press, 23–44.

——(2000) 'Taking Memetics Seriously: Memetics Will Be What We Make It', in Robert Aunger (ed.) *Darwinizing Culture: The Status of Memetics as a Science*, Oxford: Oxford University Press.

Ingham, Geoffrey (1996) 'Money is a Social Relation', *Review of Social Economy*, vol. LIV, winter, 507–30; reprinted in Steven Fleetwood (ed.) (1999) *Critical Realism in Economics: Development and Debate*, London: Routledge.

Ingrao, Bruna and Giorgio Israel (1990) *The Invisible Hand*, Cambridge MA: MIT Press.

Jacobsen, Joyce P. and Andrew A. Newman (1997) 'What Data Do Economists Use? The Case of Labour Economics and Industrial Relations', *Feminist Economics*, vol. 3, no. 2, 127–30.

Jameson, Fredric (1991) *Postmodernism or The Cultural Logic of Late Capitalism*, London: Verso.

Jones, Lyle V., Gardner Lindzey and Porter E. Coggeshall (eds) (1982) *An Assessment of Research-Doctorate Programs in the United States: Social and Behavioral Sciences*, Washington DC: National Academy of Sciences Press.

Kaldor, Nicholas (1985) *Economics Without Equilibrium*, Cardiff: University College Cardiff Press.

Kanth, Rajani K. (1997) *Against Economics: Rethinking Political Economy*, Aldershot: Ashgate.

Kaul, Nitasha (2002) 'A Critical *Post* to Critical Realism', *Cambridge Journal of Economics*, vol. 26, no. 6, 709–26.

Kay, John (1995) 'Cracks in the Crystal Ball', *Financial Times*, 29 September.

Keynes, John M. (1933) *Essays in Biography*, London: Macmillan.

——(1973a) *The Collected Writings of John Maynard Keynes, vol. VII: The General Theory*, London: Royal Economic Society.

——(1973b) *The Collected Writings of John Maynard Keynes, vol. VIII: A Treatise on Probability*, London: Royal Economic Society.

——(1973c) *The Collected Writings of John Maynard Keynes, vol. XIV: The General Theory and After. Part II: Defence and Development*, London: Royal Economic Society.

Kincaid, Harold (2001) 'The Empirical Presuppositions of Metaphysical Explanations in Economics', in Uskali Mäki (ed.) *The Economic Worldview*, Cambridge: Cambridge University Press.

Kirman, Alan (1989) 'The Intrinsic Limits of Modern Economic Theory: The Emperor Has no Clothes', *Economic Journal*, vol. 99, no. 395, 126–39.

——(1997) 'The Evolution of Economic Theory', in Antoine D'Autume and Jean Cartelier (eds) *Is Economics becoming a Hard Science?*, Cheltenham: Edward Elgar, 92–7.

——(2001) 'Letter From France. The Teaching of Economics: Signes d'Alarme', *Royal Economic Society Newsletter*, no. 112, January, 7–8.

Kline, Morris (1964) [1953] *Mathematics in Western Culture*, Oxford: Oxford University Press.

Kozul-Wright, Richard and Robert Rowthorn (1998) 'Spoilt for Choice? Multinational Corporations and the Geography of International Production', *Oxford Review of Economic Policy*, vol. 14, no. 2, 74–92.

Krugman, Paul (1998) 'Two Cheers for Formalism', *Economic Journal*, vol. 108, no. 451, November 1829–36.

Kusch, Martin (1999) *Psychological Knowledge: A Social History and Philosophy*, London and New York: Routledge.

Lachmann, Ludwig (1971) *The Legacy of Max Weber*, Berkeley: Glendessery Press.

——(1991) 'Austrian Economics: A Hermeneutic Approach', in Don Lavoie (ed.) *Expectations and the Meaning of Institutions: Essays in Economics by Ludwig Lachmann*, London and New York: Routledge.

Lamarck, Jean Baptiste Pierre Antoine de (1984) [1809] *Zoological Philosophy: An Exposition with Regard to the Natural History of Animals*, trans. Elliot from the first (French) edition of 1809, Chicago: Chicago University Press.

Langlois, Richard N. (1986) 'The New Institutional Economics: An Introductory Essay', in Richard Langlois (ed.) *Economics as a Process: essays in the new institutional economics*, Cambridge: Cambridge University Press.

Lantner, Roland (1997) 'On Scientific Pluralism: Drawing a Comparison between Economics and Theoretical Physics', in Antoine D'Autume and Jean Cartelier (eds) *Is Economics becoming a Hard Science?*, Cheltenham: Edward Elgar, 50–74.

Latsis, Spiro J. (1976) 'A Research Programme in Economics', in Spiro J. Latsis (ed.) *Method and Appraisal in Economics*, Cambridge: Cambridge University Press.

Laurent, John and John Nightingale (eds) (2001) *Darwinism and Evolutionary Economics*, Cheltenham: Edward Elgar, 87–118.

Lavoie, Marc (1992) 'Towards a New Research Programme for Post-Keynesianism and New-Ricardisanism', *Review of Political Economy*, vol. 4, no. 1, 37, 78.

Lawson, Clive (1994) 'The Transformational Model of Social Activity and Economic Analysis: A Reinterpretation of the Work of J. R. Commons', *Review of Political Economy*, vol. 6, no. 2.

——(1995) 'Realism and Institutionalism: John R. Commons, Carl Menger and Economics with Institutions', Ph.D. dissertation, University of Cambridge.

——(1996a) 'Realism, Theory and Individualism in the Work of Carl Menger', *Review of Social Economy*, vol. LIV, no. 4, winter, 445–64; reprinted in Steven Fleetwood (ed.) (1999) *Critical Realism in Economics: Development and Debate*, London: Routledge..

——(1996b) 'Holism and Collectivism in the Work of Commons', *Journal of Economic Issues*, December vol. xxx, no.4, 967–84.

——(1999a) 'Towards a Competence Theory of the Region', *Cambridge Journal of Economics*, vol. 23, no. 2, 1999.

——(1999b) 'Commons' Contribution to Political Economy', in Philip O'Hara (ed.) *Encyclopedia of Political Economy*, London: Routledge.

——(2000) 'Collective Learning System Competences and Epistemologically Significant Moments', in David Keeble and Frank Wilkinson (eds) *High-Technology Clusters Networking and Collective Learning in Europe*, Aldershot: Ashgate.

——(2002) 'Technical Consultancies and Regional Competencies', in Charles Dannreuther and Wilfred Dolfsma (eds) *Globalisation, Social Capital and Inequality*, Cheltenham: Edward Elgar.

Lawson, Clive (forthcoming) 'A Transformational Conception of Technology', mimeo, Gonville and Caius College, Cambridge.

Lawson, Clive, Mark Peacock and Stephen Pratten (1996) 'Realism, Under-labouring and Institutions', *Cambridge Journal of Economics*, vol. 20, no. 1, January, 137–51.

Lawson, Clive and Edward Lorenz (1999) 'Collective Learning, Tacit Knowledge and Regional Innovative Capacity', *Regional Studies*, vol. 33, no. 4, 305–17.

Lawson, John (2002) 'Depth Accessibility Difficulties: An Alternative Conceptualisa-tion of Autism Spectrum Conditions', MIMEO: Departments of Experimental Psychology and Psychiatry, Cambridge.

Lawson, John, Simon Baron-Cohen and Sally Wheelwright (2002) 'Empathising and Systemising in Adults with and without Asperger's Syndrome', mimeo, University of Cambridge.

Lawson, Tony (1989) 'Abstraction, Tendencies and Stylised Facts: A Realist Approach to Economic Analysis', *Cambridge Journal of Economics*, vol. 13, no. 1, March, 59–78; reprinted in Tony Lawson, Gabriel Palma and John Sender (eds) (1989) *Kaldor's Political Economy*, London and San Diego: Academic Press; also reprinted in Paul Ekins and Manfred Max-Neef (eds) (1992) *Real-Life Economics: Understanding Wealth Creation*, London: Routledge.

——(1993) 'Keynes and Conventions', *Review of Social Economy*, vol. LI, summer, 174–201.

——(1994a) 'Realism and Hayek : A Case of Continuing Transformation', in Maria Colonna, Harald Hagemann and Omar F. Hamouda (eds) *Capitalism, Socialism and Knowledge: The Economics of F. A. Hayek*, vol. 2, Cheltenham: Edward Elgar.

——(1994b) 'The Nature of Post Keynesianism and its links to other traditions', *Journal of Post Keynesian Economics*, vol. 16, no. 4, summer, 503–38; reprinted in D. L. Prychitko (ed.) (1996) *Why Economists Disagree: An Introduction to the Contemporary Schools of Thought*, New York: State University of New York Press.

——(1994c) 'Economics and Expectations', in Shiela Dow and John Hillard (eds) *Keynes, Knowledge and Uncertainty*, Cheltenham: Edward Elgar.

——(1996) 'Developments in *Economics as Realist Social Theory*', *Review of Social Economy*, vol. LIV, no. 4, 405–22; reprinted in Steven Fleetwood (ed.) (1999) *Critical Realism in Economics: Development and Debate*, London: Routledge.

——(1997a) *Economics and Reality*, London: Routledge.

——(1997b) 'Situated Rationality', *Journal of Economic Methodology*, vol. 4, no. 1, 101–25.

——(1997c) 'Horses for Courses', in Philip Arestis, Gabriel Palma and Malcolm Sawyer (eds) *Markets, Unemployment and Economic Policy: Essays in Honour of Geoff Harcourt, Volume Two*, London and New York: Routledge, 1–15.

——(1997d) 'Development in Hayek's Social Theorising', in Frowen Stephen (ed.) *Hayek the Economist and Social Philosopher: A Critical Retrospect*, London: Macmillan.

——(1997e) 'Critical Issues in *Economics as Realist Social Theory*', *Ekonomia*, special issue on critical realism, vol. 1, no. 2, 75–117; reprinted in Steven Fleetwood (ed.) (1999) *Critical Realism in Economics: Development and Debate*, London: Routledge.

——(1998) 'Tendencies', in J. Davis, W. Hands and U. Mäki (eds) *The Edward Elgar Companion to Economic Methodology*, Cheltenham: Edward Elgar.

——(1999a) 'Connections and distinctions: Post Keynesianism and Critical Realism', *Journal of Post Keynesianism*, vol. 22, no. 1, 3–14.

——(1999b) 'Keynes' Realist Orientation', *The Keizai Seminar*, no. 537, 106–14.

——(2000) 'Evaluating Trust, Competition and Cooperation', in Yuichi Shionoya and Kiichiro Yagi (eds) *Competition, Trust and Cooperation: A Comparative Study*, New York, Berlin and Tokyo: Springer Verlag.

——(2002) 'Mathematical Formalism in Economics: What Really Is the Problem?' in Philip Arestis, Meghnad Desai and Sheila Dow (eds) *Methodology, Microeconomics and Keynes: Essays in Honour of Victoria Chick, Volume Two*, London: Routledge.

Layder, Derek (1993) *New Strategies in Social Research: An Introduction and Guide*, Cambridge: Polity Press.

——(1997) *Modern Social Theory: Key Debates and New Directions*, London: UCL Press.

Lazreg, Marnia (1994) 'Women's Experience and Feminist Epistemology: A Critical Neo-rationalist Approach', in Kathleen Lennon and Margaret Whitford (eds) *Knowing the Difference: Feminist Perspectives in Methodology*, London and New York: Routledge.

Leamer, Edward E. (1978) *Specification Searches: Ad hoc Inferences with Non-experimental Data*, New York: Wiley.

——(1983) 'Let's Take the Con out of Econometrics', *American Economic Review*, vol. 73, no. 1, 31–43.

Lee, Frederic S. (1995) 'The Death of Post Keynesianism', *Post Keynesian Economics Study Group Newsletter*, 4.

——(2002) 'Theory Creation and the Methodological Foundation of Post Keynesian Economics', *Cambridge Journal of Economics*, vol. 26, no. 6, 789–804.

Leontief, Wassily (1982) letter in *Science*, vol. 217, 104–7.

Lewis, David (1986) 'Causal Explanation', in *Philosophical Papers*, vol. II, 214–40, Oxford: Oxford University Press.

Lewis, Paul (1996) 'Metaphor and Critical Realism', *Review of Social Economy*, vol. LIV, no. 4, 487–506; reprinted in Stephen Fleetwood (ed.) (1999) *Critical Realism in Economics: Development and Debate*, London: Routledge.

——(2000a) 'Realism, Causality and the Problem of Social Structure', *Journal for The Theory of Social Behaviour*, vol. 30, no. 3, 249–68.

——(2000b) 'Does Metaphor Have a Place in a Realist Methodology of Economics?', mimeo, University of Cambridge.

——(2002a) 'Recent Developments in Economic Methodology: the Rhetorical and Ontological Turns', *Foundations of Science* (forthcoming).

——(2002b) 'Naturalism and the Rhetoric of Economics', in Justin Cruickshank (ed.) *Critical Realism: The Difference It Makes*, London and New York: Routledge.

——(2003) 'Boettke, the Austrian School, and the Reclamation of Reality in Modern Economics', *Review of Austrian Economics* (forthcoming).

Lewis, Paul (ed.) (forthcoming) *Transforming Economics: Perspectives on the Critical Realist Project*, London and New York: Routledge.

Lewis, Paul and Jochen Runde (1999) 'A Critical Realist Perspective on Paul Davidson's Methodological Writings on – and Rhetorical Strategy for – Post Keynesian Economics', *Journal of Post Keynesian Economics*, vol. 22, no. 1, 35–56.

Lipsey, Richard, G. (2001) 'Successes and Failures in the Transformation of Economics', *Journal Of Economic Methodology*, vol. 8, no. 2, June, 169–201.

Lipton, Peter (1991) *Inference to the Best Explanation*, London: Routledge.

Loasby, Brian J. (1999) *Knowledge, Institutions and Evolution in Economics*, London: Routledge.

Longino, Helen (1987) 'Can there be a Feminist Science?', *Hypatia*, vol. 2, no. 3, fall; reprinted in Ann Garry and Marilyn Pearsall (eds) (1996) *Women, Knowledge and Reality: Explorations in Feminist Philosophy*, London and New York: Routledge.

——(1990) *Science as Social Knowledge: Values and Objectivity in Scientific Enquiry*, Princeton: Princeton University Press.

Louçã, Francisco and Mark Perlman (eds) (2000) *Is Economics an Evolutionary Science? The Legacy of Thorstein Veblen*, Cheltenham: Edward Elgar.

Lucas, Robert E. (1986) 'Adaptive Behaviour and Economic Theory', *Journal of Business*, vol. 59, no. 4, 401–26.

Magnussen, Lars, and Jan Ottosson (eds) (1997) *Evolutionary Economics and Path Dependence*, Cheltenham: Edward Elgar.

Mäki, Uskali (1998) 'Aspects of Realism about Economics', *Theoria*, vol. 13, no. 2, 301–19.

Mäki, Uskali (ed.) (2001) *The Economic Worldview: Studies in the Ontology of Economics*, Cambridge: Cambridge University Press.

Marshall, Alfred (1986) [1920] *Principles of Economics*, 8th edn, London: Macmillan.

——(1906) letter to Arthur Lyon Bowley, in John K. Whitaker (ed.) (1996) *The Correspondence of Alfred Marshall, Economist, Volume Three: Towards the Close, 1903–1924*, Cambridge: Cambridge University Press.

——(1961) *The Principles of Economics*, 9th variorum edn, London: Macmillan.

Marx, Karl (1974) *Capital: Volume 1: A Critical Analysis of Capitalist Productions*, ed. Frederick Engels, London: Lawrence and Wishart.

——(1981) *Grundrisse: Foundations of the Critique of Political Economy*, rough draft, Harmondsworth: Penguin Books in association with *New Left Review*.

Marx, Karl and Freidrich Engels (1952) [1848] *Manifesto of the Communist Party*, Moscow: Progress Publishers.

Mayer, Thomas (1997) 'On the Usefulness of Economics', *Options Politiques*, September, 19–21.

Mayhew, Anne (1998a) 'On the Difficulty of Evolutionary Analysis', *Cambridge Journal of Economics*, vol. 22, no. 4 July, 449–61.

——(1998b) 'Veblen and the Anthropological Perspective', in Warren Samuels (ed.) (1998) *The Founding of Institutional Economics: The Leisure Class and Sovereignty*, London and New York: Routledge.

McCloskey, Donald N. (1983) 'The Rhetoric of Economics', *Journal of Economic Literature*, vol. xxi, June, 481–517.

——(1986) *The Rhetoric of Economics*, Brighton: Wheatsheaf.

McCloskey, Dierdre N. (1990) 'Storytelling in Economics', in Don Lavoie (ed.) *Economics and Hermeneutics*, London: Routledge, 61–75.

——(1997) 'You Shouldn't Want a Realism if You Have a Rhetoric', mimeo: Erasmus University of Rotterdam and the University of Iowa.

McDonald, Martha (1995) 'The Empirical Challenges of Feminist Economics: The Example of Economic Restructuring', in Edith Kuiper and Jolande Sap (eds) *Out of the Margin: Feminist Perspectives on Economics*, London and New York: Routledge, 175–97.

McKenna, Edward. J. and Diana Zannoni (1999) 'Post Keynesian Economics and Critical Realism: A Reply to Parsons', *Journal of Post Keynesian Economics*, vol. 22, no. 1, 57–70.

Merton, Robert K. (1968) *Social Theory and Social Structure*, 3rd edn, Glencoe: Free Press.

Midgley, Mary (2001) 'Why Memes?', in Hilary and Steven Rose (eds) *Alas Poor Darwin: Arguments against Evolutionary Psychology*, London: Vintage.

Mill, John Stuart (1900) *Principles of Political Economy with Some of Their Applications To Social Philosophy*, London: George Routledge & Sons.

——(1981) *A System of Logic Ratiocinative and Inductive: Being a Connected View of the Principles of Evidence and the Methods of Scientific Investigation*, 2 vols, ed. J. M. Robson, introduction by R. F. McRae, Toronto and Buffalo: University of Toronto Press.

Miller, Edith S. (1989) 'Comment of Boettke and Samuels: Austrian and Institutionalist Economics', *Research in the History of Economic Thought and Methodology*, 151, 158.

Mills, C. Wright (1959) *The Sociological Imagination*, Oxford: Oxford University Press.

Mirowski, Philip (1994) 'What Are the Questions?', in Roger E. Backhouse (ed.) *New Directions in Economic Methodology*, London and New York: Routledge.

——(2000) 'The Evolution of Market Automata and Some Implications for Financial Markets', mimeo, University of Notre Dame.

——(2001) *Machine Dreams: economics becomes a cyborg science*, Cambridge: Cambridge University Press.

Montes, Leonides (2003) 'Smith and Newton: Some Methodological Issues concerning General Equilibrium Theory', *Cambridge Journal of Economics* (forthcoming).

Morgan, Mary S. (2001) 'Models, Stories and the Economic World', *Journal of Economic Methodology*, vol. 8, no. 3, 361–84.

——(2002) 'Seeing the World in Models', mimeo: University of Amsterdam and London School of Economics, presented at Cambridge Realist Workshop, April 2002.

Morgan, Mary S. and Rutherford, Malcolm (1998) 'American Economics: The Character of the Transformation', in M. S. Morgan and M. Rutherford (eds) *From Interwar Pluralism to Postwar Neoclassicism*, annual supplement to vol. 30, *History of Political Economy*, Duke and London: Duke University Press.

Nell, Edward, J. (1998) *The General Theory of Transformational Growth: Keynes after Sraffa*, Cambridge: Cambridge University Press.

Nelson, Julie (1993) 'Value-Free or Valueless? Notes on the pursuit of Detachment in Economics', *History of Political Economy*, vol. 25, no.4, 121–43.

——(1996) *Feminism, Objectivity and Economics*, London: Routledge.

——(2003) 'Once More, With Feeling: Feminist Economics and the Ontological Question', *Feminist Economics* vol. 9, no. 1 (forthcoming; page references to a mimeo version).

Nelson, Richard and Sidney Winter (1982) *An Evolutionary Theory of Economic Change*, Cambridge MA: Harvard University Press.

New, Caroline (1998) 'Realism, Deconstruction and the Feminist Standpoint', mimeo: Bath Spa University College.

Nicita, Antonio and Ugo Pagano (eds) (2001) *The Evolution of Economic Diversity*, London and New York: Routledge.

Nielsen, Peter (2002) 'Reflections on Critical Realism in Political Economy', *Cambridge Journal of Economics*, vol. 26, no. 6, 727–38.

Norrie, Alan (2001) *Punishment, Responsibility and Justice: A Relational Critique*, Oxford: Oxford University Press.

Northover, Patricia (1995) 'On Explaining Economic Growth: A Methodological Enquiry', Ph.D. dissertation, University of Cambridge.

Nussbaum, Martha C. (1995) 'Human Capabilities, Female Human Beings', in Martha C. Nussbaum and Jonathan Glover (eds) *Women, Culture, and Development: A Study of Human Capabilities*, Oxford: Clarendon Press.

Nussbaum, Martha C. and Amartya Sen (eds) (1993) *The Quality of Life*, Oxford: Clarendon Press.

O'Driscoll, Gerald P. and Mario J. Rizzo (1985) *The Economics of Time and Ignorance*, Oxford: Blackwell.

Olmsted Jennifer C. (1997) 'Telling Palestinian Women's Economic Stories', *Feminist Economics*, vol. 3, no. 2, 141–51.

O'Neill, John (1998) *The Market: Ethics, Knowledge and Politics*, London: Routledge.

Ormerod, Paul (1994) *The Death of Economics*, London: Faber and Faber.

Ott, Notburga (1995) 'Fertility and Division of Work in The Family: A Game Theoretic Model of Household Decisions', in Edith Kuiper and Jolonde Sap (eds) *Out of the Margin: Feminist Perspectives on Economics*, London and New York: Routledge, 148–60.

Pagano, Ugo (forthcoming) 'Critical realism and institutionalism', in Paul Lewis (ed.) *Transforming Economics: Perspectives on the Critical Realist Project*, London and New York: Routledge.

Parker, Richard (1993) 'Can Economists Save Economics?', *The American Prospect*, vol. 4, no. 13, March, 21.

Parsons, Stephen (1995) 'Post Keynesian Realism and Keynes's General Theory', *Journal of Post Keynesian Economics*, vol. 18, no. 3, fall, 419–41.

Patomäki, Heikki (2002) *After International Relations: Critical Realism and the (Re)construction of World Politics*, London and New York: Routledge.

Pawson, Ray (1999) 'Middle-Range Realism', mimeo, Department of Sociology and Social Policy, Leeds University (paper presented at annual conference of the International Association for Critical Realism, Örebro, 1999).

Penrose, Edith (1952) 'Biological Analogies in the Theory of the Firm', *American Economic Review*, vol. XLII, no. 5, December, 804–19.

Peukert, Helge (2001) 'On the Origins of Modern Evolutionary Economics: The Veblen Legend after 100 years', *Journal of Economic Issues*, vol. XXXV, no. 3, September, 543–56.

Pfouts, Ralph W. (2002) 'On the Need for a More Complete Ontology of the Consumer', in Edward Fullbrook (ed.) *Intersubjectivity in Economics: Agents and Structures*, London: Routledge.

Phelps Brown, E. H. (1972) 'The Underdevelopment of Economics', *Economic Journal*, vol. 82, no. 1, March, 1–10.

Phipps, Shelley A. and Peter S. Burton (1995) 'Social/Institutional Variables and Behaviour Within Households: An Empirical Test Using the Luxembourg Income Study', *Feminist Economics*, vol. 1, no. 1, 151–74.

Pinkstone, Brian (2002) 'Persistent Demi-regs and Robust Tendencies: Critical Realism and the Singer-Prebisch Thesis', *Cambridge Journal of Economics,* vol. 26, no. 5, 561–84.

Pisanie, Johann A. du (1997) 'Declining Enrolments in Economics', *Royal Economic Society Newsletter*, no. 96, January, 7.

Poincaré, Henri (1901) letter to Walras, in W. Jaffé (ed.) (1965) *Correspondence of Léon Walras and Related Papers*, vol. 3, letter 1496a, Amsterdam: North Holland, 162–5.

Polanyi, Karl (1971) 'The Economy as an Instituted Process', in George Dalton (ed.) *Primitive Archaic and Modern Economics: Essays of Karl Polanyi*, Boston MA: Beacon Press, 139–74.

Popper, Karl R. (1967) 'The Rationality Principle', in David Miller (ed.) (1985) *Popper Selections*, Princeton NJ: Princeton University Press.

Posner, Richard A. (1977) *Economic Analysis of Laws*, 2nd edn, Boston MA and Toronto: Little and Brown Company.

Potts, Jason (2000) *The New Evolutionary Microeconomics: Complexity, Competence and Adaptive Behaviour*, Cheltenham: Edward Elgar.

Pratten, Stephen (1994) 'Forms of Realism, Conceptions of Science And Approaches to Industrial Organisation', Ph.D. dissertation, University of Cambridge.

——(1996) 'The "Closure" Assumption as a First Step: Neo Ricardian Economics and Post Keynesianism', *Review of Social Economy*, vol. LIV, no. 4, 423–43.

——(1997a) 'The Nature of Transaction Cost Economics', *Journal of Economic Issues*, vol. 31, 781–803.

——(1997b) 'Coherence in Post Keynesian Economics', in P. Arestis, G. Palma and M. Sawyer (eds) *Capital Controversy, Post-Keynesian Economics and the History of Economic Thought: Essays in Honour of Geoff Harcourt, vol. 1,* , London: Routledge.

——(1998) 'Marshall on Tendencies, Equilibrium and the Statical Method', *History of Political Economy*, vol. 30, no. 1, 121–62.

——(2001) 'Coase on Broadcasting, Advertising and Policy', *Cambridge Journal of Economics*, vol. 25, no. 5, 617–38.

Pujol, Michèle (1995) 'Into the Margin', in Edith Kuiper and Jolande Sap (eds) *Out of the Margin: Feminist Perspectives on Economics*, London and New York: Routledge, 17–35.

——(1997) 'Broadening Economic Data and Methods', *Feminist Economics*, vol. 3, no. 2, 119–20.

Redmount, Esther (1995) 'Towards a Feminist Econometrics', in Edith Kuiper and Jolande Sap (eds) *Out of the Margin: Feminist Perspectives on Economics*, London and New York: Routledge, 216–22.

Reed, Mike J (2001) 'Organisation, Trust and Control: A Realist Analysis', *Organisational Studies*, vol. 22, no. 2, 201–28.

Reijnders, Jan (ed.) (1997) *Economics and Evolution*, Cheltenham: Edward Elgar.

Reinert, Erik S. (2000) 'The Austrians and "The Other Canon" ', in J. Backhaus (ed.) *The History of Evolutionary Economics*, Aldershot: Edward Elgar (page references to an unpublished mimeo).

Reybaud, Louis (1862) *Les économistes modernes*, Paris: Guillaumin.

Robbins, Lionel (1940) [1932] *An Essay on the Nature and Significance of Economic Science*, London: Macmillan.

Romanes, George John (1892–7) *Darwin and after Darwin: An Exposition of the Darwinian Theory and a Discussion of Post-Darwinian Questions*, 3 vols, London : Longmans, Green and Co.

Rose, Hilary and Steven Rose (eds) (2001) *Alas Poor Darwin: Arguments against Evolutionary Psychology*, London: Vintage.

Rose, Steven (2001) 'Escaping Evolutionary Psychology', in Hilary Rose and Steven Rose (eds) *Alas Poor Darwin: Arguments Against Evolutionary Psychology*, London: Vintage.

Rosenberg, Alexander (1976) *Microeconomic Laws: A Philosophical Analysis*, Pittsburgh: University of Pittsburgh Press.

——(1978) 'The Puzzle of Economic Modelling', *The Journal of Philosophy*, vol. 75, 670–83.

——(1983) 'If Economics Isn't Science, What Is It?', *The Philosophical Forum*, vol. 14, 296–314; reprinted in Daniel M. Hausman (ed.) *The Philosophy of Economics: An Anthology*, second edition, Cambridge: Cambridge University Press, 376–94 (page references to the latter).

——(1992) *Economics: Mathematical Politics or Science of Diminishing Returns?* Chicago: University of Chicago Press.

——(1994a) 'What Is the Cognitive Status of Economic Theory?' in Roger E. Backhouse (ed.) *New Directions in Economic Methodology*, London and New York: Routledge.

——(1994b) 'Does Evolutionary Theory Give Comfort or Inspiration to Economics?' in Philip Mirowski (ed.) *Natural Images in Economic Thought: Markets Read in Tooth and Claw*, Cambridge: Cambridge University Press.

Rosser Jr, J. Barkley (2001) 'Alternative Keynesian and Post Keynesian Perspectives on Uncertainty and Expectations', *Journal of Post Keynesian Economics*, vol. 23, no 4, summer, 545–66.

Rotheim, Roy J. (1998) 'On Closed Systems and the Language of Economic Discourse', *Review of Social Economy*, fall, 324–34.

——(1999) 'Post Keynesian Economics and Realist Philosophy', *Journal of Post Keynesian Economics*, vol. 22, no. 1, 71–103.

——(2002) 'Timeful Theories, Timeful Theorists', in Philip Arestis, Meghnad Desai and Sheila Dow (eds) *Methodology, Microeconomics and Keynes: Essays in Honour of Victoria Chick, Volume Two*, London: Routledge.

Rubinstein, Ariel (1991) 'Comments on the Interpretation of Game Theory', *Econometrica*, vol. 59, no.4, 909–24.

——(1995) 'John Nash: The Master of Economic Modeling', *Scandinavian Journal of Economics*, vol. 97, no. 1, 9–13.

Runde, Jochen (1996) 'On Popper, Probabilities and Propensities', *Review of Social Economy*, vol. 54, 465–85; reprinted in Steven Fleetwood (ed.) (1999) *Critical Realism in Economics: Development and Debate*, London: Routledge, 63–82.

——(1998a) 'Assessing Causal Economic Explanations', *Oxford Economic Papers*, vol. 50, 151–72.

——(1998b) 'Probability, Uncertainty and Long-term Expectations', in P. O'Hara (ed.) *Encyclopedia of Political Economy*. London: Routledge, 1189–92.

——(2001a) 'Chances and Choices: Notes on Probability and Belief in Economic Theory', in Uskali Mäki (ed.) *The Economic Worldview: Studies in the Ontology of Economics*, Cambridge: Cambridge University Press, 132–53; revised and extended version of a paper that originally appeared in *The Monist*, 1995, vol. 78, no. 3, July, 331–52.

——(2001b) 'On Stephen Parsons' Philosophical Critique of Transcendental Realism', *Review of Political Economy*, vol. 13, no. 1, 101–14.

——(2002) 'Filling in the Background', *Journal of Economic Methodology*, vol. 9, 11–30.

Rutherford, Malcolm (1998) 'Veblen's Evolutionary Programme: A Promise Unfulfilled', *Cambridge Journal of Economics*, vol. 22, July, 463–77.

Ruwanpura, Kanchana (2002) Matrilineal Communities, Patriarchal Realities: Female-headship in Eastern Sri Lanka – A Feminist Economic Reading, Ph.D. dissertation, University of Cambridge.

Salanti, Andrea and Ernesto Screpanti (eds) (1997) *Pluralism in Economics: New Perspectives in History and Methodology*, Cheltenham: Edward Elgar.

Samuels, Warren J. (1989) 'Austrian and Institutional Economics: Some Common Elements', *Research in the History of Economic Thought and Methodology*, 53, 72.

——(1990) 'The Self-referentiability of Thorstein Veblen's Theory of the Preconceptions of Economics Science', *Journal of Economic Issues*, vol. XXIV, no. 3, September, 695–718.

——(1998) 'Comment on 'Postmodernism and Institutionalism', *Journal of Economic Issues*, vol. XXXII, no. 3, September, 823–32.

Samuelson, Paul A. (1952) 'Economic Theory and Mathematics: An Appraisal', *American Economic Review*, vol. 42, no. 2, 56–66.

Sawyer, Malcolm (ed.) (1988) *Post-Keynesian Economics*, Aldershot: Edward Elgar.

Say, Jean-Baptiste (1803) 'Discours Préliminaire', in *Traité d'Economie Politique*, 1st edn, Paris: Crapelet.

——(1971) [1826] 'Discours Préliminaire', in *Traité d'économie politique*, 5th edn, with a preface by G. Tapinos, Paris: Calmann-Levy.

Sayer, Andrew (2000) *Realism and Social Science*, London: Sage.

Sayre-McCord, G. (ed.) (1988) *Essays on Moral Realism*, Ithaca NY and London: Cornell University Press.

Schumpeter, Joseph A. (1954) *History of Economic Analysis*, New York: Oxford University Press.

Searle, John R. (1995) *The Construction of Social Reality*, London: Penguin.

——(1999) *Mind, Language and Society: Doing Philosophy in the Real World*, London: Weidenfeld and Nicolson.

——(2001) *Rationality in Action* (The Jean Nicod Lectures), Cambridge MA and London: MIT Press.

Seiz, Janet (1993) 'Feminism and the History of Economic Thought', *History of Political Economy*, vol. 25, no. 4, 185–201.

——(1995) 'Epistemology and the Tasks of Feminist Economics', *Feminist Economics*, vol. 1, no. 3, 110–18.

Sen, Amartya (1993) 'Capability and Well-being', in Martha C. Nussbaum and Amartya Sen (eds) *The Quality of Life*, Oxford: Clarendon Press.

Setterfield, Mark (1997) 'Are Academic Economists Concerned about Public Policy?', *Options Politiques*, September, 22–4.

——(2000) 'Expectations, Endogenous Money, and the Business Cycle: An Exercise in Open Systems Modelling', *Journal of Post Keynesian Economics*, vol. 32, no. 1, fall, 77–107.

Siakantaris, Nikos (2000) 'Experimental Economics under the Microscope', *Cambridge Journal of Economics*, vol. 24, 267–81.

Smith, Dorothy (1987) *The Everyday World as Problematic*, Boston MA: Northeastern University Press.

——(1990) *The Conceptual Practices of Power*, Boston MA: Northeastern University Press.

Smithin, John (ed.) (2000) *What is Money?*, London and New York: Routledge.

Smithin, John (forthcoming) 'Macroeconomic Theory, Critical Realism and Capitalism', in Paul Lewis (ed.) *Transforming Economics: Perspectives on the Critical Realist Project*, London and New York: Routledge.

Sofianou, Evanthia (1995) 'Post-modernism and the Notion of Rationality in Economics', *Cambridge Journal of Economics*, vol. 19, no. 3, 373–89.

Soper, Kate (1990) *Troubled Pleasures: Writings on Politics, Gender and Hedonism*, London and New York: Verso.

——(1991) 'Postmodernism, Critical Theory and Critical Realism', in Roy Bhaskar (ed.) *A Meeting of Minds*, London: The Socialist Society.

Soskice, Janet (1985) *Metaphor and Religious Language*, Oxford: Clarendon Press.

Soskice, Janet and Rom Harré (1982) 'Metaphor in Science', in D. S. Miall (ed.) *Metaphor: Problems and Perspectives*, Brighton: Harvester.

Sperber, Dan (2000) 'Why Memes Won't Do', in Robert Aunger (ed.) *Darwinizing Culture: The Status of Memetics as a Science*, Oxford: Oxford University Press.

Staveren, Irene van (1997) 'Focus Groups: Contributing to a Gender-aware Methodology', *Feminist Economics*, vol. 3, no. 2, 131–7.

——(2001) *The Values of Economics: An Aristotelian Perspective*, London: Routledge.

Sterling, Richard W. (1974) *Macropolitics: International Relations in a Global Society*, New York: Knopf.

Stinchcombe, Arthur L. (1975) 'Merton's Theory of Social Structure', in L. Coser (ed.) *The Idea of Social Structure*, papers in honour of Robert K. Merton, New York: Harcourt, Brace Jovanorich.

Strassmann, Diana (1993a) 'Not a Free Market: The Rhetoric of Disciplinary Authority in Economics', in Marianne A. Ferber and Julie A. Nelson (eds) *Beyond Economic Man: Feminist Theory and Economics*, Chicago: University of Chicago Press, 54–68.

——(1993b) 'The Stories of Economics and the Power of the Storyteller', *History of Political Economy*, vol. 25, no. 4, 147–65.

——(1994) 'Feminist Thought and Economics; Or, What do the Visigoths Know?', *American Economic Review, Papers and Proceedings*, vol. 84, no. 2, 153–58.

——(1995) 'Editorial: Creating a Forum for Feminist Economic Inquiry', *Feminist Economics*, vol. 1, no. 1, 1–5.

Strassmann, Diana and Livia Polanyi (1995) 'The Economist as Storyteller: What Texts Reveal', in Edith Kuiper and Jolande Sap (eds) *Out of the Margin: Feminist Perspectives on Economics*, London and New York: Routledge.

Thomson, William L. (1999) 'The Young Person's Guide to Writing Economic Theory', *Journal of Economic Literature*, vol. XXXVII, no. 1 157–83.

Tiles, Mary (1987) 'A Science of Mars or of Venus?', *Philosophy*, vol. 62; reprinted in Evelyn Fox Keller and Helen E. Longino (eds) *Feminism and Science*, Oxford and New York: Oxford University Press.

Turnovsky, Stephen J. (1992) 'The next Hundred Years', in John. D. Hey (ed.) *The Future of Economics*, Oxford: Blackwell.

Twomey, Paul (1998) 'Reviving Veblenian Economic Psychology', *Cambridge Journal of Economics*, vol. 22, July, 433–48.

van Fraassen, Bas C. (1980) *The Scientific Image*, Oxford: Clarendon Press.

Veblen, Thorstein B. (1898) 'Why is Economics Not an Evolutionary Science?', *The Quarterly Journal of Economics*, vol. XII, July; reprinted in *'The Place of Science in Modern Civilization' and Other Essays*, 1919, Viking Press; republished (with a new introduction by Warren J. Samuels) in 1990 by Transaction Publishers, New Jersey (page references to the latter).

——(1899a) *Theory of the Leisure Class*, New York, Macmillan.

——(1899b) 'The Preconception of Economic Science I', *The Quarterly Journal of Economics*, vol. XIV, February; reprinted in *'The Place of Science in Modern Civilization' and Other Essays*, 1919, Viking Press; republished (with a new introduction by Warren J. Samuels) in 1990 by Transaction Publishers, New Jersey (page references to the latter).

——(1900) 'The Preconception of Economic Science III', *The Quarterly Journal of Economics*, vol. XIV, February; reprinted in *'The Place of Science in Modern Civilization' and Other Essays*, 1919, Viking Press; republished (with a new introduction by Warren J. Samuels) in 1990 by Transaction Publishers, New Jersey (page references to the latter).

——(1904) *The Theory of the Business Enterprise*, New York: Charles Scibners.

——(1906) 'The Place of Science in Modern Civilization', *The American Journal of Sociology*, vol. XI, March; reprinted in *'The Place of Science in Modern Civilization' and Other Essays*, 1919, Viking Press; republished (with a new introduction by Warren J. Samuels) in 1990 by Transaction Publishers, New Jersey (page references to the latter).

——(1908) 'The Evolution of the Scientific Point of View', *The University of California Chronicle*, vol. X, no. 4; reprinted in *'The Place of Science in Modern Civilization' and Other Essays*, 1919, Viking Press; republished (with a new introduction by Warren J. Samuels) in 1990 by Transaction Publishers, New Jersey (page references to the latter).

——(1909) 'The Limitations of Marginal Utility', *The Journal of Political Economy*, vol. XVII, no. 9, November; reprinted in *'The Place of Science in Modern Civilization' and Other Essays*, 1919, Viking Press; republished (with a new introduction by Warren J. Samuels) in 1990 by Transaction Publishers, New Jersey (page references to the latter).

——(1990) [1919] *The Place of Science in Modern Civilization and Other Essays*, New Jersey: Transaction Publishers.

——(1924)[1923] *Absentee Ownership and Business Enterprise in Recent Times; The Case of America*, London: George Allen and Unwin.

——(1954) [1925] 'Economic Theory in the Calculable future', *American Economic Review*, vol. XV, no. 1, supplement, March; reprinted in Leon Ardzrooni (ed.) *Essays in our Changing Order*, New York: Viking Press (page references to the latter).

Viskovatoff, Alex (2002) 'Critical Realism and Kantian Transcendental Arguments', *Cambridge Journal of Economics*, vol. 26, no. 6, 697–708.

Voltaire, F. M. Arouet de (1738) *Eléments de la philosophie de Newton mis à la porteé de tout le monde*, Amsterdam: Etienne Ledet and Co.

Vromen, Jack (2001) 'Ontological Commitments of Evolutionary Economics', in Uskali Mäki (ed.) *The Economic Worldview*, Cambridge: Cambridge University Press.

Walters, Bernard and David Young (1997) 'On the coherence of post Keynesian economics', *Scottish Journal of Political Economy*, vol. 44, no. 3, 329–49.

——(1999) 'Is Critical Realism the Appropriate Basis for Post Keynesianism?', *Journal of Post Keynesian Economics*, vol. 22, no. 1, fall, 105–23.

Walras, Leon (1874) 'Principe d'une théorie mathématique de l'échange', in *Compte-rendu des Séances et Travaux de l'Académie des Sciences Morales et Politique, séances du 16 et 24 Août 1873*, January 1874, 97–120.

——(1893) 'Notice autobiographique', in W. Jaffé (ed.) (1965) *Correspondence of Léon Walras and Related Papers*, vol. 1, 1–15, Amsterdam: North Holland.

Weiner, Jonathan (1994) *The Beak of the Finch: A Story of Evolution in Our Time*, London: Jonathan Cape.

Weintraub, E. Roy (1989) 'Methodology Doesn't Matter, But the History of Thought Might', *Scandinavian Journal of Economics*, vol. 91, no. 2, 477–93.

Weintraub, E. Roy and Philip Mirowski (1994) 'The Pure and the Applied: Bourbakism Comes to Mathematical Economics', *Science in Context*, vol. 7, 245–72.

Whitehead, Alfred N. (1926) *Science and the Modern World*, Cambridge: Cambridge University Press.

Wiles, Peter and Guy Routh (eds) (1984) *Economics in Disarray*, Oxford: Blackwell.

Wilkinson, Frank (1983) 'Productive Systems', *Cambridge Journal of Economics*, vol. 7, no. 3, 413–29.

Willmott, Robert (2002) *Education Policy and Realist Social Theory*, London and New York: Routledge.

Witt, Ulrich (2001) 'Evolutionary Economics', in Kurt Dopfer (ed.) *Evolutionary Economics: Programme and Scope*, Boston MA, Dordrecht and London: Kluwer Academic Publishers.

Wolowski, Louis (1848) *Etudes d'économie politique et de statistique*, Paris: Guillaumin.

Yonay, Yuval P. (1998) *The Struggle Over the Soul Of Economics: Institutionalist and Neoclassical Economists in America Between the Wars*, Princeton: Princeton University Press.

NAME INDEX

SUBJECT INDEX

abduction: from other domains 114, 116; as causal reasoning *see under* retroduction; abductionist fallacy 114

abductionist fallacy 114, 310 n

absences 17, 65, 93, 94, 210

abstraction xvii, 43, 52, 83, 177, 181, 239, 240, 290 n, 301 n, 307 n, 308 n, 325 n; contrasted with methods of isolation xvii, 83, 307 n, 308 n

action, human *see under* intentionality, human

actualism 59, 238, 303 n

agency/structure interaction 49–53, 57, 117, 118, 129, 136, 147–150, 225–228, 241, 254, 300 n; diachronic aspect of 50, 205; synchronic aspect of 50, 205; *see also* the transformational model of social activity

anti-realism 63, 67, 71, 74; *see also* irrealism

atomism 13–16, 19, 171, 286 n, 290 n

Austrianism 6, 32, 167, 169, 180, 182, 207, 234, 247, 275, 294 n, 300 n, 305 n, 324 n, 325 n; *see also* heterodox traditions of economics

biological explanation *see* explanation, biological

causal explanation *see* explanation, causal

causal sequence(s) 186, 187, 196, 326 n; relation of 14, 105, ; events standing in 14, 41, 79, 171, 296 n; closed system(s) or closure(s) of 15, 17, 23, 25, 41, 42, 83, 103, 119, 296 n, 306 n,

307 n; explanations of the form of 15; event regularity of 15, 17, 23, 24, 51, 82, 103, 143, 290 n; event correlations of 25, 41, 83

closed system(s) or closure(s) 5, 12–17, 20, 21, 22, 23, 25–27, 41, 42, 60, 67, 68, 81, 82, 83, 84, 93, 103, 105, 106, 108, 113, 119, 143, 150, 156, 171, 173, 175, 178, 179, 222, 224, 229, 284 n, 292 n, 296 n, 306 n, 307 n, 308 n, 345 n; of causal sequence 15, 17, 23, 25, 41, 42, 83, 103, 119, 296 n, 306 n, 307 n; of concomitance 15, 42, 296 n; conditions of 224–225, 296 n; of continuity 41; contrasted with demi-regs 105–107; experimental 81, 87, 93, 105, 150; of isolation 41; psychological need for 345 n; *see also* open systems

collective learning 70, 302 n

collectivities 58–59, 147, 227–228

concomitance: closed system(s) or closure(s) of 15, 42, 296 n; event regularities or variations of 14, 94, 196, 197, 296 n, 329 n

concrete xvii, 43, 51, 52, 54, 61, 79, 84, 96, 100, 109, 126, 146, 147, 152, 157, 158, 168, 177–181, 195, 212, 260, 290 n, 291 n, 299 n, 301 n, 304 n, 307 n, 308 n, 325 n, 334 n, 341 n, 342 n; concrete or applied explanation 146, 147, 152, 291 n, 307 n; fallacy of misplaced concreteness 290 n, 301 n

consciousness, human 46–48, 296 n, 298 n, 299 n, 302 n, 340 n; discursive 47, 48; practical or tacit 47, 48, 299 n; and unconsciousness 299 n

contrast explanation *see* explanation, contrast or contrastive

reductionist positions, methodologically 57, 69, 73, 132, 133, 137, 138, 177, 212, 217, 271, 273, 292 n; see also methodological evolutionism 57; methodological holism 57; methodological individualism 57; methodological institutionalism 57; Universal Darwinism 137, 317 n

relativism 243; epistemological 166, 202, 243, 298 n; judgemental, 166, 202, 235–237, 243

replicator(s) 122, 128, 129, 134–136, 138, 253, 257, 316 n, 317 n

retrodiction 291 n

retroduction 25, 34, 80, 81, 96, 120, 145–146, 149, 150, 291 n, 319 n; also sometimes called abduction 145; or 'as if' reasoning 145; operating under a logic of analogy and metaphor 80, 96; transcendental argument as a special case of 34, 319 n

routines 36, 38, 39, 132, 148, 227, 299 n, 308 n

science xxiv, 32, 33, 34, 73, 87, 98, 108, 142, 145, 147, 151, 181; abstract or pure explanatory 146, 147, 152; concrete or applied explanatory 146, 147, 152; and controlled experiments see experimental work in science; 290 n, 300 n, 301 n, 306 n, 307 n, 308 n; economics as xvii, xx, 25, 26, 78, 148, 149, 150; economics as a separate xxiv, 59, 70, 78, 141, 149, 150, 161–164, 181; evolutionary see under evolutionary science; mathematics thought to be an essential component of xx, 13, 22, 35, 82, 128, 135–136, 290 n, 295 n; event regularities regarded as essential to 13, 143, 318 n; nature of (natural) xx, 22–25, 143, 145, 146; non-neutrality of 220–221, 337 n, 338 n; practical side or application of 146, 147, 152; presuppositions of specific methods of xvii, 174, 175; Robbins's conception of 152–161; see also explanation; naturalism; retroduction

situated rationality, theory of 58–61

social economics 6, 169, 247, 294 n; see also heterodox traditions of economics

social relations 16, 56, 70–72, 117, 136, 149, 151, 152, 154, 163, 226, 240, 259, 304 n; external see external relations; internal see internal relations

social rules 36–39, 44, 70, 117, 128, 181, 225–227, 330 n

social systems 21, 43, 56, 58, 118, 119, 125, 130, 150, 227, 228, 229, 254

social theorising xv, xix, xxii, xxiii, xxiv, 8, 27, 28, 53, 57, 59, 62, 77, 78, 119, 140, 169, 184, 185, 204, 216, 217, 249, 295 n, 301 n, 302 n, 304 n; realist xix, xxii, xxiii, 27, 140, 169, 184, 185, 204, 216, 217

subjectivity, human 44–49, 215, 238, 297 n; see also consciousness, human

technology 16, 131–132 182, 279, 286 n, 302 n; meaning of 16; Veblen's theorising of 190, 193, 198, 199, 202, 206

teleology 119, and Veblen's conception of evolution 187, 199, 204, 205, 208, 212, 213, 214, 215, 217, 329 n, 330 n

tendency, conception of a 144–145, 224

totalities 68, 70, 72, 117, 177, 181, 183, 235, 307 n, 330 n; see also internal relations

transcendental argument 33, 34, 36, 37, 39, 43, 44, 45, 47, 49, 51–53, 132, 294 n, 319 n, 327 n; as a special case of retroduction 34, 319 n

transcendental idealism 294 n

transcendental realism see under realism, transcendental

transfactual(s) 68, 145, 242, 301 n

transformational model of social activity 40, 43, 45, 49, 50, 116–119, 126–129, 131, 132, 140, 204, 207, 208, 212–214, 259, 299 n, 300 n, 330 n

uncertainty 59 170, 171, 173, 182, 281, 302 n, 322 n, 324 n, 345 n

underlabourer conception of philosophy xvi, 53, 54, 57, 84, 177, 178, 301 n

Universal Darwinism see under reductionist positions, methodologically